Central Banking, Monetary Policy and Income Distribution

THE ELGAR SERIES ON CENTRAL BANKING AND MONETARY POLICY

Series Editors: Louis-Philippe Rochon, *Full Professor, Laurentian University, Canada, Editor-in-Chief,* Review of Political Economy *and Founding Editor Emeritus,* Review of Keynesian Economics, Sylvio Kappes, *Assistant Professor, Federal University of Ceará, Brazil and Coordinator, Keynesian Economics Working Group, Young Scholars Initiative* and Guillaume Vallet, *Associate Professor, Université Grenoble Alpes and Centre de Recherche en Economie de Grenoble (CREG), France*

This series explores the various topics important to the study of central banking and monetary theory and policy and the challenges surrounding them. The books in the series analyze specific aspects such as income distribution, gender and ecology and will, as a body of work, help better explain the nature and the future of central banks and their role in society and the economy.

Titles in the series include:

The Future of Central Banking
Edited by Sylvio Kappes, Louis-Philippe Rochon and Guillaume Vallet

Central Banking, Monetary Policy and the Environment
Edited by Louis-Philippe Rochon, Sylvio Kappes and Guillaume Vallet

Central Banking, Monetary Policy and Social Responsibility
Edited by Guillaume Vallet, Sylvio Kappes and Louis-Philippe Rochon

Central Banking, Monetary Policy and the Future of Money
Edited by Guillaume Vallet, Sylvio Kappes and Louis-Philippe Rochon

Central Banks and Monetary Regimes in Emerging Countries
Theoretical and Empirical Analysis of Latin America
Edited by Fernando Ferrari-Filho and Luiz Fernando de Paula

Central Banking, Monetary Policy and Income Distribution
Edited by Sylvio Kappes, Louis-Philippe Rochon and Guillaume Vallet

Future volumes will include:

COVID-19 and the Response of Central Banks
Coping with Challenges in Sub-Saharan Africa
Salewa Olawoye

Central Banking, Monetary Policy and the Political Economy of Dollarization
Edited by Sylvio Kappes and Andrés Arauz

Central Banking, Monetary Policy and Gender
Edited by Louis-Philippe Rochon, Sylvio Kappes and Guillaume Vallet

Central Banking, Monetary Policy and Financial In/Stability
Edited by Louis-Philippe Rochon, Sylvio Kappes and Guillaume Vallet

Central Banking, Monetary Policy and Income Distribution

Edited by

Sylvio Kappes

Assistant Professor, Federal University of Ceará, Brazil and Coordinator, Keynesian Economics Working Group, Young Scholars Initiative

Louis-Philippe Rochon

Full Professor, Laurentian University, Canada, Editor-in-Chief, Review of Political Economy *and Founding Editor Emeritus,* Review of Keynesian Economics

Guillaume Vallet

Associate Professor, Université Grenoble Alpes and Research Fellow, Centre de Recherche en Economie de Grenoble (CREG), France

THE ELGAR SERIES ON CENTRAL BANKING AND MONETARY POLICY

Cheltenham, UK • Northampton, MA, USA

Published by
Edward Elgar Publishing Limited
The Lypiatts
15 Lansdown Road
Cheltenham
Glos GL50 2JA
UK

Edward Elgar Publishing, Inc.
William Pratt House
9 Dewey Court
Northampton
Massachusetts 01060
USA

A catalogue record for this book
is available from the British Library

Library of Congress Control Number: 2023930053

This book is available electronically in the **Elgar**online
Economics subject collection
http://dx.doi.org/10.4337/9781800371934

ISBN 978 1 80037 192 7 (cased)
ISBN 978 1 80037 193 4 (eBook)

Printed and bound in Great Britain by TJ Books Limited, Padstow, Cornwall

Contents

PART II   EVIDENCE

PART III   POLICY

About the editors

Sylvio Kappes is Assistant Professor of Economics at the Federal University of Ceará, and Visiting Professor of the Graduate Program in Economics at the Federal University of Rio Grande do Sul, Brazil. His main areas of research are central banking, monetary policy, income distribution and stock-flow consistent models. His work has been published in a number of peer-reviewed journals, such as the *Review of Political Economy*, *Journal of Post Keynesian Economics* and the *Brazilian Keynesian Review*. He is a co-editor of the Elgar Series on Central Banking and Monetary Policy, together with Louis-Philippe Rochon and Guillaume Vallet. He is the book review editor of the *Review of Political Economy*. He sits on the editorial boards of the *Review of Political Economy*, the *Bulletin of Political Economy* and *Advances in Economics Education*. He is also a co-coordinator of the Keynesian Economics Working Group of the Young Scholars Initiative (YSI) of the Institute for New Economic Thinking (INET).

Louis-Philippe Rochon is Full Professor of Economics at Laurentian University, Canada, where he has been teaching since 2004. Before that, he taught at Kalamazoo College, in Michigan, USA. He obtained his doctorate from the New School for Social Research, New York, USA, in 1998, earning him the 'Frieda Wunderlich Award for Outstanding Dissertation' for his dissertation on endogenous money and post-Keynesian economics.

In January 2019, Louis-Philippe became the co-editor of the *Review of Political Economy*, and its Editor-in-Chief in 2021. Before that, he created the *Review of Keynesian Economics*, was its Editor from 2012 to 2018, and is now Founding Editor Emeritus. He has been Guest Editor for the *Journal of Post Keynesian Economics*, the *International Journal of Pluralism and Economics Education*, the *European Journal of Economic and Social Systems*, the *International Journal of Political Economy* and the *Journal of Banking, Finance and Sustainable Development*. He has published on monetary theory and policy, post-Keynesian economics, and fiscal policy.

He is on the editorial board of *Ola Financiera*, *International Journal of Political Economy*, the *European Journal of Economics and Economic Policies: Intervention*, *Problemas del Desarrollo*, *Cuestiones Económicas* (Central Bank of Ecuador), *Bank & Credit* (Central Bank of Poland), *Bulletin of Political Economy*, *Advances in Economics Education*, *Il Pensiero Economico*

Moderno, Journal of Banking, Finance and Sustainable Development and *Research Papers in Economics and Finance*. He is also the Editor of the following series: Elgar Series on Central Banking and Monetary Policy, and New Directions in Post-Keynesian Economics.

He has been a Visiting Professor or Visiting Scholar in Australia, Brazil, France, Italy, Mexico, Poland, South Africa and the United States, and has further lectured in China, Colombia, Ecuador, Italy, Japan, Kyrgyzstan and Peru.

He is also the author of some 150 articles in peer-reviewed journals and books, and has written or edited close to 35 books. He has received grants from the Social Sciences and Humanities Research Council in Canada (SSHRC), the Ford Foundation and the Mott Foundation, among others.

Guillaume Vallet is Associate Professor of Economics at the University of Grenoble Alpes, France (Research Fellow at Centre de Recherche en Economie de Grenoble). He was awarded a Fulbright Award in 2021 to explore the development of the social sciences during the Progressive Era (1892–1920), especially in light of economists' and sociologists' treatment of income inequality.

He holds two PhDs, one in Economics from the Université Pierre Mendès-France (Grenoble, France) and the other in Sociology obtained at the University of Geneva (Switzerland) and at the Ecole des Hautes Etudes en Sciences Sociales (Paris, France).

In his research, he studies monetary economics, the political economy of gender and the history of economy thought during the Progressive Era. He is the author of some 47 articles in peer-reviewed journals and books, and has written nine books. Specifically, he has published in several distinguished academic journals (*Revue d'Economie Politique, Economy and Society*), especially on Albion W. Small (*Business History, Journal of the History of Economic Thought*), and he has been invited to give talks by prestigious institutions such as the New School for Social Research (New York, USA), the Bank of Ecuador, the Bank of Hungary, the Bank of Israel, the Swiss National Bank, and the United Nations in Geneva.

Contributors

Michel Betancourt is a Postdoctoral Research Fellow at the Economic Research Institute, Universidad Nacional Autónoma de México (UNAM), Mexico City. He is part of the National System of Researchers at Level I. He received his PhD with honours from UNAM. He is a professor and tutor of economic theory in the PUEE-UNAM (Unique Program of Specializations in Economics). He is a member of the editorial board of the journal *El Semestre de las Especializaciones*. His main interest is economic theory in its logical, empirical and methodological dimensions. His topics of study are industrial organization and theory of the firm; inequality and finance; economic dynamics (non-linear systems); and heterodox models of general equilibrium.

Jorge Bustamante is a full-time Associate Professor in the Socioeconomic Division of the Faculty of Higher Studies Acatlán at the Universidad Nacional Autónoma de México (UNAM), Mexico. His latest publications include the books *Capital Movements and Corporate Dominance in Latin America* (Edward Elgar Publishing, 2021); *Financialisation in Latin America: Challenges of the Export-led Growth Model* (Routledge, 2020); and *América Latina: Movimiento de capitales y sus efectos sobre el modelo de crecimiento liderado por las exportaciones* [*Latin America: Capital Movement and its Effect on the Export-led Growth Model*] (UNAM, 2019). His lines of interest are the relationship between the financial sector and big corporations, profit strategies and financial structure of firms, development models and industrial policy.

Sascha Bützer is an Economist in the Middle East and Central Asia Department at the International Monetary Fund (IMF) in Washington, DC, USA. Prior to that, he was Senior Advisor to the Executive Director for Germany at the IMF and has worked for Deutsche Bundesbank and the European Central Bank. He holds graduate degrees in Economics from the Barcelona Graduate School of Economics, Spain, and Simon Fraser University, Canada, and an undergraduate degree in Economics from the University of Konstanz, Germany. His interests include monetary and fiscal policy, international economics, and economic history.

Santiago Capraro is a full-time Professor in Economics at the Economics School, Universidad Nacional Autónoma de México (UNAM), Mexico, and teaches macroeconomics in the Economics Graduate Programme at UNAM. He is part of the National System of Researchers at Level I. He received his PhD and MA in Economics from UNAM. He has a degree in Economics from the Pontifical Catholic University of Argentina. His general areas of research are the analysis of monetary policy with an emphasis on developing countries, the macroeconomic analysis of open economies, and the processes of income and wealth distribution in Latin American countries. Among his particular interests are the development of macroeconomic models of systems of differential equations to explain the processes of stagnation and stability in Latin America.

James K. Galbraith holds the Lloyd M. Bentsen Jr. Chair in Government/ Business Relations at the Lyndon B. Johnson School of Public Affairs and a professorship in Government at the University of Texas at Austin, USA. He was Executive Director of the Joint Economic Committee of the United States Congress in the early 1980s. He chaired the board of Economists for Peace and Security from 1996 to 2016 and directs the University of Texas Inequality Project. He is a Managing Editor of *Structural Change and Economic Dynamics*. In 2010, he was elected to the Accademia Nazionale dei Lincei, Rome, Italy, and in 2022 to the Russian Academy of Sciences. In 2014, he was co-winner of the Leontief Prize for Advancing the Frontiers of Economics. In 2020, he received the Veblen-Commons Award of the Association for Evolutionary Economics. He holds degrees from Harvard University (AB, *magna cum laude*), in Economics from Yale (MA, MPhil, PhD), and honorary degrees from Ecuador, France and Russia.

Noemi Levy-Orlik is Full Professor of Economics at the Economic Faculty, Universidad Nacional Autónoma de México (UNAM), Mexico. Her fields of interest are monetary theory and policy, fiscal policy, economic development in Latin America and post-Keynesian economics. She has the distinction of being National Researcher, an appointment awarded by the Mexican Council of National Research. She is the author of the book *Dinero y estructuras financieras y financiarización: un debate teórico institucional* [*Money and Financial Structures: A Theoretical and Institutional Debate*] (2013, ITACA, UNAM). She has also co-authored various books, including *Capital Movements and Corporate Dominance in Latin America*, with Jorge Bustamante and Louis-Philippe Rochon (Edward Elgar Publishing, 2021); *América Latina: movimiento de capitales y su efecto sobre el modelo liderado por las exportaciones* [*Latin America: Capital Movement and its Effect on the Export-led Growth Model*], with Jorge Bustamante (UNAM, 2019); and *Financialisation in Latin America: Challenges of the Export-led Growth Model*, with Jorge Bustamante (Routledge, 2020). Her research work has been published in the *International Journal of Political Economy*, the *Journal of Post Keynesian Economics* and the *Review of Applied Economics*.

Guillermo Matamoros Romero is currently a PhD candidate in Economics at the University of Ottawa, Canada. Previously, he studied for his master's and bachelor's degrees, both in Economics, at the Universidad Nacional Autónoma de México (UNAM) in Mexico. He published academic articles in refereed journals on macroeconomics, income distribution, and economic development.

Marcelo Milan holds a BA and an MA in Economics, both from the University of São Paulo, Brazil. He has a PhD in Economics from the University of Massachusetts, Amherst, USA. He taught economics at the Universities of Rhode Island (South Kingston) and Wisconsin (Parkside), USA, and is currently Associate Professor of Economics and International Relations at the Federal University of Rio Grande do Sul (UFRGS), Brazil. He is also a faculty member in the graduate programme in Strategic International Studies at the same institution and in the professional Master's in Economics. His research interests include heterodox macroeconomics and finance, radical political economics, international political economy, the Brazilian economy, and cultural economics. He has contributed to the heterodox community with book chapters and peer-reviewed articles, which have appeared in scholarly journals like *International Journal of Political Economy*, *International Review of Applied Economics* and *Journal of Post Keynesian Economics*.

Carlo Panico is a Professor at Universidad Nacional Autónoma de México (UNAM), Mexico. He was a professor at the University of Naples 'Federico II' (Italy). He has published articles in the *Cambridge Journal of Economics*, *Contributions to Political Economy*, *Economic Journal*, *Metroeconomica*, *European Journal of the History of Economic Thought*, *Review of Political Economy*, *Review of Keynesian Economics*, and books with Macmillan, Routledge and Edward Elgar Publishing. His major area of interest is the influence of monetary phenomena on distribution and growth. Another area is in the history of economic analysis, studying Marx, Marshall, Keynes, Myrdal, Harrod, Sraffa, Kaldor, and the nineteenth-century 'British monetary orthodoxy'. Further work has been carried out on Marshallian supply curves, the concept of rationality, the European Monetary Union, the relationship between central banks' independence and democracy, the conduct of monetary policy and its coordination with fiscal policy, and the influence on regional development of different forms of planning government intervention.

Massimo Pivetti is a former Professor of Economics at the University of Rome 'La Sapienza' and is an exponent of the neo-Marxian or Sraffian approach to political economy. He has been the Editor of the international journal *Political Economy: Studies in the Surplus Approach* (1985–90), and his bibliography includes books, book chapters and journal articles on distribution theory, monetary theory and policy, international economics, the economics of military spending, the euro system and history of economic analysis. He is presently working on the employment and distributive impact of free trade in advanced capitalism.

Sergio Rossi is Full Professor of Economics at the University of Fribourg, Switzerland, where he holds the Chair of Macroeconomics and Monetary Economics. He has a PhD degree in Economics from the University of Fribourg and a PhD degree in Economics from University College London, UK. His research interests are in macroeconomic analysis, particularly monetary and financial issues. He has authored or edited about 25 books, has widely published in academic journals, and is frequently invited on TV talk shows to discuss macroeconomic issues at both national and international levels. He is a member of the editorial boards of *Cogent Economics & Finance* and the *Review of Political Economy*. Since 2015, he has featured on the list of the most prominent economists in Switzerland.

Mario Seccareccia is Professor Emeritus at the Department of Economics, University of Ottawa, Canada, where he taught from 1978 to 2018 in the fields of macroeconomics, monetary theory, labour economics, history of economic thought, and economic history, subjects on which he has also written extensively. He has published some 130 academic articles in scientific refereed journals or book chapters, and has authored or edited a dozen books. He has also edited or co-edited some 45 special issues of journals. Many of these publications are of an interdisciplinary nature and cover many areas of political economy. He has been a visiting professor at a number of universities in France (Université de Bourgogne, Université de Grenoble, Université Paris 13, and Université Paris-Sud) and in Mexico (Universidad Nacional Autónoma de México), and participates regularly in policy debate in both Europe and North America. Among other activities, since 2004 he is Editor of the *International Journal of Political Economy*.

Jan Toporowski is Professor of Economics and Finance at the School of Oriental and African Studies, University of London, UK; Professor of Economics and Finance at the International University College, Turin, Italy; and Visiting Professor of Economics at Meiji University, Tokyo, Japan. His research is concentrated on monetary theory and policy, finance, and the work of Michał Kalecki. Jan has published over 300 books, papers and reviews, including two biographical volumes on Kalecki and *Credit and Crisis from Marx to Minsky* (Edward Elgar Publishing, 2021). His most recent book, *Interest and Capital: The Monetary Economics of Michał Kalecki*, was published by Oxford University Press in 2022. Jan studied economics at Birkbeck

College, University of London, and the University of Birmingham, UK. He has worked in fund management, international banking and central banking, and has been a consultant for the United Nations Development Programme, the United Nations Conference on Trade and Development, and the Economist Intelligence Unit.

Luis Daniel Torres-González is Adjunct Professor at Universidad Nacional Autónoma de México (UNAM) and member of the Mexican National Research System Level I (SNI-I). He received his PhD in Economics from the New School for Social Research, New York, and his MA and BA from UNAM. He did a postdoc at UNAM and at Benemérita Universidad Autónoma de Puebla, and has been a consultant for the United Nations Economic Commission for Latin America and the Caribbean. His general areas of research are input–output analysis and the theories of prices, interest rates, and real exchange rates. In particular, he is interested in probabilistic and statistical approaches to the study of productive structures; the modelling and empirical computation of multisector models of prices, growth, and technical change; the modelling of interest rates and rates of return in financial markets based on the long-period method and statistical equilibrium; and linear analysis.

Matías Vernengo is Full Professor at Bucknell University, USA. He was formerly Senior Research Manager at the Central Bank of Argentina (BCRA), Associate Professor of Economics at the University of Utah and Assistant Professor at Kalamazoo College, USA and the Federal University of Rio de Janeiro (UFRJ), Brazil. He has been an external consultant to several United Nations organizations like the Economic Commission for Latin America and the Caribbean, the International Labour Organization, the United Nations Conference on Trade and Development and the United Nations Development Programme, has edited six books and authored two books and more than 100 articles published in scientific peer-reviewed journals or book chapters. He specializes in macroeconomic issues for developing countries, in particular Latin America, international political economy and the history of economic ideas. He is also a founding co-editor of the *Review of Keynesian Economics* and co-editor-in-chief of the *New Palgrave Dictionary of Economics*.

Acknowledgements

In the making of this book, we would like to thank all the authors who contributed a chapter, therefore their time and energy. Written and put together during the worst of COVID-19, we appreciate it even more knowing that many of the authors had urgent family commitments, and we all had to navigate more difficult work conditions. We would also like to acknowledge, as always, the generous support of Alan Sturmer and the rest of the team at Edward Elgar Publishing for their continued and enthusiastic support of our work.

Introduction to *Central Banking, Monetary Policy and Income Distribution*

Sylvio Kappes, Louis-Philippe Rochon and Guillaume Vallet

INTRODUCTION

Since the 2007/08 financial crisis, central banks have been waking up to new realities concerning both the limitations of conventional policies and the impact conventional and unconventional policies may have, only to face the possibility of aggregate-demand secular stagnation. The task facing central banks today is to identify the challenges ahead and to respond to them with the right tools and policies.

This is a far cry from the Goldilocks years of the Great Moderation when central bankers and policymakers celebrated, thinking they had finally got things right. Business cycles had been vanquished, we were told, with huge and obvious implications for monetary policy. Keynes was a relic of a bygone era. This illusion was short-lived, however.

With the financial and then the pandemic crises, central banks tested the limits of monetary policy. They pushed interest rates to near zero in many countries, but the results were disappointing as the policy had very limited or even no success in generating economic growth, thus disapproving neo-classical theory. It would appear that consumption and investment decisions rely on variables other than the rate of interest. In fact, real interest rates were pushed to negative territory in the hope of stimulating demand, but this was a case of imposing a theory where the empirical evidence was clearly showing otherwise. As Storm (2019, n.p.) writes: 'As the real interest [rate] *increased* from 1.6% in 1980 to 8.1% in 1984, the investment rate *increased*' (original emphasis).

Nevertheless, there was still a belief in the loanable funds theory: if only real rates were pushed low enough, investment would pick up. This was how some, like Lawrence Summers, interpreted secular stagnation: not so much as a crisis in aggregate demand, but rather as a crisis in loanable funds, easily solved by lowering interest rates. This approach corresponded, for the past few decades, to the rise of the 'austerian' philosophy, where central banks have been made to carry most of the economic policy burden, thereby contributing to the age of monetary policy dominance, during which fiscal policy took a back seat to the pursuit of economic growth. Governments, it was assumed, overburdened us and future generations with piles of public debt. They had to assure balanced or sound finances, and leave the challenge of fine-tuning economic activity to independent central bankers.

One important conclusion we can draw from the pair of crises is that central banks are unable to carry the whole burden of recovery. With the failure of both conventional and unconventional policies, many central banks resorted to asking governments to inject stimulus given that they 'had done their job'. As Bernanke testified in front of Congress, on 7 June 2012, 'Monetary policy is not a panacea... I would feel much more comfortable if Congress would take some of this burden from us and address these issues'.

It was clearly the return of Keynes, or rather the 'return of the Master' (Skidelsky, 2009). And though Keynes did make an appearance in 2009, it was short-lived, as by 2010, many countries had resorted back to sound finance. But the Master did return in a big way during the COVID crisis, when unprecedented fiscal stimulus, including in some countries the quasi-nationalization of private sector wages, proved so historically important. Around the world, governments embraced deficit spending on a large and unprecedented scale: once again, Keynes rescued aggregate demand.

At the same time, central banks also went through a rethinking process of their own. Strict adherence to inflation targeting, which has been around since the early 1990s, started to wane, as some central banks started to adopt either dual mandates – no less New Zealand, which was ironically the first bank to inflation target – or a looser version of inflation targeting: average inflation targeting.

Particularly noteworthy, and following in the footsteps of a number of countries, like Canada, for instance, the US Federal Reserve abandoned reserve requirements in 2020 in a further attempt to update its monetary framework. This is a clear statement that reserve requirements simply don't work in giving central banks control over the supply of credit by commercial banks. In another words, the money multiplier is dead, and as a recently published paper by the Federal Reserve states, 'R.I.P. money multiplier' (Ihrig, Weinbach and Wolla, 2021).

THE OLD MODEL OF CENTRAL BANKING

But, despite these seemingly positive changes over the last decade, has there been real change in monetary thinking, or has it been more cosmetic than anything else? The answer may be a little of both.

To answer this question, let us begin with a discussion of what we call the old model of central banking, most associated with Friedman's monetarism, pre-dating the so-called New Consensus Macroeconomics model. Such an old model, we argue, is based on the following nine fundamental arguments:

1. Central banks control the supply of high-powered money or reserves.
2. Central banks exert control over the growth of monetary aggregates, the money supply.
3. Central banks control reserve requirements.
4. The money multiplier is at the core of the transmission mechanism.
5. Debate over rules vs discretion, favouring the former.
6. The natural rate of interest is a relevant variable for policy.
7. Money and inflation are linked.
8. Central banks must be independent.
9. Long-run neutrality of money.

Accordingly, central banks can control the money supply given their control over high-powered reserves and reserve requirements, a key element in the money multiplier. It is assumed that the money multiplier is stable. In this sense, if central banks want to rein in money supply growth, they need only to either decrease the supply of high-powered money or indeed increase reserve requirements. In both cases, the supply of money is assumed exogenous, and hence independent of whatever occurs in the economy, by definition. In accordance with the *quantity theory of money*, assuming stable velocity, the rate of growth of the money supply should be set according to the long-run, natural growth of the economy, also known as Friedman's rule.

According to this model, commercial banks are mere financial intermediaries, and their lending activities are at the mercy of central banks: they are severally constrained in their ability to lend – constrained by the availability of reserves and deposits. In this sense, central banks can influence lending by increasing or decreasing the availability of high-powered money to the banking system and, through the (stable and predictable) money multiplier, will impact the supply of bank loans. In essence, deposits create loans.

But if the central bank can influence the supply of loans, this is only a short-run phenomenon. Indeed, monetary policy only has short-run effects. In the long run, money is neutral, and has no impact on real variables. Money only affects prices in the long run. This is the standard way of reading the quantity theory of money equation: from left to right and if money supply growth is appropriately set, then in the long run, the price level remains constant.

This is an important function of central banks, and one that is seen as crucial given the notion that inflation is influenced by all things monetary: inflation is 'always and everywhere a monetary phenomenon' (Friedman, 1970, p. 24).

Control of the growth of the money supply therefore becomes of paramount importance: if central banks cannot control the money supply, then they must also give up on trying to control inflation.

The idea that inflation and money are linked was – and still is – considered a universal truth. This led Friedman to propose his monetary rule. There were in fact two main reasons for favouring rules over discretion: Friedman had a deep mistrust of central bankers, and in this sense always opposed the notion of independent central banks. At least, were they so independent, rules would ensure that central bankers would follow proper monetary policy etiquette.

THE NEW MODEL OF CENTRAL BANKING

In recent years, central banks themselves have come a long way in leaving at least parts of the monetarist story behind, and many have gone so far as to embrace some version of the post-Keynesian theory of endogenous money (even though post-Keynesian works and authors are seldom if ever cited). If the old model of central banking owed a debt to Friedman, the new approach owes much to the work of Wicksell.

In this new model, most now readily admit that it is the rate of interest that is the control instrument – not some monetary aggregate – and that the setting of interest rates is independent of the quantity of reserves in existence – what Borio and Disyatat (2010) have called the 'decoupling' effect. Former Bank of Canada Governor Gerald Bouey famously stated in 1982, 'We didn't abandon the monetary aggregates: they abandoned us' (Dodge, 2010, p. 4). It is perhaps because of this that central banks turned to another monetary framework, careful, however, not to stray theoretically too far from orthodox monetary thinking. Indeed, '[t]he main change is that it replaces the assumption that the central bank targets the money supply with an assumption that it follows a simple interest rate rule' (Romer, 2000, p. 154).

With that in mind, central banks then looked for a more suitable model to build, and turned to inflation targeting, a concept that goes back at least to Keynes (1923). This elegant, three-equation model (see Romer, 2000; Taylor, 1993; Woodford, 2003) contains a Taylor rule, and IS and Phillips curves. New Zealand was the first country in the world to adopt the new model, in 1990, followed by Canada the following year.

The model was widely popular with central banks and academics. Indeed, Goodfriend (2007, p. 59) claimed that 'the Taylor rule became the most common way to model monetary policy', and Taylor (2000, p. 90), heralded that 'at the practical level, a common view of macroeconomics is now pervasive in policy-research projects at universities and central banks around the world'.

The inflation target itself became the anchor for inflation, and in Wicksellian fashion, we find embedded in the model the inescapable natural rate of interest determined by productivity and thrift, and a market-determined benchmark rate set by the central bank. The model was also based on some fine-tuning: whenever the rate of inflation was above target, central banks, via a Taylor rule, would raise the benchmark rate, hoping the economy would slow down just enough to bring inflation back down to target via the well-behaved IS and Phillips curves. Without these, of course, the model falls apart. The adoption of this new model also corresponded to a period of Great Moderation, leading some to argue that '[i]n the years prior to August 2007, central banks had appeared to have almost perfected the conduct of monetary policy' (Goodhart, 2011, p. 145).

Yet, with the financial crisis, the model began falling apart and a new search for a new monetary policy framework was under way. Indeed, this model was confronted with the problem of the lower bound, where central banks were unable to push nominal interest rates below zero. Here, central banks were convinced the natural rate was below zero and hence why they needed to push the benchmark rate to such low levels. But in their model, even a zero nominal rate was still too high: real rates were still above the natural rate given low levels of inflation. Interestingly enough, the secular stagnationist view was based precisely on this view: our economies were stagnating because the natural rate had fallen below zero; austerity had nothing to do with it. As stated above, stagnation was interpreted as a crisis in loanable funds, not a crisis in aggregate demand per se. Because of this, fiscal policy was not seen initially as a possible solution: austerity made sense, according to this view.

In the continued absence of fiscal policy, central banks were struggling to be seen as still relevant, and turned to unconventional means to foster economic growth – means that proved as uninspiring as the more conventional policies. Yet, the financial crisis would eventually reveal the degree to which the monetary new emperor had no clothes: the limits of this new view were starting to emerge. In a startling new paper, 'Whither central banking?', Summers and Stanbury (2019) were now admitting 'the impotence' of the model: 'Simply put, tweaking inflation targets, communications strategies, or even balance sheets is not an adequate response to the challenges now confronting the major economies... Central banks cannot always set inflation rates through monetary policy' (n.p.).

THE HUMPTY-DUMPTYING OF THE NEW MODEL

There is no denying that the New Consensus Macroeconomics model has come under criticism in the last decade since the financial crisis, and not just from post-Keynesians, but also from a growing number of analyses from within central banks themselves. The question remains as to whether all the central banks' guards and horses can put the model back together again.

In a Bank of England paper now almost a decade old, McLeay, Radia and Thomas (2014) go to great lengths to dispel some old myths surrounding monetary creation, and clarify the 'misconceptions' from the 'reality'. In particular, they argue that lending creates deposits: 'In the modern economy, those bank deposits are mostly created by commercial banks themselves' (p. 15). More crucial, we believe, is the explanation of why reserves are not an important component of bank lending, and cannot 'be multiplied into more loans' (ibid., p. 14).

In a second paper published at the Bank of England, Jakab and Kumhof (2019) argue that 'loans come before deposits' (p. 6) and that 'a new loan involves no intermediation. No real resources need to be diverted from other uses, by other agents, in order to be able to lend to the new customer' (p. 4), which they claim is a 'more realistic framework', which is 'supported by a long and growing list of central bank publications' (p. 1). Moreover, they specify that this view 'has always been very well understood by central banks' (p. 7).

The Deutsche Bundesbank, of all banks, also contributed to this new central bank model, in 2017, with a paper entitled 'The role of banks, non-banks and the central bank in the money creation process'. Indeed, a reference to the 'money creation process' is a very telling rejection of the exogenous money story where this process is absent, in the very notion of helicopter money. The article argues that:

> [s]ight deposits are created by transactions between a bank and a non-bank (its customer) – the bank grants a loan, say, or purchases an asset and credits the corresponding amount to the non-bank's bank account in return. Banks are thus able to create book (giro) money. This form of money creation reflects the financing and portfolio decisions of banks and non-banks and is thus driven by the same factors that determine the behaviour of banks and non-banks. (Deutsche Bundesbank, 2017, p. 15)

In a 2018 speech, Christopher Kent, Assistant Governor of the Reserve Bank of Australia, discussed whether money was 'born of credit'. He makes clear that '[m]oney can be created, however, when financial intermediaries make loans. Accordingly, the concepts of money and credit are closely linked in a modern economy… The process of money creation requires a willing borrower… [and the bank must] satisfy itself that the borrower can service the loan' (n.p.). These are familiar themes for post-Keynesians, who will recognize the notion that loans create deposits, and that they are 'demand determined' by creditworthy borrowers – in other words, that money is seemingly endogenous.

Moreover, two papers recently published by the Federal Reserve show a very different side to the central bank model. In the first, Rudd (2021) argues that inflationary expectations are no ground for predicting future levels of inflation. According to the author's abstract, such an idea rests on 'extremely shaky foundations'. The conclusions are devastating, as anticipations of inflation are certainly a core principle of central banking today. The 'pugnacious paper' created a firestorm, leading *The Economist* (2021) to declare the paper 'a social-media sensation' (n.p.).

In a second paper, with the provocative subtitle 'R.I.P. money multiplier', Ihrig et al. (2021) explain the changes to monetary policy in the United States following the financial crisis and COVID. The paper is noteworthy for a few reasons. First, in light of the Federal Reserve's elimination of reserve requirements in 2020, the authors warn professors of 'mistakes' they still make in teaching money and banking. Second, the authors admonish textbooks for still teaching the ways of the old model. In this sense, the subtitle of the paper is meant to be a definitive statement (and perhaps even a warning) to economists that they are doing a disservice to students by not correctly representing (or understanding) what central banks do. Both reasons are summarized by the title of one of the sections of the paper: 'Make sure your teaching is current'.

Finally, in celebrating the 25th anniversary of the publication of Moore's (1988) *Horizontalists and Verticalists*, Bindseil and König (2013) – Bindseil works at the European Central Bank – have acknowledged that 'the last 25 years have vindicated the substance of his [Moore's] thinking in a surprising way that could hardly have been anticipated in 1988. Central bankers have by now largely buried "verticalism", at least when it comes to monetary policy implementation' (p. 385). This is an acknowledgement that the old model of central banking is dead.

Or is it? While many of the above quotes (and we could have cited a number of other papers) certainly appear, at least on the surface, as indicative of important changes in monetary thinking, we are not convinced. So while there is no doubt that central banks have come a long way in repudiating *some* of the elements of the old model, we argue they have not successfully done so in their entirety. What is left is perhaps best described as a hybrid model. In this sense, we agree with Fiebiger and Lavoie (2020, p. 78), who have argued that '[t]he NCM [New Consensus Macroeconomics] replaced money supply targeting with inflation targeting while preserving monetarist results'. This is exactly what Lavoie (2006, p. 167) meant when he wrote, almost two decades ago, that New Consensus models 'simply look like old wine in a new bottle'.

So, let us once again refer to the nine arguments above:

1. Central banks control the supply of high-powered money or reserves.
2. Central banks exert control over the growth of monetary aggregates, the money supply.
3. Central banks control reserve requirements.

4.   The money multiplier is at the core of the transmission mechanism.
5.   Debate over rules vs discretion, favouring the former.
6.   The natural rate of interest is a relevant variable for policy.
7.   Money and inflation are linked.
8.   Central banks must be independent.
9.   Long-run neutrality of money.

We can conclude that the first four elements have been abandoned by many central banks, and in New Consensus models as well. This said, despite these advances, as welcome as they are, we are still not entirely on board with the idea that mainstream thinking is any closer to the post-Keynesian story of endogenous money. In other words, the new model of central banking certainly leaves behind a number of assumptions of the old model, but from a post-Keynesian perspective, it does not go far enough. Five elements still remain at the core of the model:

5.   Regarding the debate over rules vs discretion, we can summarize that it has evolved, but perhaps not by much. The old model contains a monetary rule, while the new model contains an interest rate rule. But Taylor (1993, p. 195) defines his approach as akin to 'a responsive rule'. Indeed, Taylor (ibid., p. 196) claims that '[p]olicymakers do not, and are not evidently about to, follow policy rules mechanically', therefore leaving some room for discretion, and warns about making Taylor rules 'too complex'. So in many ways, central banks use fine-tuning to adjust interest rates in response to inflation shocks.
6.   Regarding the natural rate of interest, it is still at the heart of New Consensus models. In a Wicksellian manner, it acts as an anchor to short-term benchmark rates. The purpose of the central bank is to set the rate and to move it up or down until it reaches an inflation target, corresponding presumably with the natural rate. The question is whether we can have a theory of endogenous money while also espousing a natural rate of interest. Rochon (1999) and Smithin (1994) have always rejected the claim that a theory of endogenous money can accommodate a natural rate of interest. After all, if post-Keynesians believe the benchmark rate is truly exogenous, then that would rule out a natural rate that acts as an anchor for central bank rates. At best, as Palley (2006, p. 80) writes, the New Consensus 'is a conception of endogeneity that is fundamentally different from the Post Keynesian conception, which is rooted in the credit nature of money'. Palley calls the New Consensus approach 'central bank endogeneity'. In a similar vein, Gnos and Rochon (2007, p. 378) have claimed that the New Consensus lacked a '*theory* of endogenous money' (original emphasis). Setterfield (2004, p. 41) arrives at the

same conclusion: 'whereas the stock of money is endogenous in practice in NC [New Consensus] macroeconomics, it is endogenous in principle in PK [post-Keynesian] macroeconomics'.

7. In addition, inflation is still thought to be linked to monetary policy. As such, only central banks are equipped to regulate economic activity efficiently so as to influence inflation and achieve its target, with minimal damage to the economy. In this sense, inflation, we can say, is always and everywhere a monetary *policy* phenomenon.

8. Central bank independence is still considered a *sine qua non* of mainstream monetary policy. Advocates claim that it is at the core of current monetary thinking, especially now (at the time of writing this introduction) as inflation is starting to increase around the world. According to Goodhart (2021), if inflation persists, central banks must move to swiftly increase interest rates or risk losing credibility. Central bank independence is tied to notions of credibility: 'It is important to have in place adequate mechanisms to "guard the guardians" of monetary and financial stability' (Goodhart and Lastra, 2018, p. 49).

9. There is also a staunch defence of the long-run neutrality of money. This is particularly the case in current research on the links between monetary policy and income distribution. While some central banks recognize the income-distributive impact of monetary policy, it is said to be small and temporary (see Rochon, 2022). For instance, Romer and Romer (1999, p. 38) claim that '[i]t is certainly true that expansionary policy can generate a boom and reduce poverty temporarily. But the effect is unquestionably just that: temporary'. In a recent survey,[1] Colciago, Samarina and de Haan (2019, p. 1224) argue that '[o]ver the longer horizon, the distributional impact is likely to die out given the temporary nature of the effects of monetary policy shocks'. This is a required conclusion to a theory that insists on long-run neutrality.

The new model is thus not too far from Friedman (Fiebiger and Lavoie, 2020), well evidenced in the following quote in a speech by Bernanke (2003): 'I am ready and willing to praise Friedman's contributions wherever and whenever anyone gives me a venue… We can hardly overstate the influence of Friedman's monetary framework on contemporary monetary theory and practice…both policymakers and the public owe Milton Friedman an enormous debt' (n.p.).

THE POST-KEYNESIAN MODEL OF CENTRAL BANKING

While mainstream economists have had to face new realities and come to some realizations about how central bank policy operates, post-Keynesians have also made some changes in the way they perceive central banks and monetary policy. Of course, endogenous money is still the coping stone of post-Keynesian theory, where the rate of interest is set by central banks in a total disconnect with the natural rate, which is rejected. Loans make deposits, and banks are never constrained by a lack of deposits or reserves, but only by a lack of creditworthy borrowers. While Kaldor (1970) and Moore (1988) are central to this view, the ideas were present in many of Joan Robinson's writings, especially the *Accumulation of Capital* (1956).

Post-Keynesians have pushed the boundaries of central banking by advocating against the use of fine-tuning, and by linking monetary policy to income distribution. Regarding the first argument, the concept of fine-tuning consists of increasing and decreasing interest rates incrementally until the correct rate of interest is found, which delivers an inflation consistent with its target. However, there is much that is assumed here. Indeed, in New Consensus models, this fine-tuning is based on well-established IS and Phillips curves: central banks change interest rates in an effort to generate just the right amount of change in output, which in turn will generate just enough change in unemployment and inflation. But these are empirical relationships that need to be tested, and so far, the empirical evidence is weak.

Both Keynes and Robinson rejected fine-tuning. Keynes is famous for having said that fine-tuning 'belongs to the species of remedy which cures the disease by killing the patient' (Keynes, 1936, p. 323). In a similar vein, Robinson, in a much underappreciated essay, argues that '[t]he regulating effect of changes in the rate of interest was at best very weak' (1943, p. 26), and again in 1952, where she describes as a 'false scent' the use of counter-cyclical monetary policy, and rejects 'the conception of an economy which is automatically held on a path of steady development by the mechanism of the rate of interest... But it is by no means easy to see how the monetary mechanism is supposed to ensure how that the rate of interest actually assumes its full employment value... The automatic corrective action of the rate of interest is condemned by its very nature to be always too little and too late' (Robinson, 1952, pp. 73–4).

While recognizing this, post-Keynesians further argue that monetary policy is foremost about income distribution. While the mainstream is starting to recognize this, as stated above, there is nevertheless a stark difference with post-Keynesians. While for the mainstream, monetary policy may have income-distributive effects in the short run, for post-Keynesians, monetary policy *is* income distribution. It is for both these reasons that Lavoie (1996, p. 537), in rejecting fine-tuning, concludes that '[i]t then becomes clear that monetary policy should not so much be designed to control the level of activity, but rather to find the level of interest rates that will be proper for the economy from a distribution point of view. The aim of such a policy should be to minimize conflict over the income shares, in the hope of simultaneously keeping inflation low and activity high'.

PURPOSE OF *THE ELGAR SERIES ON CENTRAL BANKING AND MONETARY POLICY*

In early 2018, we decided to organize a small gathering on 'the future of central banking', and applied for a financial grant from the Social Sciences and Humanities Research Council (Canada) as they have a wonderful programme for that purpose. The three of us had been having discussions around this topic for a few years before, noticing what appeared to be important changes in central banking and monetary policy, from so-called 'unconventional policies' like quantitative easing and lower-bound policies, to discussions over income distribution, the environment, and the quasi-embrace of at least some version of endogenous money by some central banks.

It was in this spirit that we gathered in Talloires (France), on the shores of Lake Annecy, over a few days on 26–28 May 2019. We invited some well-known heterodox scholars, such as Elissa Braunstein, Gary Dimsky, Juliet Johnson, Marc Lavoie, Dominique Plihon, Mario Seccareccia, but also some more mainstream scholars, like Etienne Farvaque and Ulrich Bindseil, in an effort to encourage a dialogue of sorts on central bank-related topics. We also partnered with the Young Scholars Initiative from the Institute for New Economic Thinking, which funded the travel and accommodation of 11 young scholars. This partnership has proven rewarding for all those involved.

By all accounts, it was a huge success and it was from this gathering that the idea of a book on the same topic was born. To be sure, the resulting book went well beyond the initial plan, as we expanded its scope and breath. The *Future of Central Banking* is the first book of this series, and we divided it into several sections, each dealing with the relationship between central banking, monetary policy and various themes like the environment, gender, income distribution, macro-prudential policies, structural change, and central bank independence.

While we are very proud of that book, and it remains in many ways ground-breaking, it soon became apparent that there was more to be said on each of these topics, and so we began discussions with Edward Elgar Publishing to create a series dedicated to all aspects of central banking. While we signed the contract for the book in July 2019, by November we had signed a contract to create the series. That first book would then anchor the rest of the series.

From there, we felt that many of the topics from the first book needed to be developed, so we decided to do entire books on each of these themes. We agreed on the next four titles: income distribution, the environment, social responsibility, and the future of money, and quickly contacted some possible contributors.

This then launched us in new directions, and new reflections, with the aim of moving forward the critical discussion over the future of central banking, and pushing the boundaries of heterodox thought. In many ways, the mainstream was 'out-researching' us on some of these topics, and heterodox economists had to return to monetary policy and push forward. This was also the rationale for creating the Monetary Policy Institute, which we all direct.

The overall goal of this new series is to contribute to a new research agenda on central banking and monetary policy. Note, the title of the series is not simply 'Monetary Policy' as we understand it – that is, interest rates and their impact on the economy. While there is still much work to be done in this respect – for instance, understanding the impact of incremental changes in interest rates on income distribution and social classes, on gender, on the environment, and so on – we need to go beyond a mere discussion on interest rates, and consider central banks as institutions. This remains a gravely under-developed area of research in economics, though sociologists have considered this topic with great promise. In this context, economists have much to learn from sociologists, and their emphasis on power, for instance.

Indeed, sociological studies on central banking highlight that, as institutions, central banks produce rules that 'coerce' individuals and shape their lives through their policies. In that sense, central banks exert what Susan Strange (1994) called 'structural power' on the economy and society. Such a 'structural power' is personally concentrated in central bankers' hands, whose sociological profile should be put in relation to the distributive nature of monetary policy: do central bankers really serve the people? This crucial argument demonstrates that central banks reciprocally need people's confidence to gain social legitimacy: central banks' power needs to be 'socially embedded'. All in all, central banks are undoubtedly non-neutral institutions, and for that reason economics has a lot to learn from other social sciences.

In the end, the crucial question is whether central banks serve the interest of the people (see Dietsch, Claveau and Fontan, 2018). This opens up a Pandora's Box of questions and more about central banking, monetary policy and social responsibility, democracy, gender, income distribution, and structural change. One by one, these themes are covered in the books in this new series, which aims to push the boundaries of how we analyse, reflect and write about central banks today.

THE STRUCTURE OF THE BOOK

Part I of the book is devoted to theoretical debates relating to monetary policy and income distribution. In Chapter 1, Louis-Philippe Rochon and Mario Seccareccia debate 'what central banks believe they do', arguing that the usual story is that a change in interest rates will impact aggregate demand, and the resulting change in unemployment rate will ultimately affect inflation. However, there is ample evidence that none of these relations actually happen in the economy. The authors then move to 'what central banks really do', arguing that an inflation-targeting (IT) regime is actually an incomes policy, since every interest rate change alters the income of households holding interest-bearing assets. They illustrate their claim by showing that, in Canada, the labour share has declined since the adoption of an IT regime. The authors conclude by advocating for a policy change that widens the social purpose of central banking.

In Chapter 2, Marcelo Milan addresses monetary policy and income distribution from a Marxist perspective. The author highlights the class nature of central banks as capitalist state institutions and argues that this nature determines an important set of constraints over monetary policy. By sorting out the different approaches to the class nature of the capitalist state and therefore of central banks on the one hand, and the role of for-profit monetary institutions in capitalism on the other, he provides an interpretation of monetary policy's likely impacts on distribution. These effects are considered first in terms of intra-capitalist class conflicts (division of surplus between interests and profits) and then inter-capitalist class conflicts (struggles over wages and surplus, considering capital accumulation and employment). Finally, the chapter surveys empirical works showing that monetary policy generally favours capitalists' general class interests, but social struggles prevent mechanical unidirectional causal relations from policy rate movements to functional income distribution.

In Chapter 3, Matías Vernengo explores the various interpretations for the decline in interest rates in the past 40 years, a period in which income inequality increased. The author shows that ideas such as the liquidity trap as defined by Paul Krugman, the global savings glut by Ben Bernanke and the secular stagnation hypothesis of Larry Summers are all based on the notion of a natural rate of interest. After pointing to the theoretical and empirical inconsistencies around this notion, he advocates that interest rates are best seen as the product of monetary authorities' beliefs as well as their interaction with financial markets. He closes the chapter by advocating for a recovery of the ideas of old classical political economy authors, as reinterpreted by modern heterodox authors.

In Chapter 4, Michel Betancourt and co-authors examine how the literature has proposed alternative ways to integrate money within the theory of distribution. This chapter provides a historical perspective on this subject by relating the evolution of monetary analyses to that of the credit and financial structures. The authors argue that the monetary theories of distribution have always been relevant in this literature, pointing out that at the beginning of the 1970s the state of knowledge on the foundations of the economic discipline would have made it difficult to predict the subsequent spread of consensus on the neoclassical views proposed by the New Consensus Macroeconomics. They further argue that this consensus did not depend on the provision of satisfactory analytical answers to the criticisms raised against them after World War II. Those criticisms, they claim, were simply ignored.

In Chapter 5, Jan Toporowski reclaims ideas from Hartley Withers and Michał Kalecki to argue that debt can be regarded as a transfer of income from debtors to creditors once the interest payments are due. Building on the aforementioned authors' works, he then explains that government debt issued in the domestic currency should be viewed as a system of income redistribution, not as a deduction from aggregate income. Toporowski then argues that, in the case of *private* debt, the distributional effects are determined 'by the *net* borrowing or lending position of borrowers and lenders, and only marginally by the rate of interest' (his emphasis). He then concludes that '[t]he main channel by which debt and interest affect the distribution of income is through government debt and the fiscal policy that it facilitates'.

Part II of the book discusses the empirical evidence of the distributional impacts of monetary policy. James Galbraith opens Chapter 6 by revising classical, neoclassical, Keynesian and Marxist views of monetary policy and of the determination of distributive outcomes. He then discusses empirical evidence of the relationship between inequalities in the structure of pay with the unemployment rate, and also with capital asset prices. Galbraith then argues that, for developing countries, there is a relationship between the monetary policy pursued in the US, exchange rates, debt crises and income inequality. Finally, the author stresses that the existence of a link between monetary policy and income distribution has the profound theoretical implication of inverting the case for microfoundations, since, given this link, a macroeconomic policy has major implications for the behaviour of the micro agents.

In Chapter 7, Noemi Levy-Orlik and Jorge Bustamante analyse the distributive character of the interest rate in a sample of Latin American countries through the application of the Pasinetti index for Brazil, Colombia, Chile and Mexico, from 1950 to 2018. They present econometric evidence for an inverse relation between the change in the real interest rate and the growth in real wages for the period 1980–2018, and no relation between these variables for the period 1950–80. The authors provide a historical discussion of these countries' economic history to shed further light on this result, stressing the role of financial deregulation and debt crises.

Mario Seccareccia and Guillermo Matamoros Romero open Chapter 8 with a historical digression about the conceptualization of the distributional impacts of monetary policy in economic theory. After revisiting Keynes's *Tract*, they discuss the mainstream views on this matter, contrasting their positions before and after the global financial crisis (GFC). Their digression concludes with the workings of post-Keynesian authors, especially those of Luigi Pasinetti. In the empirical part of the chapter, the authors present the evolution of the Fisher real long-term rates of interest and two measures of the Pasinetti index for a selected group of industrial countries. They conclude with an analysis of the wage share, indicating that the rentier losses during the post-GFC decade were reflected primarily in increased profits of business corporations.

Finally, Part III of the book is dedicated to policy implications. In Chapter 9, Sascha Bützer argues that outright transfers (OTs) from the central bank to households would constitute a more equitable and effective monetary policy tool to stimulate aggregate demand and achieve price stability objectives than currently employed monetary policy measures, especially in an economy stuck at the effective lower bound. The author discusses a number of practical issues involved in its practical implementation, such as accounting for OTs on the central bank balance sheet, central bank solvency, negative central bank equity, seigniorage and reserve requirements and remuneration. Sascha also provides an overview of a number of important but often overlooked differences between central bank-issued liabilities and government-issued debt. Finally, the author explores legal considerations and concerns regarding central bank independence and democratic legitimacy.

In Chapter 10, Massimo Pivetti discusses the real effects of interest rate policy, as well as its impact on inflation, once the concept of a 'natural' real rate of interest is abandoned and interest is viewed as a monetary phenomenon that contributes to determining normal production costs. The author then debates the merits of cheap money, whilst it is maintained, by contrast, that a persistent zero real interest rate policy would ultimately be incompatible with capitalism. The chapter concludes by pointing out the implications of the main arguments put forward for the status of the central bank and the question of capital control.

Finally, in Chapter 11, Sergio Rossi claims that the GFC that burst in 2008 has not really induced a policy change against inflation targeting, which has been the preferred monetary policy strategy since the early 1990s in an increasing number of countries. He argues that, instead, several central banks expanded their focus beyond price stability on the goods market, to also consider financial stability, although the definition of the latter remains problematic in theory as well as in practice. His chapter then presents the essential characteristics of inflation targeting, which epitomize a revised version of monetarism *à la* Friedman. He then discusses the major shortcomings of it, both before and after the GFC, notably with regard to income and wealth distribution.

The distributive impacts of monetary policy are receiving greater attention from both academia and policymaking circles. Several studies have been published by institutions such as the International Monetary Fund, the World Bank, the Federal Reserve, the European Central Bank and the Bank for International Settlements. While there is increased recognition that monetary policy can affect income inequality, the consensus between policymakers and mainstream authors seems to be that this is a side-effect of pursuing an inflation target, which is the sole or main objective of central banks, and that this effect is temporary, netting out over the business cycle. This can be exemplified in a recent speech by Agustín Carstens (2021), in which he affirms that 'the best contribution monetary policy can make to an equitable society is to try to keep the economy on an even keel by fulfilling its mandate' (p. 1) and that 'delivering on central banks' mandate of ensuring macroeconomic stability provides the best foundation for an equitable society' (p. 3). We hope that this book provides a fruitful guide for those researchers interested in studying central banking and monetary policy beyond the simplistic mainstream view of fine-tuning and inflation targeting, and looking instead to the broader impacts of these actions, without assuming a priori that they are unfortunate side-effects that will disappear in the long run.

NOTE

1.   For a survey following a post-Keynesian perspective, see Kappes (2023).

REFERENCES

Bernanke, B.S. (2003, 24 October), 'Remarks by Governor Ben S. Bernanke at the Federal Reserve Bank of Dallas Conference on the Legacy of Milton and Rose Friedman's *Free to Choose*', accessed 23 March 2022 at https://www.federalreserve.gov/boarddocs/speeches/2003/20031024/default.htm.

Bernanke, B.S. (2012, 7 June), 'Economic outlook and policy: Chairman Ben S. Bernanke before the Joint Economic Committee, U.S. Congress, Washington, D.C.', Board of Governors of the Federal Reserve System.

Bindseil, U. and P.J. König (2013), 'Basil J. Moore's *Horizontalists and Verticalists*: an appraisal 25 years later', *Review of Keynesian Economics*, **1** (4), 383–90.

Borio, C. and P. Disyatat (2010), 'Unconventional monetary policies: an appraisal', *Manchester School*, **78**, 53–89.

Carstens, A. (2021), 'Central banks and inequality, remarks by Agustín Carstens, General Manager of the BIS at Markus' Academy, Princeton University's Bendheim

Center for Finance, Basel, 6 May, 2021', accessed 23 March 2022 at https://www.bis .org/speeches/sp210506.htm.

Colciago, A., A. Samarina, and J. de Haan (2019), 'Central bank policies and income and wealth inequality: a survey', *Journal of Economic Surveys*, **33** (4), 1199–231.

Deutsche Bundesbank (2017), *Monthly Report: April 2017. The Role of Banks, Non-banks and the Central Bank in the Money Creation Process*, Frankfurt: Deutsche Bundesbank, pp. 13–33.

Dietsch, P., F. Claveau and C. Fontan (2018), *Do Central Banks Serve the People?*, Cambridge, UK: Polity Press.

Dodge, D. (2010), '70 years of central banking in Canada', remarks by David Dodge, Governor of the Bank of Canada to the Canadian Economic Association, accessed 23 March 2022 at https://www.bankofcanada.ca/wp-content/uploads/2010/06/dodge .pdf.

Fiebiger, B. and M. Lavoie (2020), 'Helicopter Ben, monetarism, the New Keynesian credit view and loanable funds', *Journal of Economic Issues*, **54** (1), 77–96.

Friedman, M. (1970), *The Counter-Revolution in Monetary Theory: First Wincott Memorial Lecture. Occasional Papers 33*. London: Institute of Economic Affairs.

Gnos, C. and L.-P. Rochon (2007), 'The New Consensus and Post-Keynesian interest rate policy', *Review of Political Economy*, **19** (3), 369–86.

Goodfriend, M. (2007), 'How the world achieved consensus on monetary policy', *Journal of Economic Perspectives*, **21** (4), 47–68.

Goodhart, C. (2011), 'The changing role of central banks', *Financial History Review*, **18** (2), 135–54.

Goodhart, C. (2021, 25 October), 'What may happen when central banks wake up to more persistent inflation?', *Voxeu.org*, accessed 23 March 2022 at https://voxeu.org/ article/what-may-happen-when-central-banks-wake-more-persistent-inflation.

Goodhart, C. and R. Lastra (2018), 'Populism and central bank independence', *Open Economies Review*, **29**, 49–68.

Ihrig, J., G. Weinbach and S.A. Wolla (2021), 'Teaching the linkage between banks and the Fed: R.I.P. money multiplier', *Econ Primer*, September, Federal Reserve Bank of St. Louis.

Jakab, Z. and M. Kumhof (2019), 'Banks are not intermediaries of loanable funds – facts, theory and evidence', *Bank of England, Staff Working Paper No. 761*, June.

Kaldor, N. (1970), 'The new monetarism', *Lloyds Bank Review*, **97**, 1–7.

Kappes, S. A. (2023), 'Monetary policy and personal income distribution: a survey of the empirical literature', *Review of Political Economy*, **35** (1), 211–30. DOI: 10.1080/09538259.2021.1943159.

Kent, C. (2018, 19 September), 'Money – born of credit? Remarks at the Reserve Bank's Topical Talks Event for Educators, Sydney – 19 September', *RBA.gov.au*, accessed 23 March 2022 at https://www.rba.gov.au/speeches/2018/sp-ag-2018-09 -19.html.

Keynes, J.M. (1923), *A Tract on Monetary Reform*, London: Macmillan.

Keynes, J.M. (1936), *The General Theory of Employment, Interest and Money*, London: Macmillan.

Lavoie, M. (1996), 'Monetary policy in an economy with endogenous credit money', in E. Nell and G. Deleplace (eds), *Money in Motion* (pp. 532–45), London: Macmillan.

Lavoie, M. (2006), 'Post-Keynesian amendment to the new consensus on monetary policy', *Metroeconomica*, **57** (2), 165–92.

McLeay, M., A. Radia and R. Thomas (2014), 'Money creation in the modern economy', *Bank of England Quarterly Bulletin*, **54** (1), 14–27.

Moore, B.J. (1988), *Horizontalists and Verticalists: The Macroeconomics of Credit Money*, Cambridge, UK: Cambridge University Press.

Palley, T. (2006), 'A post-Keynesian framework for monetary policy: why interest rate operating procedures are not enough', in C. Gnos and L.-P. Rochon (eds), *Post-Keynesian Principles of Economic Policy* (pp. 78–98), Cheltenham, UK and Northampton, MA, USA: Edward Elgar Publishing.

Robinson, J. (1943), *The Problem of Full Employment*, London: The Workers' Educational Association & Workers' Educational Trade Union Committee.

Robinson, J. (1952), *The Rate of Interest and Other Essays*, London: Macmillan.

Robinson, J. (1956), *The Accumulation of Capital*, London: Macmillan.

Rochon, L.P. (1999), *Credit, Money and Production: An Alternative Post-Keynesian Approach*, Cheltenham, UK and Northampton, MA, USA: Edward Elgar Publishing.

Rochon, L.-P. (2022), 'The general ineffectiveness of monetary policy', in S. Kappes, L.-P. Rochon and G. Vallet (eds), *The Future of Central Banking* (pp. 20–36), Cheltenham, UK and Northampton, MA, USA: Edward Elgar Publishing.

Romer, C.D. and D.H. Romer (1999), 'Monetary policy and the well-being of the poor', *NBER Working Paper No. 6793*. National Bureau of Economic Research.

Romer, D.H. (2000), 'Keynesian macroeconomics without the LM curve', *Journal of Economic Perspectives*, **14** (2), 149–69.

Rudd, J. (2021), 'Why do we think that inflation expectations matter for inflation? (And should we?)', *Finance and Economics Discussion Series: Divisions of Research & Statistics and Monetary Affairs, Federal Reserve Board. Washington, D.C. 2021-062.*

Setterfield, M. (2004), 'Central banking, stability and macroeconomic outcomes', in M. Lavoie and M. Seccareccia (eds), *Central Banking in the Modern World: Alternative Perspectives* (pp. 35–56), Cheltenham, UK and Northampton, MA, USA: Edward Elgar Publishing.

Skidelsky, R. (2009), *Keynes: The Return of the Master*, London: Allen Lane.

Smithin, J. (1994), *Controversies in Monetary Economics: Ideas, Issues and Policy*, Aldershot, UK and Brookfield, VT, USA: Edward Elgar Publishing.

Storm, S. (2019, 3 September), 'Summers and road to Damascus', *Ineteconomics. org*, accessed 23 March 2022 at https://www.ineteconomics.org/perspectives/blog/summers-and-the-road-to-damascus.

Strange, S. (1994), 'The study of international political economy,' in U. Lehmkuhl (ed.), *Theorien Internationaler Politik* (pp. 310–30), Munich: Oldenburg Verlag.

Summers, L. and A. Stanbury (2019, 23 August), 'Whither central banking?', *Project-syndicate.org*, accessed 23 March 2022 at https://www.project-syndicate .org/commentary/central-bankers-in-jackson-hole-should-admit-impotence-by -lawrence-h-summers-and-anna-stansbury-2-2019-08?barrier=accesspaylog.

Taylor, J.B. (1993), 'Discretion vs policy rules in practice', *Carnegie-Rochester Conference Series on Public Policy*, **39**, 195–214.

Taylor, J.B. (2000), 'Teaching modern macroeconomics at the principles level', *The American Economic Review*, **90** (2), 90–94.

The Economist (2021, 9 October), 'Does anyone actually understand inflation?', accessed 23 March 2022 at https://www.economist.com/finance-and-economics/2021/10/09/does-anyone-actually-understand-inflation.

Woodford, M. (2003), *Interest and Prices: Foundations of a Theory of Monetary Policy*, Princeton, NJ: Princeton University Press.

PART I

Theory

1. A primer on monetary policy and its effect on income distribution: a heterodox perspective

Louis-Philippe Rochon and Mario Seccareccia

1. INTRODUCTION

Irrespective of where they live, most households may know of the existence of central banks, but remain in the dark with respect to precisely what they do: central banks remain a mystery to many. One possible reason may be the many confusing and often contradictory discussions economists and policymakers have around monetary policy, interest rates, money and inflation. Indeed, this reminds us of the joke attributed to Winston Churchill: 'If you put two economists in a room together, you get two opinions, unless one of them is Lord Keynes, in which case you get three opinions'.

This short chapter aims to shed light on this confusion – indeed, it is very much in the spirit of Keynes – by looking at the intricacies of monetary policy and by offering another view of what central banks really do when they change the central bank-administered interest rate. When the media talk about central bank policy, they normally describe how monetary policy decisions affect the cost of financing one's mortgage or the impact on credit card payments, which may affect one's creditworthiness both as a consumer or a small firm that needs to finance business working capital. While this may be true, the media do not normally discuss how a change in interest rate also affects the income flow of some groups, often at the expense of others. Nor do they discuss its effect over time on your own regular paycheck if, say, you are an average wage earner holding no financial assets and managing household debt. This is unfortunate, as by ignoring this important second side of the monetary policy coin, so to speak, it can lead to faulty analysis. By seeing monetary policy from the revenue side, it provides economists with an opportunity to cast monetary policy in a different light.

Contrary to popular belief, therefore, monetary policy, by which we mean primarily changes in the central bank-administered rate of interest – the 'overnight rate' in Canada, the federal funds rate in the United States or generally referred to as the benchmark rate – may not do what central banks think they do, or at least not without imposing possible collateral damage on the economy. Again, the media are often silent on this issue. We will argue that, while central bank policy does have an impact on economic activity – the so-called 'transmission mechanism' – it operates primarily through the revenue side, and more specifically, through income distribution. Indeed, the rate of interest in itself must be seen as not only a cost to the public for borrowing funds from financial institutions (one side of the coin), but also as generating income for some group – namely, recipients of investment income, who may hold, for example, a corporate bond or government securities (the other side of the coin). Seen in this way, changes in the rate of interest benefit some, while harming other income groups. In other words, when central banks raise or lower the rate of interest, they will have both a direct and, as we shall see, an indirect impact on income distribution, and there will inevitably be winners and losers.

This chapter begins with a brief discussion of what central banks do, and how they believe their policy affects the economy. We then proceed to discuss the success of their policies, and the wisdom of their current policies. Finally, we discuss a new way of looking at monetary policy that emphasizes its income-distributive nature – a topic that has grown in interest since the global financial crisis of 2008, and during the COVID-19 crisis.

2.   WHAT CENTRAL BANKS BELIEVE THEY DO

Ever since the creation of modern central banks in the nineteenth and early twentieth centuries, the overwhelming policy goal has been to maintain price stability. In this respect, the mainstream story with regard to monetary policy is quite simple: central banks aim to maintain a low and stable rate of inflation for the ultimate well-being of all households, regardless of whether you are a wage earner or a recipient of investment income. Low and stable inflation is said to contribute to a stronger economy.

Since the early 1990s, this approach has been institutionalized under the guise of 'inflation targeting', where central banks raise or lower the rate of interest to affect aggregate spending and the overall economy, which, in turn, presumably, will lower or raise the rate of inflation until a target is reached. In this perspective, what is important to note is that interest rates are considered a cost: the cost of borrowing for the purposes of consumption or investment. Indeed, as the rate of interest increases, the cost of borrowing money from banks increases, which in turn should slow down consumption and investment plans.

In most countries today, inflation-targeting central banks, such as in Canada, aim for a rate of inflation of between 1 and 3 per cent – essentially meaning an official target of 2 per cent, on average, right at the mid-point of a 1–3 per cent band. When inflation – or expected inflation – is above 2 per cent, the central bank ought to increase its administered rate of interest. According to the mainstream view, this lowers consumption and investment, and slows down economic activity. Assuming inflation and economic activity move together, a slowdown of economic activity should bring the inflation rate down to target. This 'fine-tuning' of economic activity continues until inflation reaches its target.

Monetary policy relies on two important relationships to effectuate changes in the rate of inflation via changes in the central bank-administered rate: first, the relationship between interest rate and overall spending (or 'aggregate demand'); and second, the relationship between aggregate demand (as reflected in the level of unemployment) and inflation. Those two relationships must hold for monetary policy to be effective, otherwise, monetary policy cannot do what it claims to do, with the conclusion that it is ineffective.

Over the years, there has been considerable research done on those two relationships. Unfortunately, the conclusion has not been very kind to the mainstream view. For instance, Cynamon, Fazzari and Setterfield (2013, p. 13) claim that:

> [t]he transmission mechanism from monetary policy to aggregate spending in new consensus models relies on the interest sensitivity of consumption. It is difficult, however, to find empirical evidence that households do indeed raise or lower consumption by a significant amount when interest rates change. Some authors have generalized the link to include business investments (see Fazzari, Ferri, and Greenberg, 2010 and the references provided therein) but a robust interest elasticity of investment has also been difficult to demonstrate empirically.

This suggests that the first relationship between aggregate private spending and interest rates may not be very significant, especially for small, incremental changes, which do not appear to have the intended effects: consumption and investment do not seem to respond all that well to changes in the rate of interest – what the authors refer to as the 'interest elasticity' of private spending. Of course, if inflation is higher than 2 per cent, and the central bank raises interest rates several times, eventually, of course, it will collapse the economy. Unfortunately, this is often what happens: central banks raise interest rates several times until the economy simply comes crashing down. This is because central banks are searching for just the 'right' interest rate to keep inflation at 2 per cent – what they call officially the 'neutral' rate of interest. Much like modern oracles, monetary policymakers interpret this 'neutral' rate, which is really unobservable, largely through its manifestation of the rate of inflation. The logic is the following: if inflation is above target, then it must be that policy interest rates are below the neutral rate, and the central bank should therefore raise interest rates.

However, if this quest to bring down the inflation rate by raising its policy rate to its 'neutral' level ends up collapsing the economy, because of the discontinuous/non-incremental relationship between private spending and interest rates, then there is nothing neutral about this rate. Examples abound historically about the devastating consequences of combating inflation through excessively high interest rates on modern economies. For instance, in the North American context, there was the famous Volcker high interest rate shock that triggered the catastrophic 1981–82 recession in the United States, which had direct ramifications for other countries such as Canada, since in the latter case, the Bank of Canada closely followed the American sky-high interest rate policy: short-term interest rates reached over 20 per cent by 1981! Moreover, there is a broad consensus among Canadian economists on the direct role of former Governor John Crow's overzealous policy of combating inflation through double-digit interest rates during the late 1980s, thereby triggering the so-called 'Made in Canada' recession of 1990–91.

Now, what about the second relationship – namely, between unemployment and inflation? Unfortunately, the conclusions are no better. In fact, over the last three decades or so, the relationship has completely collapsed. For instance, the Chief Economist for the Bank for International Settlements (BIS), Claudio Borio, has recently argued that 'the response of inflation to a measure of labour market slack has tended to decline and become statistically indistinguishable from zero. In other words, inflation no longer appears to be sufficiently responsive to tightness in labour markets' (Borio, 2017, p. 2). In other words, inflation no longer seems to move in response to changes in the unemployment rate (or economic activity), except perhaps in a non-incremental way, whereby only extremely low or high rates of unemployment can trigger inflation or deflation in wages and prices. This led Arestis and Sawyer (2003, p. 5) to argue, correctly, that '[i]t is a long and uncertain chain of events from an adjustment in the interest rate controlled by the central bank to a desired change in the rate of inflation'. This conclusion was also expressed by Nobel laureate, Paul Krugman (2018), who called it a 'dirty little secret of monetary analysis…[that] any direct effect on business investment is so small that it's hard even to see it in the data' (n.p.).

These are devastating conclusions for anyone who still believes in the mainstream view of monetary policy, and its expected transmission mechanism. It leaves the conduct of monetary policy in question. In other words, the policy of targeting inflation is in doubt. Yet, this has not stopped central bankers from continuing this policy, or some version of it, despite the empirical evidence against its capacity to control the inflation rate through simple changes in the cost of borrowing. This is not to say that the pursuit of an inflation target does not have consequences or implications, as we explain below. However, it is primarily through an alternative mechanism, which is somewhat different from what we are told.

In turn, this also leads to another important question: 'What then does monetary policy do?' This is what the rest of this chapter attempts to answer.

3.   WHAT CENTRAL BANKS REALLY DO

As we discussed the limited success of monetary policy above, we deal in this and following sections with the nature of monetary policy, or, rather, the dual nature of interest rates, and how changes in them affect the distribution of income and wealth among social classes. We wish to argue that this is the primary way that monetary policy actually affects income and wealth as well as their distribution over time. As readers will note, this is an entirely different explanation than the mainstream perspective. And if this is correct, it raises a number of questions, and places socioeconomic class analysis at the heart of monetary policy.

There are two ways that monetary policy can affect income and wealth distribution: (1) through the income channel; and (2) through the wealth channel. As shown in Figure 1.1, the income channel can be divided into a direct and an indirect mechanism. The direct mechanism begins with the notion that interest rates should not so much be seen as merely a cost of borrowing, but rather as an income for those who own interest-bearing assets. We can call them investment income recipients or rentiers: individuals whose incomes arise not from work, but from simply owning classes of financial assets, such as government bonds and corporate securities. Admittedly, some of us may be both receiving an employment income but also an investment income, either directly or via our accumulated contributions, say, to a group pension fund. However, given the long-term saving rate particularly of most North American households, only those in the highest quintile of income groups can actually save and live sufficiently well from such accumulated savings (see Costantini and Seccareccia, 2020). Moreover, outside the unionized sector, most of the elderly must rely primarily on direct government transfers, or demogrants, in the form of old age social security, which are not necessarily dependent on interest rate policy.

In light of this fact, changes in the rate of interest *directly* affect the distribution of income: the higher rate of interest, the higher the income from holding these financial assets, as the complete spectrum of returns tends to follow changes in the central bank-controlled interest rate. Hence, financial asset-holders from the higher quintiles of the income scale benefit from higher interest rates, and as such from policies that are based on raising interest rates when inflation increases. It is in this sense that Smithin (1996) has referred to high interest rate policies as the ultimate 'revenge of the rentiers', since inflation-fighting monetary policy tends to sustain this latter social group usually at the expense of other income groups in a modern economy.

On the other hand, the policy is detrimental to those in the lower end of the income scale who constitute the most indebted as a proportion of their incomes. This suggests that inflation-targeting policies that have been adopted by central banks since the early 1990s benefit financial asset-holders whenever central banks increase interest rates, but are detrimental to these rentiers when interest rates fall. Hence, the many years of monetary austerity, especially during the last two decades of the last century, have been described as the era of the 'the revenge of the rentiers' precisely because central banks were very kind to financial asset-holders in response to the heavy income losses that had occurred briefly during the late 1970s. Throughout that pro-rentier era that ensued, interest rates rose more quickly than the inflation rate, with a reversal occurring only after the global financial crisis of 2007–08.

The indirect mechanism is related to what was discussed above: changes in the rate of interest may affect incomes, but through their impact on labour markets. In pursuing their inflation-targeting strategy, central banks will raise the rate of interest, which may, if they persist in their policy, eventually have effects on labour markets, unemployment, and thus the income of workers. For instance, as the rate of interest falls significantly in a recession, this may encourage the hiring of workers, a drop in unemployment, and thus an increase in total wages, not to mention that as unemployment falls, workers may also be able to demand higher wages by strengthening their bargaining position. Increases in interest rates could have the opposite effects. Although this indirect effect might be quite weak, especially for short-term incremental changes, the long-term impact of persistently high interest rates would not be insignificant on long-term unemployment, as evidence for most Western industrial countries would suggest over the last two decades of the twentieth century.

As for the wealth channel, consider, for instance, when policy rates of interest diminish, as in the aftermath of the global financial crisis that erupted in 2007–08, or during the COVID-19 crisis, with the aim of supporting economic activity and employment levels. In fact, as already pointed out, neither firms nor households will be induced to increase their borrowing from the banking sector if they fear being unable to repay their debt (and the relevant interest) when it matures. Rather, this reduction in interest rates will spur financial transactions, thus inflating an asset price bubble (Figure 1.1) that is further reinforced by the so-called 'wealth effect', which consists of feeling richer when one's assets are priced more on the relevant market. Clearly, wealthy individuals whose assets are priced more because of a reduction in policy rates of interest will not increase their spending to buy a series of consumption goods, thereby supporting economic activity, but rather increase their spending on real estate and financial markets, thus increasing the relevant asset prices. Holders of these assets will therefore feel richer, giving rise to an upward spiral that could inflate a bubble, threatening the financial stability of the whole system.

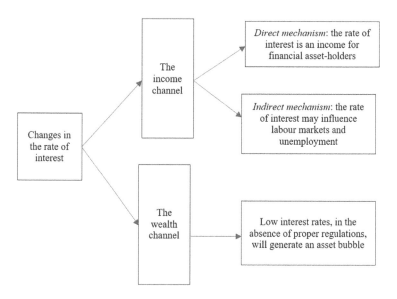

Figure 1.1   The income and wealth distributive effects of monetary policy

The immediate conclusion to be drawn from this short analysis is that monetary policy may work first through income and wealth distribution, and then eventually on aggregate spending and economic activity. Incremental changes in interest rates affect the distribution of both income and wealth between rentiers and workers, and among households. Since we know that poorer individuals spend a greater proportion of their income than wealthier ones, a policy that redistributes toward workers may encourage greater growth. In this sense, a permanent policy of low interest rates is to be considered. Indeed, this is what Rochon and Setterfield (2008) have advocated in their work on interest rate rules. Of course, this policy would then require governments to adopt a proper regulatory framework to prevent financial bubbles.

Yet, the past three decades have shown the fragility of our economic system when monetary policy is not accommodative to workers. Seccareccia and Lavoie (2016) showed that monetary policy has consistently favoured rentiers, with the exception of the global financial crisis and its aftermath, and again with the COVID-19 crisis, thereby exacerbating an already historically unequal distribution of income and wealth. In other words, monetary policy has acted as an incomes policy that protected rentiers, except over the last decade where the focus has been on preventing the collapse of asset prices in the financial markets – for instance, through unsterilized asset purchases by central banks, dubbed quantitative easing, which kept central bank rates to their historical minimum. These are the issues to which we now turn.

4.   UNDERSTANDING THE TRUE NATURE OF CANADA'S INFLATION-TARGETING REGIME

As we have suggested above, monetary policy is akin to what economists have traditionally referred to as an incomes policy. This is because, at its core, monetary policy uses a key lever – in this case, the central bank-administered rate of interest – which directly determines the income of one group, the rentiers. Ultimately, this is to effect changes in wages and prices that impact on the incomes of other social groups in an economy, both wage earners and business profit earners.

To be sure, incomes policies are hardly a new idea: government authorities have often sought to adopt some form of wage and/or price controls to prevent runaway inflation, such as during wartime, for instance. However, there are essentially two types of incomes policies that governments have adopted historically: the voluntary and the compulsory forms.

The most well-known of these voluntary forms in the North American context of decentralized wage bargaining systems were the Kennedy–Johnson Guideposts from 1962 to 1966 in the United States, as well as the federal Prices and Incomes Commission from the end of 1968 to 1972 in Canada. Under this voluntary form, government authorities would communicate a norm or 'target' for prices and incomes growth, which would normally be justified on income distributional grounds and equity considerations.

In the case of compulsory incomes policies, there were some similar features. While they were often met with legal challenges from trade unions due to the obvious fact that they overrode the right to free collective bargaining, the best examples of this compulsory form of incomes policy are the Nixon wage and price controls in the early 1970s in the United States and the Canadian federal Anti-Inflation Board (AIB) that monitored and controlled permissible income growth which lasted in Canada from 1975 to 1978. Under the AIB, the announced maximum allowable income growth imposed by the federal government was based on the principle of compensating workers for at least two important factors: the inflation factor and the national productivity factor. The maximum allowable annual wage increase permitted workers: (1) to recoup loss of purchasing power due to the expected inflation (an extrapolation based on the previous year's inflation rate); and (2) to obtain an inflation-adjusted increase in incomes linked to the long-term annual growth rate in national labour productivity. Hence, such a policy was justified on the underlying policy principle of preserving income distribution 'neutrality', which linked after-inflation (or real) wage growth to overall productivity growth, to ensure that individual income earners would be maintaining their relative share of a growing national income.

We felt it was important to mention these experiences with incomes policy because there is an aspect of the practice of a monetary policy regime of inflation targeting that is somewhat similar to a policy of voluntary guideposts in how central banks dabble with income distribution. While governments historically announced some guideline for wage growth in industries, including the public sector, so that workers and employers incorporated that norm into their negotiating practice, central banks have used a different vocabulary. Yet, the tactical logic of the 'monetary' policy is essentially the same. For instance, in Canada, every time the federal government announces, via its minister of finance, an agreement with the Bank of Canada, by defining its mandate to attain its five-year annual inflation target (as it did in 2016 and in 2021), what it is doing is officially shaping the inflation norm to anchor the latter especially in the collective bargaining arena.

Indeed, central bankers are very fond of saying that a monetary policy of inflation targeting has an impact on inflation primarily via the announcement effect of inflation targets to psychologically modify the public's inflation 'expectations'. If the inflation targets are 'credible' and provided they are marketed and repeated frequently enough, this will eventually align the public's view of inflation with that announced by the central bank. As a result, workers would demand wage compensation increases compatible with the established inflation norm. In contrast with the legal squabbling resulting especially from compulsory incomes policies, the objective of inflation targeting is to inspire public 'confidence' through a communication strategy of 'credibility' that the central bank is serious and committed to its inflation target, thereby anchoring wage demands to their target norm. As former Governor David Dodge (2005, p. 5) put it so succinctly in the case of Canada: 'With inflation targeting, our policy is more focused, our communications are clearer, and Canada's inflation expectations are more solidly anchored'.

However, as Rudd (2021) has argued recently, it is not the 'inflationary expectations' about the future that *in esse* matter. Rather, we wish to argue that it is the acceptable inflation 'norm' credibly promoted by the central bank that can ultimately influence wage demands, particularly in the collective bargaining process. Hence, in the case of Canada, what we have been seeing since the adoption of inflation targeting in 1991 is what the central bank sees as a slow and successful aligning of wage and price changes gravitating around the 2 per cent anchor. However, unlike the old types of incomes policy as under the AIB, this veiled form of incomes control does not need legal/coercive actions of the state to achieve its goal. The central bank does it primarily through a simple communication/marketing strategy of 'repetition' as used in commercial advertising. When one disentangles and tries to cut through all the central bank's mainstream jargon about why achieving its 2 per cent goal brings about maximum efficiency and welfare for participants in both the labour and product markets, ultimately the sole explicit objective is to get the public to voluntarily accept the central bank's 2 per cent norm to fulfill the government's five-year objective.[1]

What if the marketing strategy does not quite work and both workers and businesses are not complying, because the inflation rate begins to exceed the inflation target? The central bank cannot legally enforce compliance, as was the case with compulsory incomes policies during the 1970s. What the central bank does, instead, is use its interest rate lever to get workers and firms to comply through an incomes policy of 'fear'. Through the income channel of the transmission mechanism previously described in Figure 1.1, once interest rates rise significantly enough, we are told that this will eventually slow down the economy, create unemployment, and reduce wage growth and the overall rate of inflation. Unlike the older varieties of incomes policy that were often concerned about distribution neutrality, this inflation-targeting form of incomes policy is hardly neutral on equity principles. Indeed, if workers do not abide by the guideline, the central bank raises the income of one group, the recipients of investment income (or rentiers), through higher interest rates, while simultaneously seeking to reduce the income growth of the others, both wage earners and even business profit income earners.

This perverse and highly biased form of incomes policy that, until the global financial crisis, sustained the income of rentiers at the expense primarily of wage earners is perhaps the most salient feature of this monetary policy regime that placed combating inflation above all other possible goals. It is only after 2008, in a desperate attempt to sustain asset prices from complete collapse, both during the global financial crisis and during the COVID-19 pandemic, that we have seen central banks trading off a cut in the rate of return on financial assets to stabilize and sustain asset values.

5.   INFLATION TARGETING IN PRACTICE

Has this monetary/incomes policy of inflation targeting been successful? It depends on how you measure success. When looked at through the mainstream lenses of the Panglossian world of inflation-targeting central banks, Voltaire's famous expression still resonates that '*tout va pour le mieux dans le meilleur des mondes*' [everything is for the best in the best of all worlds]! With the exception of the global financial crisis of 2007–08 and the COVID-19 crises, we have indeed witnessed an era of 'wage moderation', with the rate of inflation gravitating around the 2 per cent target rate. Also, with wages and prices moving more or less in tandem, this has been associated with a relative stability of real wages over the last three decades. In that narrow sense, we can argue, or at least central banks can, that inflation targeting has been a success.

However, as we have been arguing all along, monetary policy has important income-distributive properties. What then has happened to the distribution of income and, more precisely, labour's share of national income? The answer is displayed in Figure 1.2 if we take, for example, the Canadian experience.

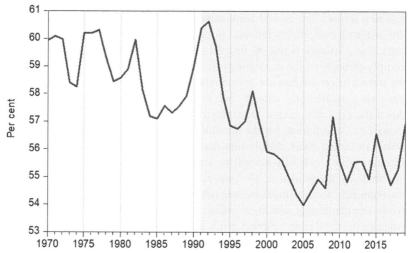

Source: AMECO database, series ALCD2. Data accessed February 2022 from the website: https://ec.europa.eu.

Figure 1.2   *Total economy labour compensation as percentages of GDP at market prices, Canada, annual observations, 1970–2019*

From its local peak in the early 1990s at close to 61 per cent of GDP, the share bottomed at around 54 per cent just before the global financial crisis of 2007–08 (recall that Canada adopted inflation targeting in 1991). Hence, while wages did keep up more or less with the rate of inflation throughout, all the gains in average labour productivity went to non-labour income, with real wage growth being continually outstripped by productivity growth (see Seccareccia and Kahn, 2019). After hitting the bottom immediately before the financial crisis, the local peak of 2009 in Figure 1.2 has more to do with the fact that the rate of inflation fell below wage growth and also the fact that labour productivity growth collapsed during the recession of 2008–09. It was certainly not because money wages were rising more quickly during the financial crisis era. In addition, although some of this decline can also be attributed to other factors during that era – namely, the spread of globalization that weakened wage growth especially of unskilled workers – it would be difficult to conclude that monetary policy did not play a significant role in the collapse of the labour share of national income.

6.   WHAT NEEDS TO BE DONE

As we have shown, the sole focus of keeping a lid on inflation over all other goals, such as full employment, in the context of inflation targeting has led to a weakening of labour's bargaining position in most industrial countries. Higher wage growth will be met with resistance not only by profit-seeking employers, as would normally be so, but also with a response of the central bank that stands ready to raise interest rates whenever the actual rate of inflation exceeds the monetary authorities' target rate of inflation. With money wages moving only commensurate with prices, which the monetary authorities tend to display as a trophy of the success of monetary policy, the whole incomes policy framework of inflation targeting is highly problematic since the policy is inherently biased against labour's share of income. A declining share of labour in a society that would increasingly value unearned rather than earned income is surely unacceptable. Moreover, since workers' wages sustain the bulk of consumption spending in an economy, this pattern of a falling share of labour income can only render future growth ever more vulnerable and dependent on the whims of the international market for its source of growth.

This is why a good number of economists internationally who do not subscribe to the mainstream perspective are now pushing for changes to central bank mandates that would consider other goals in addition to inflation targeting, as we have seen recently with the example of New Zealand (the first country to adopt inflation targeting in 1990), which, since 2018, has opted for a 'dual' mandate. The inclusion of a 'high' or full-employment monetary policy goal can potentially reverse some of the negative consequences of the single objective of inflation targeting on income distribution. This is because it can lead to a strengthening of labour's bargaining position and bring real wage growth to align more closely with productivity growth.

In addition to a strong 'dual' mandate, there are alternative interest rate operating rules that have long been proposed as options that would address the perverse income distribution effects of an 'inflation first' monetary policy. Unlike the full-employment mandate that focuses on increasing labour market tightness, these other options have also been proposed by heterodox economists to primarily address the concern over the distribution between rentier and non-rentier income. To achieve this greater stability of income distribution, it would remove altogether the ability of a central bank to engage in discretionary interest rate policy and would, instead, set the latter on automatic pilot.

As we have reviewed in greater detail elsewhere (Rochon and Setterfield, 2008; Lavoie and Seccareccia, 2019), there have been at least three such proposals that would set interest rates to follow some precise rule. The first of these is sometimes referred to as the Kansas City rule, because it is mostly associated with the originators of what became modern monetary theory (MMT), many of whom were academics based at the University of Missouri at Kansas City. The proposal simply advises that the central bank-administered policy rate, the interbank rate for funds (or overnight rate), be pegged nominally at zero, with other rates on financial assets being marked up on the zero central bank benchmark rate. One can infer that this would stabilize rentier income at a very low level (not unlike what it is presently in many countries) and keep it there permanently, so that the gains arising from increases in productivity go primarily toward non-interest income earners. It would also leave all the heavy work of stabilizing aggregate employment and prices in the economy exclusively to fiscal policy.

A similar, yet slightly different, proposal is what is described as the Smithin rule. Unlike the Kansas City proposal of setting the nominal overnight rate at zero, the Smithin rule would peg the real (or inflation-adjusted) interest rate to a very low, or even at a zero, constant level permanently. This would ensure that neither the 'euthanasia of the rentiers', as in very recent years, would ensue nor would it permit the excessive swelling of rentier income ('the revenge of the rentiers') as had occurred during the last two decades of the twentieth century before the global financial crisis (Smithin, 1996).

A third proposal, sometimes referred to as the 'fair' rate of interest rule, which was the offshoot of an analysis originally proposed by the celebrated Italian post-Keynesian economist, Luigi Pasinetti, focuses on the simple principle of fairness in maintaining unchanged income distribution between rentier and non-rentier income earners and in preserving the value of financial assets, as with individual savings or group pension funds. He believed that interest rates should be set by the central bank in such a way that financial asset value would remain constant in labour time. To preserve this asset value over time in labour time, this would mean that the real rate of interest ought to be tied to the growth of real wages. Since real wages have been relatively flat over the last four decades, a 'fair' interest rate rule in the sense of being neutral in terms of the distribution of income and wealth would have meant that the central bank would be seeking to achieve a zero real interest rate on relatively riskless assets such as long-term government bonds, not unlike the Smithin rule.

We do recognize, of course, that these various 'automatic' or 'park it' interest rate operating rules would be difficult to maintain in the face of international shocks, especially in developing and emerging economies such as in Latin America, which, for instance, face the 'original sin' of servicing debt in a currency other than their own. These 'park it' rules would be hard to sustain in such an environment, thereby necessitating discretionary monetary policy. In some ways, this is why we would be much more favourable to the dual/multi-goal mandate (see, for instance, Lavoie and Seccareccia, 2021) that allows more flexibility in one's choice of options while still being committed to high employment and a favourable income distribution despite adverse exchange rate pressures that can frustrate both the inflation and full-employment goals. This is why it is so important for the government to consider a battery of other measures for the ultimate purpose of slowly asserting a greater degree of monetary sovereignty that is under existential threat in some countries, because, without this sovereignty, the central bank will be heavily constrained. Ultimately, a government must promote the use of its own currency, including perhaps central bank digital currency, if that would facilitate and strengthen local currency use, as well as to pursue more classic options in other policy areas such as import substitution, which would sustain the demand for local currency, and capital controls. Without a significant degree of monetary sovereignty, central banks in emerging economies would be condemned to pursue defensive postures that would frustrate their ability to achieve the objectives of full employment, price stability and a more desirable distribution of income and wealth.

Hence, what is truly necessary is that we return to a policy pragmatism that has disappeared since the 1970s when central banks began to adopt a sole objective under the rubric of what became inflation targeting by the 1990s. The ability to balance policy goals to address evolving policy priorities is what the true art of central banking was once all about until the 'inflation first' policy priority reduced this art to such a single-minded policy objective. After two profound global financial shake-ups in a little over a decade, it is now time for a return to a multi-goal perspective in which employment and income distribution are given their proper place in the hierarchy of goals of central banks.

NOTE

1. By the way, readers may wonder about why 2 per cent was chosen as a goal. This is a good question, with no obvious answer. When one of the authors of this chapter asked former Governor of the Bank of Canada, John Crow, in 1989 what he meant by achieving price stability, he suggested simply 'zero inflation'. However, because of measurement bias of quality change in the Consumer Price Index, some would argue that a number slightly greater than zero might be compatible with 'price stability'. However, we have never been able to find a meaningful answer to why 2 per cent became the norm. As Benjamin Friedman claimed recently, 'there is the arbitrariness surrounding the current 2 per cent target. In retrospect, the paucity of serious empirical research underlying the

identification of the 2 per cent norm, now quite some time back is a professional embarrassment' (Friedman, 2018, p. 187).

REFERENCES

Arestis, P. and M. Sawyer (2003), 'Reinstating fiscal policy', *Journal of Post Keynesian Economics*, **26** (1), 3–25.
Borio, C. (2017), 'Through the looking glass', lecture by Claudio Borio, Head of the BIS Monetary and Economics Department, OMFIF City Lecture, 22 September, accessed February 2022 at https://www.bis.org/speeches/sp170922.pdf.
Costantini, O. and M. Seccareccia (2020), 'Income distribution, household debt and growth in modern financialized economies', *Journal of Economic Issues*, **54** (2), 440–49.
Cynamon, B., S. Fazzari and M. Setterfield (2013), *After the Great Recession: The Struggle for Economic Recovery and Growth*, Cambridge, UK: Cambridge University Press.
Dodge, D. (2005), 'Inflation targeting – a Canadian perspective', *BIS Review*, No. 20, 1–5, accessed February 2022 at https://www.bis.org/review/r050323i.pdf.
Friedman, B. (2018), 'The future of central banking', in European Central Bank, *The Future of Central Banking: Festschrift in Honour of Vítor Constâncio, Colloquium held on May 16–17, 2018*, pp. 187–90, accessed February 2022 at https://www.ecb.europa.eu/pub/pdf/other/ecb.futurecentralbankingcolloquiumconstancio201812.en.pdf.
Krugman, P. (2018, 15 November), 'Why was Trump's tax cut a fizzle?', *New York Times*, accessed February 2022 at https://www.nytimes.com/2018/11/15/opinion/tax-cut-fail-trump.html.
Lavoie, M. and M. Seccareccia (2019), 'Macroeconomics and natural rates: some reflections on Pasinetti's fair rate of interest', *Bulletin of Political Economy*, **13** (2), 139–65.
Lavoie, M. and M. Seccareccia (2021, 23 April), 'Going beyond the inflation-targeting mantra: a dual mandate', Max Bell School for Public Policy, McGill University, accessed February 2022 at https://www.mcgill.ca/maxbellschool/article/articles-choosing-right-target/going-beyond-inflation-targeting-mantra-dual-mandate.
Rochon, L.-P. and M. Setterfield (2008), 'The political economy of interest rate setting, inflation, and income distribution', *International Journal of Political Economy*, **37** (2), 2–25.
Rudd, J. (2021), 'Why do we think that inflation expectations matter for inflation? (And should we?)', *Finance and Economics Discussion Series (FEDS)*, Board of Governors of the Federal System (September), accessed February 2022 at https://www.federalreserve.gov/econres/feds/why-do-we-think-that-inflation-expectations-matter-for-Inflation-and-should-we.htm.
Seccareccia, M. and N. Kahn (2019), 'The illusion of inflation targeting: have central banks figured out what they are actually doing since the global financial crisis? An alternative to the mainstream perspective', *International Journal of Political Economy*, **48** (4), 364–80.
Seccareccia, M. and M. Lavoie (2016), 'Income distribution, rentiers and their role in a capitalist economy: a Keynes–Pasinetti perspective', *International Journal of Political Economy*, **45** (3), 200–223.
Smithin, J. (1996), *Macroeconomic Policy and the Future of Capitalism: The Revenge of the Rentiers and the Threat to Prosperity*, Cheltenham, UK and Brookfield, VT, USA: Edward Elgar Publishing.

2. Monetary policy and functional income distribution: a Marxist view

Marcelo Milan

1. INTRODUCTION

Monetary policy has a direct and simultaneous impact on functional income distribution. Unlike fiscal policy, which typically affects income flows (and wealth) with a lag (unless one assumes a supply-side perspective), monetary policy is about setting the parameter that contributes to the rhythm of real expansion of a specific type of functional income (unless one assumes a monetarist perspective). That is, pursuing a short-term interest rate affects the velocity of growth of part of rentiers' income.[1] Since, on the other hand, interest rates may affect the initial financing of capital accumulation in its different forms, and the corresponding future functional income flows of profits and wages, it can also indirectly impact the distribution. From a Marxist perspective, the relevant distribution of income is indeed the functional one, mainly in terms of profits and wages. Personal income distribution is just a consequence, given the demographics associated with the different classes determined by the concentrated private property of capital that creates functional incomes.

Marx did not offer, given his incomplete works on this subject, detailed contributions to understand these connections, and heterodox economists influenced by him have not provided them either. There is a significant literature on money, interest and credit (De Brunhoff, 1967; De Brunhoff and Foley, 2006; Itoh and Lapavitsas, 1999), but not as many works dealing with banks, central banking and monetary policy (Argitis, 2001 and Argitis and Pitelis, 2001 being exceptions). On the other hand, there is a relevant Marxist discussion about inter- and intra-class income distribution (Levine, 1988), but generally not connected to issues of monetary policy.

Therefore, there is a gap in the literature. This chapter is a contribution to this sparse research area. It proposes a Marxist interpretation of the causality running from conventional monetary policy to functional income distribution. It is the analytical emphasis of the Marxists, in their treatment of central bank and monetary issues, on class conflicts, capitalist institutions and power that is singular. Marxism has a built-in class analysis based on social relations of production and appropriation that provides general trends for functional income distributions as a normal or regular, but not totally determinate, outcome of capitalist economies.

The main argument in this chapter is that monetary policies pursued by central banks reflect a complex collection of class and fractions of class interests, influences, power, expectations and conflicts. Since the class-related aspects of monetary policy involve not only central banks but also the state at large, industrial capitalists and the organizations dealing with money and finance, there is a degree of indeterminacy over the general distributive outcomes. Hence, more concrete analyses must be pursued by looking at the effects of monetary policy for specific periods and national class struggles.

The proposed Marxist approach to the relationship between monetary policy and functional income distribution is pursued in four steps. The first, discussed in the next section, is to engage in a discussion about the class nature of the state in capitalism, given that central banks are still mostly part of the state apparatus.[2] The second step, in Section 3, involves a discussion about the roles of money, credit and banks in capitalism, highlighting the necessarily contradictory nature of central banks, as institutions dealing with reserves and other banks, but from a structured position in the state apparatus. Central banks do not deal with those industrial capitalists who need money to start the circuit of capital in the form of credit, but with banks that provide such initial finance under parameters fixed by the former. It is argued that, as capitalist institutions performing the specialized function of conducting monetary policies, among others not discussed in this chapter, with monopoly over a currency that bears the legitimacy of the capitalist state, central banks have an intrinsic class bias.

The third step in Section 4 widens the analysis by focusing on the fundamental links between credit and capital, the interest rate, and the primary functional income directly and indirectly affected by monetary policy operations: interest on capital. The interest rate is the rate at which many revenues (generated by assets like reserves and loans) and expenses (generated by liabilities like money borrowed to function as capital) grow over a specific period of time, underlining the intra-capitalist distributive conflict associated with it. In this step, the interpretation of the interest rate as a deduction of profits generated in production is assumed.

The final step in Section 5 further develops the argument that monetary policy has a direct impact on intra-capitalist income distribution, by deriving the likely consequences in terms of capital accumulation. Since expanded capital accumulation depends both on previous profits (stocks) and new credit (flows), a deduction of expected profits by interest rates might change the rhythm of capital accumulation. Moreover, as long as it indeed affects capital accumulation, and therefore accumulation of variable capital, employment and wages are also indirectly affected, providing a full impact of monetary policy on functional income distribution. That is, monetary policy changes policy interest rates and part of interest incomes, directly impacting the division of profits. If capital accumulation is modified due to this distribution, monetary policy may have an indirect effect on employment and wages. The exercise basically involves an assessment of policy-induced adjustments in income shares, with the additional difficulty that monetary policy as interest rate manipulation is only one factor impacting functional income distribution. A few empirical findings in the literature are discussed before the conclusions.

2. STATE, STATE APPARATUSES AND CENTRAL BANKS

What is the appropriate starting point to begin an investigation that aims to take us from monetary policy to functional income distribution? Although it is claimed here that monetary policy is an intrinsic mechanism of direct intra-capitalist income distribution, it is not possible to simply establish direct connections between operational procedures of central banks and the total functional distribution of all incomes. The strength of any explanation lies in the identification of relevant intermediate steps and their workings and mutual determinations. It is therefore a valid exercise to consider a more complex approach. It must include all the relevant processes to assess the impacts of monetary policy on income distribution, considering not only the downstream direct impacts on interest income and the indirect effects on capital accumulation, employment and wages, but also the upstream class-based chain of connections leading to the monetary policy in the first place.

This requires properly inserting the role of banks and central banks into capitalism and the relationship between the state and central banks. We assume that this complex route is more revealing about the distributional impacts of monetary policy than the unmediated one. Of course, this increases the degree of indeterminacy, given that the paths from monetary policy, when its class determinants are considered, to capitalist macrodynamics and finally to functional income distribution, are multiple and variegated.

To discuss monetary policy using a Marxist approach, it is important to first consider its class foundations. Monetary policy is apparently about money and policy, but it is primarily about the class politics of stocks, money as an asset and as a liability, and the class politics of flows or interest income of money capitalists as opposed to profits of industrial capitalists.[3] It is about how monetary stocks and flows impact the functional distribution of income. As long as politics (distribution) usually trumps over economics (supposed efficiency) when money is involved (Kirshner, 2003), it is important to understand the single most important structural political institution of capitalism: the state.

Indeed, money or, to be more precise, currency, is also partially a creature of the state. And since money is still mostly national or territorial (Helleiner, 2003), it cannot be legally created by non-financial corporations or households, although they can design private payment arrangements. As a representative of universal or social value, money cannot effectively be the object of private design. Only the state can legitimately perform such a function.

Banks can also create money in the form of deposits that have a fixed exchange rate with the state currency. The fixed exchange rate transfers legitimacy, or lack thereof, to the private money created by banks. Yet, even without assuming the form of a legal currency, money is eminently political, since it is unevenly distributed among groups and classes, creating hierarchies and a relevant source of purchasing power, when in motion, and of political power when it is a stock to be put in motion. Money is about politics even when no state institution is involved in its creation. Yet, when money and state institutions are intermingled, the power of politics is enhanced.

The monetarist simplification of a computer program controlling the stock of money growth in substitution to the central bank in the state apparatus is a hallucination, since it seeks to have a completely depoliticized money supply. Monetarists assume that when politics meets supposedly apolitical money, the only result is inflation, since prices bear a strong correlation with the 'excess' money stock created by politicized central banks above the 'technical' stock of money – that is, the one necessary to stabilize the growth of prices in the quantity equation. However, De Brunhoff (1971) argues that the control of money supply by central banks is possible during periods of crises.

Another illusion of a depoliticized monetary policy is to have government-independent central banks. It is a normative view: there is politics, but there should not be, to the extent that it only causes inflation by keeping interest rates below the divine coincidence level that prevents high inflation. The delusion here is to attempt to isolate central banks from governments in particular and from politics in general. However, as part of the state apparatus, the central bank cannot be run without politics since it is a centralized and hierarchical institution. Independence means setting up an institution that is operationally separated from the government, although it may formally be part of the state apparatus. But politics is not only about the state. Setting interest rates without pressures from elected politicians is still a political decision reflecting class interests, one without institutional mediation that manages class conflicts. As specialized money-dealing state institutions, central banks are intrinsically political.

Modern money is capitalist money, issued by central banks embedded in the capitalist state. That is, central banks are usually part of the state apparatus, which is a source of structural constraint for its instruments and policies. Indeed, De Brunhoff and Bruini (1973) consider monetary policy as a state practice, not a technique, and an ideology of this state activity. There is therefore a sequence going from state as framework to central bank as an apparatus and to monetary policy as a state practice. Monetary policy has institutional backward linkages. This raises the following questions: What is the nature of the state in capitalism? What is the nature of central banks established (created or nationalized) politically by the capitalist state? On the first question, three main positions can be identified in the Marxist literature:[4] instrumentalist, associated with Ralph Miliband; structuralist, linked to the work of Nicos Poulantzas; and the derivationist, first developed by German theorists in the mid-1970s.

The instrumentalist view assumes the *Communist Manifesto*'s claim that the modern executive branch is a committee for managing the common affairs of the *whole* bourgeoisie. The capitalist state is another instrument of the class struggle of capital against labour since the capitalist class dominates the state. State policies are functional to and further the interests of capitalists and strengthen their power against labour. The structuralist perspective, in turn, sees a relative autonomy of the state regarding the class struggle. It is above class conflicts and mediates them, providing social cohesiveness and avoiding political crises caused by unabated class struggle. The state maintains and reproduces the capitalist social structure, mainly the existence of wage-labour, this being necessary to stabilize capitalism.

Finally, the derivationist approach understands the state as an ideal collective capitalist, providing a legal framework for the private transactions and public goods that are difficult to commodify. The state intends to promote the general interests of the capitalist class, but cannot always achieve this goal. The underlying general logic of capital provides an interpretation for the specific historical developments of national states, in which they evolve to fulfil necessary roles that capital itself cannot functionally perform – for example, the reproduction of wage-labour (capital would tend to intensify exploitation to the point of exhausting the available pool of workers).

Regarding the second question, despite the different possible interpretations of the necessity of a state in a capitalist society, none of the previous approaches dealt with monetary policy as a typical state function. Central banks were not emphasized as parts of the capitalist state apparatuses. But, being a part, they necessarily have a class nature. Epstein (1992) complains that these perspectives do not allow the possibility that workers could have an influence on monetary policymaking.[5] He also refers to a corporatist state where policy is jointly made by all classes. State could indeed be sensitive to workers' demands if they are strong and well organized. Yet, experience suggests that central banks tend to be impervious to such interests. Anyway, since the class nature of central banks has far-reaching consequences for understanding monetary policy, Table 2.1 suggests an answer to the second question.

Table 2.1   *State theories, central banks and monetary policies*

State Theory	Central Bank as Part of the State Apparatus	Monetary Policy (setting a short-run interest rate or lending the last resort)
Instrumentalist	Instrument of the capitalist class, mainly banks	Instrument of capitalist interests against workers' interests. Causing reduced capital accumulation and higher unemployment to discipline workers. Labour is overexploited. Higher interest rates. $r > p > w$ (*)
Structuralist	Above specific capitalist interests such as banks, must stabilize capitalism's monetary system	Made from above fractions of capitalist interests, mainly banks and financial. Must provide general capitalist domination without revolt from workers. Full employment or low unemployment would be a goal. Lower interest rates. $p > r > w$. If a financially hegemonic fraction of capital forms a historical bloc and dominates the state, it can gain the upper hand and revert the policy back to $r > p > w$. It would be equivalent to an instrumentalist approach then
Derivationist	Derived from capital along with the state, which is the ideal collective capitalist. Central banks are the ideal monetary capitalist	Must allow the accumulation of capital in general and mainly avoid monetary crises. $p > w$ and $r > w$, but not to the point of starving workers or overexploiting them. Not clear how p relates to r. It probably depends on the historical circumstances. More important is to prevent substantial crises and to restore money as wealth when it gets destroyed by them. Instrumentalism leads necessarily to derivationism

Note: (*) r is the nominal interest rate, p is the nominal profit rate and w is the rate of change in nominal wages (which depends on the bargaining power of workers or employment growth, which in turn depends on expected profits and credit, and therefore on the interest rate).

The inequality symbols are intended to show the likely trends in income shares and class interests that prevail in the making of monetary policy for a given level and distribution of wealth, and are not deterministic about the ability of the central bank to fully manage the general monetary affairs of a complex capitalist economy. As Epstein (1992) argues, probably none of the three state theories can explain monetary policy all the time and across different national capitalist spaces. This means that a unified, general Marxist theory of state must be developed in the near future to cope with central banks and monetary policy. For the moment, it is important to stress the indeterminacy of distributive outcomes. If we assume that the rate of change in wages is very close to the rate of change in prices or inflation, this means that real interest and profit rates are positive for all theories. If productivity changes faster than real wages, then money capitalists and industrial capitalists are in permanent conflict over the resulting profits. Monetary policy can influence this intra-capitalist conflict by setting the policy parameter that, at every moment, and with variable degrees of intensity, influences the direction of market interest rates and the division between profits and interest.

It would be necessary to differentiate between structural or long-term features and transitory attributes of central banks. Monetary policy is an arena of changing conflicts. For instance, Russell (2007) shows how finance can be either a master or a servant to industrial capitalists, with central banks and the state acting as instruments. When the servant relation prevails, we have an interpretation close to structuralist, with industrial hegemony in alliance with labour and low interest rates. But finance may react and form a hegemonic bloc to regain control over monetary policy.[6] Industrial capital could then curb finance with other instruments, like regulation, not just by pressing for low interest rates. Financial collapses may also weaken finance in democracies.

Smithin's (1996) account of the break of the accord between entrepreneurs and rentiers, with central banks setting high interest rates can be seen as an instrumentalist central bank under financial hegemony. Also, the fair interest rule (Rochon and Setterfield, 2007) depends on a structuralist nature of central banks, although capitalism is not about fairness. If r is set close to zero, automatically $p > r$. But the 'euthanasia of the rentier' requires a complete hegemony of the industrial capitalists allied with labour, and a monetary system where the initial finance can be obtained at low interest rates, with institutions willing to provide the loans. Is it feasible to expect that interest-thirsty banks, strongly connected to central banks, would play such a role? Thus, the outcomes of monetary policy are contingent on class struggle. To reduce this uncertainty somehow, in this step of the analysis it is reasonable to assume that the class nature of a central bank is given for the relevant period of time, differentiating between expanding and crisis periods.

It is worth noting that specific industrial capitalist interests have been reflected in specialized apparatuses in the state for policymaking decisions for a long time, such as ministries, bureaus or agencies: ministry of agriculture, ministry of industry, ministry of finance or treasury, and so forth. It is not surprising that banks and financial capitalists have their interests reflected in regulatory agencies and mainly central banks. Yet, a money income is not specific to these institutions. Money as a general wealth binds capitalists, state bureaucrats, politicians and wage workers. So, it cannot be managed by banks alone. Central banks must play this general derivationist role of managing the abstract labour value represented by money.

Moreover, unlike pre-capitalist societies, the capitalist state cannot appear as a class institution, as an instrument for class domination, but as a social or universal contract. Specifically with regard to interest incomes, they are pre-capitalist (or antediluvian), following the circuit $M - M'$. Capitalism represents a change to $M - C - M'$, in which interest-bearing capital cannot be an independent source of value expansion. Capitalism therefore needs not only state management of labour relations, but also of money. That is why free banking – central bank-free capitalism – is not feasible (Itoh and Lapavitsas, 1999). This is particularly clear when central banks provide crisis management in the form of lender of last resort and show their true class nature. They must sustain the stock of money, not only flows of interest payments. If Lenin was right regarding the dependence of capitalism on a stable value of money, then of course central banks play a fundamental collective role.

Itoh and Lapavitsas (1999) mention the nature of central banks, but actually it is a treatment of the functions performed by them: bank of the banks, bank of the state, and holder of international money. They are also operators of monetary policy, and their ability to change interest rates depends on the stage of the business cycle and the relationship between reserves and liabilities. Finally, the authors discuss the functions of overseer of the credit system and lender of last resort. The latter follows the Lombard Street paradigm of Bagehot, when the central bank creates currency without the need to sell commodities or borrow with interest. It also has a derivationist flavour, as a full banking crisis would shatter the entire system. Thus, many of these functions point to actions that cannot structurally be performed by individual capitalists.

Central banks also set an important parameter for the distributive struggle over profits that cannot be fixed by the very capitals aiming at sharing these profits, only by a state-backed central bank. Goodhart (1988) has highlighted this feature by identifying the non-competitive and non-profit-maximizing attributes of modern central banks – that is, as a special bank neither competing with private banks nor driven exclusively by profits; a bank that is therefore institutionally outside the industrial circuit of capital to manage money and prevent profit-seeking competition to cause crises, or to replenish money when it gets rapidly destroyed by the latter. Goodhart claims that this is actually a natural evolution, and this is an argument similar to a modified derivationist view extended to monetary policy. Rather than a natural evolution, the history of central banks reflects the developments and needs of capitalism.

A challenge to this view is the nature of the Federal Reserve System as a hybrid, public or non-competitive, and at the same time, private or profit-seeking institution that distributes profits to banking capital.[7] It is not a central bank, but a federal reserve, a stock of liquidity managed by the federal government based on the regional economic and monetary conditions. It is a political creature, but banks are part of the governance structure. Although these features are not symmetrical, with the state function prevailing, the money capital function has to struggle with other fractions of capital for an adequate interest rate, but at the same time it is easier for the former to have its interests best represented. This institutional arrangement provides a stronger bias to an already class-based monetary policy.

Also, if the crisis of 1907 can explain the creation of the Federal Reserve System to perform the functions played by private bankers like J.P. Morgan, then the derivationist explanation seems more plausible, since the state must create conditions for a well-functioning capitalist economy. And this is carried out not by standing above the class conflicts, but by assuming a specific interest: that of money capitalists. At the same time, the dual mandate is a directive imposed on monetary policy by politics. On behalf of whom? Productive employment is a source of profits. By jointly imposing the need for price stability, it provides directives for safeguarding the interests of money capitalists and, by keeping wages under control, to productive capitals. The dual mandate is a pro-capital monetary policy.

Livingston (1986) suggests that the creation of the Federal Reserve System reflected a rising capitalist ideological coherence and class consciousness at the turbulent end of the nineteenth century. It represented the emergence of a modern ruling class. The Federal Reserve System's independence is built in, since, according to Livingston, it was the result of a reform to remove monetary policy from social control and to depoliticize money against the populist threat to gold. The goal was to achieve long-term economic stability based on a cohesive class programme, political and cultural authority, not short-term profits or temporary advantages. Promoting sound money was seen as technical, not the result of narrow interests.

3. MONEY, CREDIT, BANKS AND CENTRAL BANKS

After laying bare the backward structural connection, now it is possible to advance to the forward linkages. The relationship between state and money as reflected in the existence of central banks has an important counterpart in the relationships between central banks, private banks and credit flows. Although states may affect banks and their loans by other instruments, such as regulation, the channels of monetary policy work mainly through banks. How do central banks implement monetary policy in their connections with profit-seeking banks, given the structural class nature inscribed in the state that the former are part of, and whose apparatus is shaped by the very existence of banking but also of other capitals?

Modern central banks are structurally linked to private banks, since individually they cannot manage the entire monetary system.[8] Banks need a syndicate.

But this J.P. Morgan model is not likely to solve internal, intra-money capital disputes. A derivationist central bank fits this function well. De Brunhoff and Bruini (1973) argue that money plays a contradictory role in capitalism. It enters the circulation of capital $(M - C - M')$ but is also part of the general commodity circulation $(C - M - C)$ as a general equivalent. When it partially detaches itself from the latter to promote an expanded reproduction of the former, a risk of not reproducing the general equivalent is created. The central bank cannot force this reproduction of the general equivalent since it only passively follows the movements of commodities and capitals that are the cornerstone of capitalism. States can define the units of account and the legal status of currencies, but not control the full movements of money. Money in capitalism is not an end in itself. The stock must be permanently transformed into new flows. The end is more money (profit) and central banks can at most regulate the beginning of the circuit mainly in terms of setting the distributive parameters of the struggle between banks and industrial capitalists for the future profits.

De Brunhoff and Bruini (1973) argue that central banks must centralize the convertibility process of private credit money into national currency, to organize the monetary system and make it work. The monetary system is hierarchical, assuming a pyramidal form. Banking money is at the base, international money at the top, and national currencies in the middle. Although central banks conduct monetary policy mainly by dealing with banks in the market for reserves, where the policy interest rate is pursued given the necessity of maintaining the ability of banks to convert their money into state currency, this is not the whole history. As state institutions, central banks must contribute to guarantee the reproduction of the capitals, avoid crises, and then stabilize their distributive conflict over profits.

All these goals are related to the behaviour of credit in capitalism. Credit, in the form of loans or bond holding, creates assets and liabilities and the corresponding income flows affected by monetary policy, interest being just one. As capitalism's goals are making ever-increasing quantities of money, mirroring the interest on credit operations $(M - M')$, banks are fundamental for its functioning by providing loans to complement retained profits as primary sources of money for capital accumulation. If banks are likely to cause crises by interrupting the credit circuit (not advancing credit to industrial capitals or raising interest rates that cause over-leveraged firms to go bankrupt), central banks, acting as a collective capitalist institution, must step in to avoid it. A disorderly functioning monetary system can be harmful to individual capitals and to capital in general.

Banks as institutions dealing with capitalist money are never fully autonomous, since they can create deposits in the form of credit that must bear a fixed exchange rate with the official currency, and therefore must deal with the central bank and other competing banks in the short-term money market. Thus, central banks can affect interest paid on excess reserves, loans to industrial capitalists, bond portfolios, and on interbank loans. But money cannot circulate in the monetary system alone to sustain the reproduction of capital, even banking capital. There is a need for money capital both to start production and to sell it. Wealth matters, and so does credit.

Here uncertainty about the reproduction of money under capitalist conditions cannot be reduced by assuming a more or less fixed monetary and financial structure or policy regime. Money and money substitutes, financial and institutional innovations, banking practices and so on all make this initial movement of the capitalist reproduction chain full of unpredictable results. General money management by central banks is mostly a passive endeavour. For example, financialization was not part of the concerns of central banks in the 1950s and 1960s. As a result of changing capitalist macrodynamics, now they may not even recognize it, given their attachment to Wicksellian wonderland, but they cannot avoid it when pursuing the interest rates, in the form of 'market pressures', interest-elasticities, capital flows and so on.

Therefore, when it comes to the distributive struggle, interest rates set by monetary policy depend on previous policies, struggles and accumulation, reflected in the current distribution of assets and liabilities. Market interest rates are the result of fluctuations of, and property transfers in, stocks, mainly money, but also other capital ownership financed by credit. Despite the efforts of central banks, there seem to be autonomous movements in market interest rates irrespective of monetary policy goals. The emphasis then must be placed first on the stock of money created by credit, which must be converted into capital to create income flows.

Marx did not ignore the above issues. He identified the two fundamental functions of banks. The first is to centralize and redistribute or transfer retained profits, affecting the path of accumulation:

> [T]he banker, who receives the money as a loan from one group of the reproductive capitalists, lends it to another group of reproductive capitalists, so that the banker appears in the role of supreme benefactor; and at the same time, the control over this capital falls completely into the hands of the banker in his capacity as middleman. (Marx, [1894] 1959, p. 494)

And about the consequence in terms of incomes:

> If all capital were in the hands of the industrial capitalists there would be no such thing as interest and rate of interest. (Ibid., p. 370)

But this would limit capital accumulation to past profits (stocks) as the main source of new money. Marx argued that credit is necessary to sustain capital accumulation and commodity production on an expanded scale, although it makes the system more fragile and crisis prone. Providing credit is the second function of banks:

> By means of the banking system the distribution of capital as a special business, a social function, is taken out of the hands of the private capitalists and usurers. But at the same time, banking and credit thus become the most potent means of driving capitalist production beyond its own limits, and one of the most effective vehicles of crises and swindle. (Ibid., p. 593)

Thus the role of banks in capitalism is contradictory. Credit changes the scale of capital accumulation and production, but also of crises. Give profit-constrained capitalists (or over-confident ones) enough rope (credit) to hang themselves. But when they get hanged, the ropes are gone and banks suffer as well, without the forgone ropes and without enough flow of new candidates to be hanged:

> The credit system, which has its focus in the so-called national banks and the big money-lenders and users surrounding them, constitutes enormous centralization, which gives to the class of parasites the fabulous power, not only to periodically despoil industrial capitalists, but also to interfere in actual production in a most dangerous manner – and this gang knows nothing about production and has nothing to do with it. The Acts of 1844 and 1845 are proof of the growing power of these bandits, who are augmented by financiers and stock-jobbers. (Ibid., p. 532)

This makes the existence of a state-backed central bank inevitable. Instability follows credit, and central banks must necessarily be lenders of last resort in a capitalist economy, displaying a built-in derivationist logic. Replenish money first, because without it there is no capital nor profits, by socializing capital losses and sustaining wealth. This type of monetary policy clearly concentrates and centralizes capital, and as the economy enters the ascendant phase again, the flows will be concentrated along the same lines (De Brunhoff and Foley, 2006).

The relevant issue here is whether central banks can solve these contradictions. Since in his time central banks had not fully developed their capitalist roles, Marx engaged in a historical analysis in terms of the British capitalist state itself. For instance, he analysed the Bank Charter Act of 1844 in his rebuttals of the Currency school, siding with the Banking school. The connections with the state (parliament) are clear, as the private Bank of England was subsumed. The impact of pursuing a monetary policy of a structuralist central bank with financial hegemony is illustrated by the Act.

Marx criticized the Act, mainly considering that (1) it reinforced the 1847 and 1857 monetary crises; (2) it did so by restricting the circulation of money and causing a huge increase in interest rates; and (3) it instrumentally favoured monetary and financial interests against industrial interests.[9] However, at the same time, it prohibited issuing private bank notes and imposed the Bank of England notes as the legal tender. It was the act of a proto-derivationist state. Yet, this policy is not feasible when a major crisis occurs since it intensifies the problem. As the industrial capital enters a crisis, profits plummet, unemployment increases, wages fall. And non-performing loans affect the interest income of banks. Inasmuch as crises tend to harm different types of capital, and with them labour, the capitalist state must prevent a collapse and behave like a structuralist state. Thus, it is not straightforward to assume that functional income distribution can indefinitely shift to interest in detriment to profit and wages. It is a general trend, but the concrete result is indeterminate since other classes respond to their losses.

4. INTEREST AS DEDUCTION OF SURPLUS VALUE: MONETARY POLICY AND INTRA-CAPITALIST INCOME DISTRIBUTION

Regarding the nature of interest rates, for Marx they are pre-capitalist phenomena. How does capitalism transform them? Interest is very easily accommodated in capitalism, since it has the nature of a surplus value, an excess over the initial value of money. Thus, it is the income associated with ownership of money, the starting point of any capitalist circuit. But in capitalism, money cannot sustainably increase in value by means of redistribution, as in pre-capitalist societies, although this feature remains in the form of profit upon alienation. Money must grow by means of exploitation of labour. Since only industrial capitalists exploit productive labour, interest represents a struggle between industrial capitalists and money capitalists. Central banks, to the extent that they influence the level and direction of interest rates, shape this intra-capitalist conflict.

Yet, there is a discussion among Marxists and others about the relationship between profits and interest. Panico (1988) shows that classical economists did not treat interest separately. It was part of the bulk of profits or what Pivetti (1987) calls 'normal profits' (profits of entrepreneurs plus interest). Panico rejects the view that Marx neglected nominal interest rates and the money market. He claims that the profit rate sets a limit for the interest rate, but the latter is determined by historical and conventional factors, such as the public opinion about its normal level and the state intervention in money markets – that is, central banks. The author points out an important ambiguity in Marx's writings: assuming on the one hand a Ricardian view that the wage rate is exogenous, and therefore the profit rate determines the interest rate, and on the other hand that powerful banks influence the level of interest rates.

Panico (1988) argues that, for Marx, interest rate determination is a matter of bargaining power between lenders and borrowers. In pre-capitalist societies, usury was dominant, with monopoly power setting very high interest rates. When capitalism began to develop, industrial and commercial capitalists tried to bring interest rates down by means of state intervention, in a typical structuralist view with industrial hegemony. The development of the credit system represented another defeat for the usurers, which were replaced by bankers or money capitalists. Argitis (2001) and Hein (2004, 2006) equally argue that the rate of interest is determined by the struggle between industrial capital and finance.

In terms of distribution, there are two relevant conflicts: between real wages and profits and between profits and interest. The problem for long-term profits is not ground rent, as feared by Ricardo, but interest costs. Pivetti (1985, 1987) proposed a different view. In his view, nominal interest rates regulate first the price level and the wage rate. Thus, profits of enterprise are indirectly determined by nominal interest rates and therefore by monetary policy. Of course, if the decision to set the interest rate is political, the class nature of central banks must be made explicit. His argument is at odds with the empirical evidence, discussed below, that the Federal Reserve System sets interest rates by fully taking into account first corporate profits (financial and non-financial). It is here assumed that interest incomes are residuals deducted from profits.

Thus, interest is a portion of profits generated in the production process. This view is backed by current capitalist accounting practices. For instance, earnings before interest, taxes, depreciation and amortization (EBITDA) considers profits before interest payments are deducted (that is, interests are ex post deductions of profits), similar to a tax imposed on operating profits not by the state but by money capitalists. Intra-capitalist class conflicts do matter for monetary policy. Marx is very clear about the centrality of this distributive conflict:

> On the other hand, profit of enterprise is not related as an opposite to wage-labour, but only to interest... assuming the average profit to be given, the rate of the profit of enterprise is not determined by wages, but by the rate of interest. It is high or low in inverse proportion to it. (Marx, [1894] 1959, p. 372)

In the complete circuit of industrial capital, there is an asymmetrical access to credit between functioning capital and banks. Only the former pays net interest, and the banking sector as a whole earns net interest. To the extent that monetary policy affects the relevant rate that regulates the inflows and outflows of interest payments, the central bank temporarily settles the conflict in favour of one or another fraction of capital. Of course, functional income distribution goes beyond intra-capitalist conflicts: workers pay net interest to rentiers. This is usually not the object of bargaining or conflict, though, and can be taken as given. The same holds for credit-financed consumers and the state. In particular, public debt and its service is about fiscal policy and cannot be dealt with here.

When monetary policy favours banks, industrial capitalists lose income, and so do the indebted working class and other groups. When it is reversed, industrial capitalists win, and the other groups also tend to benefit, directly and indirectly (increasing both gross and net income). Yet, with financialization this may change and cushion the intra-class conflict: industrial capital may also earn interest from their consumers and the state. This may cause the former to support higher interest rates (Papadatos, 2009). What is lost in net earnings against banks is offset by interest earnings against customers and the Treasury. Argitis and Pitelis (2001) argue that industrial capitalists could also favour high interest rates if they facilitated reforming labour relations. As a consequence, during periods of crises, the central bank follows a derivation-ist logic, but during normal times it acquires instrumentalist features. Changes in capitalism cause changes in the capitalist state, its apparatuses and policies.

Epstein (1992) develops a political economy of central banking, focusing on four determinants of monetary policy: inter-capitalist class struggle or capital–labour relations; intra-capitalist class struggle or industry–finance relations; the relationship between the central bank and the capitalist state, or degree of central bank independence; and the structure of international capitalism or place of the country in the world economy. His model is a contested terrain of central banking. Epstein points out that the state, and therefore the central bank, are spaces of class and intra-class struggle.

Monetary policy, on the other hand, is constrained by the structure of capital and labour markets; the position of the country in the world capitalist structure; and capital accumulation. It must be noted that inter-capitalist class struggle can be a defining factor as long as central banks are not independent, and even if they are not, that workers are strong enough to affect wage growth and prices. His model indicates that the Federal Reserve System is a rentier bank since it is independent and the industry–finance link is weak (structuralism with financial hegemony). Interest rates tend to be high, suggesting that renti-ers' share is also relatively high.

In Epstein's discussion, the Deutsche Bundesbank was independent, but the industry–finance connection was strong, and monetary policy tends then towards the interests of capitalists in general. It will be restrictive if labour is strong, and accommodating if labour is weak. We can assume that rentiers' income will be high and profits and wages moderate in the first situation. If interest rates are low, rentiers' income will be smaller, but profits and wages will share a larger fraction of national income. In Sweden, industry is tied to finance, labour is cooperative and the central bank is part of the state apparatus. Thus, monetary policy is corporatist and expansionary. Wages and profits are likely to be higher, and interest income low.

The main problem with Epstein's approach is that the central bank has the ability to manage capitalism exactly according to the contending class interests. If the class struggle is such that independent central banks rule over loose industry–finance relations, it can cause unemployment regardless of profit expectations. If the central bank is under democratic control and industry–finance connections are weak, it could achieve full employment regardless of profit squeezes. The central bank has class and institutional variants, but it is deterministic in terms of what monetary policy can achieve. It lacks that chain of structural determinants that could cause the distributive outcomes to be more uncertain.

5.   MONETARY POLICY AND FUNCTIONAL INCOME DISTRIBUTION: THE IMPACT OF INTEREST ON PROFITS, CAPITAL ACCUMULATION, EMPLOYMENT AND WAGES

Building on the previous discussion, it is possible to take the final step in our gradual approach. Modern central banks consider that their technical (apolitical) task is to keep inflation low and stable. Yet, like interest rates, inflation is not an immediate channel from monetary policy to overall functional income distribution. It is not determined by the quantity of money or low interest rates (compared to a natural rate). Inflation is a complex phenomenon tied to international prices (cost of imports or international intra-industrial capitalist struggle); speculation with raw materials and exchange rates (financial profits upon alienation); and mainly domestic distributive conflicts between wages and profits.

Thus, monetary policy, to the extent that the policy interest rate affects market interest rates, the division of profits between profits of enterprise and interest, capital accumulation and employment, and therefore workers' bargaining power, can affect nominal wage growth and therefore prices, profits and real interest rates. It should be noticed that nominal wage growth, unit labour costs and raw material cost-push price growth are all related to profits of industrial capital. Adding complexity to the discussion, high interest rates aimed at boosting rentiers' income may nonetheless be in the interest of industrial capital to the extent that it slows wage growth and raw material prices more than it drags price changes. Also, a change in interest rates may cause flows of money capital across countries, and therefore changes in nominal exchange rates. This could cause another indirect change in income distribution to the extent that imported wage goods are more important in the consumption of workers than imported circulating and fixed capital and luxury goods for capitalist expenditures. Just like the export sector paying a lower wage as a means to enhance capacity to overcome competing foreign capitals.

Since the source of wages is wage-labour, its path depends on the employment needed for profit-seeking industrial capitals and on the bargaining power of workers. The latter depends on labour policies, capital accumulation and the rate of labour-saving technical progress. If the interest rate directly affects the path of capital accumulation by changing expected profits, then it can indirectly affect employment, wages and actual profits in the second round. Thus, wages depend on capital accumulation, which in turn depends on previous profits and interest rates. Capital sets the tune of income distribution (Lianos, 1987). Effective monetary policies can affect the rhythm and composition of capital accumulation.

These are only likely results, since the very class nature of central banks does not make the results of monetary policy certain, and functional income distribution is affected by other variables. The contested terrain feature, if this is the case, is not restricted to central banks. For example, a wave of labour strikes could harm profits just like high interest rates or a deep financial crisis. We can only indicate overall trends in functional income distribution. This results from the complex explanatory path taken. There are many changing issues involved, and many others not explicitly considered above.

According to Hein (2004, 2006), central banks fix exogenous interest rates that affect profit expectations. Thus, a low interest rate resulting from a structuralist central bank with industrialist hegemony, for example, means larger expected profits if banks do not reduce the flows of credit necessary to complement capital accumulation. Industrial capitalists will accumulate, and employment (assuming no jobless growth) will expand. With low unemployment rates, wages are likely to increase as well. Income distribution shifts in favour of profits and wages. If this process goes on and the industrial reserve army shrinks, at some point class struggle can cause distributional conflicts and rising prices and inflation, reducing real wages and real interests.

Under inflation targeting, nominal interest rates must be hiked. This may cause net expected profits to go down, mainly to less financialized firms. Firms with floating interest rate obligations will have reduced net earnings. Loans become more expensive. So, capital accumulation may be somewhat discouraged. Interest incomes go up. If wages drop due to harder bargaining, functional income distribution is likely to change: profits and wages drop while interest income goes up. If rates are hiked to the point of causing bankruptcies of leveraged industrial capitalists, then the share of interest income may expand faster. But profits and wages will definitely shrink, shifting income distribution towards rentiers. Yet, productivity could go up, reducing the pace of inflation. Profit expectations may give rise to a self-sustaining period of rising profits, accumulation and new profits, reducing the necessity of credit and interest payments.

Thus, monetary policy indirectly affects gross wages by means of the industrial reserve army effect (Argitis and Pitelis, 2001; Epstein, 1992; Green, 1991). As mentioned, household debt that allows the realization of profits in the wage goods industry would represent another source to the direct impact of monetary policy on income distribution, opposing labour to banks, but without any bargaining power for the former. Indeed, given the rapid growth of household debt, a full account of monetary policy impacts on functional income distribution must consider how interest payments affect net wages (Lattanzi-Silveus, 2019). This would add a new layer of complexity to the analysis, allowing innovations for interest payments out of wages, and assessing the evolution of $w - r$ and how labour would try to compensate in terms of $w - p$. This means that monetary policy is first about intra-class conflicts between money capitalists and industrial capitalists, but these conflicts can be extended to tripartite struggle involving labour, industrial capital and finance.

Is there any empirical evidence regarding the issues discussed above? Argitis and Pitelis (2001) evaluated the effects of high interest rates in the US and in the UK from the early 1960s to the mid-1990s. They show how real interest payments from industrial capitalists had grown very fast. The share of industrial profits declined steadily until the early 1990s in the US, recovering afterwards. In the UK, the share was more stable. At the same time, the wage share declined strongly in the UK. This means that in the US industrial profits were squeezed by wages and interests, explaining the high cost-push inflation rates for most of the period.

Epstein and Schor (1990) found that, in the US, for the period 1966–83, the Federal Reserve System included corporate profits in its interest rate decisions, but did not act upon the interests of labour. It provides evidence in favour of the instrumentalist approach. They criticize the liberal theory according to which central banks act in the interest of society as a whole by being inflation-averse since independent central banks tend to practise high interest rates. Thus, they take rentier interests into account, having a special relationship with the financial sector. Epstein and Schor equally reject the bureaucratic theory, claiming that central banks pursue their own internal interests against the interest of society. Central banks have an objective function responding to corporate profits, with weights that can change according to the influence of each fraction of capital. Independence matters because it is easier to pursue pro-capital policies. Finally, Epstein (1992) analysed eight Organisation for Economic Co-operation and Development (OECD) large economies for the 1970–84 period and found that a combination of independent central banks, speculative financial markets and hostile labour–capital relationships tends to strongly correlate with high interest rates and high levels of idle capacity.

6.   CONCLUSION

The discussion above suggests that a Marxist approach can shed important light on the relationship between monetary policy and functional income distribution. When analysing this relationship, it is better to stress first which class and therefore which functional income tends to get a bigger slice of the pie when monetary policy changes. And then observe how the induced distribution affects the size of the pie. The evidence presented suggests that, at least for the advanced countries, monetary policy favours capitalist interests in general, and money capital interests in particular. It is set to increase profits, either by reducing interest rates and boosting accumulation or by increasing interest rates and forcing industrial capital to overexploit labour. These trends are not random in a Marxist reading. They are inscribed in the class nature of central banks as part of the capitalist state apparatus.

But it is necessary to highlight that this structural class determination is neither unchallenged nor permanent. Different class interests at different moments and spaces can cause different outcomes. More empirical research is necessary to observe the full working of the operational part of this inter-pretation (the forward linkages): direction and intensity of changes in policy interest rates, the direction and intensity of changes in market interest rates, the direction and intensity of changes in stocks or in assets and liabilities, the direction and intensity of changes in profits and capital accumulation (also including its composition), and direction and intensity of changes in employ-ment and wages.

The focus on interest rate determination as the main goal of monetary policy is correct, but the lender-of-last-resort function seems to be increas-ingly important as a socialization-of-losses mechanism under a policy regime strongly instrumentalized by finance. Credit has fuelled speculation and destabilized capitalist economies. Central banks have recently not been an instrument of the capitalist class as a whole, but clearly of money capitalists. Monetary policy has an iterative process, favouring first the concentration and centralization of wealth in the form of money capital by high interest rates, including the crises resulting from this policy regime, and then sustaining the income flows derived and the division between industrial capital and banks. It pursues an interest rate that is satisfactory first to money capital, but without completely ignoring profit expectations of industrial capital that allows accu-mulation, employment and wages, and mainly solvency, outside the financial sector.

Monetary policy is not about an independent central bank setting interest rates according to the degree of excess demand in the economy to control the rhythm of inflation for an optimum level of income. Central banks are political institutions defining income distribution according to class interests, expectations, influence and conflicts. Central banks can never be fully independent from politics. They can loosen the leashes of the state structure, but this movement represents a central bank already pursuing a specific class interest: that of the rentiers. There is no possible technical isolation from other political bodies when the central bank is part of the state apparatus. More important, there are no technical issues involved – except the void intention of fine-tuning the velocity of growth of interest incomes that respond directly and indirectly to policy interest rates to the velocity of growth of other capitalist and non-capitalist incomes (domestic and foreign profits, reflected in prices of commodities used for final or intermediate consumption, and wages). Monetary policy is neither art nor science, but pure class politics.

NOTES

1. Throughout this chapter we aggregate different terms such as rentiers, financiers, banks, money or financial capitalists and so on into the same meaning to refer to this fraction of non-wage earners, despite their remarkable differences. By pursuing a short-term rate, the central bank impacts many interest incomes. It first affects the income of banks in the reserves market and in the credit market (creation of loans and other assets whose interest rate is marked up over policy rates). The term structure of interest rates, the value of bonds and other long-term assets and the corresponding income flows are equally affected, but only indirectly. We also do not separate capital gains and losses caused by changes in monetary policy from interest payments.
2. Not all central banks are integral parts of the state apparatus, like the rest of the civil bureaucracy or the military. The Federal Reserve System in the US, for instance, is hybrid, partly owned by the state, partly owned by bank members and financial institutions. The European Central Bank is part of a supranational economic arrangement. Other central banks were private banks nationalized in the post-World War II period (Goodhart, 1988). The choice of a chair for heading the central bank, however, is still ultimately political, and, in that sense, the chair is appointed by politicians in charge of the state apparatus, to manage official monetary affairs, but always with the blessing of the private financiers. The movement towards central bank independence is meant to remove the significance of this political degree of freedom and turn the blessing into an anointing. It is a gradual return to private central banks of the past, with all the potential for more frequent crises.
3. In this regard, works like Colander and Daane (1994) and Clarida, Galí and Gertler (1999) cause a distraction, at best, when they associate monetary policy with an art or a science, as if money and interest rates had nothing whatsoever to do with distribution and class interests and only with achieving the holy grail of macroeconomics: stable growth with inflation subdued.
4. Barrow (1993) includes two other approaches: the system-analytical and the organizational realist.
5. Some Federal Reserve System banks have labour unions on their boards, for example.

6. And credibility as a shibboleth to constrain the central bank from changing course to avoid rampant inflation seems to be valid only when finance has the upper hand.
7. The creation of the European Central Bank represents another challenge to the Marxist interpretations of monetary policy. Although the Deutsche Bundesbank and, to a lesser extent, the Bank of France, and therefore their banks and money capitalists, are the major anchors of the European monetary system, the class conflicts are necessarily more complex. The discussion needs to take into account the transnational positions of different classes and capitals. Given that the movement of industrial capital is slow, and that of money or financial capital is agile, this impacts their relative bargaining power in influencing interest rate changes. This is clearly a field to exploit in future research.
8. Original central banks were created to provide funds for the pre-capitalist states. But these states were struggling to consolidate into national units (absolutism) and also to promote primitive accumulation that would accelerate capitalist development and transform the former states into modern capitalist states and former central banks into modern central banks, oriented to capital more than to the state.
9. Marx provides evidence from the transcribed proceedings of the Parliamentary Committee on the commercial distress that this was indeed the case. Papadatos (2009) reaches a similar conclusion regarding inflation targeting and the sub-prime mortgage crisis, but opposing financial to social interests. The interest rate determination is compared with a public policy, with many conflicting demands putting pressure on it. Yet, it is not clear how central banks could serve the interests of the majority if they are considered an instrument of financial interests.

REFERENCES

Argitis, G. (2001), 'Intra-capitalist conflicts, monetary policy and income distribution', *Review of Political Economy*, **13** (4), 453–70.

Argitis, G. and C. Pitelis (2001), 'Monetary policy and the distribution of income: evidence for the United States and the United Kingdom', *Journal of Post Keynesian Economics*, **23** (4), 617–38.

Barrow, C. (1993), *Critical Theories of the State: Marxist, Neo-Marxist, Post-Marxist*, Madison, WI: University of Wisconsin Press.

Clarida, R., J. Galí and M. Gertler (1999), 'The science of monetary policy: a new Keynesian perspective', *Journal of Economic Literature*, **37**, 1661–707.

Colander, D. and D. Daane (1994), *The Art of Monetary Policy*, Armonk, NY: M.E. Sharpe.

De Brunhoff, S. (1967), *La Monnaie chez Marx*, Paris: Les Editions Sociales.

De Brunhoff, S. (1971), *L'Offre de Monnaie – Critique d'un Concept*, Paris: François Maspero.

De Brunhoff, S. and P. Bruini (1973), *La Politique Monétaire: Un Essai d'Interprétation Marxiste*, Paris: Presses Universitaires de France.

De Brunhoff, S. and D. Foley (2006), 'Karl Marx's theory of money and credit', in P. Arestis and M. Sawyer (eds), *A Handbook of Alternative Monetary Economics*, Cheltenham, UK and Northampton, MA, USA: Edward Elgar Publishing, pp. 188–204.

Epstein, G. (1992), 'Political economy and comparative central banking', *Review of Radical Political Economics*, **24** (1), 1–32.

Epstein, G. and J. Schor (1990), 'Corporate profitability as a determinant of restrictive monetary policy: estimates for the post-war U.S.', in T. Mayer (ed.), *The Political Economy of American Monetary Policy*, New York: Cambridge University Press, pp. 49–62.

Goodhart, C. (1988), *The Evolution of Central Banks*, Cambridge, MA: MIT Press.

Green, F. (1991), 'The reserve army hypothesis: a survey of empirical applications', in P. Dunne (ed.), *Quantitative Marxism*, Cambridge, UK: Polity Press, pp. 123–40.

Hein, E. (2004), 'Money, credit and the interest rate in Marx's economics. On the similarities of Marx's monetary analysis to Post-Keynesian economics', *International Papers in Political Economy*, **11** (2), 1–43.

Hein, E. (2006), 'Money, interest and capital accumulation in Karl Marx's economics: a monetary interpretation and some similarities to post-Keynesian approaches', *The European Journal of the History of Economic Thought*, **13** (1), 113–40.

Helleiner, E. (2003), *The Making of National Money: Territorial Currencies in Historical Perspective*, Ithaca, NY: Cornell University Press.

Itoh, M. and C. Lapavitsas (1999), *Political Economy of Money and Finance*, New York: Palgrave Macmillan.

Kirshner, J. (2003), *Monetary Orders: Ambiguous Economics, Ubiquitous Politics*, Ithaca, NY: Cornell University Press.

Lattanzi-Silveus, L. (2019), 'Consumer finance and labor exploitation', *Review of Radical Political Economics*, **51** (1), 95–110.

Levine, D. (1988), 'Marx's theory of income distribution', in A. Asimakopulos (ed.), *Theories of Income Distribution*, Boston, MA: Kluwer Academic Publishers, pp. 49–74.

Lianos, T.P. (1987), 'Marx on the rate of interest', *Review of Radical Political Economics*, **19** (3), 34–55.

Livingston, J. (1986), *Origins of the Federal Reserve System: Money, Class, and Corporate Capitalism (1890–1913)*, Ithaca, NY: Cornell University Press.

Marx, K. ([1894] 1959), *Capital, Vol. III*, Moscow: Foreign Languages Publishing House.

Panico, C. (1988), *Interest and Profit in the Theories of Value and Distribution*, London: Palgrave Macmillan.

Papadatos, D. (2009), 'Central banking in contemporary capitalism: monetary policy and its limits', *Research on Money and Finance Discussion Paper No. 05*.

Pivetti, M. (1985), 'On the monetary explanation of distribution', *Political Economy: Studies in the Surplus Approach*, **1** (2), 73–102.

Pivetti, M. (1987), 'Interest and profit in Smith, Ricardo and Marx', *Political Economy: Studies in the Surplus Approach*, **3** (1), 63–74.

Rochon, L.P. and M. Setterfield (2007), 'Interest rates, income distribution and monetary policy dominance: post-Keynesians and the "fair rate" of interest', *Journal of Post Keynesian Economics*, **30** (1), 13–42.

Russell, E. (2007), *New Deal Banking Reforms and Keynesian Welfare State Capitalism*, New York: Routledge Press.

Smithin, J. (1996), *Macroeconomic Policy and the Future of Capitalism: The Revenge of the Rentiers and the Threat to Prosperity*, Cheltenham, UK and Brookfield, VT, USA: Edward Elgar Publishing.

3.   Savings glut, secular stagnation, demographic reversal, and inequality: beyond conventional explanations of lower interest rates

Matías Vernengo

1.   INTRODUCTION

Interest rates in the United States have declined over the last 40 years, a period of increasing inequality. The steady decline in interest rates has been interpreted within the mainstream of the economics profession as resulting from a decline of the natural rate of interest, a concept largely abandoned with the Keynesian Revolution in the 1930s, and which was revived slowly, starting in the late 1960s with Friedman's reintroduction of the notion of a natural rate of unemployment. The dominant explanations for the decline in the natural rate of interest, following the conventional wisdom on the topic, tend to emphasize real variables, including an increase in the savings rate and a decline of investment (Goodhart and Pradhan, 2020; Summers, 2014). The argument is fully based on the old marginalist approach, suggesting that monetary factors have only temporary effects on the economy. Mian, Straub and Sufi (2021) have provided an alternative explanation that suggests that inequality is at the heart of the decline of the natural rate of interest. However, their argument also builds on the mainstream real theory of interest, which faces significant logical problems.

This chapter provides a brief overview of the conventional arguments for a lower rate of interest, and for the predictions about a coming reversal. It suggests that low interest rates are not the result of demographical changes, or real changes associated with the prospects of the current stage of industrialization, nor with the effects of inequality on savings. It is suggested that financial fragility, associated with the process of financial liberalization, which started globally with the collapse of Bretton Woods 50 years ago, is to blame. The reasons for increasing inequality, which took place initially as interest rates rose in the 1980s, and continued during the subsequent period as interest rates on average declined, are discussed briefly, and their relation to monetary policy clarified, within the context of an alternative theory of interest based on a revival of classical political economy, in particular the Sraffian tradition that emphasizes the monetary roots of long-term normal interest rates (Pivetti, 1991). Note that the mainstream has also provided extensions of the conventional model to deal with what it refers to as the global financial cycle, which still maintain the prominence of the natural rate of interest (Borio, 2012).

The rest of the chapter is divided into three sections. Section 2 analyzes the main explanations within the mainstream for the lower interest rate, associated with a lower natural rate of interest, with an emphasis on the debate between Ben Bernanke and Lawrence Summers, and the more recent contributions of Charles Goodhart and Atif Mian and their co-authors. Section 3 discusses the financial explanations, based on the notion of a global financial cycle, in particular in the work of Claudio Borio and Hélène Rey, and the continuity with the conventional notion of a natural rate of interest. In both sections, the limits of the conventional view are analyzed and the importance of the notion of an exogenous monetary rate is emphasized. A brief conclusion follows in Section 4.

2.   FROM SAVINGS GLUT TO GREAT DEMOGRAPHICAL REVERSAL

Paul Krugman's rediscovery of the liquidity trap in Japan in the late 1990s (Krugman, 1998) and his insistence that something similar could be adduced for the United States in the aftermath of the global financial crisis (GFC) of 2008 (Eggertsson and Krugman, 2012) has been, perhaps, the most visible outcome of the policy debate about the decline of interest rates over the last few decades. But Krugman did not provide any clear underlying story of the reasons for the low rates per se. Krugman's arguments were normally about the domestic economy, and the problem of the zero lower bound interest rate, or what he somewhat idiosyncratically calls the liquidity trap, and the possibility of a negative natural rate of interest.[1] Bernanke (2005) put forward the idea that interest rates are low as a result of a global savings glut. The reasons for the glut were associated with the accumulation of dollar reserves in the period that followed the financial crises in developing countries, starting with the Tequila crisis in Mexico in 1995, and ending with the Argentine crisis in 2002, also including the Asian, Russian, and Brazilian crises. In this view, the accumulation of reserves, and the depreciation of the exchange rates of foreign countries with respect to the United States, and subsequent current account deficits, led to an accumulation of foreign savings, not matched by investment in these countries, pushing the international interest rate down. The argument was fundamentally based on the traditional marginalist loanable funds theory

(LFT) of interest – with no consideration of the limitations associated with the capital debates – and the notion that the supply of funds, mostly associated with surplus countries like China, Japan, Germany and oil exporters, pushed interest rates down.

In Bernanke's (2015b) view, the solution for the savings glut would be 'to reverse the various policies that generate the savings glut – for example, working to free up international capital flows and to reduce interventions in foreign exchange markets for the purpose of gaining trade advantage' (n.p.). This would, presumably, move up the investment schedule and lead to a recovery. Bernanke used the global savings glut idea to criticize Larry Summers's secular stagnation argument. For Bernanke (ibid.), 'unless the whole world is in the grip of secular stagnation, at some point attractive investment opportunities abroad will reappear. If that's so, then any tendency to secular stagnation in the US alone should be mitigated or eliminated by foreign investment and trade. Profitable foreign investments generate capital income (and thus spending) at home; and the associated capital outflows should weaken the dollar, promoting exports. At least in principle, foreign investment and strong export performance can compensate for weak demand at home.'

Summers (2014), in contrast, argued that the reasons for the declining interest rates were to be found in the notion of secular stagnation, a concept that was originally discussed by Alvin Hansen (1939), the dean of the old neoclassical synthesis Keynesians, in his presidential address to the American Economic Association (AEA). According to Summers (2014, p. 69), 'it is a well-known fact, going back to Alvin Hansen and way before, that a declining rate of population growth…means a declining natural rate of interest. The US labor force will grow at a substantially lower rate over the next two decades than it has over the last two decades, a point that is reinforced if one uses the quality-adjusted labor force for education as one's measure.' In this view, as in Hansen's work, the effects of population growth on the natural rate of interest are positive. In this context, population growth would positively impact the need for investment, and it would lead to an increase in the marginal productivity of capital and to higher interest rates, and conversely in the case of lower population growth.[2]

The main disagreement between Bernanke and Summers was on the relative forces behind the lower natural rate of interest, with an emphasis on excess savings in a global context for Bernanke, and lack of investment, primarily in the United States for Summers.[3] Also, both authors disagreed on the solution for the savings glut or secular stagnation problems. Bernanke would prefer to promote, as noted above, capital account liberalization, and an increase in international investment. At the domestic level, depreciation would also lead to higher exports. Furthermore, capital mobility should lead to more efficient allocation of resources on a global basis, with savings increasing in

the advanced economies in the Western world, in the United States more specifically, and savings falling in the developing nations in the East, in particular
China, but also in other surplus countries.

The logic of Bernanke's position can be represented with a modified version
of the so-called Metzler diagram, presented in Figure 3.1 (Metzler, [1960]
1968). Following the conventional LFT of the rate of interest (r), it assumes
that the natural rate of interest is determined by productivity (or investment, I)
and thrift (or savings, S), and it also shows a situation in which the advanced
Western nations have a lower savings rate and a higher interest rate. This
corresponds to excess savings in the developing surplus countries, and once
capital mobility is established, flows to the advanced economies would
increase the funds available there, and reduce, and eventually eliminate, the
interest rate differential. In this sense, the allocation of capital is more efficient,
and a uniform natural rate of interest would be achieved, corresponding to
a long-standing tradition in economic theory.[4] The monetary variables, in particular the policy rate determined by the central bank, would adjust to the real
variable. In other words, the problem of the zero lower bound would be caused
by an ever lower natural rate, and the real forces would impose limitations on
the ability of the monetary authority to conduct policy.

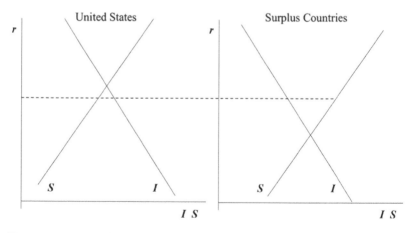

Figure 3.1   Global savings glut

The fundamental role of capital mobility, in this context, is to allow for intertemporal smoothing of savings and investment decisions, and allowing for
international lending to reduce the frictions in the functioning of the system.[5]
In addition, the existence of international financial mobility would allow for
risk sharing, in particular if countries with different patterns of productive and

trade specialization are hit by idiosyncratic shocks (Gourinchas and Rey, 2014; Obstfeld and Rogoff, 1996).[6] Bernanke's defense of free capital mobility was, in this sense, more in line with conventional economic theory than Summers's argument for more expansionary fiscal policy or higher public investment, a position he seems to have retracted in the aftermath of the expansionary programs related to the COVID-19 pandemic recession.

Both the secular stagnation, as discussed by Summers, and the savings glut, as presented by Bernanke, theories rest on the idea of an excess supply of savings. Summers (2015) was clearly skeptical about exchange rate depreciation as a solution to the US stagnation, and the empirical evidence for an external recovery on the basis of a more depreciated dollar is certainly not convincing, since the US has maintained a persistent current account deficit, in spite of fluctuations in the value of the dollar, with a clear and mild tendency to depreciation since the end of Bretton Woods. But there was no clear difference on a theoretical level. Summers (2015) said that the 'essence of secular stagnation is a chronic excess of saving over investment' and that 'secular stagnation and excess foreign saving are best seen [as] alternative ways of describing the same phenomenon' (n.p.). Further, he argued that '[s]uccessful policy approaches to a global tendency towards excess saving and stagnation will involve not only stimulating public and private investment but will also involve encouraging countries with excess saving to reduce their saving or increase their investment. Policies that seek to stimulate demand through exchange rate changes are a zero-sum game, as demand gained in one place will be lost in another' (n.p.).

Summers suggested that one of the problems with Bernanke's argument would be that competitive depreciations would make that a dead end in policy terms. His argument was not on whether depreciation, the relative price substitution effect, would be enough to boost exports or reduce imports, a proposition that might be questionable in the same way as the notion that a lower interest rate would stimulate investment,[7] Summers was essentially arguing that China and other surplus countries should boost the world economy. The so-called global imbalances should be reduced to solve the problem of a lower natural rate of interest. The position seems to suggest that the United States did not hold a privileged position, associated with the international role of the dollar as the key global currency, and that in these circumstances, as famously noted by Charles Kindleberger (1973), it would befall to the hegemon to promote the global recovery.

More recent work by Goodhart and Pradhan (2020) tends to emphasize the role of population growth and the effects of the entry of the Chinese economy into global markets, but some of their conclusions differ from the savings glut and secular stagnation hypotheses. In their view, and in contrast with the Bernanke–Summers argument, the fundamental effect of demographic factors in the last decades was to cause a significant increase in savings, and reduce the rate of interest.[8] For them, higher population growth associated with the entry of China and Eastern European economies into the world economy increased population growth and reduced dependency ratios, leading to higher economic growth, in a Solowian growth effect, and also to higher savings ratios. In this view, it is the higher savings associated with a younger labor force that explains the lower natural interest rate, and that forced the lower policy rates, which in turn have led to what the authors refer to as a debt trap. In Goodhart and Pradhan's (2020) words, '[t]he deflationary bias over recent decades, reinforced by the Global Financial Crisis (GFC), has led to massively expansionary monetary policies, with interest rates, both nominal and real, coming down to historically exceptionally low levels. This has, as was intended, led to a dramatic increase in debt ratios, both in the public and private sectors' (p. 17). But the reversal of the demographic tendencies of the last few decades should lead not only to the rise of inflation and lower growth, but also to a higher natural rate of interest. They suggest that 'real, inflation-adjusted interest rates, particularly at the longer end of the yield curve, may rise... because of the behaviour of ex-ante (expected) savings and investment. That the elderly will dissave is not controversial. Those who believe real interest rates are likely to fall or stay low clearly believe that investment will fall even further below savings – we disagree' (p. 12).

The authors also suggest that inequality was also a by-product of the increase in the labor force, reducing bargaining power, and that the reversal would not lead to lower inequality and higher risks of inflation (ibid.). In other words, the same forces that led to a lower natural interest rate caused the increase in inequality. But in their view, inequality was not instrumental in bringing about the lower natural rate of interest. This is the argument developed by Mian et al. (2021), who indicate that rising income inequality is more important than the aging and demographic forces in explaining the decline in the natural interest rate. Like Bernanke and Goodhart and Pradhan, the emphasis is on savings behavior, rather than investment.[9] They note that savings rates are higher in higher income groups, and that higher inequality since the 1980s is the main driving force in the decline of the natural rate. This has important policy implications, since if inequality has sources other than the demographical reversal, and inequality is the main driving force behind the lower natural rate, then there is little reason to expect that the great demographic reversal would lead to higher rates.[10]

In other words, Mian et al. (2021) also rely fundamentally on the marginalist LFT to explain the decline in interest rates over the last three decades. There are too many well-known logical problems with the marginalist theory of value and distribution (Dvoskin and Petri, 2017). The investment schedule and the very existence of a natural rate of interest, negative or otherwise, is plagued by logical problems and by the complete lack of empirical evidence, since investment really reacts to changes in the level of activity, in line with the acceleration principle. Also, the notion that intertemporal decisions govern consumption behavior is not without its problems, an issue raised by Keynes in the *General Theory* (GT). That is why Keynes abandoned the LFT and tried to do the same with the notion of a natural rate of interest. The capital debates show that with factor price reversals, when one good can be said to be capital-intensive at one level of the wage–profit ratio, and labor-intensive at another level of the same ratio, there is no monotonic inverse relation between investment and the rate of interest. The investment schedule might misbehave, with portions that have a negative slope and some in reverse, and there might be no interest rate that equilibrates investment with full employment savings.[11] That means that the monetary authority can set the rate of interest, what Keynes referred to as the normal rate in the GT, which was conventional not psychological, as he suggested, and that the level of employment would be determined by autonomous spending. All this is well known, or should be.

The logical problems associated with the notion of a natural interest rate are compounded by the empirical limitations for the determination of an unobservable variable. The twin notion of the natural rate of unemployment, which is achieved when the economy is at full employment in the labor market, and when investment equals savings, and, hence, a natural interest rate prevails, is a good example of the limitations of conventional measures. While initially the natural rate of unemployment was often portrayed as relatively fixed, eventually a discussion of its variability over time become central, in particular after the evidence in Nelson and Plosser (1982) that showed that output as measured by GDP follows a random walk and exhibits strong hysteresis.[12] Note that in the conventional measures of the natural rate of unemployment or the time-varying non-accelerating inflation rate of unemployment (NAIRU), it is the actual rate that is used to calculate the normal long-run variable, in a reversion of the theoretical notion according to which the short-run variable gravitates around its equilibrium position. The same is true of measures of the natural rate of interest that for the most part follow the methodology introduced by Laubach and Williams (2003). The authors use a Kalman filter measure based on the actual and optimal or natural output levels, but, as in measures of the NAIRU, these imply that the actual variables determine the estimated natural rate and not the other way around. In other words, there is no solid empirical basis for any measure of the natural rate.[13]

Keynes suggested famously in the GT that he was 'no longer of the opinion that the concept of a "natural" rate of interest…has anything very useful or significant to contribute to our analysis' ([1936] 1964, p. 243). Beyond the exegetical issues about his ability to do so in his own analytical framework, it is clear that the notion of a conventional monetary rate of interest, independent of real forces, implies an abandonment of the real rate dependent on productivity and thrift analyzed by all modern authors, which remain pre-Keynesian in that sense.[14] Keynes was building on a tradition that harked back to classical political economists on the anti-bullionist and Banking school side of the nineteenth-century debates, which emphasized the monetary nature of the interest rate. In this view, the monetary rate is not an allocative variable but a key distributive variable, determined by the monetary authority and acting as the gravitation center for the rate of profit.[15] The reasons for the fall in the rate of interest should then be searched for in the policy decisions of the monetary authorities.

The interest rate can be seen, as noted by Aspromourgos (2007, p. 514), as the result of '"history" plus the beliefs of the monetary authorities, where those beliefs may be illusory but nevertheless validated by actual outcomes.' To understand the falling trend in the interest rates, one needs to delve into the history of the interaction between monetary authorities and financial markets – in particular, the period after the financial liberalization and deregulation processes that started globally in the 1970s, increasing the importance of what the mainstream has come to refer to as global financial cycles.

3.   FREE CAPITAL MOBILITY AND CENTRAL BANK POLICY RATES IN THE CENTER AND THE PERIPHERY

The monetary and financial order built in the aftermath of World War II, during the Bretton Woods era, tried to reduce exchange rate volatility. However, the main characteristic of the Bretton Woods system was not the fixed, but adjustable, exchange rates, but the introduction of capital controls. Keynes saw these as central for the functioning of the system as a permanent feature of economic policy, and not a mere solution to reduce instability during crises (Pivetti, 1993). In an institutional framework in which the monetary authority exogenously determines the interest rate, and affects the dynamics of public debt accumulation, the ability to maintain relatively low interest rates on public debt in order to expand the scope of the welfare state was seen as a key precondition for the functioning of the system (Vernengo and Rochon, 2000).

The abandonment of Bretton Woods is often portrayed in conventional wisdom as resulting from the inability or incapacity of the United States to maintain the fixed parity, in the face of external imbalances, and discontent among key players with the inflationary policies that were exported to the rest of the world (e.g., Eichengreen, 2021). But this view has little support in practice. It was not only the decision to abandon Bretton Woods that was clearly pursued by groups within the United States and other advanced economies that had an interest in a more open financial order (Helleiner, 1994), but also the dollar hegemonic position was enhanced by the demise of Bretton Woods since the restrictions that tied the dollar to gold were eventually eliminated (Vernengo, 2021).[16] The end of Bretton Woods should not be seen as the result of the inevitable collapse of the Keynesian consensus of the so-called Golden Age. In fact, the collapse of the system by the neoliberal groups seeking free capital mobility, in part to force average higher interest rates, and higher remuneration to capital, were preconditions for the demise of Keynesian policies.

Over the last five decades since the collapse of Bretton Woods, a process of financial deregulation and liberalization has led to a large increase in flows of capital and to an increase in the relative size of the financial sector, often referred to as financialization (Epstein, 2005; Palley, 2007).[17] Although there are many characterizations of the phenomenon, not all mutually compatible, it is clear that there is an underlying fear that this process of financial liberalization, and the increasing role of finance in the functioning of the global economy, may be seen as an unproductive and speculative activity that does not contribute to economic development (Barba and DeVivo, 2012) and it may be central to understanding the global increase in inequality during this same period (Galbraith, 2016). Further, this financialization process has become clear in mainstream circles, where the idea of a global financial cycle has become widely accepted (Borio, 2012).

Borio and Disyatat (2011) was one of the seminal papers in the literature on the global financial cycle. Borio (2012) suggested that capital flows were procyclical and more regulation in general was needed to preclude the financial crises. The definition of the financial cycle was based on individual perceptions. In his view, financial cycles result from 'self-reinforcing interactions between perceptions of value and risk, attitudes towards risk and financing constraints, which translate into booms followed by busts' (ibid., p. 2). There were three analytical variables that are essential to understanding the global financial cycle. First, that financial cycles have endogenous causes, second, that debt must be present, and last, but not least, a different measure of the output gap that includes financial variables. Borio correctly noted that output gap measures only take inflation into consideration when ascertaining whether the economy is above its potential level or not, and that 'it is quite possible for inflation to remain stable while output is on an unsustainable path' (ibid., p. 9) and one could add that inflation might accelerate even if the economy is not at full employment. Borio's measure of the output gap included information about asset price inflation too – for example, property prices and measures of credit booms.

Note that his new output gap measure would indicate, for economies where there were asset bubbles like the United States before the 2008 crisis, that they were over the potential or natural level, or at least by more than in the conventional measures that did not take into consideration financial assets.

Borio (2012, p. 14) concluded that '[p]otential output and growth tend to be overestimated.' In other words, what the measure suggests is that the supply constraint of the economy is often much harsher than assumed by conventional methods. Further, Borio's point when arguing that the cycle is endogenous is that excessive booms are the cause of the collapse, so what is needed is to smooth out the boom. The prescription is to slow down growth and avoid surpassing the potential level, which is supply determined and exogenous as in conventional views about the functioning of the economy. The reasons for the excess in the boom are associated with excessive finance, which he called excess elasticity of the system, as in Shin's (2012) global banking glut, and not excessive savings, since he correctly points out that '[e]xpenditures require financing, not saving' (Borio, 2012, p. 12). In this sense, Shin seems to have, to some extent, a better picture than Bernanke about the reasons for lower interest rates, but his views are still underpinned by the notion of a natural rate of interest.[18]

It is worth noting that Borio, James and Shin (2014) also noted that in the process of trying to integrate financial flows into conventional open macroeconomic models, too much attention has been paid to the current account and not enough to the capital account. For them, the important policy implication was that '[t]his analysis has major implications for central banks. Given their primary responsibility for monetary and financial stability, central banks inevitably end up under the spotlight once the focus shifts to asset prices, balance sheets and financial crises. As long as the focus is on current accounts, central banks' role is necessarily more peripheral' (p. 21).[19] The emphasis on the current account is what is traditionally associated with the focus on net flows, while a focus on the capital account would lead to an emphasis on the gross flows, and the accumulated stocks.

It is exactly on the basis of the importance of gross flows within the global financial cycle that Rey (2013, 2015) put forward the notion that countries were not faced by a trilemma, but simply by a dilemma or tradeoff between free capital mobility and independent monetary policy, irrespective of the exchange rate regime. According to her, 'there is a potent global financial cycle in gross capital flows, credit creation and asset prices, which has tight connections with fluctuations in uncertainty and risk aversion' (2013, p. 286). Gross flows were larger, and the correlation was tighter between advanced economies in North America and Western Europe, but they were in sync globally, with the exception of Africa, and Asia in the case of foreign direct investment (FDI) flows. Rey (2013, p. 294) argued that the global financial cycle vindicates the view of Calvo, Leiderman and Reinhart (1996), according to whom the main factors behind the cyclicality of flows were related to global factors, normally referred to as push factors, which included the interest rate in the hegemonic or dominant country, meaning the United States, the rate of growth in advanced economies, and global risk-aversion factors.[20]

By contrast, domestic factors or pull factors, which include the domestic interest rate and rate of growth, and the domestic risk factors, including, for example, the level of domestic reserves, would be considered less relevant.[21] In this view, the flows to developing countries were to a great extent the result of the lower rates of interest in the United States and other advanced economies – in particular, starting in the 1990s. However, as the Federal Reserve policy rate went up after the 1992 recession, flows to the periphery still continued. Similarly, after the collapse of the dot-com bubble in the early 2000s, the higher interest rate in the United States did not seem to tame financial flows to parts of the periphery, and this gave more credence to those that emphasized pull factors. It is worth noticing that push and pull factors are interrelated, to some extent, and that it would be reasonable to assume that the influence of decisions in the center has a larger impact on domestic factors in the periphery, rather than vice versa. For example, monetary policy decisions in the United States and Europe influence the decisions in developing countries, and this can be seen by looking at the policy rates of central banks (Figure 3.2).[22]

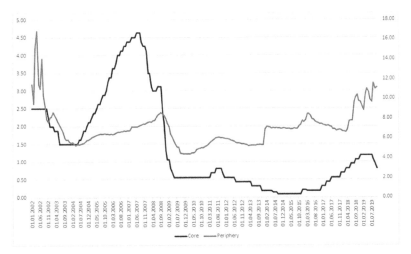

Source: Bank for International Settlements.

Figure 3.2   Policy rates of central banks

In that sense, although the predominance of global push factors is often accepted, there is an increasing consensus that 'global factors do not affect capital flows to all countries equally' (Cerruti, Claessens and Puy, 2019,

p. 134). Some countries are very sensitive to global push factors, while others are considerably less vulnerable, even if the direction of the flows remains highly correlated, and macroeconomic fundamentals do not seem to be central in explaining these differences (ibid., p. 145). The same authors suggested that 'countries with deep and liquid equity and bond markets, and with a high reliance on global mutual funds, are the most exposed to changes in global conditions' (ibid.). All these results reinforced the idea that macroprudential policies and capital account management restrictions might have a role in taming excess volatility, even for mainstream authors, which has led to the erroneous assumption that they have abandoned conventional views about the determination of economic fundamentals.

As should be clear, the mainstream literature on global financial cycles, in general, suggests that capital controls are second-best tools, since they do not address the fundamental causes of excess elasticity of financial markets, and that microprudential regulation should be utilized to constrain booms. They might be necessary only before the domestic financial market becomes more developed. Rey (2013, p. 311) argued that 'capital flows are beneficial only after a country has reached a certain amount of institutional or financial sector development' and before that presumably capital controls would be an acceptable tool. Macroprudential policies, including capital controls, should be used for that aim fundamentally in crisis situations.[23] Further, while noting that in balance sheet recessions, following the seminal contribution by Koo (2008), it is important to deal with agents' losses head on, Borio (2012, pp. 18, 20) suggested that 'fiscal policy is less effective than in normal recessions' and that as a result of excessive monetary expansion after the bust 'the central bank's autonomy and, eventually, credibility may come under threat.' In other words, the true objective of policymakers is to smooth out the booms to preclude the collapses, and there is an implicit notion that some degree of austerity in the boom might be instrumental, since nothing much beyond re-writing debt down and acting as a lender of last resort can be done afterwards.

There are some significant limitations with the global financial cycle view, even if there are some good things, not least the recognition of its relevance and the role of the hegemonic country in shaping the global cycle. But to suggest that the problem with the cycles is excessive financial elasticity and the excesses of the boom associated with a global economy beyond its capacity limit, seems an inadequate explanation for the problems both in the core and the periphery. In fact, there is abundant evidence for the notion that potential output varies with demand expansion, according to the Kaldor–Verdoorn law, and it seems that a revision of conventional methods of measuring capacity utilization would lead to the opposite conclusion (Fontanari, Palumbo and Salvatori, 2021). In advanced economies, the problem was not so much that the economies were beyond their capacity limit, and that they were overborrowing, even though private agents certainly did, as much as the fact that the accumulation of debt was less sustainable because it relied on unregulated private instruments (Barba and Pivetti, 2009), and that it was exacerbated by income inequality (Galbraith, 2012). But in advanced economies, with debt in domestic currency, the ability of their respective central bank to rescue their insolvent agents is limitless, as noted in the literature now referred to as modern money theory (MMT) (Wray, 2012).

More importantly, the literature on the global financial cycle does not sufficiently emphasize the problems associated with accruing debt in foreign currency, and the qualitative differences of the problems in peripheral countries. In particular, decisions about interest rates in the core countries, which affect asset prices and exchange rates, have a significant impact on the balance sheets of national governments and private agents in the periphery. Akyüz (2021) notes that in the last decades it has led to large international financial markets and wealth transfers from developing to advanced economies. This occurred, in part, because 'changes in interest rates, asset prices and exchange rates in major reserve-currency countries affect economic and financial conditions in emerging economies not only through their impact on international capital *flows*, but also by altering the value of their outstanding *stocks* of gross international assets and liabilities' (Akyüz, 2021, p. 233; original emphasis). In particular, a large proportion of external liabilities of developing countries are assets denominated in the currencies of advanced economies. As a result, valuation changes generated by changes in asset prices and exchange rates entail transfers of wealth from the former to the latter.[24]

Furthermore, as should be clear from the review of the literature on the mainstream on the global financial cycle, it seems that the notion of a natural rate of interest based on the LFT prevails, and that capital mobility is seen essentially in a positive light, even if sometimes in the presence of imperfections, capital controls might be temporarily needed. In other words, capital controls are for the most part rejected in dominant policy circles.[25] The reason to introduce macroprudential policies is to eliminate the excessive speculation or the global banking glut, the financial version of Bernanke's explanation for the lower natural rate of interest. In this view, central banks were forced to reduce interest rates in the last 30 years because of the financial crises and the need to rescue the financial sector, but were unable to use the traditional instruments of monetary policy, the blunt effect of raising rates, because of the lower natural rate. As Bernanke (2015a) argued, '[t]he bottom line is that the state of the economy, not the Fed, ultimately determines the real rate of return attainable by savers and investors' (n.p.).

Many authors within the mainstream associate the increase of credit necessary to maintain the expansion of aggregate demand to the increase in inequality since the 1970s, and emphasize the fact that this expansion occurred hand in hand with the reduction of interest rates. Mian and Sufi (2018) emphasize what they refer to as the credit-driven household demand model, and while they recognize the role that inequality and the importance of spillover effects, beyond asymmetric information, and the importance of investors 'neglect[ing] tail risks' (p. 49) played in the global financial crisis, it is still true that their model remains grounded in the conventional New Keynesian analysis. As they suggest, in their model, 'the downturn is driven initially by a decline in aggregate demand which is further amplified by nominal rigidities, constraints on monetary policy, banking sector disruptions, and legacy distortions from the boom. The credit-driven household demand channel is distinct from traditional financial accelerator models…primarily due to the centrality of households as opposed to firms in explaining the real effects of credit supply expansions' (p. 52).[26]

More importantly, Mian and Sufi (2018) remain tied to a view of the cycle as somewhat independent of growth, the latter being dependent on supply-side conditions presumably, and, hence, the role of monetary policy and macroprudential policy is essentially one that should be seen as smoothing out the cycle by reducing the expansion of credit and the excessive risk taking during the boom. Their policy conclusion, even if cautious, is that regulators should impose macroprudential limits on household debt and that monetary policymakers should 'lean against the wind' during credit supply expansions (p. 52). This would contrast with alternative views that emphasize the importance of credit for demand expansion, and of the latter for growth.

The work by Hyman Minsky, cited by Mian and Sufi (2018), is certainly relevant, but in ways that escape their analysis. Minsky argued that the conventional theory suggested that the financial sector could only be disrupted by the functioning of an otherwise stable economy and that was equivalent to a barter economy, while the capitalist economies discussed by Keynes and his followers corresponded to what he referred to as the Wall Street paradigm. In other words, the relevant framework was that of a capitalist economy in which the objective is the accumulation of capital in monetary form. The central idea in Minsky's financial instability hypothesis (FIH) was that the normal functioning of the capitalist economy would lead to a financial crisis, not as a result of imperfections but because the process of competition would compel firms to adopt increasingly fragile financial structures. In other words, in his famous dictum, stability was destabilizing. This view is in accordance with the so-called critical macro-finance (CMF) approach that argues that global finance is organized on interconnected, hierarchical balance sheets, increasingly subject to time-critical liquidity (e.g., Bonizzi and Kaltenbrunner, 2020; Gabor, 2020). This, of course, needs to be grounded on a monetary theory of the rate of interest, in which the central bank of the hegemonic country sets the globally relevant interest rate.

In this context, central banks have been forced to reduce interest rates, as the Federal Reserve did, as a result of the increasing financial volatility that followed the process of deregulation of domestic financial markets and liberalization of capital flows, which started in the 1970s, and culminated with the victory of the neoliberal paradigm in the 1990s. Nominal rates only remained high in the 1970s because of high inflation. Once inflation fell, as the cost pressures and the distributive conflict eased, the monetary rates went down. It is the financial instability that caused the monetary rates to come down, and that forced the average long-term rate to decline too. More importantly, financial instability is also at the root of the inequality that increased over the last 40 years, as the two processes are intertwined (Galbraith, 2020).

4.   CONCLUDING REMARKS

This chapter provides a survey of alternative interpretations of the decline in interest rates over the last 40 years. Most explanations are based on the conventional marginalist LFT, which suggests that the real forces behind productivity and thrift are the main cause for lower monetary rates. In this view, the monetary rates determined by central banks have been constrained by these developments. Paul Krugman's notion of a liquidity trap was the seminal contribution in a revival of the notion of the natural rate of interest that has its origins in Milton Friedman's presidential address to the AEA. The debate between Ben Bernanke and Larry Summers, between the global savings glut and the secular stagnation hypotheses, emphasized alternative views about the reasons for a lower natural rate of interest. Atif Mian and Charles Goodhart's contributions, with co-authors, have added new wrinkles to the traditional story.

The conventional view suffers from logical and empirical problems that are ultimately unsurmountable. Only with the Keynesian critique of the notion of a natural rate of interest, which requires the abandonment of the marginalist theory of value and distribution behind the LFT, and with the explicit understanding of the alternative monetary theory of interest rates, as determined exogenously by the monetary authority of the hegemonic country, is a coherent explanation of the low interest rates in the last four decades possible. This requires the recovery of the ideas of old classical political economy authors, together with the ideas of Keynes and his followers, as reinterpreted by modern heterodox authors. It is argued here that the exogenous interest rate, controlled by the Federal Reserve, is the ultimate cause of lower rates globally, and that ultimately the cause for the lower interest rate in the United States is the process of financial deregulation and the instability that followed.

NOTES

1.   Sumner (2021, p. 5) suggests that Krugman's paper should be compared to the famous presidential address to the American Economic Association (AEA) by Milton Friedman (Friedman, 1968) and should be seen as 'the most important macro article of the past 40 years'. He calls New Keynesian contributions by Krugman and some other key authors in the literature on the zero lower bound, including Bernanke and Krugman, but also Gauti Eggertsson, Lars Svensson and Michael Woodford (the Princeton school), and sees it as distinctive from the Chicago school. It will be contenteded here that, while there are policy differences, the main arguments within the discussion of the decline of the rate of interest are essentially Wicksellian, and that the theoretical framework is essentially the same. On the limitations of a negative natural rate of interest, see Di Bucchianico (2020) and Serrano, Summa and Garrido Moreira (2020).

2.   For Hansen (1939, p. 8), investment, and hence the natural rate of interest, could be attributed '(a) to population growth, (b) to the opening of new territory and the discovery of new resources, and (c) to technical innovations.' The closing of the frontier, the slower population growth – a preoccupation in which Hansen was influenced by Keynes's work in the *Eugenics Review* (see Backhouse and Boianovsky, 2016, p. 951) – and the reduced outlets for investment were ultimately the cause of stagnation, particularly the last two. In Hansen's words, 'it is my growing conviction that the combined effect of the decline in population growth, together with the failure of any really important innovations of a magnitude sufficient to absorb large capital outlays, weighs very heavily as an explanation for the failure of the recent recovery to reach full employment' (Hansen, 1939, p. 11). Note that in this view is the collapse of the marginal productivity or efficiency, in more Keynesian terms, of capital that explains both stagnation and a lower interest rate.

3.   Summers's argument seems to be more in line with Robert Gordon's view that the Third Industrial Revolution requires less investment and is associated with lower rates of growth than the previous two major changes in the structure of production (Gordon, 2016).

4.   In spite of significant differences that can be ascribed to both classical political economy authors of the surplus approach, like David Ricardo, and marginalist authors, like Knut Wicksell, in both cases competition would impose an equilibrium interest rate determined by real forces. In classical economics, it must be noted, the profit rate that was the center of gravitation for the monetary rate, was a residual rate, and was not related to abstinence, thriftiness, or the savings rate. There are many problems from a logical point of view with the notion of a natural rate of interest, and the notion of a well-behaved investment schedule, which are well-established in the literature. For a recent description of the main critiques of conventional marginalist theory, see Petri (2015) and Dvoskin and Petri (2017).

5.   The theoretical foundations of capital account liberalization are well-established and not difficult to understand. According to Eichengreen (2001, p. 341), '[t]he case for free capital mobility is thus the same case for free trade but for the subscripts of the model. To put the point another way, the case for international financial liberalization is the same as the case for domestic financial liberalization.' In this view, financial markets provide intermediation for intertemporal decisions to consume, and guarantee that investment adjusts to full employment

savings. The free mobility of capital leads to the adjustment of the domestic interest rate to the international rate, as much as free entry in any industry at home would equalize the domestic profit rate.

6. In the more traditional Mundell–Fleming (MF) model, a model that included some Keynesian features, capital mobility implied that monetary policy was inefficient in a context of fixed or stable exchange rates – the so-called impossible trinity or the trilemma. Some fundamental problems with the MF model are discussed in Summa and Serrano (2015).

7. There is a literature on the contractionary effects of depreciation that harks back to the work of Albert Hirschman, Carlos Díaz-Alejandro, and formalized by Krugman and Taylor (1978). In this literature, depreciations do solve external problems by causing a recession and reducing imports, rather than by boosting competitiveness and exports. In this view, the effect is mediated by income distribution effects. A depreciation by redistributing income to exporters, which are seen as wealthy capitalists, and reducing real wages by increasing the costs of basic goods consumed by workers, leads to a lower effect of spending on income and a recession. A classical view in which the foreign exchange rate should be seen as a key distributive variable is developed in Vernengo (2001).

8. For Goodhart and Pradhan (2020), '[m]any of those who argue that personal sector savings will remain high enough to keep real interest rates and aggregate demand low (the secular stagnation camp) do so on the assumption that (1) the age of retirement will rise relative to the expected age of death, and/or (2) that state benefits to the old will fall relative to the average income of workers. If either were to happen, the rate of increase of expenditure on the elderly would be less than the output generated by workers. Both are possible, but neither are likely, for social and political reasons' (p. 73).

9. In this respect, Summers is closer to heterodox traditions, as he himself recognized. He said: 'This formulation of the secular stagnation view is closely related to the economist Thomas Palley's recent critique of "zero lower bound economics": negative interest rates may not remedy Keynesian unemployment. More generally, in moving toward the secular stagnation view, we have come to agree with the point long stressed by writers in the post-Keynesian (or, perhaps more accurately, original Keynesian) tradition: the role of particular frictions and rigidities in underpinning economic fluctuations should be de-emphasized relative to a more fundamental lack of aggregate demand' (Summers and Stansbury, 2019, n.p.).

10. Mian et al. (2021, p. 34) argue that '[t]he traditional demographics view argues that measures of r^* should be expected to rise as the baby boom generation retires, a process that is already underway. More recently, there has emerged disagreement on whether shifting demographics should be expected to raise or lower r^* going forward. In contrast, the rising income inequality view explains the current situation with considerable ease. Income inequality today remains extremely high relative to its pre-1980 level, and there does not appear to be any reversion in inequality in the near future.'

11. Some Austrian authors claim that they have a purely subjective, or a pure time preference, theory of interest that is not open to the capital debate critique. They base their argument on Böhm-Bawerk's notion that there is a need for time or waiting as an independent factor in the determination of interest. Kirzner (1993, p. 104) argues that '[i]f time and waiting are not themselves to be considered productive agents, no interest could emerge as a result of the productivity of

time-consuming processes of productions.' Note, however, that this is a confusion between necessary and sufficient causes. Obviously, in the marginalist theory, a supply of savings curve based on time preferences is necessary, but it is certainly not sufficient to determine the rate of interest without saying something about the ability to produce more goods in the future. One would still need to adjust the time preferences to the ability to obtain more consumption in the future, and that would be the role of the marginal productivity of capital. One cannot escape the need for a measure of capital.

12.   The common interpretation, at least among real business cycle (RBC) authors, is that supply shocks cause the change of the natural output level, which when faced with a disturbance does not revert to its trend. The trend and the shocks that cause the cycle have a common nature, and this would explain the strong hysteresis in the data. Of course, there is a simpler explanation that is not open to the logical problems of showing that the system tends to be at the optimal output level at all times, or the empirical difficulty of suggesting that cycles are caused by supply-side shocks. That would be to accept the notion that the long-run trend is determined by autonomous, non-capacity-generating spending, as in the Sraffian supermultiplier. See Bortis (1997) and Serrano (1995).

13.   For all practical purposes, the evidence cited in Holston, Laubach and Williams (2017) that suggests that in the United States and other advanced economies the natural rate of interest has fallen to zero, is simply a reflection that actual rates have fallen. The empirical measure of the natural rate cannot be used to explain the fall of the actual rates without falling into logically circular arguments, since the data on the latter is part of the explanation of the natural rate itself.

14.   The fact that modern macroeconomics is Wicksellian, and remains pre-Keynesian, is probably the only good reason to refer to authors that try to advance the Keynesian principle of effective demand as post-Keynesian, in the sense that the theories are a development on the notions that came after Keynes, and Kalecki. On the history of the term, see Lavoie (2009).

15.   The key author in that tradition is Thomas Tooke, and the modern notion derives from the work of Piero Sraffa and has been developed by Pivetti (1991).

16.   On the role of the dollar as the key hegemonic currency, see Fields and Vernengo (2013).

17.   Some of these ideas were discussed in Latin American circles even before the literature on financialization developed, and associated with the notion of financial dependency (Vernengo, 2006). A literature on the existence of long-term debt-default cycles was relatively well established by the 1980s, after the debt crisis of the early 1980s, which hit Latin America particularly harshly, leading to stagnation, as the rest of the periphery recovered and growth even accelerated in other parts of the periphery, in particular Asia. Debt-default cycles could be seen as driven by the current account problems, and the problems of technological dependency that were emphasized by structuralist authors. Medeiros (2008) argues that financial dependency was at the center of an external cycle that was forged since the nineteenth century in the case of Latin America, and associated with the policies to promote globalization and integration into world markets. In other words, orthodox macroeconomic policies – in general associated with fiscal austerity and adherence to some form of monetary restriction that emphasized inflation as the central concern (e.g., Gold Standard, quantitative monetary controls, inflation targeting) and the independence of the central bank from the fiscal authority – were pursued to maintain the open capital and current accounts

of the balance of payments, often with some desire for relative stability of the nominal exchange rate, which was undermined by events in the center, and reversion of capital flows.

18. This literature resembles in some sense the post-GT literature on the so-called finance motive. It is worth noting that the finance motive literature, which remains relevant in some post-Keynesian circles, is very much about the demand for money, and related to conventional marginalist assumptions about it. On an early skeptical view of Keynes's liquidity preference theory (LPT) of interest rates by Piero Sraffa, see Kurz (2015). According to Kurz (2015, p. 117), 'Sraffa observes that the inverse relationship between holding cash and the rate of interest, i.e. the liquidity preference curve, is reminiscent of the usual *marginal utility curve*' (original emphasis).

19. This is certainly not new, and Kindleberger (1987, p. 18) argued that, citing Henry Wallich, 'capital flows dominate the balance of payments and exchange-rate changes,' and that they are the proverbial 'tail that wags the dog.' This is not to say that the current account is irrelevant. In fact, export performance is central for the ability to repay debt in foreign currency. For the sustainability of debt in foreign currency see Cline and Vernengo (2016).

20. Rey (2013, p. 310) argues that 'one important determinant of the global financial cycle is monetary policy in the center country, which affects leverage of global banks, credit flows and credit growth in the international financial system.'

21. Domestic factors very often include countries' macroeconomic fundamentals, including the size of reserves, current account position, fiscal position, economic growth, and its institutional environment – that is, sovereign risk, institutional quality measures. See Fratzscher (2012), who suggests that during the global financial crisis, push factors were more relevant.

22. The policy rate is a simple average of the Fed and European Central Bank (ECB) for the core and the rates of the central banks of Argentina, Brazil, Chile, China, Colombia, India, Malaysia, Mexico, Peru, Thailand, and South Africa for the periphery. The correlation is relatively weak for the period as a whole, but much stronger in the 2002–14 period. In part, this might be explained by the increasing issuance of instruments in the domestic currency in the periphery, which accelerated in the last few years (Hale, Jones and Spiegel, 2020).

23. Rey (2013, p. 315) is explicit about it, suggesting that since 'it is really excessive credit growth that is the main issue of concerns, capital controls should be viewed more as partial substitutes with macroprudential tools.' Her argument is in the context of the use of capital controls as temporary instruments, rather than permanent tools for managing capital flows. The logic of the temporary use of capital controls is well explained by Eichengreen (2003, p. 279), who suggests that emergency situations call for emergency solutions.

24. Since the problems associated with not issuing instruments in their own domestic sovereign currency, the so-called 'original sin' problem (Eichengreen and Hausmann, 1999), and the existence of a financial external restriction, are not temporary, then the question that literature raises is, ultimately, whether capital controls should be used as a permanent tool of capital account management by peripheral economies, as Keynes defended during the Bretton Woods negotiations.

25. Krustev (2019) provides a model that adds the global financial cycle, as discussed by Borio and co-authors, to the Laubach and Williams (2003) methodology for measuring the natural rate of interest.

26. The conventional view on the mechanism relating household debt to the demand boom has been compellingly challenged by Mason and Jayadev (2014) and Mason (2018), who suggest that the bulk of the increase in household debt was not associated with demand expansion, but simply resulting from on average higher interest rates, in particular in the period before the 2000s. Note that another fundamental channel through which debt affects household consumption would be through the mortgage market.

REFERENCES

Akyüz, Y. 2021. 'External balance sheets of emerging economies: low-yielding assets, high-yielding liabilities.' *Review of Keynesian Economics*, **9** (2), 232–52.

Aspromourgos, T. 2007. 'Interest as an artefact of self-validating central bank beliefs.' *Metroeconomica*, **58** (4), 514–35.

Backhouse, R. and Boianovsky, M. 2016. 'Secular stagnation: the history of a macroeconomic heresy.' *European Journal of the History of Economic Thought*, **23** (6), 946–70.

Barba, A. and DeVivo, G. 2012. 'An "unproductive labour" view of finance.' *Cambridge Journal of Economics*, **36** (6), 1479–96.

Barba, A. and Pivetti, M. 2009. 'Rising household debt: its causes and macroeconomic implications – a long-period analysis.' *Cambridge Journal of Economics*, **33** (1), 113–37.

Bernanke, B. 2005. 'The global saving glut and the U.S. current account deficit.' Remarks by Governor Ben S. Bernanke at the Sandridge Lecture, Virginia Association of Economists, Richmond, Virginia, March 10. Accessed November 2021 at https://www.federalreserve.gov/boarddocs/speeches/2005/200503102/.

Bernanke, B. 2015a. 'Why are interest rates so low?' *Brookings.edu*. Accessed November 2021 at https://www.brookings.edu/blog/ben-bernanke/2015/03/30/why-are-interest-rates-so-low/.

Bernanke, B. 2015b. 'Why are interest rates so low, part 3: the global savings glut.' *Brookings.edu*. Accessed November 2021 at https://www.brookings.edu/blog/ben-bernanke/2015/04/01/why-are-interest-rates-so-low-part-3-the-global-savings-glut/.

Bonizzi, B. and Kaltenbrunner, A. 2020. 'Critical macro-finance, Post Keynesian monetary theory and emerging economies.' *Finance and Society*, **6** (1), 76–86.

Borio, C. 2012. 'The financial cycle and macroeconomics: what have we learnt?' *BIS Working Papers, No. 395*. Bank for International Settlements.

Borio, C. and Disyatat, P. 2011. 'Global imbalances and the financial crisis: link or no link?' *BIS Working Papers No. 346*. Bank for International Settlements.

Borio, C., James, H. and Shin, H.-S. 2014. 'The international monetary and financial system: a capital account historical perspective.' *BIS Working Papers No. 457*. Bank for International Settlements.

Bortis, H. 1997. *Institutions, Behaviour and Economic Theory: A Contribution to Classical-Keynesian Political Economy*. Cambridge, UK: Cambridge University Press.

Calvo, G., Leiderman, L. and Reinhart, C. 1996. 'Capital flows to developing countries in the 1990s: causes and effects.' *Journal of Economic Perspectives*, **10**, 123–39.

Cerruti, E., Claessens, S. and Puy, D. 2019. 'Push factors and capital flows to emerging markets: why knowing your lender matters more than fundamentals.' *Journal of International Economics*, **119**, 133–49.

Cline, N. and Vernengo, M. 2016. 'Interest rates, terms of trade and currency crises: are we on the verge of a new crisis in the periphery?' In A. Gevorkyan and O. Canuto (eds), *Financial Deepening and Post-Crisis Development in Emerging Markets: Current Perils and Future Dawns*. London: Palgrave Macmillan, pp. 41–62.

Di Bucchianico, S. 2020. 'A note on Krugman's liquidity trap and monetary policy at the zero lower bound.' *Review of Political Economy*, **32** (1), 99–120.

Dvoskin, A. and Petri, F. 2017. 'Again on the relevance of reverse capital deepening and reswitching.' *Metroeconomica*, **68** (4), 625–59.

Eggertsson, G. and Krugman, P. 2012. 'Debt, deleveraging, and the liquidity trap: a Fisher–Minsky–Koo approach.' *Quarterly Journal of Economics*, **127** (3), 1469–513.

Eichengreen, B. 2001. 'Capital account liberalization: what do cross-country studies tell us?' *World Bank Economic Review*, **15** (3), 341–65.

Eichengreen, B. 2003. 'Capital controls: capital idea or capital folly?' In B. Eichengreen (ed.), *Capital Flows and Crises*. Cambridge, MA: MIT Press, pp. 279–88.

Eichengreen, B. 2021. 'Bretton Woods after 50.' *Review of Political Economy*, **33** (4), 552–69.

Eichengreen, B. and Hausmann, R. 1999. 'Exchange rates and financial fragility.' In *New Challenges for Monetary Policy: A Symposium Sponsored by the Federal Reserve Bank of Kansas City, Jackson Hole, Wyoming, August 26–28*, pp. 329–68.

Epstein, G. 2005. 'Introduction: financialization and the world economy.' In G. Epstein (ed.), *Financialization and the World Economy*. Cheltenham, UK and Northampton, MA, USA: Edward Elgar Publishing, pp. 3–16.

Fields, D. and Vernengo, M. 2013. 'Hegemonic currencies during the crisis: the dollar versus the euro in a Cartalist perspective.' *Review of International Political Economy*, **20** (4), 740–59.

Fontanari, C., Palumbo, A. and Salvatori, C. 2021. 'The updated Okun method for estimation of potential output with broad measures of labor underutilization: an empirical analysis.' *INET Working Paper No. 158*. Institute for New Economic Thinking.

Fratzscher, M. 2012. 'Capital flows, push versus pull factors and the global financial crisis.' *Journal of International Economics*, **88**, 341–56.

Friedman, M. 1968. 'The role of monetary policy.' *American Economic Review*, **58** (1), 1–17.

Gabor, D. 2020. 'Critical macro-finance: a theoretical lens.' *Finance and Society*, **6** (1), 45–55.

Galbraith, J. 2012. *Inequality and Instability: A Study of the World Economy Just Before the Great Crisis*. Oxford: Oxford University Press.

Galbraith, J. 2016. *Inequality: What Everyone Needs to Know*. Cambridge, UK: Cambridge University Press.

Galbraith, J. 2020. 'Inequality and instability.' In J. Barkley-Rosser, E. Pérez Caldentey and M. Vernengo (eds), *The New Palgrave Dictionary of Economics*. London: Palgrave Macmillan.

Goodhart, C. and Pradhan, M. 2020. *The Great Demographic Reversal: Ageing Societies, Waning Inequality, and an Inflation*. London: Palgrave Macmillan.

Gordon, R. 2016. *The Rise and Fall of American Growth: The US Standard of Living since the Civil War*. Princeton, NJ: Princeton University Press.

Gourinchas, P.-O. and Rey, H. 2014. 'External adjustment, global: imbalances, valuation effects.' In G. Gopinath, E. Helpman and K. Rogoff (eds), *Handbook of International Economics, Vol. 4*. Amsterdam: North-Holland, pp. 585–645.

Hale, G., Jones, P. and Spiegel, M. 2020. 'Home currency issuance in international bond markets.' *Journal of International Economics*, **122**, Article 103256.

Hansen, A. 1939. 'Economic progress and declining population growth.' *American Economic Review*, **29** (1), 1–15.

Helleiner, E. 1994. *States and the Re-Emergence of Global Finance: From Bretton Woods to the 1990s*. Ithaca, NY: Cornell University Press.

Holston, K., Laubach, T. and Williams. J. 2017. 'Measuring the natural rate of interest: international trends and determinants.' *Journal of International Economics*, **108** (1), 39–75.

Keynes, J.M. [1936] 1964. *The General Theory of Employment, Interest and Money*. London: Harcourt Brace Jovanovich.

Kindleberger, C.P. 1973. *The World in Depression, 1929–1939*. London: Allen Lane.

Kindleberger, C.P. 1987. *International Capital Movements*, Cambridge, UK: Cambridge University Press.

Kirzner, I. 1993. 'The pure time-preference theory of interest: an attempt at clarification.' In J.M. Herbener (ed.), *The Pure Time-Preference Theory of Interest*. Auburn, AL: Mises Institute, pp. 99–126.

Koo, R. 2008. *The Holy Grail of Macroeconomics: Lessons from Japan's Great Recession*. Chichester: Wiley.

Krugman, P. 1998. 'It's baaack: Japan's slump and the return of the liquidity trap.' *Brookings Papers on Economic Activity*, **2**, 137–87.

Krugman, P. and Taylor, L. 1978. 'Contractionary effect of devaluation.' *Journal of International Economics*, **8** (3), 445–56.

Krustev, G. 2019. 'The natural rate of interest and the financial cycle.' *Journal of Economic Behavior and Organization*, **162**, 193–210.

Kurz, H. 2015. 'Keynes, Sraffa, and the latter's "secret skepticism".' In H. Kurz and N. Salvadori (eds), *Revisiting Classical Economics: Studies in Long-Period Analysis*. London: Routledge, pp. 102–21.

Laubach, T. and Williams, J. 2003. 'Measuring the natural rate of interest.' *Review of Economics and Statistics*, **85** (4), 1063–70.

Lavoie, M. 2009. *Introduction to Post-Keynesian Economics*. London: Palgrave Macmillan.

Mason, J.W. 2018. 'Income distribution, household debt, and aggregate demand: a critical assessment.' *Working Paper No. 901*. Levy Institute of Bard College.

Mason, J.W. and Jayadev, A. 2014. '"Fisher dynamics" in US household debt, 1929–2011.' *American Economic Journal: Macroeconomics*, **6** (3), 214–34.

Medeiros, C. 2008. 'Financial dependency and growth cycles in Latin American countries.' *Journal of Post Keynesian Economics*, **31** (1), 79–99.

Metzler, L. [1960] 1968. 'The process of international adjustment under conditions of full employment: a Keynesian view.' In R. Caves and H. Johnson (eds), *Readings in International Economics*. Chicago, IL: Irwin, pp. 1407–29.

Mian, A., Straub, L. and Sufi, A. 2021. 'What explains the decline in r^*? Rising income inequality versus demographic shifts.' Accessed November 2021 at https://www.kansascityfed.org/documents/8337/JH_paper_Sufi_3.pdf.

Mian, A. and Sufi, A. 2018. 'Finance and business cycles: the credit-driven household demand channel.' *Journal of Economic Perspectives*, **32** (3), 31–58.

Nelson, C. and Plosser, C. 1982. 'Trends and random walks in macroeconomic time series: some evidence and implications.' *Journal of Monetary Economics*, **10** (2), 139–62.

Obstfeld, M. and Rogoff, K. 1996. *Foundations of International Macroeconomics*. Cambridge, MA: MIT Press.

Palley, T. 2007. 'Financialization: what it is and why it matters.' *Levy Economics Institute, Working Paper No. 525.*

Petri, F. 2015. 'Neglected implications of neoclassical capital–labour substitution for investment theory: another criticism of Say's Law.' *Review of Political Economy*, **27** (3), 308–40.

Pivetti, M. 1991. *An Essay on Money and Distribution*. London: Palgrave Macmillan.

Pivetti, M. 1993. 'Bretton Woods, through the lens of state-of-the-art macrotheory and the European monetary system.' *Contributions to Political Economics*, **12** (1), 99–110.

Rey, H. 2013. 'Dilemma not trilemma: the global financial cycle and monetary policy independence.' In *Global Dimensions of Unconventional Monetary Policy*: *Proceedings of the Economic Policy Symposium, Jackson Hole, August 21–23, Federal Reserve Bank of Kansas City*, pp. 285–333.

Rey, H. 2015. 'Dilemma not trilemma: the global financial cycle and monetary policy independence.' *NBER Working Paper No. 21162*, revised 2018. National Bureau of Economic Research.

Serrano, F. 1995. 'Long period effective demand and the Sraffian supermultiplier.' *Contributions to Political Economy*, **14**, 67–90.

Serrano, F., Summa, R. and Garrido Moreira, V. 2020. 'Stagnation and unnaturally low interest rates: a simple critique of the amended New Consensus and the Sraffian supermultiplier alternative.' *Review of Keynesian Economics*, **8** (3), 365–84.

Shin, H.-S. 2012. 'Global banking glut and loan risk premium.' *IMF Economic Review*, **60** (2), 155–92.

Summa, R. and Serrano, F. 2015. 'Mundell–Fleming without the LM curve: the exogenous interest rate in an open economy.' *Review of Keynesian Economics*, **3** (2), 248–68.

Summers, L. 2014. 'U.S. economic prospects: secular stagnation, hysteresis and the zero-lower bound.' *Business Economics*, **49** (2), 65–73.

Summers, L. 2015. 'On secular stagnation: Larry Summers responds to Ben Bernanke.' *Brookings.edu*. Accessed November 2021 at https://www.brookings.edu/blog/ben-bernanke/2015/04/01/on-secular-stagnation-larry-summers-responds-to-ben-bernanke/.

Summers, L. and Stansbury, A. 2019. 'Whither central banking?' *Project-syndicate. org*. Accessed November 2021 at https://www.project-syndicate.org/commentary/central-bankers-in-jackson-hole-should-admit-impotence-by-lawrence-h-summers-and-anna-stansbury-2-2019-08?barrier=accesspaylog.

Sumner, S. 2021. 'The Princeton School and the zero lower bound.' *Mercatus Center Working Paper*. George Mason University.

Vernengo, M. 2001. 'Foreign exchange, interest and prices: the conventional exchange rate.' In L.-P. Rochon and M. Vernengo (eds), *Credit, Interest Rates and the Open Economy: Essays on Horizontalism*. Cheltenham, UK and Northampton, MA, USA: Edward Elgar Publishing, pp. 256–70.

Vernengo, M. 2006. 'Technology, finance, and dependency: Latin American radical political economy in retrospect.' *Review of Radical Political Economics*, **38** (4), 551–68.

Vernengo, M. 2021. 'The consolidation of dollar hegemony after the collapse of Bretton Woods: bringing power back in.' *Review of Political Economy*, **33** (4), 529–51.

Vernengo, M. and Rochon, L.-P. 2000. 'Exchange rate regimes and capital controls.' *Challenge*, **43** (6), 76–92.

Wray, L.R. 2012. *Modern Money Theory: A Primer on Macroeconomics for Sovereign Monetary Systems*. London: Palgrave Macmillan.

4. The evolution of monetary institutions and of the theory of money: the value of a monetary theory of production and distribution[1]

Michel Betancourt, Santiago Capraro, Carlo Panico and Luis Daniel Torres-González

1. INTRODUCTION

This chapter moves from the standpoint that the evolution of monetary theories reflects that of the payments system and of the credit and financial structures. It recalls some events that were relevant for the development of monetary theories, focussing on how money can be integrated within the theoretical foundations of the economic discipline – that is, within the theory of value, distribution and production. No attempt is made to give a comprehensive account of the history of financial institutions and monetary theories.[2]

The solution regarding how to integrate money in the theoretical foundations of the economic discipline is related to a crucial point of the enduring debates over the theories of distribution. This is the role of the restrictions posed by technological knowledge and the availability of resources and that of the political-institutional organization of society in determining the rates of wages, profits and rents.

According to some theories, the constraints set by technological knowledge and the availability of resources define both the relationship between distributive variables and their levels.[3] These theories reduce the space for political and institutional regulation. Some of them refer to 'natural' rates of wage and interest to argue that legislation and policy interventions, overlooking the existence of 'natural' rates, are harmful for the economy. In neoclassical theory, the 'natural' interest rate, a distributive variable depending on the marginal productivity of the last unit of capital employed in the economy, indicates how monetary policy must be conducted. The authorities must drive the 'market' rate towards the 'natural' one to avoid unemployment or inflation.

According to other theories, the constraints set by technological knowledge and the availability of resources only influence the relationship between distributive variables without determining their levels. In these theories, monetary events and political and institutional agreements among social groups play a relevant role in determining the levels of distributive variables both directly – setting some reference rates of remuneration, like the policy interest rate – and, indirectly – establishing rules for the content of contracts and contributing to the formation of conventions on what is normal or equitable to pay for labour services and for the use of loanable capital, two elements that have an influence on the rate of profits.

In discussing how money can be integrated within the theoretical foundations of the economic discipline, this chapter highlights the following points:

1. In the literature, there have always been alternative perspectives on how money can be integrated within the theory of value, distribution and production.
2. Monetary theories of distribution have always occupied a relevant position in the scientific development of the discipline, and in some historical periods they gathered a large consensus.
3. Those holding a monetary theory of distribution refuse Say's Law and accept the non-neutrality of money in long-run analyses – that is, they accept that money affects the potential output of the economy.
4. Within the analysis of the demand for money, speculation on financial assets had limited importance until World War I. The nineteenth-century literature considered it of no great concern and consequently represented the financial sector as an industry selling services to the rest of the economy. The speculative motive of the demand for money was analytically expounded and became a significant element of the theory of distribution after World War I.
5. At the beginning of the 1970s, the state of knowledge on the foundations of the economic discipline would have made it difficult to predict the subsequent spread of consensus on Say's Law and on the neutrality of money in long-run analyses. The debates of the previous years had undermined the traditional neoclassical parables – in particular, the belief that variations in relative prices lead the economy to full employment positions of equilibrium.
6. The New Macroeconomics, developed since the 1970s, represents a return to the traditional neoclassical views on the theory of income distribution.
7. The return to these views is not due to the provision of satisfactory analytical answers to the criticisms raised against them after World War II. Those criticisms are simply ignored.

2.   MONETARY INSTITUTIONS AND THEORIES BEFORE WORLD WAR I

In spite of the importance that can be attributed to Petty, historians consider that political economy became a scientific discipline during the eighteenth century. The idea that the economy is a system – that is, something showing systematic behaviour that can be represented through accounting identities (see Quesnay, [1758] 1972), favoured the development of political economy as a scientific discipline. Smith improved on this knowledge by extending the analyses of Quesnay and the physiocrats to an economy where the Industrial Revolution was taking place.

The construction of monetary theories took a slower pace. Historians claim that the changes that occurred in Great Britain at the end of the seventeenth century[4] represented a 'financial revolution'.[5] Nonetheless, in the seventeenth century, the payments and credit systems were still in embryonic form. When the specie payments by the Bank of England were suspended on 27 February 1797, there was 'no generally accepted theory of monetary and banking system. There were only laws and institutions, inadequate and in some cases inconsistent' (Fetter, 1965, p. 1). Analyses of the relation of bank credit to money supply and of the effects of the growth of banking on the economy were in their initial stages:

> The evolution of banking from the early goldsmith's receipt of deposit and issue of notes against which a 100 per cent reserve was held, to the mid-nineteenth century situation of England, in which an overwhelming proportion of total payments was made by the transfer of bank liabilities, either bank notes or deposit currency, equal to many times the country's specie supply, emerged out of the convenience of business and the desire of banks to make profits. The explanation of what was taking place, and the changes in public opinion and in the law necessary to regulate these banking private institutions in a larger public interest, came later. (Fetter, 1965, pp. 6–7)

The changes in legislation and in the financial system that had been occurring since the beginning of the nineteenth century favoured the funding of the British industry, its growth, and the achievements of the Victorian period. One can submit that these changes generated a second financial revolution.

The positive effects of these changes were accompanied by a series of systemic crises, which originated within the banks on account of the sudden expansion of non-performing loans. The debates that followed those events led to the formation of what can be considered the first nucleus of monetary theory in the history of economic thought. Fetter (1965) named it 'British monetary orthodoxy', underlining that its formation developed from 1797 to 1873, when Bagehot's *Lombard Street* was published (see Fetter, 1965, p. 1).[6]

Different positions, relevant for the discussion of the relationship between money and the theories of value, distribution and production, were proposed in those years. Several authors queried Ricardo's view that the rate of profits determines the interest rate and focussed on the introduction of a monetary theory of distribution. Joplin (1823, 1832), Tooke (1826) and Mill ([1844] 1948 – written in 1829–30) were the first (see Caminati, 1981; Panico, 1988, pp. 29–32; Pivetti, 1985, 1991, 1998). Gilbart (1834) highlighted the existence of two positions in the literature, one asserting that the rate of profits determines the rate of interest and the other claiming the opposite. Later on, Tooke, Fullarton and Wilson argued in favour of a monetary determination of the rates of interest and profits, although with some ambiguities on the role of banks' intermediation (see Panico, 1988, pp. 31–41).

Another debated point was the existence of permanent influences of monetary events on the overall activity of the economy – that is, a monetary theory of production. Henry Thornton, who had a notable impact on the Bullion Committee of 1810, considered that monetary events could permanently influence the level of production of the economy.[7] Ricardo and James Mill, on the contrary, abided by Say's Law and sustained that the potential output does not depend on monetary factors. This debate was on what is nowadays called 'the long-run neutrality of money'. The non-neutrality during the different phases of the cycles was never disputed.

The analyses of the British monetary orthodoxy continued to be at the basis of the monetary positions of the Cambridge school (see Keynes, [1923] 1971; Marshall, 1923; Pigou, 1917). Like the nineteenth-century literature, these contributions describe the demand for money by following the distinction between 'circulation of income' and 'circulation of capital' introduced by Smith in the eighteenth century. The former refers to the payments used in the transactions between consumers and producers; the latter to the payments used in the transactions between producers and producers, merchants and producers, and merchants and merchants.

The nineteenth-century literature dealt with monetary events by focussing on the demand and supply of credit. These analyses can, however, be presented in terms of demand and supply of money.

Marx's writings also focussed on demand and supply of credit and adopted the distinction between 'circulation of income' and 'circulation of capital', although he preferred to refer to them as 'expenditure of revenue' and 'transfer of capital' (see Marx, 1972a, p. 443; Panico, 1988, pp. 64–70, 78–9). He did not formalize the results of his examinations. Nonetheless, it is possible to present them through the following equalities, which consider M, M_c, M_b, C and L_b as measured in monetary terms:

$$M = M_c + M_b \tag{4.1}$$

$$M_c = v_c\, C \tag{4.2}$$

$$M_b = c_r\, L_b, \tag{4.3}$$

where M is the supply of money, consisting of coins and bank notes of the Bank of England (see Marx, 1972a, p. 499); M_c is the demand for money due to the 'expenditure of revenue'; M_b is the demand for money for the 'transfer of capital'; v_c is the velocity of circulation of the money used for the 'expenditure of revenue'; C is the 'expenditure of revenue', which for Marx (1972a, p. 446) and the nineteenth-century British literature coincided with the expenditure for consumption; c_r is the ratio between the banks' reserves and advances; and L_b is the demand for banks advances.

In Marx's work L_b came from:

- firms needing short-term loans to solve their cash-flow problems;
- firms needing short-term loans to speculate on inventories;
- firms needing long-term loans for their investment expenditure;
- stockjobbers; and
- government.

He assumed that the relation between M_c and C is stable and can be captured by a parameter, v_c, which depends on institutional arrangements, like the dating of wage payments. He also assumed that workers had no access to credit (see Marx, 1972a, pp. 488, 496), so that banks could not influence M_c (see Marx, 1972a, pp. 445, 454).

As for the demand for the 'transfer of capital', $M_b = c_r\, L_b$, like the nineteenth-century literature, Marx focussed on the cash-flow problems of the firms, which were considered the main source of the demand for bank loans. His analysis concentrated on the decisions of the firms to solve the cash-flow problems and on those of the banks regarding the ratio between their reserves and advances, c_r. Marx related both decisions to the institutional organization of the payments and credit systems (see Panico, 1988, pp. 66, 70, 72, 76, 77). Moreover, he linked these decisions to the movements of the interest rates during the different phases of the cycle.

During the prosperous phase, he contended, banks and the other firms experience a sense of security on the stability of the financial system. These feelings lead the former to reduce their reserve ratio – increasing the leverage and the supply of loans – and the latter to promote the circulation of bills of exchange, thus reducing the demand for bank loans. Under these conditions, the market interest rate tends to remain below the average value.

In the subsequent phase of the cycle, firms start to have difficulties selling and tend to increase the demand for bank loans to recuperate the means of payments that are not coming from the sale of commodities. Banks, on the other hand, being unaware of the problems of firms, do not increase their reserves, keeping constant the supply of loans.

In a third phase, banks realize that some firms have solvency problems and increase their reserve ratio (see Marx, 1972a, p. 536). Under these conditions, the market interest rate rises above the average one. In the absence of an institution playing the role of a timely and reliable 'lender of last resort', the uncertainty characterizing this phase of the cycle can lead to a credit crunch.

Like a large part of the nineteenth-century literature, Marx considered that the demand for money for the 'transfer of capital' is unstable owing to its dependence on the conditions of uncertainty about the economic and financial situation prevailing in the near future (see Panico, 1988, pp. 65–70). The presence of this element in the analysis amounts to acknowledging the existence of a demand for money as a reserve of value used for precautionary motives.

Marx and the nineteenth-century literature recognized the existence of other sources of demand for bank loans, but assumed that they played a minor role in the working of the payments and credit systems. The demand for credit coming from stockjobbers and related to speculation on financial assets was considered of limited concern (see Panico, 1988, pp. 69–70). This assumption was still present in the writings of the Cambridge school at the beginning of the twentieth century.[8] In *A Tract on Monetary Reform*, Keynes ([1923] 1971, pp. 61–70) considers that the demand for money due to speculation on financial assets was underdeveloped.

Marx and the nineteenth-century literature instead attributed a prominent role to speculation on inventories in the analysis of the transmission mechanism of the monetary impulses to the rest of the economy (see Panico, 1988, pp. 27, 42–3). At that time, the literature had not elaborated the neoclassical notion of the demand for capital based on the assumption that the marginal productivity is decreasing. Thus, an increase in monetary circulation could raise the demand for commodities through growing speculative purchases of inventories.

Signs of this analysis can be found in some writings of the Cambridge school. In *A Treatise on Money*, Keynes ([1930a] 1971, pp. 173–6; [1930b] 1971, pp. 116–18) highlighted that Hawtrey had based his analysis of the transmission mechanism on this assumption. Moreover, after noticing that Marshall's evidence before the Gold and Silver Commission (1887) and the Indian Currency Committee (1898) presents some ambiguities on this point, Keynes ([1930a] 1971, pp. 171–2) suggested that Marshall's reference to speculation had to be interpreted in an extended way – that is, by considering as speculative activity the demand for both fixed capital and inventories. Keynes ([1930a] 1971, pp. 176–8) concluded this review of the literature by saying that the clearest exposition was provided by Wicksell, who unambiguously claimed that a reduction in the interest rate increases the investment in fixed capital.

The limited relevance attributed to speculation on financial assets by the nineteenth-century literature highlights that these authors considered the financial sector as an industry providing services to the rest of the economy.

Marx used the previous analysis to deal with the relationship between the rates of interest and profits, the factors affecting the interest rates, and the responsibilities of the Bank of England. This set of notes, which were posthumously presented in Volume III of *Capital*, led him to conclusions that do not match those of the theory of distribution he had presented in Volume I.

On the relationship between the rates of interest and profits, Marx argued that 'the average rate of profit is to be regarded as the ultimate determinant of the maximum limit to interest' (Marx, 1972a, p. 360). Moreover, and despite the presence of contradictory statements (see Panico, 1988, pp. 55–60), he stated that the average, or common, rate of interest and the general rate of profits tend to move in the same direction and that the former governs the latter.

Indications of the view that the rates of interest and profits move together can be found in the following statement:

> The average rate of interest appears in every country over fairly long periods as a constant magnitude, because the general rate of profit varies only at longer intervals... And its relative constancy is revealed precisely in this more or less constant nature of the average, or common, rate of interest. (Marx, 1972a, p. 366)

The view that the rate of interest governs the rate of profits can be found in his critique of the notion of the 'natural' interest rate and in his analysis of the factors affecting the average, or common, rate. He said that 'there is no such thing as a natural rate of interest' (Marx, 1972a, p. 362) and claimed that the competitive forces of demand and supply of bank loans govern the interest rate, just as those of demand and supply of commodities regulate market prices:

> But the difference here is just as apparent as the analogy. If supply and demand coincide, the market-price of commodities corresponds to their price of production, i.e., their price then appears to be regulated by the immanent laws of capitalist production, independently of competition, since the fluctuation of supply and demand explain nothing but deviations of market-prices from prices of production... But it is different with the interest of money-capital. Competition does not, in this case, determine the deviations from the rule. There is rather no law of division except that

enforced by competition because, as we shall see later, no such thing as a 'natural' rate of interest exists. (Marx, 1972a, pp. 355–6)

Following this standpoint, he refused the conclusion that the average interest rate depends on the demand and supply of real capital (see Panico, 1988, pp. 71, 74–80), criticized the discussions about the 'real rate produced' – an expression used in those days – and ironically rejected Karl Arndt's position that the natural interest rate is determined by the annual rate of growth of timber in European forests (see Marx, 1972a, p. 363).

He argued that the way to proceed in relation to the average interest rate is to examine the historical settings under which changes in this rate take place. For him, the theory of the average interest rate must focus on the historical circumstances bringing about permanent variations in the average conditions of competition in the money market.

Marx developed this analysis by moving from the claim that the average interest rate depends on the 'common opinion' on what its level will be. He referred approvingly to what Joseph Massie had written in 1750 on this point:

> Massie has rightly said in this respect: 'the only thing which any man can be in doubt about on this occasion is what proportion of these profits belongs to the borrower, and what to the lender; and thus there is no other method of determining than by opinions of borrowers and lenders in general; for, right or wrong in this respect, are only what common consent makes so'. (Marx, 1972a, pp. 362–3)

Describing the elements affecting the common opinion, Marx indicated some economic factors, like the improvements in the organization of the credit system, which allow permanent changes in the ratio between banks' reserves and their advances, c_r (see Marx, 1972a, p. 362). Moreover, he recalled the influence of international forces, such as 'the greater or lesser approximate equalisation of the rate of interest in the world market' (Marx, 1972a, p. 358)[9] and the working of competition leading to the equalization of the rate of profits in the different sectors of the economy.

Marx's notes on the role played by bankers in the process of the equalization of the rate of profits are scattered in different parts of his works. They offer two clues on how bankers' activities influence this process. First, the presence of the credit system makes this process more effective.[10] Second, it affects the cost of production of commodities and the general rate of profits.[11]

The existence of the credit system affects the costs of production and the rate of profits because 'in the production of commodities, circulation is as necessary as production itself, so that circulation agents are just as needed as production agents' (Marx, 1970, p. 129). He also underscored that with the development of the credit system at the beginning of the nineteenth century, bankers had replaced individual moneylenders, and money was mainly borrowed to solve the cash-flow problems of the firms engaged in production (see Marx, 1972a, p. 600). This description contributed to clarifying how bankers appropriate their share of surplus value and the forms assumed by the relationship between the rates of interest and profits (see Panico, 1980; 1988, Chapter 3).

Marx not only referred to economic factors to explain the variations in the average interest rate. He also recalled that conventional elements, like custom or juristic tradition, affect this rate (see Marx, 1972a, pp. 363–4), arguing that the influence of these elements reflects the distribution of power in society.

In Part III of *Theories of Surplus Value*, he recalled the role played by the state in the early periods of capitalist society, when the emerging industrial bourgeoisie was able to restrain the power of individual moneylenders and obtain, through 'usury laws', forced reductions of the interest rate (see Marx, 1972b, pp. 456, 467, 469; also Marx, 1972a, pp. 602–3). However, Marx argued, in the subsequent years, the use of usury laws was replaced by the creation of the credit system (see Marx, 1972b, pp. 468–9; also Marx, 1972a, p. 600).

Marx argued that monetary legislation, which may reflect the ability of the financial sector to exert pressure on the political world, influences the common opinion on the level of the average interest rate. He was deeply concerned with the growing importance of this sector and contended that the purpose of the Bank Act of 1844 was to increase the profits of the bankers. For him, the content of this law, which reflected the strong position of this group of capitalists in the distribution of power (see Marx, 1972a, pp. 558–60), affected the rates of interest and profits.[12]

The reference to historical and conventional elements in the analysis of the rates of interest and profits and the adoption of what can be called a 'monetary theory of distribution' highlight the existence of some similarities between Marx and Keynes's *General Theory* (see Panico, 1988). More than Keynes, however, Marx conceived the influence of historical and institutional factors as reflecting the distribution of power in society, which in turn affects the formation of laws regulating the working of the payments and credit systems.

Finally, his writings characterize the financial sector as an industry – that is, a set of firms performing the following activities:

• It provides the other industries with 'intermediate' services (e.g., bank loans), which solve the cash-flow problems that firms encounter to manufacture and sell their commodities. These services are necessary inputs affecting the cost of production of commodities.
• It is organized to exert pressure on the political world to obtain legislation favouring its interests.

- It pays to the owners of its capital (e.g., to shareholders) a rate of profit that bears some relation to the general rate of profits and to the rates of remuneration of financial assets.

Other writings of the nineteenth century recognized that the financial industry can put pressure on the political world.[13] Unlike those works, however, Marx made this element an integral part of his theorizing.

Marx supported the Banking school's ideas on the role and responsibilities of the Bank of England against the positions of the Currency school, which requested the imposition of rigid rules on monetary issues. The Currency school dominated the formation of the Peel Act of 1844, which ruled out discretion on the issue of money. The Act had to be suspended during the crises of 1847, 1857 and 1866. Moreover, its constraints on the monetary issue of the Bank favoured the uses of cheques and deposits, which became a major form of payment in Great Britain.[14]

In those years, the debate on the responsibilities of the Bank of England was still open. The Bank was reluctant to accept the role of lender of last resort. Fetter (1965, p. 273) pointed out that even after the crisis of 1866, powerful voices within the Bank 'gave no assurance that it would do the same in another crisis'. He mentioned that over the 1860s, Bagehot had been advocating in *The Economist* that the country needed an institution that played the role of lender of last resort with certainty. Yet, only in Bagehot's 1873 book *Lombard Street* was he able to persuade those adhering to the principles of free trade to accept this point (see Fetter, 1965, p. 274). From the mid-1870s, the Bagehot principle was no longer in doubt inside and outside the Bank. 'The Bank of England as a lender of last resort was...accepted as the foundation of monetary and banking orthodoxy' (Fetter, 1965, p. 275).

The nineteenth-century British payment and credit systems developed in the form of 'specialized banking', which was characterized by correspondence in the term structure of assets and liabilities. Commercial banks and discount houses collected deposits and 'money at call' (i.e., commercial banks' loans whose repayment could be obtained at very short notice) and only gave short-term loans. The other specialized financial institutions, which offered medium- and long-term loans, collected funds through medium- and long-term liabilities. This system guaranteed a reduction in the risks assumed by the banking system. Yet, systemic crises only disappeared when there was certainty that the Bank of England was a timely lender of last resort.

A different organization of the banking system was realized in Germany after the 1871 unification. Instead of promoting the specialized system, the Germans decided to organize a 'mixed' system, in which banks could collect short-term deposits and take on a long-term involvement in industrial investments. The term structure of the assets and liabilities of these institutions was riskier than that of the British banks. Yet, the German authorities thought that the mixed system could favour the industrial development of the country.

As Sraffa pointed out in the notes prepared for the lectures on continental banking he gave in Cambridge in the spring terms of 1929 and 1930 (Sraffa Papers, D2/5), the working of the mixed system (which has some features in common with the 'universal' system that dominates today) requires forms of regulation that are different from those used in Great Britain. He pointed out that the Reichsbank had developed closer cooperative relations with credit institutions than those built up by the Bank of England (Sraffa Papers, D/2/5/14–16). These relations had to ensure that the mixed banks could fund industrial development without running into financial problems.

For Sraffa, the Reichsbank worked as an entity of a planned economy in which the mixed banks took a long-term concern in industrial firms by promoting their formation, providing the rating and the certification of their balance sheets, and favouring the sale of their shares in the market. While the banks funded and participated in the organization of production in the strategic sectors of the economy, the Reichsbank assisted them with funds, which were systematically anticipated to stimulate economic development, rather than given as an emergency provision, as occurred in Britain (Sraffa Papers, D/2/5/14–16). As De Cecco (2005, pp. 355, 358) points out, until World War I, the Reichsbank acted as 'lender of first resort', rather than of last resort. Yet, this functioning had to change after the war.[15]

The success of the German mixed banks led the Italian authorities to introduce this organization of the banking system in their country towards the end of the nineteenth century. The Italian experience was fruitful until World War I, contributing to the first industrial development of Northwest regions. Yet, the problems created by the rising financial needs of the firms engaged in war production and by the downturn caused by the post-war transition to peace triggered the financial crisis of 1921. In his essay on this crisis, Sraffa (1922) argued that the mixed system tends to generate embroiled relations between financial and industrial firms and the consequent formation of large groups or 'concentrations' able to control sections of the economy, of the media and of the political world and to attain monetary legislation and policies favourable to their own interests. He also pointed out that the weak financial regulation of the Italian legislation was unable to counteract the power of the concentrations and avoid the crisis.

Sraffa's thoughts on the roles of central banks and financial regulation in the different organizations of the banking system are relevant for the interpretation of the conduct of monetary policy and the origins of the crisis in recent years (see below).

3.   MONETARY INSTITUTIONS AND THEORIES AFTER WORLD WAR I

The funding of World War I marked the evolution of the financial systems and the progress of monetary theories. It generated a gigantic debt that after the war freely circulated among the international financial centres. Moreover, the disruptions in the defeated countries made it necessary a financial reconstruction of Europe. The solution of these problems was a challenge for the authorities and the profession. It stimulated new thinking on money and on the organization and conduct of monetary policy.

The return to the Gold Standard, which in Great Britain was considered as functioning well for almost a century before the war, was a debated issue in those years. The documents of the international conferences of Brussels (1920) and Genoa (1922) show that the political and technical authorities wanted to resume it (see Sayers, 1976, pp. 153–203).

The Gold Standard was reintroduced in Great Britain in 1925 but, unlike what had happened before the war, it generated problems and was abandoned in 1931. The reasons were the increased dimension of the international financial markets and the expansion of new centres, like New York. Before World War I, the smooth working of the Gold Standard had depended on the existence of equilibrium conditions in the balance of payments of different countries and on the ability of the Bank of England to control the daily movements of gold between London and Paris.

According to De Cecco (1974), the British Empire, more than the spontaneous working of market forces, promoted the maintenance of equilibrium conditions in the international flows of commodities and capital. Examining the working of the Gold Standard from 1890 to 1913, De Cecco describes how Great Britain maintained a persistent deficit in its trade balance with the USA, which in turn had a persistent deficit with some Asian colonies. Using its political power, the Empire obliged the Asian colonies to deposit in London the international reserves coming from the USA, thus re-establishing equilibrium conditions in the balance of payments of the countries involved.

As for the control of the daily movements, the dimension of the capital flows and the primacy of London and Paris as financial centres allowed the Bank of England to successfully perform this duty before the war. Through small variations of the interest rate in London, which did not interfere with the funding needs of the private and the government sectors, the bank rate policy had been able to induce daily adjustments that restored safe levels of gold reserves and a sound monetary circulation.

After the war, the increased size of financial flows and the progress of new financial centres reduced the effectiveness of the adjusting mechanism previously used. Moreover, the feebleness of international coordination among monetary policies further weakened the ability of small variations of the interest rate in London to control the movements of financial capital. The result was that, unlike what had happened before the war, the resumption of the Gold Standard obliged the Bank of England to employ large variations of the interest rate. The bank rate policy became problematic and the political tensions over the maintenance of the Gold Standard led to its abandonment in 1931 (see Panico and Piccioni, 2016, 2018; Sayers, 1976, pp. 314–73). After World War I, the economic profession did not attribute a strong position to the Gold Standard within monetary and banking theory.

According to Sayers (1976, p. 66), World War I marked the transformation of the Bank of England into a central bank. Before the war, the Bank had performed functions implying public responsibilities and had gradually given them priority over its commercial interests. Yet, it 'was not a central bank according to the mid-twentieth usage of this term' (Sayers, 1976, p. 1). The complexity of the problems posed by the size of the debt, by the reconstruction of the European financial system, and by the need to counteract the intense processes of speculation and inflation, induced the political authorities to delegate the management of monetary policy to technical experts. The conduct and the institutional organization of monetary policy changed. The major alterations in the activities of the Bank can be found in the operations concerning the funding of the government sector and the consolidation of the British position in the international financial system.

The Treasury had enlarged its powers on monetary issues during the war and the transition to peace. At the beginning of the 1920s, the Bank firmly advocated that the government had to discipline itself if the Gold Standard had to be restored. The rate of interest depended in those years on the financial needs of the government and the Bank could not control it. By 1923, however, the Bank had taken advantage of the enlarged size of the market for Treasury Bills to control the short-term interest rates through open market operations, which Keynes ([1930b] 1971, p. 208) considered the best device hitherto evolved to conduct monetary policy.

The operations concerning the consolidation of the British position in the international financial system also underwent important variations (see Sayers, 1976, pp. 153–209). The need to reconstruct the financial structures impaired by the war in some European nations led the Bank of England to take on new tasks. It became a leading actor in the reorganization of the international financial system. The Bank, the Federal Reserve (Fed) and the Financial Committee of the League of Nations directed the process leading to the re-establishment of the financial system in Austria, Hungary, Germany and Poland and to the design of central banks in those countries and in the Dominions.[16]

The onset of central banks was accompanied by a forceful demand for independence by the monetary authorities. They asked for the attribution of some forms of independence to guarantee that their professional activity could be free from the pressures of economic and political groups (see Panico and Piccioni, 2016, 2018). In their activities, the president of the Federal Reserve of New York, Benjamin Strong, and the Governor of the Bank of England, Montague Norman, had as a common objective 'to bind [central bankers] together in a professional caste of mutual support and comfort' (Sayers, 1976, p. 156). They believed that central bankers 'had more chance than any politicians of guiding the peoples of the world, both nationally and internationally, in the adoption and maintenance of policies needing time and patience' (Sayers, 1976, pp. 154–5). These elements promoted the institution of the Bank for International Settlements, which was conceived as a place where the financial problems of the world economy were discussed, and as an institution complying with the principle that it had to be independent of governments and able to analyse and regulate the international payments system (see Sayers, 1976, p. 353). These aspirations were realized in 1930 when the Bank for International Settlements started to operate.

The delegation of monetary policy to technical experts raised the issue of how to regulate the relations among the institutions participating in the management of public policy. Keynes conceived the institutional setting as a network of bodies in which the independence of each should be balanced by coordination based on reciprocal cooperation and deliberate division of labour (see Panico and Piccioni, 2016, 2018). Moreover, he defended the right of the Bank of England to advocate the freedom of its professional activity from the pressures of economic and political groups, saying that 'its independence and its prestige are assets' (Keynes, [1932a] 1982, p. 132) for society.

He was in favour of attributing to the Bank three forms of independence, which nowadays are referred to as 'personnel or staff independence', 'financial and administrative independence' and 'technical or instrumental independence'.[17] By contrast, he was against attributing what can be defined as 'goals and priorities independence', which is the power of central banks to decide the value of the variables representing the objectives of monetary policy (for instance, the rate of inflation that policy must achieve) and the order of priority over different goals when they are considered antagonistic. Keynes ([1932a] 1982, p. 131) stated that in a representative democracy, elected bodies must make the fundamental decisions on the objectives that society wants to achieve. According to him, these decisions establish 'the main lines of policy, the choice of which, as distinct from the execution, was not properly [the Bank's] affair at all' (Keynes, [1932a] 1982, p. 132).

Keynes's views coincide with those dominating the profession until the 1970s. Then, the contributions of Kydland and Prescott (1977), Rogoff (1985) and the 'institutional design literature' proposed attributing to central banks the power to decide the goals and priorities of monetary policy, assuming it is beneficial for society that the preferences of the technical authorities systematically prevail over those expressed by citizens in the electoral process. This position had an impact on recent literature, influencing the 'Washington Consensus' and the 'New Consensus in Macroeconomics'. Yet, it generated strong reactions. Some outstanding economists criticized it for misrepresenting the workings of the institutions taking policy decisions (see Blinder, 1997, 1998; McCallum, 1996; Stiglitz, 1998) and for being incompatible with the functioning of representative democracy (see Greenspan, 1996; Samuelson, 1994; Tobin, 1994). These reactions have limited its acceptance in recent debates on monetary theory and policy (see Capraro and Panico, 2021).

The growth of speculative activities on financial assets also led to some new developments in the analysis of the demand for money. The intensification of speculation affected the level of production in some countries, inducing the profession to reconsider its role in the working of the economy. In Great Britain, the participation of the banking system in international speculation was seen as an element contributing to the stagnation of production.[18] Economists like Lavington and Keynes focussed on this issue, presenting in the 1920s an analysis of the speculative demand for money.

The exposition of the quantity theory of money in *A Tract* followed those of Pigou and Marshall (see Keynes, [1923] 1971, pp. 61–70, in particular p. 63, fn. 1), which dealt with the demand for money by using the traditional distinction between 'circulation of income' and 'circulation of capital' (see Keynes, [1930a] 1971, p. 31, fn. 1). No reference can be found to the demand for money for anticipating variations in the price of financial assets.

As Moggridge points out in the Preface to *A Tract*, in the section 'The forward market in exchanges', Keynes presented 'one of the clearest expositions ever written' (Keynes, [1923] 1971, p. i) of the working of hedging operations in the forward market for exchanges, which were developing in those years. Keynes ([1923] 1971, pp. 100–101) did not attribute a relevant role to these activities in the analysis of the demand for money because the business world had only begun to adapt to them. He wrote: 'in practice merchants do not avail themselves of these facilities to the extent that might have been expected' (Keynes, [1923] 1971, p. 100). They were unavailable until the 1919 'unpegging' of the leading exchanges. Moreover, even after that date, banks had not learnt to offer them at reasonable rates.

Keynes's remarks on hedging operations confirm that financial markets were changing in those years. The collapse of the German mark in 1923 brought about further progress in the innovating activities of financial firms. It led to the substitution of professional for amateur speculators, which reduced the opportunities to gain from arbitrage operations (see Sraffa Papers D2/3, containing the conference on the 'Revaluation of the Lira' Sraffa gave at the Emmanuel Economics Society in Cambridge on 3 November 1927).

In *A Treatise* and in the *General Theory*, the analysis of the speculative demand for money was instead present. 'Financial circulation' was added to the 'circulation of income' and 'circulation of capital' (see Keynes, [1930a] 1971, pp. 31, 217, 218). The idea that savings deposits could earn a higher rate of return than other financial assets was made a central part of the movements of the economy (see Keynes, [1930a] 1971, pp. 31, 35, 38, 42, 43, 127–8, 223–5).

The relevance attributed to the speculative demand for money did not lead Keynes to abandon the dominant theory. *A Treatise* still belongs to the neo-classical tradition. It accepts the dichotomy between the real and the monetary departments of economic analysis; the long-run neutrality of money; the neoclassical theory of value, distribution and production; and the notion of the 'natural interest rate' determined independently of monetary influences (see Panico, 1988, pp. 102–41). As we argue in the next section, whilst the analysis of the demand for money remained the same, Keynes's work after the crisis of 1929 introduced major changes in the relation between money and the theory of value, distribution and production. He moved from a theory where the constraints set by technological knowledge and the availability of resources define the relationship between distributive variables and their levels to a theory where these constraints only define the relationship between distributive variables.

4.   THE CRISIS OF 1929 AND WORLD WAR II

The crisis of 1929 was the result of speculation on financial assets. Unlike those that occurred in England in the nineteenth century, it began in the stock exchange and moved to the banking sector two years later owing to the recession and the difficulty of borrowers to pay back their debt.

In the final parts of *A Treatise* and in the writings of 1930–32, Keynes proposed an interpretation of the crisis in line with the neoclassical tradition (see Panico, 1988, pp. 102–41). He argued that the monetary authorities were finding it difficult to equalize the market interest rate with the natural one and recalled that their attempts to reduce the market rate were forborne by the banking industry on account of the rigidity of the costs of production of their loans (see Keynes, [1931] 1981; [1932b] 1982). The persistence of the crisis and the critical appraisals of this interpretation submitted by his colleagues in the Cambridge Circus persuaded Keynes that a radical change in the relation between money and the theory of value, distribution and production was necessary.

Keynes (1979, pp. 49–57) introduced the concept of 'monetary theory of production' during the autumn of 1932. On 14 November, he wrote a note to describe the content of the new book he wanted to publish. He clarified his intention to reject the neoclassical theoretical foundations of the economic discipline and propose an alternative one, according to which monetary events and policies can directly influence the equilibrium level of the income produced and of the interest rate (see Keynes, 1979, pp. 54–7). The book, initially titled *A Monetary Theory of Production*, was published as *The General Theory of Employment, Interest and Money*.

The major area of work for the development of the new theory was the establishment of three points: (1) rejection of the concept of the natural interest rate representing the 'ideal maxim for monetary policy'; (2) proposal of an alternative theory of the interest rate; (3) critique of the logical consistency of the neoclassical one.

Keynes considered the long-run neutrality of money, the dichotomy between the real and the monetary departments and the natural interest rate as abstract concepts leading to mistaken interpretations of the working of the economic system. Referring to *A Treatise*, he said that 'I am now no longer of the opinion that the concept of a "natural" rate of interest, which previously seemed to me a most promising idea, has anything very useful or significant to contribute to our analysis' (Keynes, [1936] 1973, p. 243).

In *A Treatise*, Keynes had stated that the central bank fixes the durable or average interest rate at its natural level. In the *General Theory*, he claimed that the policy of the monetary authorities, rather than depending on an abstract and not directly observable natural rate, is the result of their evaluations of what is convenient for the economy under the current historical circumstances. For him, the average interest rate is a historical and conventional phenomenon (see Panico, 1988, pp. 102–41; 2021). It can be set at the level that the authorities judge convenient, provided that financial operators consider their policy 'credible' (see Keynes, [1936] 1973, pp. 202–4).

In the third step of his work, Keynes attempted to prove that the neoclassical theory lacks logical coherence. He tried to reach this result in different ways that the colleagues reading his writings systematically demolished (see Panico, 1988, pp. 133–7; 2021). In 'Poverty in plenty' ([1934] 1973) he confirmed that this critique was necessary to persuade the profession to abandon the dominant school. The reference to empirical facts, including the effects of the crisis, cannot achieve this objective (see Keynes, [1934] 1973, pp. 489–92).

When the *General Theory* was published, a watertight critique of neoclassical theory had not been developed. Some of the first signs of Sraffa's critique can be found in his notes of the early 1940s (see Panico, 2001, p. 300). He argued that in the analysis of an economy where more than one commodity is produced, the marginal productivity of the factors, and thus their demand functions, might not be monotonically decreasing. This result introduces instability problems for the equilibrium solutions of the model and undermines the neoclassical parable that price variations enforce Say's Law by leading the economy to full employment.

After the publication of *Production of Commodities by Means of Commodities* (Sraffa, 1960) this critique was at the centre of the 1966 Symposium on 'Paradoxes in Capital Theory' published in the *Quarterly Journal of Economics*. Samuelson summarized the result of this debate by recognizing the validity and relevance of the critique as follows:

> If all this causes headaches for those nostalgic for the old-time parables of neo-classical writing, we must remind ourselves that scholars are not born to live an easy existence. We must respect, and appraise, the facts of life. (Samuelson, 1966, p. 583)

Sraffa's analysis of *Production of Commodities* offers a solution to Keynes's attempt to criticize the logical consistency of the neoclassical theory of interest and the foundations of the economic discipline.

The crisis of 1929 affected the confidence that professional people, voters and governments had in the working of competitive market forces. This limited confidence led to a new 'discretionary' approach to financial regulation, intro-duced in the USA after the banking crisis of 1931. Congress approved a set of measures, including the Glass–Steagall Act of 1933, to fortify the discretion-ary powers of the authorities over the managers of financial firms to avoid the financial sector growing at a higher rate than the other sectors (see Panico et al., 2016).

The strategy followed by this discretionary regime tended to integrate different interests and to secure a consensual participation of as many sectors as possible in the benefits generated by the growth of the economy. The new regulatory framework focussed on the relations between the authorities and financial firms and the fact that the economy can be damaged if the financial sector supersedes the others. An increasing size of the financial sector can generate a situation in which speculation dominates over enterprise and can exacerbate conflicts over the distributive shares by leading to policies favour-ing the interests of this sector (see Panico and Pinto, 2018; Panico et al., 2012).

It is widely acknowledged (see Eichengreen and Bordo, 2003; Goodhart, 2010; White, 2009) that the discretionary approach to regulation achieved positive results. The management of financial firms was adequately controlled and bank crises disappeared. The few banks that failed were small and most of them had been involved in frauds that regulators unearthed. Commenting on the results of the discretionary approach, White (2009, p. 28) stated that 'this tight regulatory and supervisory regime helped to prevent bank failures, which as a percentage of all banks or deposits, fail to show up on the radar'.

World War II further undermined the confidence in the working of competitive market forces. There was consensus on the idea that international capital movements and speculation had been a major cause of the 1929 recession that led to the rise of aggressive forms of nationalism and to the war. This idea piloted the Bretton Woods Agreements towards the imposition of controls on capital movements. By doing so, the Agreements allowed national policies to focus on full employment and social justice. The results were positive and Piketty (2014, p. 11) recalls the post-war period as 'the thirty glorious years from 1945 to 1975'.

During those years, important work was devoted to saying more on the theoretical foundations of the economic discipline. Some authors proposed alternative theories of growth and distribution (see Kaldor, 1955–56; Pasinetti, 1962; Robinson, 1956) and expounded a monetary theory of distribution (see Dobb, 1973; Kaldor [1958] 1964; Nuti, 1971; Sraffa, 1960). Others criticized the neoclassical theory, arguing that the assumption of diminishing marginal product introduces logical inconsistencies in a model where more than one commodity is produced and that the presence of a non-monotonically decreasing marginal product generates problems of instability of the equilibrium solutions (Garegnani, 1970; Pasinetti, 1966; Sraffa, 1960). These problems undermine the traditional neoclassical parable that price variations lead the economy to full employment.

During the 1950s, monetary policy was resumed to counteract the inflation raised by the Korean War. The restrictive measures implemented, however, failed to achieve this result, stirring a debate on the working of monetary policy. Minsky's (1957) essay on financial innovation is an outcome of this debate. It argued that restrained issues of monetary base trim down the ability of the banking industry to expand its turnover. Under these conditions, competition within the financial sector intensifies. Like the firms of any other industry, banks tend to accelerate financial innovation to attract the customers of their competitors and avoid the negative effects of the restrictive policy. The acceleration of financial innovation leads to the creation of new forms of payments and investments, which neutralize the tight monetary policy.

The Radcliffe Report was another product of the debate that followed the failure of monetary policy to control the rise in inflation after the Korean War. To assess the causes of this failure, the British government set up the Radcliffe Committee in 1958, whose report, published in 1959, became a reference point for students and professional people, testifying to the wide consensus achieved by Keynesian positions and to the discredit surrounding the quantity theory of money and the use of rigid rules in monetary policy.

This situation induced Friedman and his monetarist colleagues to work on a project aiming at restoring confidence in the working of competitive market forces. They proposed a rehabilitation of the quantity theory of money, an empirical re-evaluation of transmission mechanisms, and an analysis of the monetary cycle emphasizing the damage caused by discretionary policies overlooking the effects of inflation. Moreover, they proposed to restore the neoclassical views on the relation between money and the theory of value, distribution and output by supporting the dichotomy between the real and the monetary departments, the long-run neutrality of money, and the idea that market forces lead the economy to full employment, which manifests itself as a 'natural rate of unemployment'.

Friedman claimed that his views were based on the results of the 'Walrasian system' – that is, the axiomatic version of the neoclassical general equilibrium model proposed in the 1950s by Arrow, Debreu, Hahn, Malinvaud and McKenzie, and submitted that the natural rate of unemployment is the rate that 'would be ground out by the Walrasian system of general equilibrium equations' (Friedman, 1969, p. 102).

Hahn (1971) criticized Friedman's views. He stated that for the world with market imperfections to which Friedman referred, 'no one has ever succeeded in writing down such equations nor in "grinding out" the natural level of unemployment from them' (Hahn, 1971, p. 62). According to Hahn, the Walrasian general equilibrium model deals with an economy where the conditions for the existence of money are ruled out. It cannot provide a theoretical underpinning for the neutrality of money and Friedman's natural rate of unemployment. Moreover, by presenting a long-run analysis to test Friedman's view, Hahn (1971, p. 74) concluded that 'monetary policy can affect long-run equilibrium'.

The state of scientific knowledge at the beginning of the 1970s did not favour the re-establishment of the neoclassical views on the relation between money and the theory of value, distribution and production. The debate on the version of the neoclassical theory of distribution considering capital as a homogeneous factor had shown the validity of the critique of the neoclassical parables stating that the level of distributive variables depend on the relative scarcity of the productive factors and that variations in relative prices lead the economy to full employment (see Samuelson, 1966). Friedman's attempt to support his views by using the Walrasian general equilibrium version of the neoclassical theory, which considers capital as a heterogeneous set of factors of production, had been disallowed by Hahn's clarifications. Those proposing the Walrasian system proved the 'existence' of solutions under restrictive assumptions. They could not demonstrate the *stability* of the equilibrium solutions. The subsequent literature could not show the 'existence' of solutions under less restrictive assumptions and demonstrated that the Walrasian model cannot be used to verify the parable that price variations lead the economy to full employment.[19]

The state of scientific knowledge at the beginning of the 1970s made it difficult to foresee the changes in the dominant positions that occurred in the subsequent years.

5. MONETARY INSTITUTIONS AND THEORIES IN THE ERA OF LIBERALIZATIONS

The events of the 1970s created new changes in the history of monetary institutions. The breakdown of the Bretton Woods Agreements and the oil shocks were followed by forms of liberalizations and by a new approach to financial regulation, which favoured the dominance of finance.

The clearest change in economic theory was the return of the neoclassical parables and of the related views on how to integrate money within the foundations of the economic discipline. The reappearance of confidence in the working of market forces was not the result of analytical answers to the criticisms previously recalled. Their content was simply ignored as if the analyses proposing them, which Hahn (1971) elucidated and Samuelson (1966, p. 583) considered 'facts' that the scientific community had to respect and appraise, had not been developed.

All versions of the New Macroeconomics neglect these criticisms. They attribute validity to the neutrality of money in long-period analyses and to the belief that price variations lead the economy towards positions of equilibrium corresponding to full employment. In what follows, we recall some events that led to the dominance of finance and some contents of the New Macroeconomics.

President Nixon put an end to the Bretton Woods Agreements on 15 August 1971 by repelling the official gold parity and the fixed exchange regime. During the 1970s, controls on capital movements remained in force. Some literature, however, highlighted the need to abandon them, arguing that they caused 'financial repression', a phenomenon preventing capital from moving from more to less rich countries. The promise of this literature was that the elimination of this phenomenon would have promoted growth in low- and medium-income countries (see McKinnon, 1973; Shaw, 1973). The process of liberalization of capital movements started later, when Margaret Thatcher became prime minister in 1979 in the UK.

The breakdown of the Bretton Woods Agreements was accompanied by the gradual introduction of other changes in monetary institutions. In spite of its positive functioning, after 1970 the discretionary approach to financial regulation was gradually replaced by a new 'rules-based' regime, dominated by the introduction of capital and liquidity requirements and characterized by an ongoing erosion of the powers of the authorities. As White (2009) states, in the USA this process went through a 'transition period' (1971–90) and a 'contemporary era' (1991–2007). During the first it primarily occurred by relaxing the application of administrative measures (see Panico et al., 2016; White, 2009). During the 1990s, new legislation formalized the dismissal of the discretionary approach and the conversion of specialized into universal banks. This change favoured the introduction of complex financial instruments and made it more difficult for the authorities to control the systemic risk:

> By ruling out discretion, banks were able to develop new complex financial instruments that are not subject to statutory standards and allow them to assume more risk with existing capital. The most notorious of these were, of course, the mortgage-backed securities that were held off-balance sheet in structured investment vehicles (SIVs) that skirted the rules-based control system that was sufficiently rigid that it was difficult to quickly adjust to innovations. Banks were able to increase their risk and hence their return, while regulators appeared to be faithfully executing their mandates. (White, 2009, p. 36).

Dealing with the crisis of 2007–08, White (2009, p. 36) claims that 'the genesis of the most recent collapse has part of its root' in the shift to the rules-based regime.

The transformation of the specialized into the universal banking system forced the central bank to add to the role of lender of last resort that of lender of first resort (see De Cecco, 1999). The Fed was forced to systematically issue abundant liquidity to avoid the occurrence of credit crunches due to increasing risks assumed by universal banks. This can have set in motion the recent tendency of the interest rate to fall.

Other elements of the conduct of monetary policy started to change during the 1970s. The central banks of the German Federal Republic and Switzerland introduced policies focussing more on monetary targets and inflation in 1974. The United States, Canada, Great Britain, France and Australia made similar choices from 1976. Yet, it was in October 1979, after the second oil shock, that the Fed announced the introduction of new operative procedures. As prescribed by monetarism, the Fed introduced rigid controls on monetary issues, leaving aside the concern for the stability of the interest rates. A few months later, the Bank of England also adopted the 'monetarist experiment', which went on up to 1982, when consequences similar to those foreseen by the Radcliffe Report imposed its abandonment.[20]

After the repudiation of the monetarist experiment, the conduct of monetary policy followed a pragmatic approach. It rejected the use of rigid rules on monetary issue and gradually began to systematically provide abundant liquidity to the interbank markets to counteract the risks assumed by universal banks. At the same time, it gave priority to price stability over full employment. They decided to control the very short-term interest rate, while before they stabilized a long-term interest rate. This change indicates that they have become more preoccupied with financial stability than with the growth of product. Moreover, they succeeded in obtaining the approval of legislation attributing to the monetary authorities the role of leader and to the fiscal authorities that of followers in the process of coordination of economic policies. During the 1990s, the New Macroeconomics used its theoretical views to formalize this spontaneous behaviour of central banks, thus elaborating the analytical framework called 'inflation targeting'. This model recognizes that the supply of money depends on demand for it coming from the markets at an established interest rate. Yet, it could not expound the role of lender of first resort played by the central bank.

The start of the process that led to the formation of the New Macroeconomics can be traced in a series of essays published in the 1970s. Lucas motivated his work in this direction by saying that, although it had been investigated since Hume, the relationship between monetary expansions and the level of production during the cycle was still an unresolved problem:

> The work for which I have received the Nobel Prize was part of an effort to understand how changes in the conduct of monetary policy can influence inflation, employment, and production. So much thought has been devoted to this question and so much evidence is available that one might reasonably assume that it had been solved long ago. But this is not the case: It had not been solved in the 1970s when I began my work on it. (Lucas, 1996, p. 661)

In the Nobel Lecture, Lucas (1996, pp. 663–4, 668–70) stated that the analysis of the long-run neutrality of money, which can be carried out through comparative statics, had been 'stated with increasing precision and worked through rigorously, using the latest equipment of static general equilibrium theory' (Lucas, 1996, p. 669). On the contrary, the influence of money on output during the cycle, which must be analysed through dynamic methods, needed improvement. Hume and the subsequent literature were equipped with verbal method and could not solve this problem. The Depression of the 1930s led the economic profession to further concentrate on this subject. Keynes's *General Theory* was one product of this change of focus (ibid.). Nonetheless, in spite of the progress of the analysis of inter-temporal decisions, up to the 1960s the literature kept studying the cycle through verbal descriptions that 'underscore the futility of attempting to talk through hard dynamic problems without any of the equipment of modern mathematical economics' (ibid.). He resolved that the aim of the work for which he received the Nobel Prize was to take advantage of the progress of dynamic analysis to search for acceptable solutions for the problem of the short-run non-neutrality of money (Lucas, 1996, p. 671).

The Nobel Lecture clarifies some relevant features of Lucas's work. He postulated the validity of the long-run neutrality of money and of the dichotomy between the real and monetary departments of economics (see Lucas, 1996, pp. 674–6; 1972, p. 103; 1973, pp. 326, 333–4). He interpreted Keynes's *General Theory* as an analysis of the fluctuations of the economy, rather than as an attempt to change the theoretical foundations of the economic discipline by rejecting the long-run neutrality of money, the former dichotomy, Say's Law and the tendency to full employment. Moreover, Lucas used the assumption of the neoclassical theory of distribution that the marginal productivities of the factors of production are monotonically decreasing (see Lucas, 1981, p. 44; Lucas and Rapping, 1969, p. 723).

Lucas's postulates were not based on the presentation of analytical answers to the criticisms that had been raised. He ignored Samuelson's (1966) warnings that the critiques raised against the versions of the neoclassical theory of distribution representing capital as a homogeneous magnitude were analytical 'facts' that the nostalgic of the traditional neoclassical parables could not overlook. Likewise, he ignored Hahn's (1971) reproach of Friedman's claims that the Walrasian general equilibrium model can 'grind out' the tendency towards the 'natural rate of unemployment' and the long-run neutrality of money. Finally, he snubbed Keynes's aim to part with the long-run neutrality of money and the neoclassical foundations of the economic discipline.

In spite of these omissions, Lucas's beliefs became the starting point of all New Macroeconomics. Authors belonging to the New Neoclassical Macroeconomics returned to the doctrine 'that markets worked well, and that accordingly policy intervention was unnecessary' (Stiglitz, 2014, p. 24). Authors of the New Keynesian Macroeconomics promoted analyses that admitted the existence of unemployment by assuming that prices and wages adjust with delay to their equilibrium levels (see Stiglitz, 2014, p. 26). Both groups, however, agreed that in the absence of rigidities, 'market economies must be Pareto-efficient, and that, in particular, the kinds of massive under-utilisation of resources associated with recessions and depressions simply could not occur' (Stiglitz, 1992, p. 42). The convergence on these beliefs facilitated the formation of the New Consensus in Macroeconomics, which in the 1990s elaborated the inflation-targeting framework describing how economic policy should operate.

Besides the neutrality of money, the Nobel Lecture clarified that Lucas (1996, pp. 670–71) also wanted to enhance the existing studies on two points: to provide complete microfoundations for macroeconomics and to adopt an 'endogenous' method, named 'rational', for the determination of expected variables. The New Macroeconomics agreed on the necessity to develop complete microfoundations, mostly relying 'on variants of the representative agent model, maximizing utility over an infinite lifetime, with rational expectations'

(Stiglitz, 2014, p. 25). These developments generated analyses that enriched the inquiry into specific aspects of the economic system. Nonetheless, they did not justify the assumption of the long-run neutrality of money and the neoclassical views on the integration of money into the theoretical foundations of the economic discipline.

The search for complete microfoundations and the use of the endogenous method for the expected variables raised some analytical problems. To justify the need for complete microfoundations, Lucas claimed that during the 1950s and 1960s two groups of macroeconomic analyses had been developed. The first, which tried to integrate money in a temporal general equilibrium model (see Patinkin, 1956), derived demand and supply functions from the maximizing decisions of the agents but could not benefit from the use of econometric evaluations. The second, the investment-savings and liquidity preference-money supply (IS–LM) models, enhanced the use of econometric evaluations but placed less emphasis on the search for microfoundations. According to Lucas (1996, p. 670), at the beginning of the 1970s 'no one... regarded this situation as healthy'.

Tobin disagreed with Lucas's opinion. His stated that the most useful approach in macroeconomics is the use of equations that are an amalgam of individual behaviour and aggregation across a multitude of diverse individuals (see Tobin, 1982, pp. 173–5). While it is convenient to integrate micro- and macroeconomic analyses, the attempts to provide complete microfoundations pose problems of aggregation known since the 1930s (see Hicks, 1939; Leontief, 1936, 1947). Fisher's assessment of these problems clarifies that:

> such results show that the analytic use of such aggregates as 'capital', 'output', 'labour' or 'investment' as though the production side of the economy could be treated as a single firm is without sound foundations. This has not discouraged macroeconomists from continuing to work in such terms. (Fisher, 2018, p. 169; see also Felipe and Fisher, 2003; Fisher, 1993)

The existence of aggregation problems emerges in Lucas's (1972) initial attempt to provide microfoundations for macroeconomics. He assumed 'that all agents are alike or fall into two or three classes (old and young, for instance) internally homogeneous but differing from each other in arbitrary specified ways' (Tobin, 1982, p. 174). These devices are 'so abstract and arbitrary as to be useless for policy analysis and econometric model building' (ibid.). In spite of the problems of aggregation, the road set by Lucas became the norm of most subsequent analyses.

Initially the New Macroeconomics also asserted the superiority of the 'endogenous' method for the determination of expected variables. This assertion was, however, queried. For the Nobel laureate Robert Shiller, economic operators cannot count on the distribution of official forecasts, as occurs for the weather. The uncertainty generated by this situation makes it unwarranted to qualify as 'irrational' the behaviour of operators using simple approximate rules to anticipate the future trend of the variables. The empirical analyses presented by Shiller and McCulloch (1987) show that the exogenous methods can provide forecasts as good as the endogenous one:

> Empirical work on the term structure has produced consensus on little more than that the rational expectations model, while perhaps containing an element of truth, can be rejected. There is no consensus on why term premia vary. There does not seem even to be agreement on how to describe the correlation of the term premia with other variables. A lot more research could be done leading to consensus on, for example, the senses in which long rates may be influenced by government fiscal policy, term premia are related to some measures of risk, interest rates overreact or underreact to short rates, or be influenced by or depend on rules of thumb or 'satisficing' behavior. (Shiller and McCulloch, 1987, p. 61)[21]

The search for complete microfoundations and the use of endogenous methods for the expected variables have widened the analytical knowledge on specific aspects of the economy. Yet, they have not proved the validity of the postulations on the long-period neutrality of money, on the tendency to full employment and on the other elements characterizing the neoclassical theoretical foundations of the economic discipline.

6.   CONCLUSIONS

The idea that monetary elements can permanently affect distribution and production has always been relevant in the economic literature. While all subscribed to the idea that the amount of money in circulation influences the level of production during the cycle, some major nineteenth-century economists, who opposed Say's Law, admitted the non-neutrality of money in long-period analyses and monetary influences on distribution. Marx (1972a, pp. 492–3) considered those writings the most valuable part of the economic literature since 1830 and presented in Volume III of *Capital* a 'monetary theory of distribution' through a 'monetary theory of the average interest rate'.

   World War I was a watershed for the evolution of monetary institutions and for the analysis of money. It led to an increase in the extent of speculation on financial assets, which influenced economic life and caused the 1929 crisis. Keynes introduced in *A Treatise* the analysis of the speculative demand for money, integrating it within the neoclassical views on the neutrality of money in long-period analyses, the dichotomy between the real and the monetary departments, Say's Law, the tendency to full employment, and the role of the natural interest rate in monetary policy. In the *General Theory* he rejected the neoclassical theoretical foundations of the discipline, proposing a 'monetary theory of production and distribution'.

After World War II, theories of distribution and production, alternative to the neoclassical one, were presented. At the same time, analytical critiques of the neoclassical theory of distribution considering capital as a homogeneous factor were put forward. The debate proved the validity of these critiques and the problems of the neoclassical belief that variations in relative prices lead to full employment (see Samuelson, 1966). A few years later, Hahn (1971) rejected Friedman's attempts to use the Walrasian general equilibrium model to justify the long-run non-neutrality of money and the belief that price variations lead the economy towards the natural rate of unemployment.

In spite of that, the New Macroeconomics postulated the validity of the long-run neutrality of money, of the dichotomy, and of the neoclassical parable attributing to price variations the ability to lead the economy towards full employment. No analytical answers were given to the critiques raised in previous years. They were simply ignored, upsetting the scientific value of the dominant theory and playing up that of the monetary theories of distribution and production.

NOTES

1. Daniel Torres acknowledges financial support from the Dirección General de Asuntos del Personal Académico (DGAPA) of UNAM [Postdoc scholarship].
2. Other works, like Rist (1940), Morgan (1943) and Fetter (1965), investigated this subject.
3. In neoclassical theory, the constraint set by individuals' preferences is also important.
4. England introduced bills of exchange as a means of payment at the end of the seventeenth century. The government started to issue bonds in 1693 and promoted the creation of the Bank of England in 1694.
5. For an account of this debate among historians, see Temin and Voth (2004, 2013).
6. The *British Monetary Orthodoxy* studied the role of the banking system, the relationship between the business and credit cycles, the crises, the responsibilities of the Bank of England, the factors affecting the interest rates, and the relationship between the rates of interest and profits.
7. Fetter (1965, pp. 40–42, 74–5 and 101–2) recalls other authors of that period claiming that monetary events could permanently influence the overall product of the economy. Among them, he refers to Baring and to the Birmingham school spokesmen (Thomas Attwood, Matthias Attwood, Henry James, etc.).
8. In *A Treatise*, Keynes recognized that in *A Tract* the deposits of the economy were divided into 'income deposits' and 'business deposits'. This distinction, he said, was similar to that between 'circulation of income' and 'circulation of capital' introduced by Adam Smith and used by the nineteenth-century monetary literature (see Keynes, [1930a] 1971, p. 31, fn. 1).

9.   Marx agreed with the Banking school that variations of the interest rate represented the most effective way to adjust the balance of payments and restore a sound monetary circulation. The Currency school held instead the view that variations in commodities' prices were the most effective way to restore equilibrium conditions in the balance of payments.

10. See Marx (1972a, p. 435). For an analysis of his writings on this point, see Panico (1988, pp. 84–8).

11. The latter point was examined in Chapters 17–19 of Part IV of Book III of *Capital* (see Panico, 1980; 1988, pp. 82–101).

12. Marx, like the nineteenth-century literature, referred to the influence of monetary legislation, rather than of monetary policy, on the interest rate. As will be argued in Section 3 below, at the time the banks of issue had not yet become central banks. So, the monetary events that could influence the average interest rate were mainly those related to monetary legislation.

13. Fetter (1965, pp. 15, 77–9, 157–8) recalls that the British monetary orthodoxy acknowledged the role of banks' lobbying activity.

14. Like Keynes ([1930b] 1971, p. 192), in the lectures on 'continental banking', given in Cambridge in 1929 and 1930, Sraffa stated that the restrictions on monetary issues imposed by the Peel Act stimulated commercial banks to develop the use of cheques (see Panico, 2001, p. 296).

15. De Cecco (2005, pp. 356–8) points out that after World War I, the Reichsbank could not operate as before owing to the burden imposed by the Treaty of Versailles, the hyperinflation, and the restrictions on the working of the central bank set by the Dawes Plan.

16. Sayers (1976, p. 169) points out that in those years the Bank of England took initiatives that had no parallel in its history. It gave a loan to the Austrian government on a non-commercial basis to persuade the international operators to channel funds to this country.

17. 'Staff independence' refers to the rules for the naming, duration, removal and remuneration of governing body members. 'Financial and administrative independence' refers to the central bank's capacity to fund its activity with its own resources, rather than depending on transfers from the public sectors or other entities that could influence the decisions made by its executive bodies, and to manage them pursuant to their own criteria. 'Technical independence' refers to a central bank's ability to manage monetary policy on the basis of its technical evaluation, without the interference of other national or international political or economy bodies, and considering what is best for society as a whole and not only a portion of it.

18. Harrod (1951, ch. IX, para. 3) recalls Keynes's article in the *Nation*, 24 May 1924, where, after considering the negative effects of the international speculative activities of the British banks on domestic production, the Cambridge economist presented his proposals for public works for the first time.

19. The literature proved that equilibrium models assuming an economy with complete markets and no frictions can generate endogenous cycles and irregular chaotic dynamics (see Benhabib, 2008; Boldrin and Montrucchio, 1986; Fisher, 1983).

20. The halt to the experiment was caused by increases in interest rates, which enlarged government and foreign debts, causing balance-sheet problems for the banks, which also found it difficult to recover their loans, economic recession and unemployment. There was a broad consensus on this interpretation (see

Musella and Panico, 1995). Even authors who had favoured the development of monetarism accepted it. Cobham (1992, p. 266), for instance, stated that the idea of separating the goals and the functions of monetary and fiscal policy was an aberration of the early 1980s.

21. Shiller (2018, p. 4194) confirms that 'it has certainly not been established empirically that rational expectations models can predict better'.

REFERENCES

Bagehot, W. (1873), *Lombard Street: A Description of the Money Market*, London: Kegan, Paul & Co.

Benhabib, J. (2008), 'Chaotic dynamics in economics', in S.N. Durlauf and L.E. Blume (eds), *The New Palgrave Dictionary of Economics* (2nd edition), London: Palgrave Macmillan, pp. 745–7.

Blinder, A.S. (1997), 'What central bankers could learn from academics – and vice versa', *Journal of Economic Perspectives*, **11** (2), 3–19.

Blinder, A.S. (1998), *Central Banking in Theory and Practice*, Cambridge, MA: MIT Press.

Boldrin, M. and L. Montrucchio (1986), 'On the indeterminacy of capital accumulation paths', *Journal of Economic Theory*, **40**, 24–39.

Caminati, M. (1981), 'The theory of interest in the Classical economists', *Metroeconomica*, **33** (1–3), 79–104.

Capraro, S. and C. Panico (2021), 'Monetary policy in liberalized financial markets: the Mexican case', *Review of Keynesian Economics*, **9** (1), 109–38.

Cobham, D. (1992), 'Radcliffe Committee', in J.L. Eatwell, M. Milgate and P. Newman (eds), *The New Palgrave Dictionary of Money and Finance, Vol. III*, London: Macmillan, pp. 265–6.

De Cecco, M. (1974), *Money and Empire: The International Gold Standard 1890–1914*, Oxford: Blackwell.

De Cecco, M. (1999), 'The lender of last resort', *Economic Notes*, **28** (1), 1–14.

De Cecco, M. (2005), 'Sraffa's lectures on Continental banking: a preliminary appraisal', *Review of Political Economy, Special Issue: Piero Sraffa 1898–1983*, **17** (3), 349–58.

Dobb, M. (1973), *Theories of Value Since Adam Smith*, Cambridge, UK: Cambridge University Press.

Eichengreen, B. and M. Bordo (2003), 'Crisis now and then: what lessons from the last era of financial globalisation?', in P. Mizen (ed.), *Monetary History, Exchange Rates and Financial Markets: Essays in Honour of Charles Goodhart, Volume 2*, Cheltenham, UK and Northampton, MA, USA: Edward Elgar Publishing, pp. 52–91.

Felipe, J. and F.M. Fisher (2003), 'Aggregation in production functions: what applied economists should know', *Metroeconomica*, **54** (2&3), 208–62.

Fetter, F.W. (1965), *Development of the British Monetary Orthodoxy*, Cambridge, MA: Harvard University Press.

Fisher, F.M. (1983), *Disequilibrium Foundations of Equilibrium Economics*, Cambridge, UK: Cambridge University Press.

Fisher, F.M. (1993), *Aggregation: Aggregate Production Functions and Related Topics*, Cambridge, MA: MIT Press.

Fisher, F.M. (2018). 'Aggregation problem', in, *The New Palgrave Dictionary of Economics*, London: Palgrave Macmillan, pp. 167–70. https://doi.org/10.1057/978-1-349-95189-5_586.

Friedman, M. (1969), *The Optimum Quantity of Money*, London: Macmillan.

Garegnani, P. (1970), 'Heterogeneous capital, the production function and the theory of distribution', *Review of Economic Studies*, **37**, 407–36.

Gilbart, J.W. (1834), *The History and Principles of Banking*, London: Longman.

Goodhart, C.A.E. (2010), 'The changing role of central banks', *BIS Working Papers No. 326*. Bank for International Settlements.

Greenspan, A. (1996), 'The challenge of central banking in a democratic society', remarks at the Annual Dinner and Francis Boyer Lecture of the American Enterprise Institute for Public Policy Research, Washington, DC, 5 December, accessed 18 November 2022 at https://www.federalreserve.gov/boarddocs/speeches/1996/19961205.htm.

Hahn, F.H. (1971), 'Professor Friedman's views on money', *Economica*, **38** (149), 61–80.

Harrod, R.F. (1951), *The Life of John Maynard Keynes*, Oxford: Oxford University Press.

Hicks, J.R. (1939), *Value and Capital: An Inquiry into some Fundamental Principles of Economic Theory*, Oxford: Clarendon Press.

Joplin, T. (1823), *Outlines of a System of Political Economy*, London: Baldwin, Cradock & Joy.

Joplin, T. (1832), *An Analysis and History of the Currency Question*, London: James Ridgway.

Kaldor, N. (1955–56), 'Alternative theories of distribution', *Review of Economic Studies*, **23** (2), 83–100.

Kaldor, N. ([1958] 1964), 'Monetary policy, economic stability and growth, memorandum submitted to the Radcliffe Committee on the Working of the Monetary System, 23 June', in N. Kaldor, *Essays on Economic Policy Volume I*, London: Duckworth, pp. 128–53.

Keynes, J.M. ([1923] 1971), *A Tract on Monetary Reform*, in *The Collected Writings of J.M. Keynes, Vol. IV*, edited by D.E. Moggridge, London: Macmillan.

Keynes, J.M. ([1930a] 1971), *A Treatise on Money: The Pure Theory of Money*, in *The Collected Writings of J.M. Keynes, Vol. V*, edited by D.E. Moggridge, London: Macmillan.

Keynes, J.M. ([1930b] 1971), *A Treatise on Money: The Applied Theory of Money*, in *The Collected Writings of J.M. Keynes, Vol. VI*, edited by D.E. Moggridge, London: Macmillan.

Keynes, J.M. ([1931] 1981), 'Is it possible for Governments and Central Banks to do anything on purpose to remedy unemployment?', in *The Collected Writings of J.M. Keynes. Vol. XX: Activities 1929–1931: Rethinking Employment and Unemployment Policies*, edited by D.E. Moggridge, London: Macmillan and Cambridge University Press for the Royal Economic Society, pp. 529–53.

Keynes, J.M. ([1932a] 1982), 'The monetary policy of the Labour Party', in *The Collected Writings of J.M. Keynes, Activities 1931–1939. Vol. XXI : World Crises and Policies in Britain and in America*, edited by D.E. Moggridge, London: Macmillan, pp. 128–37.

Keynes, J.M. ([1932b] 1982), 'A note on the long-term rate of interest in relation to the conversion scheme', in *The Collected Writings of J.M. Keynes. Vol. XXI: Activities*

1931–1939: World Crises and Policies in Britain and America, edited by D.E. Moggridge, London: Macmillan, pp. 114–25.

Keynes, J.M. ([1934] 1973), 'Poverty in plenty: is the economic system self-adjusting?', in *The Collected Writings of J.M. Keynes, The General Theory and After. Part I: Preparation, Vol. XIII*, edited by D.E. Moggridge, London: Macmillan and Cambridge University Press for the Royal Economic Society, 485–92.

Keynes, J.M. ([1936] 1973), *The General Theory of Employment, Interest and Money*, in *The Collected Writings of J.M. Keynes, Vol. VII*, edited by A. Robinson and D.E. Moggridge, London: Macmillan.

Keynes, J.M. (1979), 'Towards the General Theory', in *The General Theory and After. A Supplement (The Collected Writings of J.M. Keynes, Vol. XXIX)*, edited by D.E. Moggridge, London: Macmillan, pp. 35–160.

Kydland, F.E. and E.C. Prescott (1977), 'Rules rather than discretion: the inconsistency of optimal plans', *Journal of Political Economy*, **85** (3), 473–91.

Leontief, W.W. (1936), 'Composite commodities and the problem of index numbers', *Econometrica*, **4** (1), 39–59.

Leontief, W.W. (1947), 'Introduction to a theory of the internal structure of functional relationships', *Econometrica*, **15** (4), 361–73.

Lucas, R.E. Jr. (1972), 'Expectations and the neutrality of money', *Journal of Economic Theory*, **4**, 103–24.

Lucas, R.E. Jr. (1973), 'Some international evidence on output–inflation trade-offs', *The American Economic Review*, **63** (3), 326–34.

Lucas, R.E. Jr. (1981), 'Distributed lags and optimal investment policy', in R.E. Lucas Jr. and T.J. Sargent (eds), *Rational Expectations and Econometric Practice*, Minneapolis, MN: University of Minnesota Press, pp. 39–54.

Lucas, R.E. Jr. (1996), 'Nobel Lecture: monetary neutrality', *Journal of Political Economy*, **104** (4), 661–82.

Lucas, R.E. Jr. and L.A. Rapping (1969), 'Real wages, employment, and inflation', *Journal of Political Economy*, **77** (5), 721–54.

Marshall, A. (1923), *Money, Credit and Commerce*, London: Macmillan.

Marx, K. (1970), *Capital, Vol. 2*, London: Lawrence & Wishart.

Marx, K. (1972a), *Capital, Vol. 3*, London: Lawrence & Wishart.

Marx, K. (1972b), *Theories of Surplus Value, Part 3*, London: Lawrence & Wishart.

McCallum, B. (1996), 'Crucial issues concerning central bank independence', *NBER Working Paper No. 5597*. National Bureau of Economic Research.

McKinnon, R.I. (1973), *Money and Capital in Economic Development*, Washington, DC: Brookings Institution.

Mill, J.S. ([1844] 1948), *Essays on some Unsettled Questions of Political Economy*, reprint, London: London School of Economics and Political Science.

Minsky, H.P. (1957), 'Central banking and money market changes', *Quarterly Journal of Economics*, **71** (2), 171–87.

Morgan, E.V. (1943), *The Theory and Practice of Central Banking: 1797–1913*, Cambridge, UK: Cambridge University Press.

Musella, M. and C. Panico (1995), *The Money Supply in the Economic Process*, Aldershot, UK and Brookfield, VT, USA: Edward Elgar Publishing.

Nuti, D.M. (1971), '"Vulgar economy" in the theory of income distribution', *Science and Society*, **35**, 27–33.

Panico, C. (1980), 'Marx's analysis of the relationship between the rate of interest and the rate of profits', *Cambridge Journal of Economics*, **4** (4), 363–78.

Panico, C. (1988), *Interest and Profit in the Theories of Value and Distribution*, London: Macmillan.

Panico, C. (2001), 'Monetary analysis in Sraffa's writings', in T. Cozzi and R. Marchionatti (eds), *Piero Sraffa's Political Economy: A Centenary Estimate*, London: Routledge, pp. 285–310.

Panico, C. (2021), 'Sraffa's monetary writings, objectivism and the Cambridge tradition', in A. Sinha (ed.), *A Reflection on Sraffa's Revolution in Economic Theory*, London: Palgrave Macmillan, pp. 419–53.

Panico, C. and M. Piccioni (2016), 'Keynes on central bank independence', *Studi Economici*, **1** (3), 190–216.

Panico, C. and M. Piccioni (2018), 'Keynes, the Labour Party and central bank independence', in N. Naldi, A. Rosselli and E. Sanfilippo (eds), *Money, Finance and Crises in Economic History: The Long-Term Impact of Economic Ideas*, London: Routledge, pp. 173–86.

Panico, C. and A. Pinto (2018), 'Income inequality and the financial industry', *Metroeconomica*, **69** (1), 39–59.

Panico, C., A. Pinto and M. Puchet Anyul (2012), 'Income distribution and the size of the financial sector: a Sraffian analysis', *Cambridge Journal of Economics*, **36**, 1455–77.

Panico, C., A. Pinto, M. Puchet Anyul and M. Vazquez Suarez (2016), 'A Sraffian approach to financial regulation', in G. Freni, H.D. Kurz, M. Lavezzi and R. Signorino (eds), *Economic Theory and Its History: Essays in Honour of Neri Salvadori*, London: Routledge, pp. 249–70.

Pasinetti, L.L. (1962), 'Rate of profit and income distribution in relation to the rate of economic growth', *Review of Economic Studies*, **29** (4), 103–20.

Pasinetti, L.L. (1966), 'Changes in the rate of profit and switches of techniques', *Quarterly Journal of Economics*, **80** (4), 503–17.

Patinkin, D. (1956), *Money, Interest and Prices*, New York: Harper & Row.

Pigou, A.C. (1917), 'The value of money', *Quarterly Journal of Economics*, **32**, 38–65.

Piketty, T. (2014), *Capital in the Twenty-First Century*, Cambridge, MA: The Belknap Press of Harvard University Press.

Pivetti, M. (1985), 'On the monetary explanation of distribution', *Political Economy: Studies in the Surplus Approach*, **1** (2), 78–81.

Pivetti, M. (1991), *An Essay on Money and Distribution*, London: Palgrave Macmillan.

Pivetti, M. (1998), 'Thomas Tooke and the influence of the rate of interest on prices: implications for distribution theory', *Contributions to Political Economy*, **17** (1), 39–52.

Quesnay, F. ([1758] 1972), *Tableau économique* (with English translation), edited by M. Kuczynski and R.L. Meek, London: Macmillan.

Radcliffe Committee (1959), *Report of the Committee on the Working of the Monetary System*, Cmnd. 827, London: HMSO.

Rist, C. (1940), *History of Monetary and Credit Theory from John Law to Present Day*, New York: Sentry Press.

Robinson, J.V. (1956), *The Accumulation of Capital*, London: Macmillan.

Rogoff, K. (1985), 'The optimal degree of commitment to an intermediate monetary target', *Quarterly Journal of Economics*, **100** (4), 1169–89.

Samuelson, P.A. (1966), 'A summing up', *Quarterly Journal of Economics*, **80** (4), 568–83.

Samuelson, P.A. (1994), 'Panel discussion: how can monetary policy be improved?', in J.C. Fuhrer (ed.), *Conference Series No. 38: Goals, Guidelines, and Constraints*

Facing Monetary Policymakers: Proceedings of a Conference held in June 1994, Boston, MA: Federal Reserve Bank of Boston, pp. 229–31.

Sayers, R.S. (1976), *The Bank of England: 1891–1944*, Cambridge, UK: Cambridge University Press.

Shaw, E.S. (1973), *Financial Deepening in Economic Development*, Oxford: Oxford University Press.

Shiller, H. (2018), 'Expectations', in Macmillan Publishers Ltd (eds), *The New Palgrave Dictionary of Economics* (3rd edition), London: Palgrave Macmillan, pp. 4186–97.

Shiller, H. and J.H. McCulloch (1987), 'The term structure of interest rates', *NBER Working Paper No. 2341*, National Bureau of Economic Research.

Sraffa, P. (1922), 'The bank crisis in Italy', *Economic Journal*, **XXXII** (126), 178–97.

Sraffa, P. (1960), *Production of Commodities by Means of Commodities*, Cambridge, UK: Cambridge University Press.

Stiglitz, J.E. (1992), 'Methodological issues and the New Keynesian Economics', in A. Vercelli and N. Dimitri (eds), *Macroeconomics: A Survey of Research Strategies*, Oxford: Oxford University Press, pp. 38–86.

Stiglitz, J.E. (1998), 'Central banking in a democratic society', *De Economist*, **146** (2), 196–226.

Stiglitz, J.E. (2014), 'Reconstructing macroeconomic theory to manage economic policy', in E. Laurent and J. Le Cacheux (eds), *Fruitful Economics, Papers in Honor of and by Jean-Paul Fitoussi*, London: Palgrave Macmillan, pp. 20–56.

Temin, P. and H.J. Voth (2004), 'The speed of financial revolution: evidence from Hoare's Bank', *Working Paper No. 04–12*, MIT, Department of Economics.

Temin, P. and H.J. Voth (2013), *Prometheus Shackled: Goldsmith Banks and England's Financial Revolution after 1700*, Oxford: Oxford University Press.

Tobin, J. (1982), 'Money and finance in the macroeconomic process', *Journal of Money, Credit and Banking*, **14**, 171–204.

Tobin, J. (1994), 'Panel discussion: how can monetary policy be improved?', in J.C. Fuhrer (ed.), *Conference Series No. 38: Goals, Guidelines, and Constraints Facing Monetary Policymakers: Proceedings of a Conference held in June 1994*, Boston, MA: Federal Reserve Bank of Boston, pp. 232–6.

Tooke, T. (1826), *Considerations on the State of the Currency*, London: John Murray.

White, E.N. (2009), 'Lessons from the history of bank examination and supervision in the United States, 1863–2008', in A. Gigliobianco and G. Toniolo (eds), *Financial Market Regulation in the Wake of Financial Crises: The Historical Experience (Banca d'Italia Workshops and Conferences)*, Rome: Banca d'Italia, pp. 15–44.

5. Monetary policy and the distribution of income in a transfer theory of debt

Jan Toporowski

1. INTRODUCTION

Up to the middle of the last century, the management of government debt was considered an important part of central banking, if not quite the reason for the existence of central banks, as it was in early modern times (Toporowski, 2019). This function of central banking was reinforced in the twentieth century by the problems of government debt arising out of the two World Wars, and this position was endorsed in the Radcliffe Committee report (1959, Chapter VII). However, shortly after this, James Tobin published his influential 'Essay on the principles of debt management', in which the management of the government's debt by the US Treasury was accorded a role alongside explicit monetary policy conducted by the central bank, in determining the money supply, thus linking monetary with fiscal policy (Tobin, [1963] 1987). In concentrating the discussion on the money supply, the influence of government debt and its management on the distribution of income was lost. This chapter aims to remedy this loss by showing how Michał Kalecki and, before him, Hartley Withers, explained the additional demands on fiscal policy, in respect of the distribution of income, that were made by government debt and its management. It is no coincidence that both these writers produced their reflections on debt management in wartime, when sensitivity to income distribution was at the forefront of popular considerations.

2. FINANCING FULL EMPLOYMENT

In 1944, the Oxford University Institute of Statistics prepared a set of studies under the title *The Economics of Full Employment*. Michał Kalecki, at that time working in the Institute, contributed to this set with a chapter entitled 'Three ways to full employment'. The three ways were deficit spending on public investment and social welfare, financed by borrowing; stimulating private investment; and redistributing income from those on higher incomes to households on lower incomes.

Kalecki reiterated his previous arguments that a fiscal deficit always finances itself, in the sense that the spending ensures that funds accrue in bank accounts to finance the government borrowing. The problem is merely an intertemporal one of securing the funds for the government to spend before they arrive in the bank accounts of the beneficiaries of government expenditure (pensioners, welfare recipients, public employees and private contractors). But this is made easy by the fact that the capitalists who hold bank accounts have money in them in the first place. The rate of interest would not rise as long as the central bank expanded commercial banks reserves sufficiently to allow commercial banks to maintain their cash ratios. If the rate of interest on government bonds started to rise, then the government could always switch its financing to shorter-term bills. In this way, as with the wartime fiscal deficit, the government borrowing could continue without affecting the rate of interest. Wage pressure on prices of consumer goods could be regulated by a combination of price controls, subsidies and income tax. Concerns about the 'burden' of the national debt could be met by servicing it from the proceeds of a capital levy, or a tax on profits with the amounts of fixed capital investment deducted from the profits liable to tax. This last Kalecki called a modified income tax that would have a neutral effect on output and employment. The capital levy idea cannot have failed to appeal to John Maynard Keynes, working on government finances in the British Treasury. In the footsteps of David Ricardo, Joseph Schumpeter, John A. Hobson and Otto Bauer, Keynes had been a long-standing advocate of a capital levy ('the scientific, expedient...rational, the deliberate method' of financing government debt; Keynes, 1923, p. 65; see also Balogh, 1944).

Kalecki found the regulation of private investment to be the most problematic way of securing full employment. The optimal amount of such investment was the amount that would keep productive capacity growing with the level of consumption and total expenditure. However, investment is the least stable part of expenditure in an economy. It was therefore unlikely to be regulated by the rate of interest, where the relevant long-term rate of interest is relatively stable, indicating only a very weak relationship between policy rates of interest, which are short term, and the level of private investment, or by tax allowances. Either of these measures would require cumulative reductions to maintain their effect so that, in time, a government would be unable to reduce interest rates or taxes any further. Another way may be to use public investment to augment and stimulate private investment. But such public investment depends on social need and, if that need is not there, it may be preferable to subsidize consumption with welfare payments. The problem with relying on private investment is that it also adds to productive capacity. Excess capacity emerges, because the rate of investment required to maintain full employment is less than that required to maintain full capacity utilization. In this situation, excess capacity will tend to depress private investment.

Relying on private investment to achieve full employment was, in Kalecki's view, a 'fundamental error':

> The proper role of private investment is to provide tools for consumption goods, and not to provide enough work to employ all available labour... Both public and private investment should be carried out only to the extent to which they are considered useful. If the effective demand thus generated fails to provide full employment, the gap should be filled by increasing consumption [by subsidizing consumption and welfare payments] and not by piling up unwanted public or private capital equipment. (Kalecki, 1944, pp. 52–3)

There was, moreover, 'a technical but important disadvantage', relative to government expenditure, of using private investment to secure full employment:

> Government spending can never fail to achieve immediately the desired employment if it is on a sufficient scale, because it generates effective demand directly. The effects of stimuli to private investment depend, however, on the reaction of entrepreneurs, and it is quite possible that when they are in a very pessimistic mood they may not respond even to considerable inducements. This may happen, for instance, if they do not feel confidence in the political situation. (Kalecki, 1944, p. 53)

Private investment, therefore, cannot be regarded as a 'satisfactory' policy for achieving full employment.

The third way of achieving full employment is by redistributing income to achieve higher consumption by taxing higher incomes and subsidizing, with welfare payments, those on lower incomes. The tax on higher incomes would have to be 'modified' by allowing deductions for business investment, so that the redistribution does not adversely affect private investment. The redistribution would result in a more equal distribution of income after tax. Such redistribution was likely to meet with much stronger opposition than the policy of deficit financing. It may therefore be necessary to reinforce redistribution with deficit spending by the government.

Kalecki noted two further distributional aspects of full employment. Wage bargaining, he argued, would have a different role in a regime of full employment. With the economy operating at full capacity, maintaining demand at the level of the output of consumer goods may require taxation to be higher than planned for under a policy of fiscal stimulus. Prices could be kept constant by price controls. The other aspect concerned the distribution of income between profits and wages. Price controls would have the effect of redistributing income from profits to wages, by increasing real wages. Here too, price controls may need to be supplemented by increased taxation on higher incomes.

This will also mean 'linking up trade union bargaining with general economic bargaining' over price controls (Kalecki, 1944, pp. 56–7).

Kalecki concluded that the most reliable way of securing full employment was by a combination of deficit financing and redistribution through taxes, subsidies, price controls and welfare payments. At the same time, it would be necessary to ensure that private investment provided sufficient capacity for demand, given full employment and labour productivity. Private investment could be encouraged by making fixed investment deductible against tax, or by replacing income tax by wealth taxes, which will have no effect on the profitability of investment. Such incentives to investment could be supplemented by public investment – for example, in slum clearance (Kalecki, 1944, pp. 57–8).

Keynes, who had urged in his *General Theory* 'the socialisation of investment' (1936, p. 378) as a solution to the problem of unemployment, was impressed. He wrote to Kalecki to thank him for the book:

> Your own contribution seems to me most striking and original, particularly pages 44–46; also most beautifully compressed. It is a great comfort to read something so short and so much to the point. I am very much taken with your modified income-tax [i.e., the tax on profits]. It will be alleged, I am afraid, that the difficulties of transition would be excessive, since it would mean that a new business might have next to no tax to pay for years, which would appear to give it a great competitive advantage. Nevertheless, there is, I think, a good answer to this, and such criticisms, which would be certain to arise, would be based on a fallacy. (Letter of J.M. Keynes to M. Kalecki dated 30 December 1944, in Keynes, 1980, pp. 381–2)

3.   'INSIDE' AND 'OUTSIDE' DEBT

Pages 44–46 in Kalecki's essay that so impressed Keynes were where Kalecki advanced the idea of the national debt as not 'a burden to society as a whole because in essence it constitutes an internal transfer' and proposed a wealth tax, or a tax on profits from which investment could be deducted. Kalecki clearly had in mind debt issued in the domestic currency, in the fiscal jurisdiction of the government. Such *inside* debt needs to be distinguished from *outside* debt owed to residents in a foreign country. The most salient difference between the two kinds of debt concerns their effect on the financial resources of a country. *Internal* debt conserves financial resources, because the counterpart of the government's liability is the asset held by residents who are owed money by the governments. Such government debt merely requires regular transfers of money from taxpayers to holders of government bonds in the form of interest and agreed repayments. By contrast, *external* debt drains the financial resources of the economy: these liabilities of a government are assets for foreign residents and interest and repayments are transfers from taxpayers in the economy to residents outside the country.

The distinction between internal and external debt highlights the ingenuity of Keynes's and Kalecki's proposals for a capital levy to pay for the servicing of government debt. The national debt, in Kalecki's approach, is a system for redistributing monetary resources from taxpayers in general to the smaller, wealthier group of government bondholders (although today, in the twenty-first century, a significant proportion of government bonds are held on behalf of the less wealthy in pension funds and insurance companies). Such transfers are in general regressive. However, a tax levied on capital wealth, or a wealth tax, to pay for servicing the government's debt, would reverse this regressive transfer by making the transfer from wealthy taxpayers to wealthy bondholders. Since the asset counterpart of government debt is wealth, a capital levy effectively mobilizes the monetary assets of the wealthy to pay interest to the wealthy and repay bonds held by them. Kalecki had already argued for that in his earlier paper on 'Political aspects of full employment', pointing out an additional advantage of this financing, that it does not affect the incentive to invest (Kalecki, 1943). Similarly, the tax on profits, with deductions for investment, would not reduce the returns from investment.

4.   THE WITHERS CONNECTION

Kalecki's analysis of internal government debt as a system of income transfers, rather than just deductions from income, should not have come as any surprise to Keynes. The analysis had been put forward 27 years earlier by the distinguished economic journalist and editor of *The Economist* magazine, Hartley Withers, in a set of lectures on 'Public Finance' that he gave at the London School of Economics in February and March 1917. Withers had already distinguished himself as a monetary economist with his book *The Meaning of Money* (Withers, 1909). In this book, he first articulated the principle that, in a credit economy, bank deposits come into existence through banks' loan advances, rather than through public deposits of money. According to Schumpeter (1954, p. 1111), this 'was considered as a novel and somewhat heretical doctrine'. But it found its way into Keynes's *Treatise on Money* (Keynes, 1930, Chapter 2) and was espoused by his colleague at Cambridge, Dennis Robertson (Robertson, 1926).

Keynes was also impressed by Withers's 'masterly account of the English financial system' for the United States Senate Commission that, in 1911, was preparing the establishment of the US Federal Reserve (Keynes, 1983, p. 368). But apart from using this account of the British financial system, and *The Meaning of Money*, in his Cambridge lectures, there is no evidence that Keynes knew of Withers's lectures in public finance, which were published in 1917 under the title *Our Money and the State* (Withers, 1917). Indeed, with the exception of the chapter dealing with the national debt, the book is rather conventional, although, perhaps because of the fiscal effort in financing World War I, singularly free of the hostility towards government expenditure and debt that one would expect of an economic journalist of his generation (Withers was born in 1867) and an editor of *The Economist*.

This lack of hostility towards government expenditure comes from Withers's clear recognition that when the government taxes the population in order to finance its expenditure, it is creating income for the public. The government draws on the monetary resources of the subscribers to its bonds; returns that money to the public in the course of expenditure; draws on that money again in the form of taxation to pay the interest cost of the bonds; returns those taxes to the holders of the bonds in the form of interest on those bonds; before drawing on the monetary resources of the public through taxation again to repay the bonds, returning that money to the subscribers of the bond. In this way, 'the view that borrowing at home puts the burden [of current expenditure] on posterity is a delusion…whatever posterity pays, it pays to itself' (Withers, 1917, pp. 45 and 35). In the case of government borrowing in the form of what were known as *consols* ('consolidated funds', or perpetual bonds), payment continues indefinitely: 'the interest charge will continue to be a burden to the citizens as a whole and an Income to the heirs of those who originally subscribed' (ibid., p. 40).

A consequence of this is that the national debt is not 'net wealth' – that is:

> [the] existence of a national debt, held by the citizens, does not affect the wealth of the nation as a whole. The wealth of a nation consists of its material assets in the way of industrial plant, agricultural estates and stock, houses, roads, railways, canals, and so on, and its holding, if any, of foreign investments, and its income consists of the annual produce of these material assets as organized and worked as a going concern by the nation's brains and sinews. (Withers, 1917, p. 41)

However, the debt does involve a transfer of incomes. On the one hand:

> the system has this advantage in a community in which wealth is unequally distributed, that it enables those who have a margin of income above the necessaries of life to pay for whatever be the object that the Government wants without at the time feeling any poorer, because they get a security that makes them think they are actually richer. If taxation is equitably imposed they will afterwards be taxed to pay themselves interest in proportion to the amount that they ought to have put into the loan when appealed to by the Government.

However:

> if those with a margin, who can save without serious discomfort, take up all or the greater part of the loan, and then taxes are imposed on all, whether they have a margin or no, then the system of financing Government spending by loan tends to

accumulate more and more wealth in the hands of those who are well off. (Withers, 1917, pp. 40–41)

Perhaps because of this income transfer from the general mass of taxpayers to the smaller minority of wealthy bondholders, Withers did not recognize any reluctance in the financial markets or among the wealthy to lend money to the government. Implicit in his (and perhaps Kalecki's) argument is the notion that the regressive redistribution of income that is effected by government debt requires more progressive taxation. The logical conclusion of such reasoning is Kalecki's capital levy to pay the annual costs of servicing the government's debt: reducing the redistribution of income effected by government debt to a redistribution entirely within the class of the wealthy – that is, making the wealthy pay the cost of servicing the debt owed to the wealthy. Withers's analysis suggests why even the prospect of having to pay taxes may not deter the enthusiasm of the wealthy for more government bonds. If they recognize that their tax liability is increased by government debt, they will buy even more government bonds: their tax liability will not increase, because their total wealth has not increased (they have merely swapped money for bonds), but their *after-tax* income will rise, providing the government bonds pay a sufficient interest margin over the rate of interest on bank deposits. The reaction against government borrowing was more likely from taxpayers than bondholders:

> High taxes, due to a big debt charge produced by home borrowing, will only go out of one pocket into another, but the taxpayers will not all recognize this, and if they are not also debt-holders it will not console them if they do. (Withers, 1917, pp. 47–8)

Withers concluded that it may be too easy for governments to finance expenditure by borrowing, and recommended as a progressive financing system that borrowing should only be undertaken where it was not possible to finance by means of taxation:

> A well-informed and benevolent despot, with a perfectly docile people, would see that if there is money in the country that he can get by borrowing he can also get it by taxing if he sets about it in the right way, and that by doing so he not only cheapens the war by reducing his subjects' demand for goods which competes with that of his War Minister, but also makes industrial recovery in peace more rapid and hearty, by the absence of after-war taxation. All the money that he wanted for war he would just take from his people in taxes as the war went on, without going through the cumbrous process of borrowing it from them and afterwards taxing them to pay themselves back. But in order to do so he would have to be able to rely on a truly equitable system of taxation, which would curtail the power even of the richest to waste money on things that are not really needed at a time of national crisis, without

taking food out of the mouths and clothes off the backs of those who are hungry and ill-clad. (Withers, 1917, pp. 48–9)

So far, Withers was lecturing/writing about 'internal' or domestic debt. His view of external debt was more critical. In his view, foreign borrowing wherever possible should be avoided because, in contrast to domestic borrowing, it drained financial resources by redistributing income from domestic sources, via taxation, to foreign holders of government bonds. Borrowing abroad was only worthwhile if it promoted economic development:

> Borrowing abroad, except for reproductive purposes such as railway building, is so evidently 'bad business' that it is only done by Governments of economically backward countries, or by Governments which are impelled into this course, against their will, by the force of circumstances, as happened to ours in the present war. (Withers, 1917, p. 50)

5.   DEBT AS REAL OR MONETARY CLAIM?

An ambiguity remains in Withers's exposition as to whether government debt is a claim on *real* resources (a deduction from the real output of the economy) or merely a claim on the monetary resources of the economy. In some passages, he regarded debt charges as being claims on the money in the economy (e.g., the phrase above about 'high taxes, due to a big debt charge produced by home borrowing, will only go out of one pocket into another') while at the same time regarding it as a claim or the real output of the economy ('debt-holders, without making any further effort, get for all time, as long as the loan is outstanding, a large slice of the nation's revenue, which has to be found out of its annual produce' (Withers, 1917, p. 42).

There is no doubt that the 'external debt' that Withers warned against is a claim on real resources, in the sense that borrowing from abroad then requires income from abroad for servicing its interest and repayment. That income, as Withers pointed out, can only be obtained from either investments abroad – for example, using foreign borrowing to invest abroad, what might be called today a perfect 'hedge' for the borrowing, but of little economic use to a government or a country unless the foreign investment entails buying equipment from that country, as Withers noted – or by exporting goods and services abroad to generate the foreign currency to repay the foreign borrowing.

With internal debt, the situation is more complicated. Withers explained the sources of government debt finance as follows:

> When we subscribe to the loan we either do so out of money that we borrow...or by drawing down our bank balances, in which case, unless we have been stupid enough to keep unnecessarily big ones, we shall save to replenish them. If we save

we have so much less to spend on our own comforts and amusements, or so much less to invest in other directions, from which we should have received interest and repayment that would not have come out of our pockets. So by subscribing we hand over our money. (Withers, 1917, p. 38)

Here Withers reveals himself as one of Keynes's 'neoclassicals' – that is, someone who still believes that the financial system intermediates between 'saving' and investment (but who differs from the 'classicals', according to Keynes, 1936, p. 177, in believing that 'saving' and investment can be actually unequal). To give Withers his due, at the time he was writing, Keynes himself was a 'neoclassical'. In fact, there is no reason to believe that the amount of money available to take up government bond sales is limited to saving out of current income. But this is also the same Withers who had earlier argued that bank loans, rather than saving, create deposits and, in the following chapter of *Our Money and the State*, went on to argue for the quantity theory of money, that the price level in the economy is determined by the quantity of money because the velocity of circulation of that money may be taken to be constant (Withers, 1917, pp. 55–6). Perhaps Schumpeter was right in paying him a double-edged compliment, describing the London *Economist* as being 'the most valuable part' of a 'vast literature' on credit and banking, despite it being 'written by…financial writers…who knew all about the facts, the techniques and the current practical problems of banking, but who cared little about "principles" – except that they never failed to refer to established slogans – and cannot be said to have had any very clear ideas about the institutional trends they beheld' (Schumpeter, 1954, p. 1110).

6.   MONETARY POLICY AND PRIVATE SECTOR DEBT

The transfer principles underlying the management of government debt also apply to private sector debt. Debt contracts are commitments to transfer money between private sector agents. Like government debt, those transfers are influenced by the size of the debt and the rate of interest. The setting of interest rates is the primary way in which central banks can influence such transfers.

In the classical theory of interest, of the Gold Standard, monetary policy affects the distribution of income through its control of the rate of interest that determines the portion of the productive surplus that is transferred to lenders who advance the finance for production (Toporowski, 2020a). In this way, monetary policy also determines the scale of the transfers required to service government debt. With production dominated by corporations, and the proliferation of debt among property-owning households (Toporowski, 2014), the situation becomes more complex. Indebted corporations and households hedge their debts with monetary and financial assets, on which they receive interest. The notional distinction between borrowers and lenders from which the theory of interest starts, ceases to represent a social reality in which the borrower also has an interest in higher rates of interest, in respect of the borrowers' holdings of monetary assets. The rates of interest fixed by central banks now determine the scale of transfers, not so much between discrete classes of borrowers and lenders as between *net* borrowers and *net* lenders.

The hedging of debts is usually done by scaling up a balance sheet, by adding more debt on the liabilities side in order to hold more liquid assets (Toporowski, 2008). Once it is recognized that, at the margin, changes in the rate of interest merely affect the scale of transfers – that is, the amount of 'churn' of liquid assets on interest-payment days, and not the net borrowing or lending – it becomes obvious that, in respect of private sector debt, those changes in the rate of interest do not affect the distribution of income. This is determined by the *net* borrowing or lending position of borrowers and lenders, and only marginally by the rate of interest.

However, as with government, the central bank does, by its open market operations, affect the liquidity of debt markets. This is important because the liquidity of debt markets determines the ability of borrowers to refinance their debts. In countries with sophisticated debt markets, the vast bulk of debt transactions are not for investment in the real economy (as assumed by the 'classics'), or even for 'speculation' as postulated by Keynes, but simply to refinance old debts. This is most obvious in what was called in Keynes's time the 'floating debt' technique of government borrowing through the issue of short-term Treasury Bills, most of which were used to repay bills issued earlier. This was known as 'floating debt' because it ends up as long-term debt at whatever is the short-term rate of interest at the time of the interest payment. Although less commonly used in the case of household debt, refinancing allows net debt to be sustained on a more or less permanent basis.

7.   CONCLUSION

The transfer approach to debt and interest shows that monetary policy has only a marginal effect on the distribution of income. The canonical impoverished citizen burdened by debt would be at the bottom of the income distribution whether the rate of interest was high or low, in much the same way that the stockholder enjoying the stock market boom brought on by quantitative easing would still be among the wealthiest whether the central bank bought bonds or not. The main channel by which debt and interest affect the distribution of income is through government debt and the fiscal policy that it facilitates. This was demonstrated by Michał Kalecki and Hartley Withers in their critique of the classical theory of government debt.

The difference between the classical and the transfer approach is essentially about where the money comes from to pay interest and repay loans. In the transfer approach, the money to pay interest and repay loans comes from existing money hoards: in the case of government debt, taxpayers run down their money hoards to pay the government, which in turn returns the money to holders of government bonds. The amount of money held by 'the public' has not changed; it has simply been redistributed or transferred from the pockets or (as Keynes and Kalecki would have it) the portfolios of taxpayers to the pockets or portfolios of bondholders. By contrast, in classical theory, the public are deemed not to hold money, but must sell commodities to raise the money to pay the taxes. But even in that situation, the money raised returns to holders of government bonds. Interest here is, in effect, a Ricardian rent that comes out of the surplus currently generated from production. In Withers's words (1917, p. 51) 'the interest we shall have to provide out of our annual production of goods and services…we shall have to work harder to provide for our own wants'.

Would the classical theory still apply if the money holdings of taxpayers were insufficient to pay the taxes required to defray the interest and repayment costs of government debt? To some degree, the classical theory would hold. But then a market would have to be found with the monetary resources to buy the commodities being sold to pay taxes. This may be the case if taxpayers (including firms and banks) do not have the liquid assets necessary to pay their taxes. However, in the case of wealthy individuals and institutions, this is not the case. In this situation, the commercial banking system and the central bank have a very specific function in maintaining the liquidity of the assets portfolios of the wealthy: the commercial banks by creating bank deposits through lending against the security of other assets in those portfolios; and the central bank by buying in securities in exchange for the reserves that the commercial banks may need to support their lending.

The transfer approach to government debt shows that the sustainability of debt is reinforced by a progressive tax system that levies the taxes necessary for the servicing of government debt on wealthy individuals, firms and financial institutions. The more progressive is the tax system, the less is the drain of government debt on current income. The banking system plays its part in advancing credit to maintain the monetary hoards that are transferred in the process of debt payments and creating, through securitization and buying government debt, the debt securities that the central bank can buy in order to maintain the liquidity of banks. In this respect financialization is good.

The transfer approach to debt also brings clarity where the discussion on government debt confuses 'inside' debt, where debt is simply a commitment to transfer money in the future from taxpayers to bondholders, with 'outside' debt, which drains monetary and financial resources, output and income.

Under the Gold Standard, such confusion was to some degree understandable, because the gold for debt repayments had to either be mined at some cost, or imported in exchange for exports. In this situation, it was easy to mistake what, for an individual, may be 'outside' debt but which, for an economy as a whole, is merely a transfer of existing monetary resources.

The relevance of these considerations in 2021, in the midst of the COVID-19 pandemic, is fairly clear. It is worth bearing in mind that Withers's, Keynes's and Kalecki's reflections on debt management were not an abstract theoretical consideration, but were evoked by the practical requirements of financing a military effort that was beyond the tax capacity of the British population at the time. COVID presents a similar financing challenge, exacerbated by the impact of the disease, and of the measures being taken to control it, on an already unequal distribution of income (Jump and Toporowski, 2020). In these circumstances, the financing recommended by Keynes and Kalecki, through the issue of long-term bonds serviced and eventually repaid by taxes on higher incomes and wealth, has a renewed currency (Kalecki, 1944; Keynes, 1940). Such financing may not only maintain living standards through the extraordinary economic recession resulting from the pandemic; the placing of the tax burden on the rich may also go some way towards remedying the egregious economic inequalities of our time. It was Kalecki's achievement in public finance to show that this progressive fiscal redistribution is also an economically efficient way of financing government expenditure on the scale required (Toporowski, 2020b). But it is fiscal rather than monetary policy that may influence the distribution of income for better or worse.

ACKNOWLEDGEMENT

For comments on an earlier draft of this chapter I am grateful to Charles Goodhart, Penelope Hawkins, David Laidler and Marc Lavoie.

REFERENCES

Balogh, T. (1944), 'The unimportance of a capital levy', *Bulletin of the Oxford Institute of Statistics*, **6** (3), 44–8.

Jump, R.C. and Toporowski, J. (2020, 30 June), 'The COVID-19 bailout and its financing dilemmas' [Perspectives Blog], Institute for New Economic Thinking, accessed 28 November 2022 at https://www.ineteconomics.org/perspectives/blog/covid-19-the-financing-dilemmas.

Kalecki, M. (1943), 'Political aspects of full employment', *Political Quarterly*, **14** (4), 322–31.

Kalecki, M. (1944), 'Three ways to full employment', in Oxford University Institute of Statistics, *The Economics of Full Employment*, Oxford: Blackwell, pp. 39–58.

Keynes, J.M. (1923), *A Tract on Monetary Reform*, London: Macmillan.

Keynes, J.M. (1930), *A Treatise on Money in Two Volumes. Volume 1: The Pure Theory of Money*, London: Macmillan.

Keynes, J.M. (1936), *The General Theory of Employment, Interest and Money*, London: Macmillan.

Keynes, J.M. (1940), *How to Pay for the War*, London: Macmillan.

Keynes, J.M. (1980), *The Collected Writings of John Maynard Keynes. Volume 25, Activities 1940–1946: Shaping the Post-War World: Employment and Commodities*, edited by D.E. Moggridge, London: Palgrave Macmillan.

Keynes, J.M. (1983), *The Collected Writings of John Maynard Keynes. Volume 11, Economic Articles and Correspondence: Academic*, edited by D.E. Moggridge, London: Macmillan.

Oxford University Institute of Statistics (1944), *The Economics of Full Employment*, Oxford: Blackwell.

Radcliffe Committee (1959), *Report of the Committee on the Working of the Monetary System*, Cmnd. 827, London: HMSO.

Robertson, D.H. (1926), *Banking Policy and the Price Level*, London: Macmillan.

Schumpeter, J.A. (1954), *History of Economic Analysis*, London: Allen & Unwin.

Tobin, J. ([1963] 1987), 'An essay on the principles of debt management' in J. Tobin, *Essays in Economics, Volume 1: Macroeconomics*, Cambridge, MA: MIT Press, pp. 378–455.

Toporowski, J. (2008), 'Excess capital and liquidity management', *Working Paper No. 549*, Levy Economics Institute of Bard College, November, pp. 1–10.

Toporowski, J. (2014), 'Debt, class and asset inflation', in R. Bellofiore and G. Vertova (eds), *The Great Recession and the Contradictions of Contemporary Capitalism*, Cheltenham, UK and Northampton, MA, USA: Edward Elgar Publishing, pp. 100–111.

Toporowski, J. (2019), 'Open market operations', in D.G. Mayes, P.L. Siklos and J.-E. Sturm (eds), *The Oxford Handbook of the Economics of Central Banking*, Oxford: Oxford University Press, pp. 436–53.

Toporowski, J. (2020a), 'Anwar Shaikh and the classical theory of interest: a critical note', *Cambridge Journal of Economics*, **44** (2), 465–4.

Toporowski, J. (2020b), 'Debt management and the fiscal balance', *Review of Political Economy*, **32** (4), 596–603.

Withers, H. (1909), *The Meaning of Money*, London: John Murray.

Withers, H. (1917), *Our Money and the State*, London: John Murray.

PART II

Evidence

6. Monetary policy and income distribution

James K. Galbraith

The hypothesis of a connection between the conduct of monetary policy and the evolution of economic inequalities poses a profound challenge to established ideas and to the organization of economics itself – to the conventional division of the field into 'micro' and 'macro' spheres. This division has been under challenge for a half-century (Lucas, 1976), but from a perspective that holds monetary policy to be strictly epiphenomenal, and hence denies the possibility of any connection between the distribution of income and the decisions of the central bank. To assert the possibility of a link, let alone a dominant or determinative causal relationship, is to invert the case for microfoundations and to assert, instead, a key role for macro policy in the central mission usually reserved for microeconomics – that of explaining the allocation of resources to different households, groups and social classes. The stakes are therefore very high.

There is, moreover, a further dimension, raising the stakes another notch. Practically all economic models and empirical analyses treat the nation-state as the frame of observation and analysis. This is a matter partly of habit, partly of convenience; habit dating to the origin of national income statistics in the interwar period and convenience due to their ongoing proliferation as a source of measures. It is emphatically not how classical political economy, in the age of colonies and empires, viewed the world. The possibility that monetary policy influences distributive outcomes leads to an auxiliary question: whose monetary policy and whose outcomes? In a world of global finance, it is not a given that the national central bank is necessarily an autonomous actor. It may rather prove that the ecology of global finance is governed by a hegemon, with a handful of exceptions that, like that tiny village in Gaul, resist control by the imperial power (Goscinny and Uderzo, 1961).

In this chapter, we shall first review the entirely conventional and familiar mainstream views of monetary policy, both neoclassical and 'Keynesian,' and the equally conventional and familiar notions of the determination of distributive outcomes in 'labor markets' governed by supply-and-demand and institutional arrangements. We will then advance an alternative theory of the connection, rooted in a systematic analysis of distributive evidence across time and space – a case of measurement *leading to* theory. A brief Appendix covers the effort by Piketty (2014) and his colleagues to bridge the macro–micro divide without making a firm commitment to either side.

In the classical and neoclassical economics – the real-exchange economics of Ricardo and Walras – money is 'a veil.' The quantity of circulating medium determines the price level in equilibrium and no real variables or relative prices are affected. Since relative prices aren't affected, distributions cannot be. This tradition persisted through the twentieth century, was embedded in models of rational expectations and the real business cycle, to the point where the neutrality and even the super-neutrality of money became points of dogma. Written into the charters of numerous central banks, these doctrines instructed the monetary authorities to target the inflation rate over all other economic policy objectives, leaving growth to be governed by technical and demographic factors and employment by the adjustment of real wages.

In the postwar version of Keynesian economics – the Hicks–Hansen IS–LM model – monetary policy acquired a new role. Depending on the slope of the equilibrium relationship between interest rates and nominal GDP, a central bank might have power over total income, and depending on the margin of unused labor and other resources, also on the level of unemployment, at least in the short run. Whether these results held in the face of adjustments to inflation expectations was a source of intense controversy, leading in the end to the embedding of the natural rate of unemployment (or NAIRU) in the thinking of a generation. But this is beside the point. At no time in the troubled reign of neo-Keynesian macroeconomic models was a link drawn between monetary policy and distribution, neither in theory nor in the spotty domain of empirical work.

Neoclassical growth theory did, of course, postulate a role for the 'real' rate of interest in the division of output between investment and consumption goods; a lower rate of interest would increase demand for investment but reduce the supply of saving, with equilibrium – and ultimately the rate of profit on capital – determined by the balance of these forces. This process had an unquestionable bearing on the functional distribution of income between classes of economic actors, typically capital and labor. But the interest rate so conceived was detached from monetary policy and central banking; its relation to 'bank rate' in the real world was at best unclear.

In Marx, the central distributive concept is the extraction of surplus value, and the rate of extraction, s/v, is connected to the rate of profit by a transformation not adequately worked out until Sraffa (1960). This rate and its derivatives have no connection to the policies of a central bank. Nor does the neoclassical theory of marginal productivities, according to which each factor – and indeed, each worker – is compensated according to their contribution to physical output, a contribution entirely governed by technical factors. In both the Marxian and neoclassical theories, the evolution of income distribution was treated as, at most, a long-term process, such as in the thesis of a falling rate of profit as capitalism matured and began to decay. The general presumption of the neoclassical theory was of equilibrium – the persistence of present patterns into the indefinite future unless disturbed by 'exogenous shocks.'

Settled expectations were forced to change beginning in the early 1990s, as a pattern of increasing inequalities, mainly in the United States and dating to the late 1970s, began to penetrate the consciousness of the economic mainstream. The mainstream responded by adjusting the terms of their underlying marginal productivity theory. While previously, relative factor supplies and technical conditions were supposed to determine the price of a homogeneous factor called 'labor,' now the market was said to distinguish labor of differing degrees of skill, and rising inequality could therefore be attributed to an increasing 'bias' of employers in favor of higher grades of skill (Bound and Johnson, 1992). There was in fact essentially no direct evidence for this proposition – and when evidence did emerge it was largely inconsistent with the hypothesis (Galbraith, 1998). But the alignment of the underlying concept with previous doctrine gave it a dominant role in mainstream discourse for at least 20 years.

The dominance of the 'skill-biased technological change' hypothesis was not unchallenged. Wood (1994) notably tried to argue that the rise in North–South trade, hence the effective supply of unskilled labor in relevantly defined product markets – was a superior explanation of apparent shifts in the skill differential. Baker et al. (2005) called attention to shifts in institutions and power dynamics, especially the relative decline of trade unions and their bargaining power. While these challenges had the merit of being connected to demonstrable events in the evolution of productive structures and class relations, they shared with their mainstream adversary a focus on the 'real' as opposed to the 'monetary' or 'financial' economy, and hence drew no link between the conduct of monetary policy and the evolving distribution of income.

I began to engage with the issue of economic inequality in the United States in the mid-1990s, in consequence of a request and modest grant from the Twentieth Century Fund (now the Century Foundation) for a monograph on the dispute over technology, trade, and the rise of inequality since the 1970s. This seemingly straightforward task became complicated on examination of the data underlying the contesting hypotheses – they were (to put it generously) so spotty that they could barely cover the sensitive parts of the argument, let alone discern between them. To make any contribution worth reading, better evidence would be required.

Two bits of intellectual background now came into play. The first and more immediately useful was a fascination, almost 20 years previously, with exploratory data analysis, numerical taxonomy, and the tools of pattern recognition in categorical and hierarchical data sets, such as public budgets and standard industrial classification schemes. My PhD dissertation in Economics at Yale (Galbraith, 1981) had suggested the use of proportionate-change time-series data – in this particular case, annual percentage change in public expenditure on all the various items in the federal budget – as a unit-free observational variable for the classification of hierarchically organized categories into behaviorally consistent groups. Later work identified discriminant function analysis on the resulting group structures as an effective way to isolate the principal economic and social forces underlying such changes, and of measuring the relative importance of each (Galbraith and Lu, 2001). For a study of divergent forces in an industrial economy, average wage payments were an appropriate parallel variable. In this way, dense, widely available, accurate annual (or even monthly) information on changes in the structure of the major forces underlying the income distribution could be brought to bear, without further recourse to the limited stock of household surveys on incomes.

The second bit of baggage was practically fortuitous, dating back to a year of reading among the Cambridge Keynesians in 1974–75 and the subsequent years, through 1980, as a staff member of the House Banking Committee charged with oversight of monetary policy under House Concurrent Resolution 133 and, after 1978, the Humphrey–Hawkins Full Employment and Balanced Growth Act. In these roles I'd found myself in steadfast (and sometimes lonely) opposition to the rising tides of monetarism, rational expectations and the new classical economics, rooted in natural rates of unemployment and the neutrality of money. Cambridge had given me some appreciation of Keynes as a theorist of the monetary-production economy – a viewpoint practically inaccessible through the lens of 'Keynesian economics' as then taught in North America. Capitol Hill was a vantage point for observing the real-world consequences of monetary policy in the recession of 1974–75 and especially after the Volcker Revolution beginning in the summer of 1979. The connection between monetary policy and rising inequality – the micro consequences of a macro tool – would only emerge from the data much later. But when it did, it was not difficult to recognize.

Numerical taxonomy, in the form of cluster analysis on annual rates of change in average wages by industrial or sectoral category – combined with discriminant function decomposition of the between-groups variations into their principal components or factors – provided an effective portrait of the patterns of economic change in the United States in the interwar and postwar years (Ferguson and Galbraith, 2001; Galbraith, 1998), and clearly showed the importance of macroeconomic forces to distributive outcomes.

To measure inequality *as such* from categorical data sets, a group formed in the mid-1990s, eventually the University of Texas Inequality Project (UTIP),[1] took up the work of Henri Theil (1967, 1972), itself based on the information theory of Claude Shannon (1948). In a series of papers, we demonstrated that measures of inequality between groups – industries, sectors, geographical units such as counties, provinces, or states – converge to micro-level measures as groups are subdivided, and that even relatively coarse and partial category structures (such as industrial classification schemes at the 2- and 3-digit level) can be exploited to generate inequality measures that are dense, consistent, and track well against the expensive and sparse alternative of high-quality household survey instruments (Conceição, Galbraith and Bradford, 2001; Galbraith et al., 2016; Galbraith and Kum, 2005).

Our measures, computed as the between-groups component of Theil's 'T' statistic, provide both credible time-series measures of the evolution of inequality for given geographic regions, such as countries or continents, but also consistent and credible estimates of differentials between regions, so long as the underlying data are organized in the same categorical schema. The advantages of the technique are accuracy, extremely low cost, and the ability to construct a year-to-year (and in some cases, month-to-month) picture of changing economic inequalities. This permits almost pinpoint historical analysis of trends and turning points, as well as a wide range of inter-regional and international comparisons, and very precise decomposition of the specific sources of income concentration within a given economy at any given moment.

For the sake of convenience and easier comparison with other measures of economic inequality, the UTIP group also demonstrated that (in most cases) a simple two-variable regression model can convert the Theil measure of inter-industry pay inequality (along with a measure of the share of manufacturing employment in total population) to a conventional Gini coefficient for gross household income inequality (Galbraith and Kum, 2005). This measure, the Estimated Household Income Inequality (EHII) data set, now covers the years 1963–2014 for over 150 countries in a definitive edition, and compares favorably in both coverage and consistency to all other large-scale inequality data sets; it is also a basis of Frederick Solt's widely used Standardized World Income Inequality Database (SWIID),[2] which relies on interpolations between years and countries to fill in gaps in the record. But as the Gini coefficient is damped by its 0–1 range, the underlying data set of Theil statistics remains preferable for cross-country and intertemporal pattern recognition.

Two early and dramatic findings suggested that rising inequality in the United States should be interpreted as primarily a phenomenon of the macroeconomic sphere – and not of vague forces of technology, the skill mix, or international trade. The first was that inequalities in the structure of pay track very closely to the unemployment rate (Galbraith, 1998). This is not because hourly wage rates vary – such rates are not measured directly in any standard data set – but because weekly earnings, the closest proxy, vary more for low- than for high-wage workers. Changing inequalities in the wage structure are therefore largely a simple extension of the prevalence or absence of involuntary unemployment; inequalities expand in slumps and close up rapidly in booms. Here the connection to monetary policy is self-evident to anyone living in the real world of the 1970s and 1980s.

The second finding was that – in the United States – income inequality, measured with tax records (from Local Area Personal Income Statistics, closely tracking surveys and top-shares measures) and therefore including incomes generated by the capital markets rather than strictly by business cash flow, varies very directly with capital asset prices (Galbraith and Hale, 2006). Thus, the proportional change in stock prices tracks an income inequality measure with stunning precision, peaking in 2000, 2007, and rising again after 2011 as the stock market recovered from the global financial crisis. Since the truly stratospheric incomes in America almost all derive from capital assets, this effect is a dominating counter-pattern to that observed within the structures of ordinary pay. Credit booms, in short, tighten up the distribution of pay to workers, but generate an overwhelming compensation to finance, technology, and other leading sectors, so that *income inequality* rises as *pay inequality* declines. In slumps, the reverse pattern prevails. Again the connection to monetary policy is fairly self-evident.

Data for the United States are rich, dense and, given the authority of the Internal Revenue Service, they include reasonably accurate measures of capital incomes – accuracy that is relatively rare in the world at large. For most other countries, data on incomes (mostly from surveys) and data on wages (measured by Theil statistics across industries) track each other reasonably well. And we have little alternative to treating them as if they give us a reasonably true picture of the world as a whole. The advantage of a dense, consistent global data set is, therefore, whether it can reveal a pattern that applies trans-nationally – and if so, whether that pattern corresponds to recognizable events in the common history of the world. The UTIP team approached that problem with a simple two-way fixed-effects regression, extracting both a hierarchy of levels of inequality, independent of the time frame, and a pattern of movement through time, common broadly to most (though not all) of the countries in the data set. The time pattern has the following characteristics (Galbraith and Choi, 2020).

Beginning in about 1971, and allowing for a spike in the oil crisis year of 1973, the dominant trend, reflecting the numerical predominance of developing countries in the world system, and even though inequalities in the US and Europe were beginning to rise at this time, is of moderately declining inequalities through 1979 or 1980. This reflected the strong commodity prices and easy credit of the decade, which fueled economic growth, and which came to an end with the global debt crisis in 1981–82. Thereafter, inequalities grew swiftly, for about 20 years, with distinct regional phases. Latin America and Africa took the lead in the early 1980s, followed by Eastern Europe and the former Soviet Union after 1989, and then the liberalizing economies of Asia, including China, in the mid-1990s. After 2000, the general upward movement of inequalities came to a halt, and modest declines are registered in much of the world through the end of the data set in 2014.

Making general sense of this pattern isn't difficult. The Third World debt crisis, precipitated by the sharp rise in US interest rates in 1979 and 1981, accounts for the surge of inequality in developing countries in the early 1980s, as import-substituting industrialization strategies collapsed, and along with them the previously emerging middle class of factory workers. Pressures of international debt contributed, at the end of the decade, to the collapse of the broadly (though obviously imperfectly) egalitarian regimes in Eastern Europe and the USSR at the end of the decade. And the fever of deregulation, liberalization, and reform spread to India in 1992, to Korea, to China in the mid-1990s and elsewhere in Asia, peaking with the Asian debt crisis of 1997 and the Russian default of 1998. Thereafter, the fever broke. Interest rates tumbled in 2001, and commodity prices then recovered thanks to strong demand from China, social-democratic governments came to power in Latin America and parts of Africa, and neoliberalism, while still dominant, was tempered by new initiatives in housing, health, education, and income support. Inequalities never fell to their pre-neoliberal values, but they ceased their remorseless rise, at least for a time.

How significant was the common factor in these developments? A calculation by Kum determined that it was the dominant force (Galbraith, 2008, Figure 7). If the common factor is subtracted from the actual values, inequality in general in the world economy would not have risen at all. This is, of course, a mathematical tautology, but it points to an underlying conclusion: that there was, in fact, a common global force underpinning the rise of economic inequalities in the crucial years from 1980 through 2000. The search for an explanation must therefore focus on economic pressures of global reach, corresponding to the precise timing observed in the data. Interest rates and debt crises – the fruit of monetary policy in the global financial center – fit the bill exactly. Nothing else does. The fact that there are certain clear exceptions, including revolutionary Iran after 1979, the delayed rise of inequalities in China and India until the early 1990s, and the relative stability of a few robust social democracies in Northern Europe, underscores the diagnosis.

In general terms, the link between external credit conditions, internal economic performance, and inequality is not hard to visualize, but one may wonder why the economic effects of a credit crunch show up as increases in inequality...why the differential effect on lower-income workers and their households? An answer emerges from a consideration of how debt crises affect exchange rates and how exchange rates affect inequality in most countries outside the world's dominant industrial and financial centers (Galbraith and Rossi, 2016). The following stylized facts are pertinent. (1) Generally, in open economies, countries export the highest value-added products that they are capable of producing. (2) These industries generally pay the highest wages in the local economy. Sectors that do not participate in the export trades, unless protected or locally monopolistic, are generally much less well paid. (3) A credit crisis, whether prompted by or precipitating capital flight, typically produces a sharp exchange rate depreciation. (4) This has an immediate effect of increasing the local currency earnings of the exporting sectors, since their foreign sales translate instantly into more local currency units, while the local currency earnings of those who sell only into local markets are unaffected. (5) Inequality, therefore, rises.

One should thus expect a preponderance of positive correlation between exchange rate devaluation against a core-country currency – the US dollar. And inequality increases in non-core countries, allowing for exceptions due to autarky, sanctions and capital controls, is broadly the case. Where two countries are close partners, such as Mexico or Canada with the US, exchange rate movements account for virtually the whole of increases in industrial pay inequalities over a span of roughly 50 years, and industrial pay inequalities play a strong role in the determination of inequalities overall.

Policy conclusions should be drawn carefully. Exchange rate manipulation to maintain an overvalued currency is not a solution to inequality. On the contrary, as Bresser Pereira (2010) and others have argued, it is an invitation to capital inflow, Dutch Disease, a debt trap and a currency collapse. Policy should therefore focus on insulating domestic financial systems and development strategies from predatory external forces and the shock effects of core-economy monetary decisions, while building institutions that can sustain a degree of social-democratic egalitarianism and associated gains in public health, education, public safety and the quality of the infrastructure. For this, maintaining a competitive exchange rate, capital controls, relative openness to trade and to technology transfer, while financing growth from internal savings, appear to be the tested and proven elements of a successful path.

So far as the core economies, and specifically that of the United States, are concerned, it is problematic to start the chain of causality with monetary policy. The central bank is not a fully autonomous force, but a recognized extension of the power of the financial sector. And as a few policymakers have had the courage to state bluntly, the predatory and rapacious nature of Big Finance is a feature, not a defect, of the system, which maintains both the stratospheric wealth and power of financial titans and, via a strong dollar, the purchasing power of a broad spectrum of the public. Unraveling this coalition of uneven mutual advantage in the interest of justice, or sustainability, or any other higher goal, is no simple matter. To do so would require first that analysts conceptualize the underlying role of financial power and define an alternative capable of being visualized by those who might benefit in the medium and long run. It may prove easier merely to wait for the rickety structure to collapse, a possibility neither history nor theory can exclude.

NOTES

1. See University of Texas Inequality Project, accessed February 12, 2021 at http:// utip.lbj.utexas.edu. Working papers and data sets available on site.
2. Accessed February 12, 2021 at https://fsolt.org/swiid/.

REFERENCES

Baker, D., A. Glyn, D. Howell and J. Schmitt (2005), 'Labor market institutions and unemployment: a critical assessment of the cross-country evidence,' in D.R. Howell (ed.), *Fighting Unemployment: The Limits of Free Market Orthodoxy*, New York: Oxford University Press, pp. 72–118.

Bound, J. and G. Johnson (1992), 'Changes in the structure of wages in the 1980s: an evaluation of alternative explanations,' *American Economic Review*, **82**, 371–92.

Bresser Pereira, L.C. (2010), *Globalization and Competition*, Cambridge, UK: Cambridge University Press.

Conceição, P., J.K. Galbraith and P. Bradford (2001), 'The Theil index in sequences of nested and hierarchic grouping structures,' *Eastern Economic Journal*, **27** (4), 491–514.

Ferguson, T. and J.K. Galbraith (2001), 'The American wage structure: 1920–1947,' in J.K. Galbraith and M. Berner (eds), *Inequality and Industrial Change*, Cambridge, UK: Cambridge University Press, pp. 33–78.

Galbraith, J.K. (1981), 'A theory of the government budget process,' PhD dissertation submitted to the Department of Economics, Yale University, unpublished.

Galbraith, J.K. (1998), *Created Unequal: The Crisis in American Pay*, New York: Free Press.

Galbraith, J.K. (2008), 'Inequality, unemployment and growth: new measures for old controversies,' *The Journal of Economic Inequality*, **7** (2), 189–206.

Galbraith, J.K. (2019), 'Sparse, inconsistent and unreliable: tax records and the *World Inequality Report 2018*,' *Development and Change: FORUM 2019*, **50** (2), 329–46.

Galbraith, J.K. and J. Choi (2020, June 29), 'Inequality under globalization: state of knowledge and implications for economics,' *Real-World Economics Review*, (92), 84–102.

Galbraith, J.K., J. Choi, B. Halbach et al. (2016), 'A comparison of major world inequality data sets: LIS, OECD, EU-SILC, WDI and EHII,' in L. Cappellari, S.W. Polachek and K. Tatsiramos (eds), *Income Inequality Around the World (Research in Labor Economics, 44)*, Bingley, UK: Emerald, pp. 1–48.

Galbraith, J.K. and J.T. Hale (2006), 'American inequality: from IT bust to big government boom,' *The Economists' Voice*, **3** (8), 1–4.

Galbraith, J.K. and H. Kum (2005), 'Estimating the inequality of household incomes: a statistical approach to the creation of a dense and consistent global data set,' *Review of Income and Wealth*, **51** (1), 115–43.

Galbraith, J.K. and J. Lu (2001), 'Cluster and discriminant analysis of time series as a research tool,' in J.K. Galbraith and M. Berner (eds), *Inequality and Industrial Change*, Cambridge, UK: Cambridge University Press, pp. 280–86.

Galbraith, J.K. and D. Rossi (2016), 'Exchange rates and industrial wage inequality in open economies,' *UTIP Working Paper No. 71*, accessed November 18, 2022 at http://utip.gov.utexas.edu/papers/utip_71.pdf.

Goscinny, R. and A. Uderzo (1961), *Astérix le Gaulois*, Paris: Hachette.

Lucas, R. (1976), 'Econometric policy evaluation: a critique,' in K. Brunner and A. Meltzer (eds), *The Phillips Curve and Labor Markets*, New York: Elsevier, pp. 19–46.

Piketty, T. (2014), *Capital in the Twenty-First Century*, trans. A. Goldhammer, Cambridge, MA: Belknap Press of Harvard University Press.

Shannon, C. (1948), 'A mathematical theory of communication,' *Bell System Technical Journal*, **27**, 379–423.

Sraffa, P. (1960), *Production of Commodities by Means of Commodities*, Cambridge, UK: Cambridge University Press.

Theil, H. (1967), *Economics and Information Theory*, Amsterdam: North-Holland.

Theil, H. (1972), *Statistical Decomposition Analysis: With Applications in the Social and Administrative Sciences*, Amsterdam: North-Holland.

Wood, A. (1994), *North–South Trade, Employment and Inequality*, Oxford: Clarendon Press.

Wright, N. (2015), 'Data visualization in capital in the XXIst century,' *World Social and Economic Review*. No. 5, July. Accessed February 12, 2021 at http://wser.world economicsassociation.org/papers/data-visualization-in-capital-in-the-21st-century/.

APPENDIX: PIKETTY'S NEOCLASSICAL MACROECONOMICS OF INEQUALITY

In his recent and celebrated work, Thomas Piketty advanced a hypothesis relating interest rates (r) and the rate of economic growth (g), and economic inequality. The hypothesis simply states that when $r > g$, inequality will rise, and when $r < g$, inequality will fall. Piketty thus attributes the recent increases of inequalities largely to a return to a nineteenth-century pattern of $r > g$, following an inequality-lowering interregnum, punctuated by global wars, in the twentieth century.

This hypothesis has the modest virtue of attracting mainstream opinion to the possibility that broad macroeconomic forces condition and determine the trajectory of income distribution. However, it should not be confused with the arguments in this chapter with regard to monetary policy and income distribution, for the following reasons:

- First, Piketty's theory of the interest rate is a confused version of the neoclassical marginal productivity theory, relating interest to the quantity and efficiency of the capital stock. Like most mainstream economists, he ignores (or more precisely, brushes off) the Cambridge capital critique, which demolished that theory on logical grounds.
- Second, Piketty's notion of a capitalist class whose interest incomes grow more rapidly than ordinary wage incomes is essentially that of a representative, infinitely-lived-agent model, ignoring changes in the allocation of capital incomes over time, the dissipation of fortunes through split inheritances, and consumption out of capital and taxes on capital incomes, all of which weaken the $r > g$ relationship.
- Third, the empirical claim for Piketty's reversion to nineteenth-century $r > g$ is unsupported by his own evidence, and only made to appear convincing to uncritical readers by a systematic pattern of distorted graphical presentations and fanciful projections into the far future (Wright, 2015). And so far as international historical and comparative data are concerned, there is essentially nothing in the work of Piketty's associates in the World Inequality Database to support his hypothesis (Galbraith, 2019).

For these reasons, while '$r > g$' provides a simple and superficially appealing way to cut through the fog of conventional labor market explanations for rising inequality, ultimately it amounts to no more than an unsupported slogan, backed by an energetic public relations campaign and an elegantly presented website.

7. The rate of interest and income distribution: an examination of the Pasinetti index in Latin America

Noemi Levy-Orlik and Jorge Bustamante

1. INTRODUCTION

One of the most important discussions in economic theory is the effect of interest rates on economic activity, particularly on investment, economic cycles and income distribution. Conventional (neoclassical-marginalist) theory defines interest rates as a real phenomenon that has an impact on savings and investment, and when both variables are equal, the economic system achieves full employment of the factors of production. Interest rates are determined in the capital market, or are set by the central bank, as a function of the natural interest rate. Divergences from this rate give rise to limited financial cycles (inflation or deflation), without triggering a crisis. Alternatively, the heterodox, post-Keynesian view attributes a monetary character to interest rates, the main effect of which is to alter liquidity. Monetary policy can affect the entire interest rate structure, and therefore portfolio decisions, indebtedness and income distribution, and indirectly affect investment via the profit margin.

A distinctive element of this theoretic approach is the relationship between interest rates and income distribution, via the distribution of surplus among the owners of capital and the entrepreneurs, which modifies the weight of wages in aggregate income. Pasinetti (1980) constructs an index (based on the real long-term interest rate and productivity) which relates high real interest rates with greater wealth in favour of financial capital, which concentrates wealth in favour of the owners of capital to the detriment of wage earners.

This chapter discusses the distributive nature of interest rates via the Pasinetti index, in the context of Brazil, Chile, Colombia and Mexico, for the 1960–2018 period. To this end, through a panel data econometric model, it endeavours to show the distributive effects of interest rates in the region during the period of industrialization by import substitution and of financial globalization.

The chapter is divided into four sections. Section 2 provides a brief discussion of the various theoretic approaches to the rate of interest, contrasting the neoclassical-marginalist, heterodox and post-Keynesian schools. Section 3 trends in interest rates, wages and productivity in Brazil, Chile, Colombia and Mexico, applying the Pasinetti index, and highlighting the particularities of the regulation period (1950–80) and the globalization-financialization period (1990–2018). Section 4 provides a panel data econometric model for the purpose of testing the hypothesis of the distributive nature of interest rates, which favours financial gains to the detriment of real wages. Finally, Section 5 sums up the central proposals of this chapter.

2.   INTEREST RATES, ECONOMIC ACTIVITY AND INCOME DISTRIBUTION

2.1   The Conventional Approach to the Rate of Interest

This approach sustains that the rate of interest is a real phenomenon, determined by individuals' savings and investment preferences, built on a financial system (banking sector and non-bank financial sector) which serves as an intermediary between surplus units (families) and deficit units (companies). This means that the financial sector captures savings and distributes them efficiently among investment projects with the highest capital productivity. Consumers provide savings based on their preference for present or future consumption, and this intertemporal relationship determines the level of interest rate necessary to guarantee the savings required for present investment (Wicksell, 1954; Woodford, 2003). Thus, individuals, based on the maximization of consumption over time, define savings, which is limited by agents' wealth and their impatience for present consumption. The real nature of the rate of interest is explained by the agents' decision to give up a set of real goods in the present to increase their consumption in the future.

The investment decision falls to companies, which access individuals' unconsumed savings to finance their investment projects according to the productivity of capital, and the limit on investment is given by the equality between interest rates and the marginal product of capital. Under this scheme, the equilibrium interest rate is achieved when there is a maximization of consumer utility and a maximization of investors' profits, therefore the rate of interest is the payment for refraining from consuming in the present, and represents the gains obtained from the productivity of the investment. The collection and distribution of the surplus is channelled through the financial system, which leads to the conclusion that the interest rate is a mechanism for distributing social capital productivity among the set of consumers.

The intervention of a central bank in setting interest rates can trigger financial cycles (inflationary or deflationary) in the case of erroneous (artificial) setting of the rate, or error in approximating the interest rate (Hayek, 1929). In this context, it is argued that the best monetary policy is one that reduces inflation to very low levels (or zero) and preserves the equilibrium between investment and savings, with the highest level of employment (or minimum unemployment) given the supply of existing factors of production (potential output). Thus, the interest rate set by the central authority is a monetary variable that does not affect the real level of productive activity over the long term; in other words, it is neutral. Monetary imbalances result from the impact of credit on demand. In this context, the New Monetary Consensus (which is the mainstream theoretic approach today) maintains that central banks should determine the interest rate through monetary rules, the central objective of which is to achieve a given level of inflation given a potential output. And the non-accelerating inflation rate of unemployment is achieved when the monetary interest rate is equal to the natural interest rate.

The role of the financial system (non-bank and bank institutions) is to create a space where capital can move freely and where savings can be efficiently allocated among the most productive activities. The aim is to make the financial system more complex to ensure a wider diversity of financial institutions and actors, with many and varying types of financial instruments, and thus to increase the depth and completeness of that system. In other words, the financial system places various financial assets at the disposal of savers, with varying terms, which broadens portfolio options and thus channels savings to their most productive use.

This process is accompanied by financial innovations that, from this perspective, increase market efficiency and reduce information asymmetries and risk. The various instruments and hedges distribute risk homogeneously and globally on the assumption that the arbitrage is perfect. Higher-risk financial assets cede a growing proportion of productivity gains, which guarantees an efficient distribution of risks and profits. Even if the information is not complete, and employment fluctuates, these are distributed randomly, with a mean equal to zero, because all agents have access to the same level of information and use a similar methodology in assessing and adjusting their portfolios (Fama, 1991).

From the conventional standpoint, then, the rate of interest is the payment for postponing present consumption to the future, which is repaid through capital gains. This means that investment surpluses are distributed among the factors of production involved in creating them, and in turn, because the rate of interest determines the limit on investment, it also defines the potential output and the maximum level of non-inflationary employment. Thus, the central authority's decision is to define a rule for setting the rate based on real factors, the level of which should be equal to the natural-neutral rate that guarantees clearing of the markets. This implies an interest rate that does not alter relative prices and attains zero inflation (Woodford, 2003).

2.2   The Interest Rate and its Distributive Nature

The heterodox approach maintains that the rate of interest affects investment, not through costs but rather through the profit margin (Rochon, 1999), based on which a mechanism is deployed for extracting surplus from productive to financial capital. This in turn influences the weight of wages in income. In this case, the interest rate is not neutral because it influences the expansion of economic activity and employment levels through demand for money. Kaldor (1985, p. 5) writes that 'demand for money, from the very beginning, was a reflection of the demand for commodities and not the source of that demand'.

In a monetary economy, where debt operates as money, causality runs from financing to investment, then income, followed by savings. In this context, given unused capacity or idle resources, a reduction in the interest rate increases demand, raises utilization of capacity or directly increases production capacity in an economy (i.e., investment), and lifts income.

This view rejects the concept of equilibrium interest rates and market clearing. And although the interest rate does not necessarily affect the investment decision directly (Kalecki, 1954), it is a fundamental variable for explaining economic dynamics and cycles (Hawtrey, 1930; Hilferding, [1910] 1981; Minsky, 2004). The interest rate affects the cost of liquidity, and with it, expectations of return on various financial assets at various terms, which prompts a reshuffling of short- and long-term investment portfolios, screened for the change in perceived level of risk for the different agents (Keynes, 1936; Minsky, 1975).

The interest rate set by the central bank represents the cost of supplying liquidity to commercial banks, which is how it affects the yield curve of various terms, and the long-term interest rate (Keynes, 1936), through its influence on expected returns in the financial market, on financing strategies, investment costs, and corporate gains (Toporowski, 1995).

Regarding the effect that the short-term interest rate has on the long-term rate, Keynes (1930) points out that the short-term rate has a significant impact on the terms of long-term loan rates (an assertion backed by statistics that American economist, Winfield W. Riefler compiled for the United States between 1919 and 1928, which Keynes himself replicated for England). Along the same lines, Kaldor (1939) explains that the long-term interest rate is constructed as an average of the interest rates of various terms, and concludes that the short-term interest rate can influence the long-term rate if its movements upward or downward are sustained over time, which alters risk perceptions and valuations of short- and long-term instruments (e.g., stock and bond prices), which can influence the level and confidence in productive investment and therefore agents' willingness to maintain stock in their investment portfolios, or extend credit without raising the premium. For this reason, the short-term interest rate alters both the financial sector and the dynamics of the real sector and level of investment.

Therefore, according to the heterodox view, the limit on the interest rate depends on the rate of return on capital, which expresses the distributive nature of that variable, because financial returns are limited by the productivity of capital, and this correlation of forces is a determining factor in setting the interest rate. Keynes, in discussion with the 'classics' regarding the determination of interest rate levels, says that idle capital should not be recompensed with gains, proposing instead a 'euthanasia of the rentier' (Keynes, 1936, Chapter 24). In his words:

> Interest today rewards no genuine sacrifice, any more than does the rent of land. The owner of capital can obtain interest because capital is scarce, just as the owner of land can obtain rent because land is scarce. But whilst there may be intrinsic reasons for the scarcity of land, there are no intrinsic reasons for the scarcity of capital.

He adds:

> [W]e might aim in practice (there being nothing in this which is unattainable) at an increase in the volume of capital until it ceases to be scarce, so that the functionless investor will no longer receive a bonus; and at a scheme of direct taxation which allows the intelligence and determination and executive skill of the financier, the entrepreneur *et hoc genus omne*...to be harnessed to the service of the community on reasonable terms of reward. (Keynes, 1936, pp. 303–4)

This view of the distributive nature or appropriate level of the interest rate has been taken into account by a series of post-Keynesian rules to determine the interest rate. First, there is Pasinetti (1980) who proposes the 'fair rate rule', which should be equal to the growth rate of productivity. Smithin (2007) argues that the real interest rate should be positive but close to zero. And finally, the 'Kansas rule' proposes that the nominal interest rate should be equal to zero (Wray, 2007). The central tenet of these rules is that the rentier class should not access wealth or receive a minimal amount for its ownership of financial capital, which is considered idle capital, and would favour the accumulation of capital. This is congruent with Keynes's 'euthanasia'. In these approaches, in the absence of a rate that guarantees a Wicksellian or neo-Wicksellian equilibrium, the determination of the level and movement of the interest rate depends on the correlation of forces within the capitalist class and between social classes and its influence on economic policy decisions.

On this basis, it can be said that the Pasinetti rule is a tool for analysing the distribution of wealth between the social classes, on the assumption that the real fair interest rate is that which is equal to the growth rate of output per employee. In his analysis, Pasinetti assumes that labour is the only factor that creates value, and therefore the growth rate of wages should be the factor that is discounted from the interest rate in real terms (this assumes that the growth rate of the real wage is equal to the growth rate of productivity) so equality between the real interest rate and the growth rate of wages is called the 'natural rate of interest'. Pasinetti says:

> [A] higher than natural rate of interest distorts the distribution of income in favour of creditors (who would be able through time to 'command' more labour than they have contributed); and, conversely, a lower than natural rate of interest distorts the distribution of income in favour of the debtors (who would repay through time an amount which can 'command' less labour than they have been able to use). Only a natural rate of interest (provided, of course, that natural prices prevail) ensures that no distortion takes place in the distribution of income. (Pasinetti, 1980, p. 176)

The Pasinetti rule or index can be summed up as follows:

$$Pindx = \lambda - \rho \tag{7.1}$$

Where:

$Pindx$ = Pasinetti index;
λ = growth rate of productivity; and
$\rho = i - \pi$ real interest rate.

Accordingly, if $\lambda < \rho$, the distribution of the surplus favours the rentier class; and if, in contrast, $\lambda > \rho$, the distribution is to the detriment of the rentier class; and if $\lambda = \rho$, a 'fair' real interest rate is obtained.

In other words, a real interest rate that exceeds the rate of productivity gains transfers the surplus to the rentiers, while a real interest rate below that level would favour the productive sector and wage earners. Thus, according to this view, the real interest rate is determined based on the conflict over distribution of the economic surplus. In this context, the rate of interest does not merely represent the cost of liquidity or level of financial risk, and there is no sense in conceptualizing it as the 'equilibrium price' that guarantees maximum use of the factors, equating investment with savings and guaranteeing full employment.

3. THE RATE OF INTEREST AND ITS DISTRIBUTIVE NATURE: BRAZIL, COLOMBIA, CHILE AND MEXICO (1950–2018)

3.1 The Distributive Nature of the Interest Rate in the Period of Regulation and the ISI Model (1950–80)

The financial regulation and industrial promotion policies of the Roosevelt era and the post-war expansion of American capitalism are a frame of reference for the model of regulation of global capitalism, and specifically for most Latin American countries, during the processes of import substitution industrialization (ISI). At the international level, capital control prevailed, under the aegis of the dollar as the international reserve unit, pegged to the value of gold but more flexibly than in the classical period of the Gold Standard, in a context in which international capital movements were limited. During the post-war period, industrial capitalism was imposed in countries of the centre (developed) and periphery (developing economies), under the direction of a mixed economy, in which nation-states played a prominent role in economic development under the dominion of productive capital.

Developmentalist models were deployed in Latin America, based on the theoretic proposals of the Economic Commission for Latin America and Caribbean (ECLAC, or CEPAL in Spanish), which considered industrialization to be the path to economic development. In this context, the productive structure was transformed to overcome regional structural issues, including productive heterogeneity, unemployment, low wages, external dependence, and inflation (see ECLAC, 1949; Palma, 1989).

Specifically, the regulation phase in Latin America was marked by intense intervention by the state in the economic system, including protectionist policies (tariffs and quotas); development financing policies (for mobilizing financial resources toward strategic sectors); industrial policy (tax breaks for industrial promotion); accompanied by expansive fiscal policy (significant budget deficits) and lax monetary policy, in line with the goal of industrial expansion. Exchange rates were fixed, with capital control in some countries, and low and basically stable interest rates. Financial disequilibria were caused by foreign trade and external debt deficits, which government attempted (and failed) to neutralize with massive devaluations (e.g., Chile and Mexico, 1954). International financial market disequilibria emerged in the 1970s, produced by the expansion of the Euromarket and industrial recession in developed countries, which flooded the region with external credit at low but flexible rates (positive terms of trade) accompanied by capital flight to developed countries.

During the ISI period, productivity grow steadily, particularly between 1950 and the mid-1960s (Brazil and Chile), prolonged until late 1970 for the Mexican and Colombian economies (Figure 7.1).

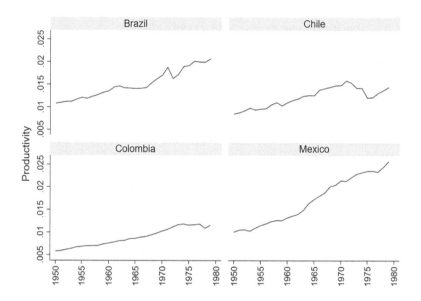

Sources: Own elaboration with data retrieved from ECLAC/CEPAL: https://estadisticas.cepal .org/cepalstat (accessed 10 October 2019); Instituto Brasileiro de Geografia e Estatística (IGBE): http://www.sidra.ibge.gov.br/bda (accessed 10 October 2019); Instituto Nacional de Estadísticas de Chile: http://www.ine.cl/ (accessed 5 October 2019); Departamento Administrativo Nacional de Estadística (DANE): http://www.dane.gov.co/ (accessed 8 October 2019); Banco de México (BANXICO): http://www.banxico.org.mx/ (accessed 20 September 2019); Instituto Nacional de Estadística, Geografía e Informática (INEGI): http://www.inegi.org.mx/ (accessed 20 September 2019).

Figure 7.1   Productivity, selected countries (1950–80) (production per worker, constant millions of dollars, 2010 = 100)

Evidently, the ISI process, based on the model of regulation, was successful in terms of the growth rate of productivity and output, but it was incapable of fully stimulating the development of endogenous productive forces because it excluded the sector that produces production goods, which remains highly dependent on external capital and intermediate goods. Fajnzylber (1983) coined the concept of 'truncated industrialization' to describe the ISI model, stating that despite the progress made in industrial development, particularly the production of final goods (first phase of the ISI), it was not strong enough to promote the capital and intermediate goods sector, which in the context of industrialization, keeps an economy dependent on external technology. This in turn prevented it from correcting external structural deficits and, as a result, the industrial process did not succeed in expanding the domestic market (Kaldor, 1959), excluding most of the population from the benefits of industrialization.

Additionally, the trade protections deployed during the ISI period bolstered monopolistic structures in fast-growing economic sectors, including foreign direct investment (FDI), which grew on the basis of obsolete fixed capital goods that had been discarded in industrialized countries in the wake of intense technological innovation. This caused the development of major capital (most notably FDI), supported by significant tax benefits and preferential exchange rates, with captive domestic markets, in the context of reduced international competition, and high prices in the domestic sphere.

The ISI, then, sparked great economic vigour with positive distributive effects for the working class, laying the basis for a middle class that, nevertheless, had limited opportunities, and the industrialization processes were violently disrupted by military coups in Brazil in 1964 and Chile in 1973, and iron-handed political controls in Mexico. This ultimately caused huge setbacks in industrialization (Rodrik, 2017) and in the inclusion of the middle and lower classes in economic development.

In terms of the real interest rate, between 1950 and 1980, the average for that variable was negative in Brazil, Chile and Colombia and 2.4 per cent for Mexico. The average rate of growth in real wages was positive but low in Brazil (0.15 per cent), Colombia (0.3 per cent) and Chile (1.82 per cent), while for Mexico it was 4.38 per cent, substantially higher than the mean interest rate. At the same time, average productivity growth rates were as follows: 2.2 per cent for Brazil; 1.8 per cent for Chile; 2.3 per cent for Colombia; and 3.2 per cent for Mexico.

The Pasinetti index does not indicate that productivity gains in the regulation period would benefit the rentier class in the Latin American countries analysed, mainly because in this period there was still a dominant oligarchical class linked to massive landholdings, with little development of a rentier class linked to financial capital. This can be explained by the low and relatively stable level of interest rates (Figure 7.2) and an almost non-existent capital market, with little activity in the stock and bond markets (Levy-Orlik, 2010; Mántey de Anguiano, 2010). In fact, again, in the countries analysed, on average, real interest rates were negative during the regulation period, and also below the growth rate of productivity (in terms of employed workers). Despite this, we can conclude that the income distribution generated by productivity growth favoured the productive sector, although we must bear in mind that financial markets in this period had very limited room for manoeuvre.

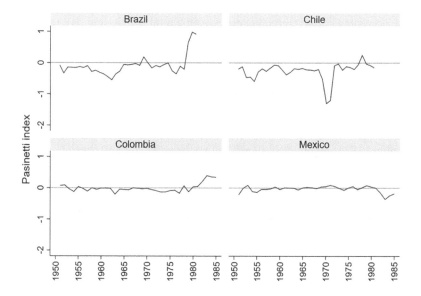

Sources: Own elaboration with data retrieved from ECLAC/CEPAL: https://estadisticas.cepal
.org/cepalstat (accessed 10 October 2019); Instituto Brasileiro de Geografia e Estatística (IGBE):
http://www.sidra.ibge.gov.br/bda (accessed 10 October 2019); Instituto Nacional de Estadísticas
de Chile: http://www.ine.cl/ (accessed 5 October 2019); Departamento Administrativo Nacional
de Estadística (DANE): http://www.dane.gov.co/ (accessed 8 October 2019); Banco de México
(BANXICO): http://www.banxico.org.mx/ (accessed 20 September 2019); Instituto Nacional de
Estadística, Geografía e Informática (INEGI): http://www.inegi.org.mx/ (accessed 20 September
2019).

Figure 7.2 Pasinetti index, selected countries (1950–86)

3.2 Interest Rates and Income Distribution in the Period of Financial Globalization (1990–2018)

The exhaustion of the regulation model was the result of a crisis in industrial countries, combined with the collapse of the Bretton Woods system,
the first expression of which was an unimaginable combination of inflation
and productive stagnation that, in Latin America, was manifest in growing
foreign-currency debt, high trade deficits and capital flight. The divorce
between money and merchandise (demonetization of gold) together with
industrial crisis in the developed world channelled excess financial capital
toward the region (which was experiencing a period of positive terms of trade).
This triggered massive indebtedness in the region, which it was unable to repay
when the United States retook control of its monetary policy and raised interest

rates to fortify its financial core. This unleashed the Latin American foreign debt crisis of the 1980s, often known as 'The Lost Decade'.

Nevertheless, the foreign debt crisis in Latin America was considered proof that the strategy of industrialization by import substitution led by the state, in a framework of economic regulation, had failed, and this became the pretext for questioning the intervention of the state in the economy and eliminating the public deficit, especially in the primary account. The most vocal critics came from neoliberal theory, whose core argument was that the industrialization policy promoted inefficiency and channelled financial resources toward low-yield companies, with reduced and fragmented financial markets (McKinnon, 1973; Shaw, 1973), and excessive trade protection that generated inefficiency (crony capitalism), the result of which was a combination of growing public deficit and external indebtedness. This current of theory coined the term 'financial repression' (McKinnon, 1973; Shaw, 1973) to refer to the idea that state intervention discouraged savings by investing in unproductive companies, and the savings of private financial agents were not channelled to the financial system for intermediation, but rather used to purchase real property as a store of value for wealth. The neoliberal school of thought assumed that reduced real interest rates repress savings and growing public intervention shuttles financial resources to inefficient productive sectors, so they therefore favoured raising interest rates in order to channel the financing to more profitable productive projects (McKinnon, 1973; Shaw, 1973) and open regional economies to foreign capital in the productive and financial sector in order to increase savings and productivity. On this basis, they proposed the productive, financial and commercial liberalization of Latin American economies, with policies that should have strengthened the financial and productive market prior to the financial and industrial opening – but this was not done.

One of the central features of globalization and financial complexity was the strengthening of the financial market, particularly non-bank financial institutions of various types, with a wide variety of financial instruments, dominated by complex financial innovations, guided by institutional investors, shadow banking, non-bank banks and others. This increased liquidity worldwide, but it was highly unstable because capital also became highly mobile in the context of financial options and hedges to reduce the risk of changes in valuation conditions (prices), which in turn made it easier to make money in the financial sphere through global speculation.

Among the results of this rising tide of liquidity and increasing prices of financial instruments was the reduction in US interest rates, most particularly in the 1980s after they reached record highs (averaging 16.38 per cent in 1980) and further inflated the financial markets because cheap credit could be acquired to purchase financial instruments at rising prices, boosting company valuations and making them eligible for further credit. This dimmed the appeal of investment in the productive sector.

The deregulation period of the 1980s also set the stage for a new international division of labour that, in Latin America, promoted the liberal export-led model based on raw materials or manufacturing with low added value, with the presence of multinational firms whose expansion was deployed through global production chains. The region's biggest disadvantage was that it entered the global market in the simplest sectors, those with low technological requirements, organizing its labour around the in-bond manufacturing or *maquila* work (Lazonick and O'Sullivan, 2000). The domination of foreign capital had its counterpart in economic privatization, with withdrawal of the state from productive activities, and the channelling of financing to production, which empowered market mechanics in the distribution of wealth, on the assumption that arbitrage worked, and based on balanced public finances in the primary account. This set of policies gave way to a process of de-industrialization before achieving full development of the productive forces (Rodrik, 2017).

In this context, financial deregulation moved toward flexible exchange-rate policies, administered by the central bank's interest rate and accumulation of reserves, in order to control inflation. Thus, monetary policy was governed by neo-Wicksellian monetary rules, the intermediate purpose of which was to stabilize the interest rate by managing exchange rates.

And in fact, around the world and in Latin America, inflation was controlled. But this was not due to interest rate management based on potential product and a target inflation rate, which would guarantee equality between an interest rate in real terms and a natural rate. The central variable for controlling inflation was wages, and keeping them low through impoverishment and precarization of the workforce. So containing wages, together with combating inflation, became a defensive policy for protecting capital gains. Another factor holding down inflation was China's entry into international trade, which made manufactured goods cheaper (Skidelsky, 2018).

At the Latin American level, in the countries analysed, specifically Brazil, Colombia and Mexico, productivity saw very limited growth, and the Mexican economy even contracted. The notable exception was Chile, which saw a growing trend (Figure 7.3). In this context, the conformation of huge corporations (either foreign – FDI – or local – trans-Latin) did nothing to activate the productive dynamics of the region. Mexico's case is a good illustration: there was a massive inflow of FDI and major foreign enterprises took hold in the fastest-growing segments of manufacturing (automotive, electronics and transport), but there was no increase in productivity. This may be because of the *maquiladora* nature of labour organization. In other countries, FDI was concentrated in the service sector and control of strategic natural resources, particularly mining.

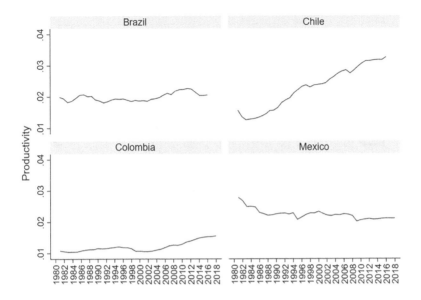

Sources: Own elaboration with data retrieved from ECLAC/CEPAL: https://estadisticas.cepal
.org/cepalstat (accessed 10 October 2019); Instituto Brasileiro de Geografia e Estatística (IGBE):
http://www.sidra.ibge.gov.br/bda (accessed 10 October 2019); Instituto Nacional de Estadísticas
de Chile: http://www.ine.cl/ (accessed 5 October 2019); Departamento Administrativo Nacional
de Estadística (DANE): http://www.dane.gov.co/ (accessed 8 October 2019); Banco de México
(BANXICO): http://www.banxico.org.mx/ (accessed 20 September 2019); Instituto Nacional de
Estadística, Geografía e Informática (INEGI): http://www.inegi.org.mx/ (accessed 20 September
2019).

Figure 7.3   *Productivity, selected countries (1980–2018) (production per
worker, constant millions of dollars, 2010 = 100)*

We might add that during the period of globalization, the financial sphere, and
particularly interest rates, became the new mechanism for surplus extraction,
which can be seen in the spread between interest rates in these countries and
the interest rate of the US central bank (the Federal Reserve) (Figure 7.4), and
domestic monetary policies aligned to increase the return on financial capital
by maintaining an accumulation of reserve that overvalued the local currency
(Bresser Pereira, 2009; Huerta, 2017). Based on this logic, it may be deduced
that in Latin America, surplus distribution did not favour wage-earners'
income; it led to the formation of a rentier class linked to the non-financial
and financial sector, which has had access to increasing surplus through the
financial channel.

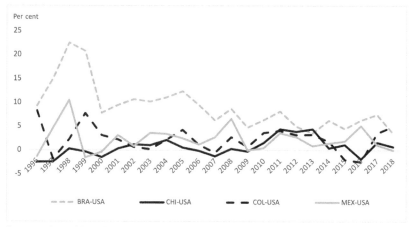

Source: Own elaboration, with data retrieved from Federal Reserve Economic Data and
ECLAC/CEPAL.

Figure 7.4   *Spread between selected countries' real interest rate and the
Federal Reserve's real interest rate (1996–2018)*

Overall, between 1995 and 2018, the average growth rate of real wages was
low: 0.7 per cent in Brazil, 2.1 per cent in Chile, 1.1 per cent in Colombia and
0.6 per cent in Mexico; while the average real interest rate was 9.5 per cent
in Brazil, 0.8 per cent in Chile, 2.8 per cent in Colombia and 2.9 per cent in
Mexico. During the same period, the average growth of productivity was 0.29
per cent for Brazil, 1.7 per cent for Chile, 1.2 per cent for Colombia and –0.08
per cent for Mexico.

On this basis, we can see that the interest rate was positive in real terms for
all four countries in the sample, higher than the growth rate of real wages or of
productivity. In fact, productivity growth was generally lower than during the
regulation period, even in Chile's case. Mexico's case is particularly interesting – despite being the fastest-growing recipient of FDI in the manufacturing
industry, productivity growth plummeted.

Along the same line of analysis, the Pasinetti index shows evidence that the
distribution of income favoured the rentier class in all four countries during
the period analysed, especially starting in the second half of the 1990s (Figure
7.5). This would validate the hypothesis that income distribution favoured the
rentier class during the period of financial globalization.

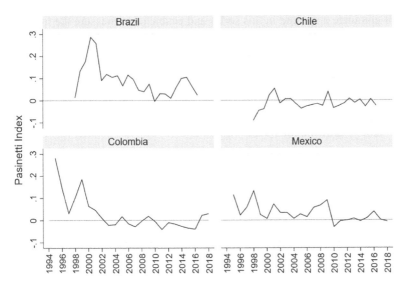

Sources: Own elaboration with data retrieved from ECLAC/CEPAL: https://estadisticas.cepal
.org/cepalstat (accessed 10 October 2019); Instituto Brasileiro de Geografia e Estatística (IGBE):
http://www.sidra.ibge.gov.br/bda (accessed 10 October 2019); Instituto Nacional de Estadísticas
de Chile: http://www.ine.cl/ (accessed 5 October 2019); Departamento Administrativo Nacional
de Estadística (DANE): http://www.dane.gov.co/ (accessed 8 October 2019); Banco de México
(BANXICO): http://www.banxico.org.mx/ (accessed 20 September 2019); Instituto Nacional de
Estadística, Geografía e Informática (INEGI): http://www.inegi.org.mx/ (accessed 20 September
2019).

Figure 7.5   Pasinetti index, selected countries (1994–2018)

4.   THE DISTRIBUTIVE NATURE OF INTEREST RATES: AN ECONOMETRIC ANALYSIS FOR BRAZIL, CHILE, COLOMBIA AND MEXICO (1950–2018)

The Pasinetti index offers a methodology for discussing the distribution of the benefits of productivity among the main social classes and segments, which can be reinforced by an analysis of empirical causality. This section uses an econometric model that supports the theoretical conclusions.

The proposed model involves a panel data methodology. Since the time horizon (T) is greater than the number of countries (N), an estimation will be made using a generalized method to control problems of serial-correlation and heteroskedasticity. Additionally, to avoid the problem of spurious regression, the variables are presented as logarithmic differences, which can be interpreted as semi-elasticities. Using the logarithmic difference of the real interest rate will eliminate any trend in this series and enable us to measure the impact of the change in that rate with respect to the dependent variable.

The model is specified by the following equation:

$$\Delta wr_{it} = \widehat{\alpha_0}\Delta\lambda_{it} + \widehat{\alpha_1}\rho_{it} + \varepsilon_{it}, \tag{7.2}$$

where:

Δwr_{it} = growth rate in real wages;

$\Delta\lambda_{it}$ = growth rate of productivity;

$\Delta\rho_{it}$ = growth rate of the real interest rate;

$\widehat{\alpha_0}$, $\widehat{\alpha_1}$ = estimated parameters; and

ε_{it} = stochastic variable.

Equation 7.2 expresses the growth rate of wages as a function of the growth rate of productivity and the growth rate of the real interest rate. The productivity coefficient is expected to be positive and the coefficient of the growth rate of real interest is expected to be negative; in other words, the increase in the real interest rate redistributes income from wage earners to rentiers. This test is applied separately for the two periods studied (1950–80 and 1980–2018). The model worked best using the pooled estimation, which nevertheless showed problems of self-correlation and heteroskedasticity, so we then used the panel correlated standard errors (PCSE) methodology to avoid errors in the hypothesis of regression coefficients, and added the robust pooled estimation to the heteroskedasticity. The results of the econometric estimations are summarized in Table 7.1.

Table 7.1 allows us to make the following observations. The conclusion of the first estimation, in all three econometric methodologies, is that the coefficient of the rate of change in the real interest rate is negative, but not significant (confidence level 99 per cent). That is, for the period 1950–80, changes in interest rates had no effect on the behaviour of real wages. The growth rate of productivity did have a positive impact on the growth rate of wages: specifically, for every 1 per cent increase in productivity, the growth rate of real wages increased by 0.53 per cent.

For the period 1980–2018, using all three methodologies, the growth of the real interest rate had a negative impact on the growth rate of wages, which can be seen in the significant negative coefficients (with a confidence level of 95 per cent), including with higher coefficients compared to the regulation period. At the same time, the effect of the growth rate of productivity on wages, expressed by the coefficient of the growth rate of productivity, was significant and positive, as expected, albeit lower than in the regulation period.

Table 7.1   *Econometric estimations*

		Equation 7.2, First Estimation (1950–80)					
Dependent	Model 1: Pool			Model 2: Pool robust		Model 2: PCSE	
Variable		$\alpha0$	$\alpha1$	$\alpha0$	$\alpha1$	$\alpha0$	$\alpha1$
ΔWr	Coef.	0.579129	−0.0112975	0.579129	−0.0112975	0.5761852	−0.0050375
	P-value	0.041	0.83	0.018	0.879	0.04	0.924
		Equation 7.2, Second Estimation (1980–2018)					
Dependent	Model 1: Pool			Model 2: Pool Robust		Model 2: PCSE	
Variable		$\alpha0$	$\alpha1$	$\alpha0$	$\alpha1$	$\alpha0$	$\alpha1$
ΔWr	Coef.	0.5357123	−0.030123	0.5357123	−0.030123	0.4964539	−0.0344094
	P-value	0.00	0.00	0.004	0.016	0.00	0.00

Source: Own elaboration (see Appendix A).

Based on the foregoing analysis, we may infer that there is evidence of the effect that the real interest rate has on income distribution, based on the inverse relation between the change in the real interest rate and the growth in real wages. There is also evidence that during the period of financial liberalization and globalization the influence of productivity increases on wage dynamics diminished, primarily due to the stagnation of productivity observed in the period analysed. This complements the analysis performed by applying the Pasinetti index, which confirms that during the period of liberalization and financial globalization, the interest rate distributed surplus toward the financial sector, at the cost of a progressive erosion of wages.

5.   CONCLUSIONS

Conventional marginalist neoclassical theory conceives the rate of interest as the payment for postponing present consumption to the future, and in this sense the interest rate is a real variable that guarantees market equilibrium and clearing, guaranteeing the allocation of savings to its most efficient uses. So the rate of interest may be viewed as a variable that permits the distribution of global productivity gains among the various savers, meaning from companies to families, through the intermediation of bank and non-bank institutions in the financial system. From this perspective, central banks should focus their activities on keeping inflation low, because this would achieve a neutral monetary policy, avoiding short-term monetary disequilibria, because it is assumed that monetary policy does not influence the real sector. That is why it is crucial to establish Wicksellian-type rules to this end.

From the heterodox viewpoint, on the other hand, interest rates are a non-neutral variable, because in a monetary economy, debt operates as money, and as a result, the rate of interest influences the demand for credit and this brings about an expansion of demand, investment, employment and income, and productive capacity becomes a dynamic variable. But interest rates also possess a distributive nature that is capable of modifying the yield curve of financial assets at different terms, and this in turn influences systemic liquidity and the level of profit in the financial markets. Discussions of the distributive nature of interest rates analyse its level over the long term, which cannot exceed the return on capital. The Kansas and Smithin rules are prominent in this discussion, setting interest rates for the purpose of reducing the surplus of the rentier class, consistent with the Keynesian 'euthanasia of the rentier'. The Pasinetti index, for its part, provides a methodology for analysing the dynamics of surplus appropriation by the rentier class, defined on the basis of a 'fair rate' that is achieved when it is equal to the growth of labour productivity.

From this analysis of the successive periods of regulation and deregulation/ financial globalization, we can conclude that there is evidence that during the former period, the real interest rate did not affect the wage dynamic, and despite a high rate of growth in wages most of the gains were appropriated by the owners of productive capital, mainly because in that period the financial markets had developed little depth and rentiers were landowners linked to control of large tracts of land; in the second period, there was a radical shift in economic policy, but specifically monetary policy, the basic purpose of which was to combat inflation by establishing neo-Wicksellian rules, under which the exchange rate could be administered to favour financial returns, evident in the movement of the Pasinetti index and other indicators presented for this period.

Finally, using econometric methodology, statistical evidence is confirmed of the inverse causality between changes in the real interest rate and wage dynamics, meaning not only that higher income flowed toward the rentier class during the period of deregulation and financial globalization, but that this flow was also to the detriment of income for the wage-earning class.

REFERENCES

Bresser Pereira, L.C. (2009), 'La tendencia a la sobrevaluacion del tipo de cambio', *Economía-UNAM*, **6** (18), 75–88.
ECLAC (1949), 'Estudio Económico de América Latina' (Economic studies of Latin America, United Nations), reproduced *Cincuenta Años de Pensamiento en la CEPAL, Textos Seleccionados* (*Fifty Years of Economic Thought of ECLAC, Selected Essays*), R. Bielschowsky (ed.), CEPAL, Fondo de Cultura Económica 1998, Volume I, 131–72.
Fajnzylber, F. (1983), *La industrialización trunca de América Latina*, Mexico: Nueva Imagen.

Fama, E. (1991), 'Efficient capital markets: II', *The Journal of Finance*, **46** (5), 1575–617.

Hawtrey, R. (1930), *Currency and Credit*, London: Longmans, Green & Co.

Hayek, F.A. (1929), *Monetary Theory and the Trade Cycle*, New York: Sentry Press.

Hilferding, R. ([1910] 1981), *Finance Capital*, ed. T. Bottomore, trans. M. Watnick and S. Gordon, London: Routledge & Kegan Paul.

Huerta, A. (2017), *El ocaso de la globalización*, Mexico: Facultad de Economía UNAM.

Kaldor, N. (1939), 'Speculation and economic stability', *The Review of Economic Studies*, **7** (1), 1–27.

Kaldor, N. (1959), 'Problemas económicos de Chile', *Trimestre Económico*, **102** (2), 170–221.

Kaldor, N. (1985), 'How monetarism failed', *Challenge*, **28** (2), 4–13.

Kalecki, M. (1954). *Theory of Economic Dynamics*, London: George Allen & Unwin Ltd.

Keynes, J.M. (1930), *A Treatise on Money*, Cambridge, UK: Cambridge University Press.

Keynes, J.M. (1936), *The General Theory of Employment, Interest and Money*, New York: Harcourt, Brace & Co.

Lazonick, W. and O'Sullivan, M. (2000), 'Maximizing shareholder value: a new ideology for corporate governance', *Economy and Society*, **29** (1), 13–35.

Levy-Orlik, N. (2010), 'Instituciones financieras para el desarrollo económico: comparación del periodo de "sustitución de importaciones" y el "secundario exportador"', in N. Levy-Orlik and G. Mántey de Anguiano (eds), *Cincuenta Años de Políticas Financieras para el Desarrollo en México*, Mexico: Plaza y Valdéz, pp. 149–78.

Mántey de Anguiano, G. (2010), 'Políticas financieras para el desarrollo en México', in N. Levy-Orlik and G. Mántey de Anguiano (eds), *Cincuenta Años de Políticas Financieras para el Desarrollo en México*, Mexico: Plaza y Valdéz, pp. 15–44.

McKinnon, R. (1973), *Money and Capital in Economic Development*, Washington, DC: The Brookings Institution.

Minsky, H.P. (1975), *John Maynard Keynes*, London: Palgrave Macmillan.

Minsky, H.P. (2004), *Induced Investment and Business Cycles*, Cheltenham, UK and Northampton, MA, USA: Edward Elgar Publishing.

Palma, G. (1989), 'Dependencia y desarrollo una visión crítica', in D. Seers (ed.), *Teoría de la dependencia una revaluación crítica*, Mexico: FCE, pp. 21–89.

Pasinetti, L.L. (1980), 'The rate of interest and the distribution of income in a pure labor economy', *Journal of Post Keynesian Economics*, **3** (2), 170–82.

Rochon, L.-P. (1999), *Credit, Money and Production: An Alternative Post-Keynesian Approach*, Cheltenham, UK and Northampton, MA, USA: Edward Elgar Publishing.

Rodrik, D. (2017), 'Premature deindustrialization', *Journal of Economic Growth*, **21** (1), 1–33.

Shaw, E.S. (1973), *Financial Deepening in Economic Development*, New York: Oxford University Press.

Skidelsky, R. (2018), *Money and Government*, New Haven, CT: Yale University Press.

Smithin, J. (2007), 'A real interest rate rule for monetary policy?', *Journal of Post Keynesian Economics*, **30** (1), 101–18.

Toporowski, J. (1995), *The Economics of Financial Markets and the 1987 Crash*, Aldershot, UK and Brookfield, VT, USA: Edward Elgar Publishing.

Wicksell, K. (1954), *Value, Capital and Rent*, London: George Allen & Unwin Ltd.

Woodford, M. (2003), *Interest and Prices: Foundations of a Theory of Monetary Policy*, Princeton, NJ: Princeton University Press.

Wray, R. (2007), 'A Post Keynesian view of central bank independence, policy targets, and the rules versus discretion debate', *Journal of Post Keynesian Economics*, **30** (1), 119–41.

APPENDIX A　　ECONOMETRIC ESTIMATIONS

Estimations 1950–80

reg tcw tcprod tctir if t<=1980, noconstant

Source	SS	df	MS		Number of obs	=	116
					F(2, 114)	=	2.29
Model	0.0890061	2	0.04450305		Prob > F	=	0.1059
Residual	2.21579928	114	0.01943684		R-squared	=	0.0386
					Adj R-squared	=	0.0218
Total	2.30480538	116	0.01986901		Root MSE	=	0.13942

tcw	Coef.	Std. Err.	t	P>t	[95% Conf. Interval]	
tcprod	0.579129	0.2801664	2.07	0.041	0.0241216	1.134136
tctir	-0.0112975	0.0525556	-0.21	0.83	-0.1154097	0.0928147

reg tcw tcprod tctir if t<=1980, noconstant vce(r)

Linear regression					Number of obs	=	116
					F(2, 114)	=	2.91
					Prob > F	=	0.0585
					R-squared	=	0.0386
					Root MSE	=	0.13942

tcw	Coef.	Robust Std. Err.	t	P>t	[95% Conf. Interval]	
tcprod	0.579129	0.2407532	2.41	0.018	0.1021988	1.056059
tctir	-0.0112975	0.0743532	-0.15	0.879	-0.1585907	0.1359956

. xtpcse tcw tcprod tctir if t<=1980, noconstant correlation(ar1) rhotype(dw)

Prais-Winsten regression, correlated panels corrected standard errors (PCSEs)

Group variable: ident				Number of obs	=	116
Time variable: t				Number of groups	=	4
Panels: correlated (balanced)				Obs per group:		
Autocorrelation: common AR(1)				min	=	29
				avg	=	29
				max	=	29
Estimated covariances	10			R-squared	=	0.0362
Estimated autocorrelations	1			Wald chi2(2)	=	4.34
Estimated coefficients	2			Prob > chi2	=	0.1139

tcw	Coef.	Std. Err.	z	P>z	[95% Conf. Interval]	
tcprod	0.5761852	0.2806358	2.05	0.04	0.0261491	1.126221
tctir	-0.0050375	0.0525866	0.1	0.924	-0.1081054	0.0980304
rho	0.0550239					

Estimations 1980–2018

reg tcw tcprod tctir if t>=1980, noconstant

Source	SS	df	MS		Number of obs =	156
					F(2, 154) =	21.16
Model	0.11260743	2	0.05630371		Prob > F =	0
Residual	0.40981131	154	0.00266111		R-squared =	0.2156
					Adj R-squared =	0.2054
Total	0.52241873	156	0.00334884		Root MSE =	0.05159
tcw	Coef.	Std. Err.	t	P>t	[95% Conf. Interval]	
tcprod	0.5357123	0.1196999	4.48	0	0.2992465	0.772178
tctir	-0.030123	0.0067839	-4.44	0	-0.0435244	-0.0167216

reg tcw tcprod tctir if t>=1980, noconstant vce(r)

Linear regression					Number of obs =	156
					F(2, 154) =	6.42
					Prob > F =	0.0021
					R-squared =	0.2156
					Root MSE =	0.05159
		Robust				
tcw	Coef.	Std. Err.	t	P>t	[95% Conf. Interval]	
tcprod	0.5357123	0.1822643	2.94	0.004	0.1756513	0.8957732
tctir	-0.030123	0.0123288	-2.44	0.016	-0.0544784	-0.0057677

xtpcse tcw tcprod tctir if >=1980, noconstant correlation(ar1) rhotype(dw)

Prais-Winsten regression, correlated panels corrected standard errors (PCSEs)

Group variable: ident					Number of obs	=	156
Time variable: t					Number of groups	=	4
Panels: correlated (balanced)					Obs per group:		
Autocorrelation: common AR(1)					min	=	39
					avg	=	39
					max	=	39
Estimated covariances	10				R-squared	=	0.2403
Estimated autocorrelations	1				Wald chi2(2)	=	36.79
Estimated coefficients	2				Prob > chi2	=	0
tcw	Coef.	Std. Err.	z	P>z	[95% Conf. Interval]		
tcprod	0.4964539	0.1254754	3.96	0	0.2505266	0.7423811	
tctir	-0.0344094	0.0079848	-4.31	0	-0.0500594	-0.0187595	
rho	0.3069783						

APPENDIX B   TESTS SELECTION MODEL

xtreg tcw tcprod tctir if t<1980

Random-effects GLS regression				Number of obs		=	112
Group variable: ident				Number of groups		=	4
R-sq:				Obs per group:			
within = 0.0314				min		=	28
between = 0.3356				avg		=	28
overall = 0.0346				max		=	28
				Wald chi2(2)		=	3.66
corr(u_i, X) = 0 (assumed)				Prob > chi2		=	0.1605

tcw	Coef.	Std. Err.	z	P>|z|	[95% Conf. Interval]	
tcprod	0.6098501	0.348246	1.75	0.08	-0.0726996	1.2924
tctir	-0.0106978	0.0567949	-0.19	0.851	-0.1220138	0.1006182
_cons	-0.0016904	0.0247115	-0.07	0.945	-0.050124	0.0467433
sigma_u	0.03715045					
sigma_e	0.14109872					
rho	0.0648295 (fraction of variance due to u_i)					

xttest0
Breusch and Pagan Lagrangian multiplier test for random effects
tcw[ident,t] = Xb + u[ident] + e[ident,t]

Estimated results:

	Var	sd=sqrt(Var)
tcw	0.0204499	0.1430033
e	0.0199088	0.1410987
u	0.0013802	0.0371504

Test: Var(u) = 0
                chibar2(01)   =   0.00
            Prob > chibar2 =   0.4844

```
xtreg tcw tcprod tctir if t>1980
```

Random-effects GLS regression				Number of obs		=	152
Group variable: ident				Number of groups		=	4
R-sq:				Obs per group:			
within = 0.2099				min		=	38
between = 0.7292				avg		=	38
overall = 0.2249				max		=	38
				Wald chi2(2)		=	41.56
corr(u_i, X) = 0 (assumed)				Prob > chi2		=	0

tcw	Coef.	Std. Err.	z	P>|z|	[95% Conf. Interval]	
tcprod	0.5523713	0.1243096	4.44	0	0.308729	0.7960136
tctir	-0.0297935	0.0066747	-4.46	0	-0.0428756	-0.0167114
_cons	0.002757	0.0056397	0.49	0.625	-0.0082966	0.0138105
sigma_u	0.00762479					
sigma_e	0.05083512					
rho	0.0220022 (fraction of variance due to u_i)					

```
xttest0
```
Breusch and Pagan Lagrangian multiplier test for random effects
$tcw[ident,t] = Xb + u[ident] + e[ident,t]$

Estimated results:

	Var	sd=sqrt(Var)
tcw	0.0032922	0.0573773
e	0.0025842	0.0508351
u	0.0000581	0.0076248

Test: Var(u) = 0

　　　　　　　chibar2(01).   =   0.11
　　　　　　Prob > chibar2 = 0.3685

xtreg tcw tcprod tctir if t<1980, fe

Fixed-effects (within) regression			Number of obs	=	112
Group variable: ident			Number of groups	=	4

R-sq:			Obs per group:		
within = 0.0314			min	=	28
between = 0.3356			avg	=	28
overall = 0.0346			max	=	28

				F(2,106)	=	1.72
corr(u_i, X) = 0.0592				Prob > F	=	0.1846

tcw	Coef.	Std. Err.	t	P>|t|	[95% Conf. Interval]	
tcprod	0.5913759	0.352117	1.68	0.096	-0.10673	1.289482
tctir	-0.0125269	0.0573208	-0.22	0.827	-0.12617	0.1011172
_cons	-0.001147	0.0165998	-0.07	0.945	-0.03406	0.0317637

sigma_u	0.03113049	
sigma_e	0.14109872	
rho	0.04641774	(fraction of variance due to u_i)

F test that all u_i=0: F(3, 106) = 1.35   Prob > F = 0.2608

xtreg tcw tcprod tctir if t>1980, fe

Fixed-effects (within) regression			Number of obs	=	152
Group variable: ident			Number of groups	=	4

R-sq:			Obs per group:		
within = 0.2100			min	=	38
between = 0.7298			avg	=	38
overall = 0.2247			max	=	38

				F(2,146)	=	19.41
corr(u_i, X) = 0.1204				Prob > F	=	0

tcw	Coef.	Std. Err.	t	P>|t|	[95% Conf. Interval]	
tcprod	0.530832	0.1281225	4.14	0	0.2776177	0.7840463
tctir	-0.0298401	0.0067053	-4.45	0	-0.0430921	-0.0165882
_cons	0.0028757	0.0041926	0.69	0.494	-0.0054103	0.0111618

sigma_u	0.00850568	
sigma_e	0.05083512	
rho	0.02723325	(fraction of variance due to u_i)

F test that all u_i=0: F(3, 146) = 1.03   Prob > F = 0.3807

8. Why central bank policy is not income-distribution 'neutral': history, theory and practice

Mario Seccareccia and Guillermo Matamoros Romero

1. INTRODUCTION

On April 29, 2019, one of the authors of this chapter, together with a group of a half-dozen well-known Canadian economists, including a member of the Senate of Canada, met with the former Deputy Governor of the Bank of Canada, Carolyn Wilkins, as well as some of her advisors, to convey our discomfort and explain to her our specific concerns with the existing central bank's monetary policy objective.[1] This arose in the context of public discussions over the Canadian federal government's five-year mandate renewal taking place just prior to the COVID-19 crisis. Indeed, this was part of our lobbying effort to broaden the mandate of the Bank of Canada that we deemed too narrow, with the Bank's focus on a single macroeconomic variable – the inflation rate.

Over the last three decades, a large number of central banks – including the Bank of Canada (since 1991) and, among approximately three-dozen others, the Banco de México (since 2001), the Bank of Japan (since 2013) and the European Central Bank (in 2021) (see Tooze, 2021) – joined the inflation-targeting (IT) bandwagon with an official focus on stabilizing the inflation rate around some numerical value, usually a 2 percent target. While this focus on combating inflation above all other possible goals actually started in the late 1970s with most central banks, the majority of the countries that moved *officially* toward IT policy had done so during the two decades from 1990 until just before the global financial crisis (GFC), with one of the important exceptions being the US Fed that only adopted officially an *explicit* 2 percent inflation target in January 2012 under the then Chair Ben Bernanke, even though the Fed had been engaged in conducting monetary policy within a somewhat *implicit* IT policy framework much before 2012 (see Shapiro and

Wilson, 2019, p. 1). In fact, there was a further significant redefining of its inflation objective and how to achieve it since August 2020. However, unlike Canada and other IT central banks that have as a sole focus the goal of fighting inflation in their official five-year mandates, this was not quite the case at the US Fed historically, which has shown greater policy pragmatism than the Bank of Canada and less tolerance to accepting high levels of unemployment over the last four decades. To confirm this difference, one simple indication is to observe the historical long-term evolution of the unemployment rates between Canada and the US.

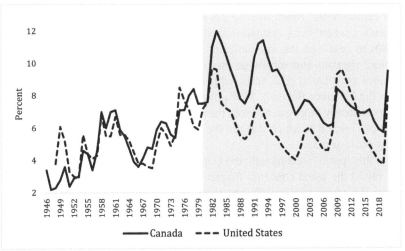

Sources: Statistics Canada, *Historical Statistics of Canada*, Series D223–235: https://www150 .statcan.gc.ca/n1/pub/11-516-x/sectiond/D223_235-eng.csv; CANSIM Series V2461224 and V2062815; Federal Reserve Bank of St. Louis, FRED Database: https://fred.stlouisfed.org/series/ UNRATE. Accessed July 11, 2021.

Figure 8.1   *Long-term evolution of the official unemployment rates in Canada (1946–2020) and the United States (1948–2020), annual averages*

From Figure 8.1, we can easily infer that, with the exception of the very early years of demobilization of their respective armed forces after World War II, where Canada faced somewhat lower rates of unemployment than the US (in the late 1940s),[2] during the remaining early postwar years of the 1950s and all the way to the 1970s, both series closely aligned until the post-1970s era. As can be seen, the series bifurcated since the early 1980s with the Canadian unemployment rate being systematically above the US rate, with the exception of the years during and immediately following the GFC and perhaps during the recent COVID-19 crisis when both unemployment series responded in a similar way to the shock in 2020.

Indeed, unlike the situation in Canada, in the US there was one clear vestige of the New Deal policy views that was able to survive the monetarist and New Classical onslaught of the 1980s, albeit highly weakened by it, and this was the commitment to low unemployment rates that managed to live on until today. We believe that this is because, despite its changing policy orientation, the US Fed never officially rejected the politically hard-fought 1978 legislated 'dual mandate' of full employment *and* reasonable price stability to which Galbraith (2020, p. 288) refers as 'the most Keynesian and most successful charter of any central bank'. Much like the US Fed under the direction of Paul Volcker, Canada's central bank first swallowed some hybrid monetarism until the early 1980s to deal with the international oil price shocks. Canada then opted for a more rigorous and somewhat less pragmatic IT policy framework that, to achieve an inflation goal, accepted persistently higher rates of unemployment than the US since the early 1990s, thereby offering a possible explanation of the persistently large gap between the two countries, as displayed in the shaded area of Figure 8.1, which was not the case during the first few decades of the early postwar era.

At this special meeting with the Deputy Governor of Canada's central bank, we raised the usual concerns frequently expressed by heterodox economists about the narrowness and limited scope of IT policy and lobbied to consider adopting either a dual mandate, with an official full-employment objective, or perhaps, even more notably, a multi-goal mandate that could also include other official objectives, such as a desirable income-distribution outcome. As was pointed out, the reason we were opposed to IT policy was because of its long-term effects on the rates of unemployment and growth that ensued from prioritizing the control of the inflation rate over all other possible goals, but also because of the undesirable consequences on both the functional and personal distributions of income resulting from a monetary policy framework that necessarily benefits certain income groups at the expense of others.

In her response, the Deputy Governor completely brushed aside our income-distribution concern and asserted that monetary policy conducted at the Bank of Canada was, to use her expression, 'neutral' with respect to income distribution. Because of the nature of the criticism and the obvious political consequences, this official denial of central bank income-distribution bias was hardly surprising to us, despite the fact that there is a long historical tradition going back at least to Keynes even before the *General Theory* that pointed to the *non-neutrality* of monetary policy effects on income distribution. This is especially so if one chooses to divide income flows by regrouping and linking them to certain more traditional socio-economic classes of economic agents, such as wage earners, profit and rentier income earners, based on a conflicting-claims class analysis. As we know, this class analysis is quite foreign to the individualistic methodology of the representative agent, which remains so ubiquitous in mainstream theory.

The object of this chapter is, in some way, a response to the position taken by central banks, such as the Bank of Canada, about the so-called 'neutrality' of monetary policy and to show that there is a very long history within macroeconomics of recognizing the non-neutrality of monetary policy on income distribution going back at least to Keynes from almost a century ago, if not even earlier, particularly in regard to the broad concerns raised by institutionalist economists such as Thorstein Veblen before Keynes (see Seccareccia, 2017). Moreover, as we shall see, since the GFC, there have appeared some significant research findings and interesting discussions within the mainstream that suggest that monetary policy can lead to unacceptable consequences on the distribution of both income and wealth. Let us first review this broad literature and then we shall consider an alternative perspective on the effect of monetary policy to show that monetary/interest rate policy is absolutely *not* neutral with respect to income distribution.

2.   A HISTORICAL DIGRESSION ON KEYNES'S *TRACT*

Notwithstanding the little attention that has been paid by central bankers, as mentioned above, the link between monetary policy and income distribution is hardly new. Undeniably, it goes back nearly a century to John Maynard Keynes in the early 1920s, not only after the hyperinflationary episodes during and right after World War I – involving Germany, Austria, Poland and Russia – but also, and perhaps more importantly, the deflationary incidents experienced by Great Britain, Czechoslovakia and the United States, due to the return to currency convertibility (Dimand, 2019). In those convulsive years just prior to the return to the prewar Gold Standard in 1926, Keynes came to recognize that discretionary monetary policy can have an impact through both the usual interest cost mechanism and the income/wealth distribution mechanism, which he explored in his famous *A Tract on Monetary Reform* in 1923 (hereafter, the *Tract*) within the established framework of Marshallian quantity theory orthodoxy.

In the *Tract*, particularly in the first chapter ('The consequences to society of changes in the value of money'), Keynes ([1923] 2013) developed a three-class model exploring the implications of monetary policy on the production and distribution of wealth in modern economies, characterized by the prevalence of interest-bearing (usually fixed) contracts, as exemplified by bonds, mortgages, among others. The model assumes three classes that differ both in their class interests and productive functions: the lending or rentier class, the borrowing or industrial class, and the wage-earning or working class. Lenders are supposed to make a living from buying interest-bearing assets and receiving interest payments on a yearly basis, while borrowers are expected to pay those interest payments out of the profits they made after selling commodities and covering costs – including the wage bill, which is the income of workers.

Being both similar and yet somewhat different from the Marxian two-class analysis, in Keynes's model, diverging interests arise, at a first stage, between the industrialist (who is a borrower) and the worker (who is not, since consumer credit was non-existent as it is today in our modern financialized society) over the distribution of revenue, split into profits and wages. At a second stage, class interests also clash between the borrower (or industrialist) and the lender (or rentier), this time over the distribution of profits, divided into interest payments and net profits, whereby the rate of interest turns out to be the key variable in dispute.

Furthermore, Keynes put forth the distributive role played by the money rate of interest, but, most importantly, by the rate of interest that is discounted by the rate of change in the level of prices – that is, the Fisher real rate of interest. For him, it was clear that lenders (borrowers) reap a corresponding extra benefit if the real rate of interest significantly increases (decreases). In other words, the income and wealth of the borrower is inversely related to that of the lender, and this is reflected in the changes in the real rate of interest.

At the very beginning of the *Tract*, when Keynes ([1923] 2013, p. 1) claims that 'a change in the value of money, that is to say in the level of prices, is important to society only in so far as its incidence is unequal', he then proceeds to explain in detail why this unequal incidence would depend on the extent to which the stability of the income flows and wealth-stocks accruing to these three classes is more or less preserved in the long run, whereby a stable real rate of interest turns out to be a necessary condition.

The *Tract* shows a special concern with periods of significant inflation and deflation primarily insofar as these events are imperfectly followed by changes in the money rate of interest. What the British economist exposed was that periods of high inflation are associated with negative real rates of interest, while times of deflation are associated with positive and high real rates of interest. As such, high inflation periods meant borrowers reaping extraordinary benefits due to a too low real rate of interest. Conversely, deflation periods meant lenders extracting abnormal gains due to a too high real rate of interest. In a way, the extraordinary benefits are owed solely to significant changes in real rates of interest, enriching one class over the others with no moral justification since the members of this class are viewed by the rest of society as either profiteers or rentiers who hardly contribute to production. Borrowers who are socially perceived as profiteers or speculators rather than entrepreneurs, or lenders who are seen as greedy rentiers, both of which, when viewed as excessive, break down the stability of a society by means of affecting the distribution of income and wealth to an extent that it is no longer morally justified by the public.

The important role that the *Tract* assigned to the real rate of interest in distributional matters is acutely contrasted with his analysis of the wage-earning class. He did not see much of a problem with the implications of inflation for workers as long as they are well organized so as to protect the purchasing power of wages. Workers, at least in appearance, were not perceived as a threat to the stability of society regardless of their degree of organization or bargaining power. On the other hand, the primary root of instability was identified in the conflicting claims arising between borrowers (the industrial class of entrepreneurs) and lenders (rentiers) over the distribution of profits. Although for somewhat different reasons due to rentier excessive preference for liquidity, this conflict between entrepreneurs and rentiers persisted even in Keynes's three-class analysis in the *General Theory*.

One of the main policy proposals derived directly from the *Tract* is that monetary policy must be conducted toward the stabilization of the real rate of interest at some reasonably low level to preserve over time the distribution of income between rentiers and other income groups, not unlike what modern heterodox economists such as John Smithin have argued in more recent times (see Smithin, 1996, 2014). Arguably, since Keynes stuck to the Marshallian quantity theory orthodoxy in his *Tract*, he suggested a money supply-side policy of controlling the level of prices rather than arguing in favor of central bank stabilization directly through interest rate adjustment as modern New Keynesian/neo-Wicksellian economists would suggest nowadays. Back then, he thought *à la* Marshall that by supposedly managing the supply of money, with an emphasis on the supply of credit as opposed to currency (Skidelsky, 1983), it would be possible to control prices, thus affecting real rates of interest. The objective of monetary policy would be to maintain societal stability by minimizing 'unacceptable' gains among the socio-economic classes that take part in the distribution of income and wealth.

Not unlike in the *General Theory*, Keynes of the *Tract* believed in the exogeneity of money and the endogeneity of the rate of interest. Therefore, the understanding of the rate of interest found in the *Tract* is fairly attached to the Marshallian orthodoxy. For this reason, Keynes focuses on controlling the rate of change in prices, something perceived as a feasible policy goal, instead of targeting the rates of interest, which he thought were determined primarily by market forces, but, very importantly, mediated by expectations in the evolution of prices. Indeed, following the analysis of the *Tract* by Skidelsky (1983, p. 155), the 'most distinctive feature in Keynes's account is his stress on expectations', and in particular his approach of expectations-driven money rates of interest:

> It is true that, in so far as a rise of prices is foreseen, attempts to get advantage from this by increased borrowing force the money rates of interest to move upwards. It is for this reason, amongst others, that a high bank rate should be associated with a period of rising prices, and a low bank rate with a period of falling prices. The apparent abnormality of the money rate of interest at such times is merely the other side of the attempt of the real rate of interest to steady itself. (Keynes, [1923] 2013, p. 20)

As an aside, it is not hard to notice the special attention that Keynes pays to the stability of capitalism as dependent on the long-run stability of prices and rates of interest, which is nothing but the declaration that monetary policy has long-lasting influences on production and income distribution in an economy. Perhaps there is a touch of irony considering that the *Tract* is rather popular for supposedly disregarding the 'long-run' issues. However, behind the immortal phrase 'In the long run we are all dead' (Keynes, [1923] 2013, p. 65), which by the way is used in the context of the quantity theory of money, the *Tract* rather establishes profound connections between the short- and long-run events – that is, there is a constant sense that one cannot be explained without the other temporally. While that early work did have some repercussions in the modeling of price and monetary behavior, such as what is found among such disparate writers as Aujac (1950), Lavoie and Seccareccia (1988) and Smithin (1996, 2018), much of the income-distribution dynamics of class behavior became lost within the mainstream literature on inflation and monetary policy, at least until the GFC.

3.   THE MAINSTREAM PERSPECTIVE

Following the GFC of 2007–08, the mainstream New Keynesian economics was the object of much criticism for not foreseeing the crisis. Notwithstanding the attacks, New Keynesian economics proved somewhat resilient and continued to be the mainstream theoretical perspective in macroeconomics in the post-GFC world (see, for instance, Storm, 2021). Prominent frontline policymakers and prestigious mainstream economists belong to the New Keynesian school, such as Ben Bernanke, Janet Yellen, Lawrence Summers, Olivier Blanchard, among others. In addition, 'the New Keynesian model arguably remains the dominant framework in the classroom, in academic research, and in policy modeling' (Galí, 2018, p. 88),

New Keynesian economics recognizes the existence of nominal rigidities in the form of sticky wages or price mark-ups, thereby changes in nominal variables – prices, wages, interest rate – have significant effects on real variables – such as the output level and real wages – but only in the short run. Accordingly, monetary policy plays a crucial role in the determination of output fluctuations through exogenous changes (shocks) in the nominal rate of interest, whence monetary policy is not 'neutral' in the short run. Nevertheless, the effects of monetary policy are transitory; by no means can the latter modify the 'natural' levels of output and interest rate that are given by long-run equilibrium conditions (Galí, 2018). In the words of Ben Bernanke, 'Most economists would agree that monetary policy is "neutral" or nearly so in the longer term, meaning that it has limited long-term effects on "real" outcomes like the distribution of income and wealth' (Bernanke, 2015, n.p.). Henceforth, the consensus among mainstream economists claims that, due to the momentary nature of monetary policy shocks, their impact on any economic variable, including income distribution, must be also short-lived (Colciago, Samarina and de Haan, 2019), whereby monetary policy 'by construction cannot explain the trends in economic inequality' (Coibion et al., 2017, p. 71).

Conversely, most New Keynesians believe that the only effect monetary policy can have in the long run is on inflation. However, persistently high inflation would result in inefficiencies, leading to a lower steady-state output level compared with the natural output level, which is the level of output consistent with the natural rate of interest in the absence of nominal rigidities (Galí, 2018). In this line of argument, the main role of monetary policy is limited to minimizing short-run fluctuations in aggregate demand around the natural level of output. The question that follows is, what are the short-run effects of monetary policy on income distribution? To some extent, the answer to that changed as a result of post-GFC developments in New Keynesian economics. Finally, one may wonder whether these new developments really marked a breakthrough with respect to the previous conventional wisdom in monetary policy and income distribution.

3.1   The Mainstream Perspective Before the GFC

Before the GFC, the assumption of a representative agent in New Keynesian models implied that monetary policy shocks do not have any impact on the distribution of income (Galí, 2018). Since all households are equal, changes in the rate of interest affect households symmetrically, and the transmission mechanisms of monetary policy – the different ways it might impact aggregate demand in the short run – consist of the two distinct effects of a change in the rate of interest on the level of output: the so-called substitution effect (given by the change in the opportunity cost of current consumption), and the income effect (which is nothing but the traditional multiplier effect). Partly because of that, very few mainstream economists tried to investigate the relationship between monetary policy and income distribution. Any redistributive effect of monetary policy was seen as a 'side effect of monetary policy, separate from the issue of aggregate demand management' (Colciago et al., 2019, p. 1202). In other words, monetary policy was only relevant to income distribution as far as it affected inflation – back then something unquestionable for the mainstream. Hence, the relevant question for the mainstream was not whether monetary policy impacts distribution but whether inflation does so, which then produces changes in income and wealth distribution.

In this line of argument, one of the few articles that addressed this question before the GFC concludes that the '[m]onetary policy that aims to restrain inflation and minimize output fluctuations is the most likely to permanently improve conditions for the poor' (Romer and Romer, 1999, p. 22). To make things clearer, consider the canonical three-equation New Keynesian model (Galí, 2018):

$$\tilde{y}_t = \ln y_t - \ln y_t^n \left(i_t^n \right) \tag{8.1}$$

$$\Pi_t = \beta \Pi_{t+1} + \kappa \tilde{y}_t \tag{8.2}$$

$$i_t = \varphi_\pi \Pi_t + \varphi_y \hat{y}_t + v_t, \tag{8.3}$$

where equation (8.1) is the dynamic IS equation that portrays the output gap ($\tilde{y}_t$) between the actual output level (y_t) and the natural output level (y_t^n), the latter depending negatively on the natural rate of interest (i_t^n). Equation (8.2) is the New Keynesian Phillips curve (NKPC), which depicts actual inflation (Π_t) as a function of expected inflation at $t + 1$ (Π_{t+1}), and the output gap. Finally, equation (8.3) is the Taylor rule monetary policy equation that defines the nominal rate of interest (i_t) as a function of current inflation, an estimated output gap ($\hat{y}_t$), and a stochastic term (v_t) through which monetary policy shocks are introduced (β, κ, φ_π, φ_y are conventional parameters).

The NKPC says that the larger the output gap as defined in equation (8.1), the higher the inflation rate, while merging the dynamic IS with the Taylor rule (assuming $\tilde{y}_t = \hat{y}_t$), yields a traditional AD curve depicting a negative relation between inflation and the output gap. For New Keynesians, the optimal monetary policy would be such that minimizes both inflation and output fluctuations from their natural long-run levels. Take, for example, the equilibrium output gap ($\tilde{y}_t^*$) given by the intersection of the NKPC and AD curves:

$$\tilde{y}_t^* = \frac{i_t - \varphi_\pi \beta \Pi_{t+1} - v_t}{\varphi_y + \kappa \varphi_\pi} \tag{8.4}$$

Assuming a positive output gap in equilibrium, a contractionary monetary policy shock – reflected in a persistent increase in v_t – would reduce the output gap and inflation rate in the short run. Apart from that, the model does not say a word with respect to inequality, since all households are equally endowed, but mainstream economists claimed that this shock might increase inequality as long as cyclical unemployment tends to affect more low-income households. However, due to the fact that natural levels of output and interest rate are unaffected by a monetary policy shock, inequality in the long run is also unaltered. Conversely, they also point out that expansionary monetary policy could benefit indebted households due to unexpected inflation, but that this benefit would be likely offset by the reduction of real wages and income transfers (Romer and Romer, 1999). It follows that the best monetary policy for everyone was the one that keeps inflation low and stable.

3.2   The Mainstream Views After the GFC

In the aftermath of the GFC, the many criticisms of the representative agent New Keynesian model forced its advocates to explore the implications of relaxing that assumption, giving rise to a new literature on heterogeneous agent New Keynesian (HANK) models. HANK models allow for differences in the level of income and wealth across households, which means that each agent will have a different marginal propensity to consume (MPC) at the moment of the shock. The differences arise from assuming random shocks in labor productivity among the distribution of households (idiosyncratic shocks) and incomplete credit markets, whereby a number of households cannot fully insure against idiosyncratic shocks. Naturally, the distribution of income will alter the effects of monetary policy and vice versa. Thus, the mainstream literature has been focused on identifying the various channels through which monetary policy affects income distribution in the short run – called distributional channels (Colciago et al., 2019).

Considering differences among households implies that it becomes much more complex to aggregate household behavior; hence, the above IS equation does not hold anymore. Nonetheless, the NKPC and the Taylor rule are not affected. Another difference derived from HANK models is that there will be creditors and debtors in equilibrium. As a result, the distributional channels are not only the income, substitution and wealth effects – the latter being the change in consumption due to a change in the asset balance sheet (ibid.) – that are characteristic of representative agent models, but there will also be various other distributional channels associated with the heterogeneous distribution of income and wealth among households.

Examples of distributional channels (see Coibion et al., 2017) are the earnings heterogeneity channel, which claims that income gains are going to be unequal depending on the MPC of each household – that is, an expansionary monetary policy would benefit more those households with higher MPCs – that is, the low-income households (Auclert, 2019). Moreover, the savings channel focuses on redistribution occurring between borrowers and lenders. Recently, Auclert (2019) pointed out that the wealth channel (also known as the Fisher channel) must be distinguished from what he calls the interest rate exposure channel. While the former reflects the change in the asset balance sheet caused by inflation, the latter captures the extent to which asset-holders are affected by changes in both interest payments and asset prices, taking into account the net position in maturing assets and liabilities. Numerous studies have pointed to these channels, especially in evaluating the effects of quantitative easing (QE) on income and wealth distribution (see, for instance, Lenza and Slačálek, 2018).

Broadly speaking, the consideration of all the possible distributional channels in HANK models has two main implications. First, the effects of monetary policy shocks to aggregate demand fluctuations are either amplified or dampened depending on the distribution of income before the shock. Second, the net effect of the shock in the distribution of income will be ambiguous. In other words, the combination of all viable channels implies a number of possibilities for the net distributional outcome as a whole depending on the pre-shock distribution, which is unpredictable due to the stochastic nature of the idiosyncratic shocks.

Hand in hand with HANK models, two-agent New Keynesian (TANK) models were developed to make heterogeneity among households more tractable. Usually, TANK models take distribution as given between two types of households: liquidity-constrained households that do not save ('hand-to-mouth' households in the mainstream jargon), and liquidity-unconstrained households that have access to financial markets. Consequently, the effects of monetary policy on distribution are less ambiguous. Recently, for example, Hohberger, Priftis and Vogel (2020) used a TANK model to show that expansionary monetary policy shocks might reduce inequality in the short and medium run due to a temporary increase in employment and a reduction in interest payments, although the effects on inequality are not permanent since steady-state values are unaffected by monetary variables.

Therefore, it is not surprising that recent empirical work on the part of the mainstream has found interesting or even puzzling the evidence that portrays significant and persistent effects of monetary policy on the distribution of income, something that escapes the boundaries imposed by New Keynesian models (see Cantore, Ferroni and León-Ledesma, 2021). For example, Furceri, Loungani and Zdzienicka (2018) provide econometric evidence showing that unexpected monetary policy shocks not only impact income distribution incrementally on a medium-term horizon, but their estimates also suggest that the effects are asymmetric over the business cycle. Specifically, they found that contractionary monetary policy shocks have greater effects in increasing income inequality than expansionary shocks reducing it, particularly during the expansions of the business cycle. Therefore, the empirical evidence clearly indicates that monetary policy effects on inequality might well persist beyond the medium term (Kappes, 2021), despite defying the mainstream models.

As explained above, the analysis of monetary policy and income distribution before the GFC is very poor. It is attached to the view of the effects of inflation on inequality, but nothing more. Then, after the GFC, the application of HANK and TANK models yielded more possible distributional channels, which is logical given the relaxation of the representative agent assumption. However, the fundamental insights did not change at all. For the mainstream, monetary policy has very little to say with respect to income inequality trends. This is because no matter how sophisticated the model is, the attachment to the natural levels of output and interest rate inhibits the mainstream to construct a long-lasting link between monetary policy and income distribution. This short-sighted perspective on the subject results in roughly the same pre-GFC conventional wisdom that perceives inflation as the root of all evils, which now includes inequality as one of them. Thus, monetary policy should be oriented toward the unique goal of combating inflation as the best strategy for central banks to contribute to the reduction of inequality, given that 'there seems to be a consensus that higher inflation, at least above some threshold, increases inequality' (Colciago et al., 2019, p. 1224; also see Kappes, 2021 for a survey on the empirical findings that challenges the view by Colciago et al., 2019).

Overall, there is a clear sense that despite a change in the official discourse toward incorporating inequality aspects in the policy agenda, including monetary policy, the reality is that it has hardly gone much beyond the discourse. The current mainstream consensus among policymakers is basically the same as before the GFC; but what has changed is the vocabulary, which means nothing but old wine in new bottles. For the mainstream, monetary policy is neutral in the long run; it simply cannot affect any real variables like income and wealth distribution. Perhaps no one has stated it more clearly than Agustín Carstens, the current General Manager of the Bank for International Settlements, who just recently claimed that 'over the long run, inequality is not a monetary phenomenon… Therefore, the best contribution monetary policy can make to an equitable society is to try to keep the economy on an even keel by fulfilling its mandate' (Carstens, 2021, p. 1).

4.   THE HETERODOX PERSPECTIVE ON THE NON-NEUTRALITY OF MONETARY POLICY ON INCOME DISTRIBUTION

The heterodox position regarding the effect of monetary policy on income distribution, which has finally been discussed and debated recently in certain policy circles outside of just strict academic exchanges among non-mainstream economists (see Lavoie and Seccareccia, 2021; Rochon and Seccareccia, 2021), starts from the triple socio-economic class division of the economy that was familiar to Keynes already a century ago. If one were to strip away the Marshallian quantity theory veneer from the *Tract* and situate the analysis within an endogenous money perspective with the interest rate being largely set by the central bank, we quickly arrive at a view of monetary policy as being in the nature of an incomes policy conducted under the direction of central banks.

The consequences of changes in the rate of interest on the level and composition of aggregate demand, and thus on the level and structure of production because of the possible interest elasticity of private spending, are well described, albeit overly emphasized, in the mainstream literature on the transmission mechanism of monetary policy. What is not usually discussed, except in some limited circles since the GFC, which in heterodox circles has actually been analyzed for a very long time, dubbed the income distribution channel (see, for instance, Seccareccia and Lavoie, 2016), is that interest rate changes also affect the terms under which production takes place via the payment of wages, profits and interest whose changing income shares can also influence economic activity, particularly because of differential propensities to consume/save. This is because changes in the rate of interest impact not only the income of rentiers directly but also the income of wage earners and entrepreneurial profit indirectly, owing to how monetary policy can modify expenditure flows in an economy due to how the incomes derived in both the product and labor markets are affected.

Abstracting from the work of Keynes and post-Keynesian economists that one can trace back almost a century, it took the mainstream until the GFC to acknowledge that monetary policy might not be neutral in the short or medium term, due at least to the recognition of this income distribution channel of monetary policy by means of introducing additional assumptions, such as heterogeneous agents in HANK models. This is so even though the mainstream is still trapped in the bogus distinction between short- and long-run effects. Hence, in the short run, changes in interest rates can have undesirable effects on factor shares, but these changes cannot persist in the long run, because mainstream theorists continue to cling to equilibrium analysis based on some 'marginal product' principle about the 'natural' determinants of factor shares. While we do recognize that an economy could have distinct structural features that may persist over time, mainstream theory prevents these economists from seeing that what the long run is, in the Kaleckian sense, merely a sequence or a 'moving picture' of such short-period snapshots as an economy evolves over actual historical time – a problem, as we have mentioned earlier, that was also originally raised by Keynes in his *Tract* with regard to Marshallian economics.

4.1 Monetary Policy as an Incomes Policy

Let us take the standard Keynesian income flows described in the triple income-class analyses inferred from the *Tract* that include wages, profits and rentier income, and defining the total money income flow, Y, at time t in the following way:

$$Y_t = p_t y_t = wL_t + rK_t + iD_{t-1}, \tag{8.5}$$

where p is price, y, is real output, w is the average money wage, L is employment, r is the rate of profit after interest is paid out that is multiplied by K, the nominal value of the capital stock to obtain the profit flow, i is the interest rate and D is the nominal value of financial assets/liabilities (debt) outstanding originating from the previous period, which when multiplied we shall approximate as rentier income, as contrasted with labor and profit income flows. Dividing by Y and taking the natural logarithm of each term similar to what is found in Smithin (2018, p. 117), by definition, the evolution of the logarithm of the rentier share (ρ) mirrors in reverse the dynamics of the evolution of the logarithm of the share of labor ($\omega - a$) (that is, the logarithmic gap between real wage and labor productivity) as well as that of the share of profit (π) in equation (8.6) below:

$$\rho_t = a_t - \omega_t - \pi_t \tag{8.6}$$

Any policy measure that attempts to control money incomes, thereby impacting on ω, π, and ρ, can be termed an incomes policy. Historically, such a policy has been used as an adjunct to fiscal and monetary policy often for the purpose of either controlling prices and especially labor costs, so as to render the latter less responsive to aggregate demand and employment growth in an economy, or modifying the evolution of unit labor costs, for instance, in order to prevent balance of payments crises in countries facing competitiveness problems, especially during the Bretton Woods era of fixed exchange rates (see, inter alia, 'classic' authors such as Romanis Braun, 1975). Hence, it can be argued that any direct policy changes affecting one of those terms in equation (8.6) would be considered in the nature of an incomes policy.

Historically, incomes policies have been usually restricted to some form of wage controls or 'wage compression' (for a discussion, see UNCTAD, 2011, Chapter 1), which have been: (1) either 'top down' with the nominal wage growth norm set *ex cathedra* for policy purposes by a government authority; or (2) via 'bottom up' as used to be the case with the early postwar 'solidaristic wage' incomes policies arrived at through economy-wide wage bargaining between trade union representatives and those of employers' associations in social-democratic regimes in Scandinavian countries. Also, of the more common 'top-down' policies, we have seen voluntary norms for permissible wage growth established in the form of 'guideposts' during the 1960s as well as legally enforced/compulsory incomes policies, for instance, in the 1970s in North America, which all sought to impact on the value of the wage growth component, w, in equation (8.5).

However, contrary to the mainstream perspective about income-distribution 'neutrality', monetary policy via interest rate setting, as within a Taylor rule reaction function, impacts directly on i in equation (8.5) or the ρ term of equation (8.6), which, in our definition, would also entail a specific form of incomes policy. Under the rubric of a monetary policy, what we have, in reality, is a very peculiar type of incomes policy pursued by government by delegating, usually through an official mandate, its monetary policy arm, the central bank, to implement it. More precisely, in the case of IT regimes, the monetary authorities follow a simple rule of adjusting central bank-administered interest rates in the same direction as the rate of inflation, thereby seeking to sustain rentier income, ρ, and simultaneously, via the transmission mechanism, by slowing down nominal and real wage growth and further compounding its downward effect on the evolution of the share of labor, $\omega - a$.

While there is a noticeable similarity between all these various historical and current types of incomes policy that target a reduction in the inflation rate through its consequences on wage growth, there is an obvious perversity in the conduct of monetary policy on income distribution that is focused on 'inflation-first' policy prioritization. In contrast to the voluntary 'guidepost' types or even the compulsory forms of incomes policy in Western Europe and North America that would set permissible wage increases in such a way as not to be blatantly biased over time in favor of any one socio-economic group (this is why these types of incomes policy would specify, for example, that wage change should be tied to a, the long-term change in labor productivity), there is nothing in the 'inflation-first' monetary policy framework to ensure some broad income-distribution neutrality. Indeed, in what sense or on what moral basis can it be considered fair to combat inflation by raising the income of rentiers, ρ, in order to restrain the growth of wage income and compress the labor share? Yet, such was the nature of the high interest rate policy of combating inflation, which began to be implemented ever since the 'inflation-first' monetary policy perspective took hold, which has now been entrenched for over four decades since the 1970s within most central bank policy circles. Despite the technocratic façade of pursuing a 'monetary' policy, there is a striking continuum in the control of inflation. IT monetary policy regimes conduct precisely the same form of incomes policy constituting genealogically the voluntary 'guidepost' family of incomes control (see Seccareccia and Lavoie, 2010). However, it is now administered usually within a renewable five-year mandate by central bank technocrats rather than being temporarily put in place by the elected authorities, as was the case with, say, voluntary or compulsory wage controls of the earlier postwar era in Western Europe and North America. More conspicuously, these policies were also quickly put in place without any concern for the distributional consequences of the policy, which was of crucial political importance to earlier pre-IT policymakers.

Let us now discuss a bit more precisely this question of fairness that has been a matter primarily discoursed outside of mainstream views since, as we have argued for the latter, monetary policy is 'neutral' on income distribution in the long run.

4.2   The Pasinetti 'Fair' Interest Rate Measures and Alternative Indicators of the Impact of Monetary Policy on Income Distribution

Though quite different from the analytical framework of Keynes's *Tract*, it is exactly this question of fairness that a celebrated Cambridge post-Keynesian economist, Luigi Pasinetti (1981), some four decades ago, first posed the problem of an income-distribution-neutral interest rate policy compatible with the socio-economic class analysis put forth by Keynes in his various writings. Let us describe the essentials, since a more comprehensive analysis of Pasinetti's precise model and its analytics has already been presented in significant detail elsewhere (see, for instance, Lavoie and Seccareccia, 1988, 1999 and 2019; Seccareccia and Lavoie, 1989, 2016). Suffice to say that Pasinetti posed a fundamental normative question of commutative justice pertaining to interest rate determination. This was done by conceptualizing an interest rate rule that would preserve the value intertemporally of a financial asset on the basis of a Smithian 'labor-command' perspective, in such a way that the value of a person's savings would remain constant in terms of the labor units that the monetary value would command. Pasinetti, therefore, delved into an issue that harks back to the medieval debates over what should a rate of interest be appropriately compensating. Namely, he posed the question of whether a financial wealth-holder should preserve over time more than the labor that the initial value of those savings commands, which remains of concern even today (see Pilkington, 2021).

Although, as we shall see, this leads to a specific conclusion as to what this Pasinetti reference rate of interest should be, actually, historically, there have emerged two ways of defining the latter. Indeed, the first formulation of the Pasinetti 'fair' rate of interest, as summarized in Lavoie and Seccareccia (1999), was actually derived differently from the way the question was posed originally in Pasinetti (1980–81, 1981). While this was an obvious genealogical offshoot arising from a particular reading of Pasinetti's works, it was actually framed initially analogous to how it is discussed within the early postwar period incomes-policy perspective that sought to answer the question of what appropriate income growth would maintain the share of labor constant, which, in this case, ought to be when real wages are growing commensurate with average labor productivity. However, since the rate of interest is already a percentage ratio, analogous to that of the share of labor, it ensued that the calculated Fisher real rate of interest could directly be equated to the growth rate of labor productivity to stabilize the share of rentier to non-rentier income. This is because a real interest rate claim on a growing overall real output would either exceed the growth of the latter or would fall short of it, thereby building rentier wealth or reducing it over time.

As discussed in Lavoie and Seccareccia (2019, pp. 150–53), there are certain problems with this norm that are not altogether consistent with the original meaning and purpose of what Pasinetti had intended, which was to obtain a reference real interest rate that would keep rentier wealth unchanged in labor units. This latter definition of the reference (or 'fair') rate of interest would thus link real interest rate movement to real wage growth. Accordingly, this brings us to two indicators discussed historically to try to capture over time the changing distribution of rentier income and wealth with regard to non-interest income earners. These are calculated and depicted graphically below for a selected group of countries. These two Pasinetti reference rates should, however, first be contrasted with the way Keynes of the *Tract* saw it by focusing on the Fisher real rate of interest, which has found its expression in the recent work of Smithin (2018), and which appears to extend Keynesian reasoning from the *Tract* by concluding that the 'fair' real rate of interest ought to be zero rather than just a very low real rate (for a discussion, see Lavoie and Seccareccia, 2019).

Let us look at the evolution of these series by seeking to infer the effect of monetary policy on income distribution by starting with Keynes's concern with the Fisher relation in the *Tract* as an indicator of income distribution. We chose the evolution of long-term rates of interest as being most representative of what was happening to 'rentier' income for a selected group of industrial countries, including the G-7 countries together with Australia and New

Zealand, for the half-century following the breakdown of the Bretton Woods system from 1971 to 2020, with the exception of Japan and Italy where the data were available from 1989 and 1992, respectively.

Figure 8.2 traces how these Fisher rates deviate from Smithin's zero real interest rate reference point. What we can conclude broadly from the clustering of these Fisher real interest rate series is that the patterns for each country are strikingly similar regardless of the institutional changes that many of these countries underwent, especially in the case of the continental European countries that experienced significant institutional changes in the monetary landscape over the last half-century. Indeed, after the collapse of the Bretton Woods system in 1971, these European countries temporarily floated their national currencies until 1979 when they began to reintegrate under the umbrella of the European Monetary System (EMS) of fixed exchange rates (the so-called European exchange rate serpent, the ERM), followed by the eventual founding of the Eurozone with the adoption of a single currency in 1999. With the only significant outlier in Figure 8.2 being Germany in the 1970s that at the time sustained positive and relatively high real interest rates, what mattered most to central bank real-interest rate policy in these mostly Western industrial countries was the commitment to 'inflation first' by the early 1980s as herd behavior dominated regardless of the different institutional arrangements in place. Hence, except for Germany's Bundesbank, which maintained relatively high real interest rates throughout the 1970s, Figure 8.2 reveals the early collapse of our indicator of rentier income flow arising from the high inflation that struck fear in the financial markets following the oil price shocks.

This spooking of rentier wealth-holders was an important political factor leading to the policy reversal of high real interest rates, which would corroborate Smithin's perspective on the 'revenge of the rentiers', whose policy dominance of 'inflation first' within central banks persisted until the GFC. It was only after the 2007–08 crisis that one witnesses a return to very low or even negative real interest rates but not of the magnitude of the decline in the 1970s.

We observe similar patterns when viewing the experience of these countries through the prism of the Pasinetti indicators previously discussed. The first of these Pasinetti series, calculated as simply the spread between real interest rates and average labor productivity growth for this same group of countries, is graphed in Figure 8.3.

As one would expect, while Figure 8.3 reproduces a similar pattern as found in Figure 8.2, there are sometimes greater fluctuations since higher interest rate policy, such as, for example, just preceding the GFC, the ensuing recession had negative consequences on productivity growth for Kaldorian reasons relating to Verdoorn's law. This would tend to magnify during recessions the cyclical patterns obtained from the simple Fisher real interest rate series. One revealing example of these wild swings in the series is the delayed pattern for

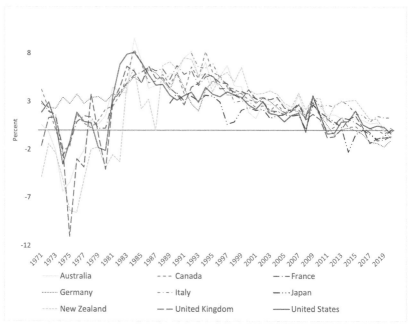

Source: OECD.Stat, *Key Short-Term Economic Indicators*, https://stats.oecd.org/index.aspx
?DatasetCode=KEI (data extracted in June 2021).

Figure 8.2   *Evolution of Fisher real long-term rates of interest of selected
industrial countries, 1971–2020, annual observations*

New Zealand, which shows in the figure how its specific Pasinetti measure was
the very last to recover only after the 1981–82 recession in the world from the
negative range throughout the previous era and then peaking immediately after
1990 when the New Zealand Reserve Bank was the first central bank to adopt
a rigorous IT policy. Also, the experience during the first year of the pandemic
in 2020 reveals some interesting bifurcation for the countries where the data
were available. In the case of Canada and the United States, the Pasinetti
measure collapsed, while in Europe it jumped sharply. Indeed, in Europe,
long-term interest rates also tended to be very low or even negative in the core
Eurozone countries, which was coupled with a mild deflation and a strong
collapse of productivity. In North America, interest rates also fell significantly
but remained positive, and productivity rose significantly due primarily to the
way government emergency support was provided during the pandemic. On
the European continent, government transfers went to firms to retain workers,
while in North America, workers tended to be laid off and then supported

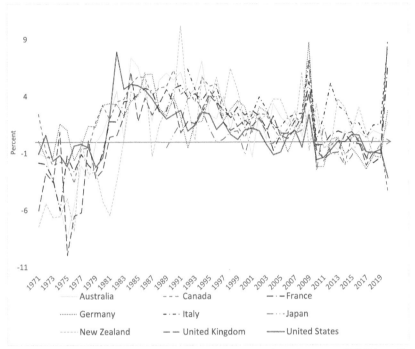

Source: OECD.Stat, *Key Short-Term Economic Indicators* and *Productivity and ULC*, https://
stats.oecd.org/index.aspx?DatasetCode=KEI and https://stats.oecd.org/Index.aspx?DataSetCode
=PDBI_I4 (data extracted June 2021).

Figure 8.3   *Evolution of the traditional Pasinetti spread between real*
                 long-term rates of interest and labor productivity growth
                 for selected industrial countries, 1971–2020, annual
                 observations

through unemployment insurance benefits, resulting in conflicting measured patterns of productivity change.

Finally, we can briefly observe the evolution of the labor-command version of the Pasinetti measure calculating the spread between long-term interest rates and an index of labor compensation. Although Figure 8.4 reveals a similar pattern, the scantiness of information on labor compensation for the early years makes it less reliable for the purpose of generalization. However, what can be said when looking at the three charts, is that the broad evidence conforms to the scenario described by Smithin (1996). After the relatively high growth and low inflation of the earlier postwar era, there was a rentier scare as the inflation rate rose and the share of rentier income declined during the 1970s, which was

followed by the 'revenge of the rentiers' during most of the three decades that
followed until the GFC, as inflation fighting became the priority of central
bankers who had been spooked by the high inflation. It was only during the
inter-crises decade following the GFC that we see a collapse of the share of
rentier income, not because of high inflation but because of the central bank
policy to combat the recession. However, the final question to be addressed is:
which social group was the beneficiary of the reversal of the fortunes of rentier
income earners after the GFC?

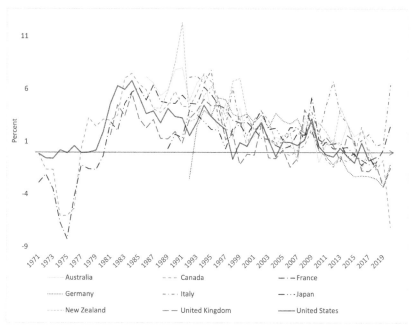

Source: OECD.Stat, *Key Short-Term Economic Indicators* and *Productivity and ULC*, https://
stats.oecd.org/index.aspx?DatasetCode=KEI and https://stats.oecd.org/Index.aspx?DataSetCode
=PDBI_I4 (data extracted June 2021).

Figure 8.4   *Evolution of the Pasinetti labor-command measure*
                  for selected industrial countries, 1971–2020, annual
                  observations

To answer the question of who the beneficiaries were, we need to consider
what happened to the wage share with regard to that of profit both before and
after the GFC. Concomitantly with the sustained high values until the GFC, in
our indicators of the rentier share we generally also observe a collapse of the
share of wage income during the 'inflation-first' era. Because of the overlap

and the clustering, it is difficult to decipher in Figure 8.5 which countries suffered the most. In varying degrees, all countries witnessed a collapse after the 1970s, with IT countries such as Canada and New Zealand seeing a significant decline in the wage share and then hit bottom before the GFC. On the other hand, the US (the top series delineated in Figure 8.5), whose central bank was faced with a dual mandate since 1978 and, therefore, politically indicating a lower tolerance for high unemployment, displays a much milder decline than any other country represented in Figure 8.5. Generally, the US was also the country displaying a lower average unemployment rate throughout that whole era, as we already observed in Figure 8.1, say, in the case of Canada and the US.

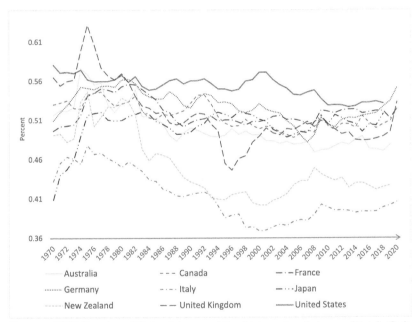

Source: OECD.Stat, *Annual National Accounts*, https://stats.oecd.org/Index.aspx?DataSetCode =NAAG (data extracted June 2021).

Figure 8.5   *Evolution of the share of labor income for selected industrial countries, 1970–2020, annual observations*

What can be inferred from Figure 8.5 is that the wage share declined, especially for IT regimes such as Canada and New Zealand, and then it bottomed out even before the GFC, as these central banks began to loosen their restrictive monetary policy through the adoption of what came to be described as 'flexible' IT. While there was some mild reversal in some countries, what seems apparent is that the rentier losses during the post-GFC decade were reflected primarily in increasing the profit mark-ups of business corporations internationally.

5.   CONCLUDING REMARKS

To conclude, what can be asserted categorically is that monetary policy is by its nature 'non-neutral' with respect to income distribution. Via the control of the key central bank-administered interest rate variable, monetary policy affects the incomes of certain groups at the expense of others. This arises not only because interest rates are a cost to borrowers that can increase the servicing cost of debt but also because they are incomes to lenders that influence economic activity through the income distribution channel of monetary policy, even more so than through the traditional interest cost channel of the monetary transmission mechanism. Because of its overwhelming importance, policy-makers can neither pretend that the collateral damage on income distribution is non-existent nor that income distribution should not be within the strict domain of policy concerns of central bank policy. As we enter a new post-pandemic era, more than ever it is time for central bankers to consider policy objectives other than merely being concerned with the control of inflation, which largely remains a relic of a quantity theory tradition in macroeconomics that has long been discredited and gone.

NOTES

1.   Our delegation included the Honorable Senator Diane Bellemare from Quebec, as well as six Canadian economists from central Canada, listed alphabetically: Mathieu Dufour (Université du Québec en Outaouais, Gatineau); Pierre Fortin (Université du Québec à Montréal, Montreal); Mario Seccareccia (University of Ottawa, Ottawa); Andrew Sharpe (Centre for the Study of Living Standards, Ottawa); John Smithin (York University, Toronto); and Brenda Spotton Visano (York University, Toronto).
2.   Given Canada's higher share of the primary sector with regard to the US at the time, the Canadian economy was perhaps able to absorb the soldiers returning from Europe more easily as many of them presumably went back directly to gainful employment in the primary sector characterized by higher Lewis-type disguised unemployment.

REFERENCES

Auclert, A. (2019), 'Monetary policy and the redistribution channel', *American Economic Review*, **109** (6), 2333–67.

Aujac, H. (1950), 'Une hypothèse de travail: l'inflation, conséquence monétaire du comportement des groupes sociaux', *Économie appliquée*, **3** (2), 279–300.

Bernanke, B. (2015, June 1), 'Monetary policy and inequality', *Brookings.edu*, accessed November 21, 2020 at https://www.brookings.edu/blog/ben-bernanke/2015/06/01/monetary-policy-and-inequality/.

Cantore, C., F. Ferroni and M. León-Ledesma (2021), 'The missing link: monetary policy and the labor share', *Journal of the European Economic Association*, **19** (3), 1592–620.

Carstens, A. (2021, May 6), 'Central banks and inequality', remarks by Agustín Carstens, General Manager of the BIS at the Markus' Academy, Princeton University's Bendheim Center for Finance, Basel, accessed May 15, 2021 at https://www.bis.org/speeches/sp210506.htm.

Coibion, O., Y. Gorodnichenko, L. Kueng and J. Silvia (2017), 'Innocent bystanders? Monetary policy and inequality', *Journal of Monetary Economics*, **88**, 70–89.

Colciago, A., A. Samarina and J. de Haan (2019), 'Central bank policies and income and wealth inequality: a survey', *Journal of Economic Surveys*, **33** (4), 1199–231.

Dimand, R.W. (2019), 'A tract on monetary reform', in R.W. Dimand and H. Hagemann (eds), *The Elgar Companion to John Maynard Keynes* (pp. 139–44), Cheltenham, UK and Northampton, MA, USA: Edward Elgar Publishing.

Furceri, D., P. Loungani and A. Zdzienicka (2018), 'The effects of monetary policy shocks on inequality', *Journal of International Money and Finance*, **85**, 168–86.

Galbraith, J.K. (2020), 'Backwater economics: a life story', *Journal of Economic Issues*, **54** (2), 287–93.

Galí, J. (2018), 'The state of New Keynesian economics: a partial assessment', *Journal of Economic Perspectives*, **32** (3), 87–112.

Hohberger, S., R. Priftis and L. Vogel (2020), 'The distributional effects of conventional monetary policy and quantitative easing: evidence from an estimated DSGE model', *Journal of Banking and Finance*, **113**, Article 105483.

Kappes, S.A. (2021), 'Monetary policy and personal income distribution: a survey of the empirical literature', *Review of Political Economy*, ahead-of-print, http://doi.org/10.1080/09538259.2021.1943159.

Keynes, J.M. ([1923] 2013), *A Tract on Monetary Reform. Vol. IV, The Collected Writings of John Maynard Keynes*, edited by E. Johnson and D.E. Moggridge, Cambridge, UK: Cambridge University Press for the Royal Economic Society.

Lavoie, M. and M. Seccareccia (1988), 'Money, interest and rentiers: the twilight of rentier capitalism in Keynes's *General Theory*', in O. Hamouda and J.N. Smithin (eds), *Keynes and Public Policy after Fifty Years, Vol. 2* (pp. 145–58), Aldershot, UK and Brookfield, VT, USA: Edward Elgar Publishing.

Lavoie, M. and M. Seccareccia (1999), 'Fair interest rates', in P.A. O'Hara (ed.), *Encyclopedia of Political Economy, Vol. 1* (pp. 543–5), London/New York: Routledge.

Lavoie, M. and M. Seccareccia (2019), 'Macroeconomics and natural rates: some reflections on Pasinetti's fair rate of interest', *Bulletin of Political Economy*, **13** (2), 139–65.

Lavoie, M. and M. Seccareccia (2021, April 23), *Going Beyond the Inflation-targeting Mantra: A Dual Mandate*, Max Bell School for Public Policy, McGill University, pp. 5–40, accessed April 24, 2021 at https://www.mcgill.ca/maxbellschool/files/maxbellschool/7_lavoie_0.pdf.

Lenza, M. and J. Slačálek (2018), 'How does monetary policy affect income and wealth inequality? Evidence from quantitative easing in the Euro Area', *European Central Bank Working Paper No. 2190*, accessed July 11, 2021 at https://www.ecb.europa.eu/pub/pdf/scpwps/ecb.wp2190.en.pdf?form=MY01SV&OCID=MY01SV.

Pasinetti, L.L. (1980–81), 'The rate of interest and the distribution of income in a pure labor economy', *Journal of Post Keynesian Economics*, **3** (2), 170–82.

Pasinetti, L.L. (1981), *Structural Change and Economic Growth*, Cambridge, UK: Cambridge University Press.

Pilkington, P. (2021), 'Monetary faith', *Inference*, **6** (1), June, accessed July 11, 2021 at https://inference-review.com/article/monetary-faith.

Rochon, L.-P. and M. Seccareccia (2021), 'Un ensayo sobre política monetaria y distribución del ingreso: una perspectiva heterodoxa' [A primer on monetary policy and income distribution: a heterodox perspective], *Ensayos Económicos*, 76, 1–22, Banco Central de la República Argentina, accessed July 11, 2021 at https://www.bcra.gob.ar/PublicacionesEstadisticas/Resumen_ensayos.asp?id=1532.

Romanis Braun, A. (1975), 'The role of incomes policy in industrial countries since World War II', *International Monetary Fund Staff Papers*, **22** (1), 1–36.

Romer, C.D. and D.H. Romer (1999), 'Monetary policy and the well-being of the poor', *Economic Review – Federal Reserve Bank of Kansas City*, **84** (1), 21–49.

Seccareccia, M. (2017), 'Which vested interests do central banks really serve? Understanding central bank policy since the global financial crisis', *Journal of Economic Issues*, **51** (2), 341–50.

Seccareccia, M. and M. Lavoie (1989), 'Les idées révolutionnaires de Keynes en politique économique et le déclin du capitalisme rentier', *Économie Appliquée*, **42** (1), 47–70.

Seccareccia, M. and M. Lavoie (2010), 'Inflation targeting in Canada: myth versus reality', in G. Fontana, J. McCombie and M. Sawyer (eds), *Macroeconomics, Finance and Money: Essays in Honour of Philip Arestis* (pp. 35–53), London: Palgrave Macmillan.

Seccareccia, M. and M. Lavoie (2016), 'Income distribution, rentiers, and their role in the capitalist economy: a Keynes–Pasinetti perspective', *International Journal of Political Economy*, **45** (3), 200–223.

Shapiro, A, and D.J. Wilson (2019, April 15), 'The evolution of the FOMC's explicit inflation target', *FRBSF Economic Letter No. 2019-12*, Federal Reserve Bank of San Francisco, pp. 1–5, accessed July 11, 2021 at https://www.frbsf.org/economic-research/files/el2019-12.pdf.

Skidelsky, R. (1983), *John Maynard Keynes: A Biography. Vol. 2: The Economist as Saviour 1920–1937*, New York: Penguin Books.

Smithin, J. (1996), *Macroeconomic Policy and the Future of Capitalism: The Revenge of the Rentiers and the Threat to Prosperity*, Cheltenham, UK and Brookfield, VT: Edward Elgar Publishing.

Smithin, J. (2014), *Essays in the Fundamental Theory of Monetary Economics and Macroeconomics*, Singapore: World Scientific.

Smithin, J. (2018), *Rethinking the Theory of Money, Credit and Macroeconomics: A New Statement for the Twenty-First Century*, Lanham, MD: Lexington Books.

Storm, S. (2021), 'Cordon of conformity: why DSGE models are not the future of macroeconomics', *International Journal of Political Economy*, **50** (2), 77–98.

Tooze, A. (2021, July 12), 'Climate crisis offers way out of monetary orthodoxy', *Socialeurope.eu*, accessed July 12, 2021 at https://socialeurope.eu/climate-crisis -offers-way-out-of-monetary-orthodoxy.
United Nations Conference on Trade and Development (UNCTAD) (2011), *Trade and Development Report, 2011*, Geneva and New York: United Nations, accessed July 11, 2021 at https://unctad.org/system/files/official-document/tdr2011_en.pdf.

PART III

Policy

9. Advancing the monetary policy toolkit through outright transfers and tiered reserve remuneration

Sascha Bützer[1]

1. INTRODUCTION

Even prior to the outbreak of COVID-19, most advanced economies had been stuck at or close to the effective lower bound (ELB) for several years. Due to persistently sluggish demand and insufficient fiscal support, central banks have been resorting to an ever expanding array of unconventional monetary policies to meet their price stability target and broader economic goals (Bützer, 2017). While expansionary monetary policy has been needed to stem off deflationary pressures, support growth, and stabilize employment, the employed measures – in particular, negative interest rates, large-scale asset purchases, and long-term lending operations – have been relatively untargeted and therefore limited in their effectiveness. They have also given rise to financial stability risks while exacerbating large pre-existing wealth inequalities.

As the link between monetary policy and inequality has been receiving increasing attention among the general public and in the literature, this chapter will focus on an alternative tool for monetary policy implementation that is both more effective and more equitable in achieving monetary policy objectives. In an economy at the ELB with spare capacity, outright transfer (OT) from the central bank to private households would allow for a much more direct monetary policy transmission on prices and the real economy without creating undesirable financial stability risks such as asset price inflation or unsustainable credit growth. Moreover, in contrast to quantitative easing (QE),[2] OT would not contribute to greater wealth inequality and reduce, rather than increase, risks of fiscal dominance. It would also allow for a faster and less disruptive liftoff from the ELB. OT could be implemented within the existing payments infrastructure although the emergence of central bank-issued digital currencies (CBDCs) could facilitate its use and allow for a more structural integration in central banks' monetary policy toolkits (cf. Barrdear and Kumhof, 2016; Bindseil, 2020).

OT constitutes a special case of 'helicopter money' that has been proposed as an addition to the monetary policy toolkit by many scholars such as Galí (2020), Boivin et al. (2019), Bernanke (2016), Sims (2016), Turner (2015a), Caballero, Farhi and Gourinchas (2015), and Woodford (2012).[3] However, these papers have not focused on the inequality-related aspects of different monetary policy tools and generally considered helicopter money in the form of monetary financing, which is distinctly different from OT with respect to its political economy and institutional implications. In particular, it requires fiscal policy cooperation, although a lack of fiscal support, often more politically than economically driven, has given rise to the problem and debate on unconventional monetary policy tools in the first place. Moreover, outright monetary financing – or even closer monetary–fiscal cooperation – is either taboo or explicitly prohibited in advanced economy jurisdictions such as the euro area. While legal complexities loom large in the case of OT, it could potentially be implemented within existing institutional frameworks in the euro area, a currency area where it could play a particularly useful role, as outlined in this chapter. A policy paper by Martin, Monnet and Ragot (2021) touches on these euro area-specific circumstances, although it does not contain a detailed assessment of the consequences for the European Central Bank (ECB)[4] balance sheet or policy solvency more generally, a gap that this chapter tries to close.

The contribution of this chapter to the literature is fivefold. It (1) adds a new monetary policy instrument to the discussion on whether – and how – monetary policy can take inequality concerns into account (Section 2); (2) discusses the expected macroeconomic and distributional effects of OT, its calibration, and practical implementation, including central bank balance sheet accounting options (Section 3); (3) presents policy solvency constraints and reserve remuneration considerations (Section 4); (4) elucidates the differences between a debt- or money-financed fiscal stimulus (Section 5); and (5) assesses broader institutional and legal considerations (Section 6). Section 7 concludes.

2.   INTEREST RATES, ASSET PURCHASES, AND INEQUALITY

The key monetary policy tools employed by advanced economy central banks over the past years, lower interest rates and asset purchases, ultimately aim to lower the cost of credit and stimulate credit growth in the hope that this will lead to increased nominal demand and price pressures.[5] While this approach has been met with some success in supporting economic activity, it is a very indirect way of influencing broad money growth, inflation, and domestic demand (Figures 9.1 and 9.2). In the euro area, inflation has remained subdued and far below its medium-term target of close to but below 2 percent since the start of QE in March 2015, despite the recent uptick.[6]

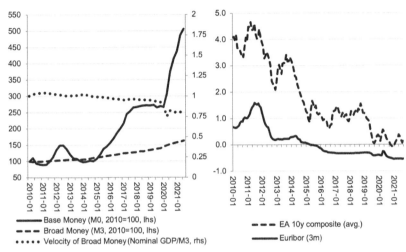

Source: Haver, ECB.

Figure 9.1   Monetary policy transmission in the euro area (EA): indexes (left); % (right)

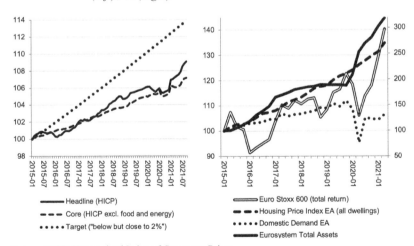

Note: HICP: Harmonized Index of Consumer Prices.
Source: Haver, ECB.

Figure 9.2   Consumer and asset prices, 2015–21 (indexes)

At the same time, asset purchases have contributed to a strong increase in asset prices (Figure 9.2), with financial assets mostly concentrated in the hands of households at the very top of the wealth distribution, while real estate ownership is more evenly distributed. The effects of QE on income inequality can be expected to be more evenly distributed due to the positive impact on employment and since income inequality tends to be much less pronounced than wealth inequality to begin with (Figure 9.3). Accordingly, Andersen et al. (2020) find a large impact on *wealth* inequality in a case study for Denmark based on household microdata, while other studies (cf. Ampudia et al., 2018; Bonifacio et al., 2021; Kappes, 2021) find mixed results, particularly for *income* inequality. The mixed evidence attests to the very heterogeneous effects of QE on households across the income and wealth distribution, depending on individual households' assets and liability structure (cf. Bunn et al., 2018), generally benefiting borrowers over creditors and owners of real estate over renters for example.[7] Moreover, it is important to distinguish between absolute and relative measures of wealth inequality. A hypothetical 1 percent increase in net wealth for each household would not alter relative measures of wealth inequality but would imply a huge rise in absolute inequality.[8] For instance, between the beginning of 2015 and the end of 2021, annual average growth rates of stock and housing prices in Europe have amounted to

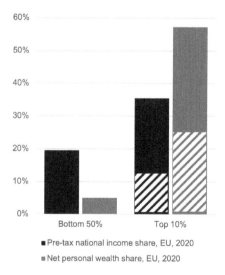

Note: The shaded area indicates the top 1%.
Source: World Inequality Database.

Figure 9.3   Wealth and income inequality in the European Union

Table 9.1 *Monetary aggregates in the euro area (end-2020, in € billion)*

	Base Money (M0)	Broad Money (M3)*	
Bank reserves (minimum and excess reserves)	3,513		
Currency in circulation (banknotes, coins)	1,435	1,359	M1
Overnight deposits		8,895	
Other short-term deposits			M2
Deposits with an agreed maturity of up to two years		1,041	
Deposits redeemable at notice of up to three months		2,448	
Marketable instruments			
Repurchase agreements		100	
Money market fund shares		649	
Debt securities issued with a maturity of up to two years		29	
Total	4,947	14,521	

Note: * Seasonally adjusted.
Source: ECB: consolidated financial statement of the Eurosystem (base money), monetary developments in the euro area (broad money).

5.8 percent and 5.1 percent, respectively, contributing to a substantial increase in absolute wealth inequality between households. This can exacerbate the perception of 'winners and losers' while the impact on relative indicators of inequality such as the Gini coefficient can be muted.[9] OT, on the other hand, would have no such extreme heterogeneous effects on absolute inequality.

It is widely recognized that expansionary monetary policy measures such as QE played an important role in supporting growth and employment in response to negative shocks and weakening demand. This does not mean, however, that there aren't other expansionary monetary policy options, such as OT, that could have achieved better results in a more equitable and less distortionary fashion. While the ratio of (commercially created) broad money[10] to (central bank-created) base money has collapsed in the aftermath of the financial crisis, the velocity of broad money has generally remained very stable except for a level shift at the beginning of the COVID-19 crisis due to the sudden fall in spending opportunities (Figure 9.1 and Table 9.1 provide an overview of monetary aggregates in the euro area). This indicates that the effect of a QE-driven expansion of base money on real activity has been limited, while providing households with purchasing power directly through direct transfers would likely lead them to increase their spending in line with their pre-existing preferences to save and consume in a mostly reopened economy. In the presence of an underutilization of resources, an increased broad money supply would have both real and price effects, such that the real demand for money increases.

A discussion of the drivers of the secular decline in real interest rates, including the role of central banks (Juselius et al., 2017), ultra-long-run trends (Schmelzing, 2020), or the retrenchment of more redistributive fiscal policies since the early 1980s, declining effective demand (Blanchard, 2021), and rising wealth inequality (Mian, Straub and Sufi, 2020) would go beyond the scope of this chapter.

It is clear, however, that the decline in interest rates has had very heterogeneous effects on the wealth of individual households, which has led to discontent among certain parts of the population, particularly in Northern European countries such as Germany where a commonly heard narrative has been the 'expropriation of the saver.' While it would not be fair to criticize central banks for pursuing a data-driven monetary policy stance, one could ask the legitimate question of whether central banks could have employed other expansionary monetary policy tools instead of pushing on an interest rate string at the ELB (cf. Bernanke, 2020; Brunnermeier and Koby, 2018). Not only is the effectiveness of the interest rate channel heavily impaired in a deep economic downturn when confidence is low and yields are depressed across the spectrum (Koo, 2011), it also creates new vulnerabilities through a potentially excessive increase in public and private debt. While not problematic per se if put to good use, such as investment in physical infrastructure or human capital that increases an economy's potential output, much of the newly created private debt does not finance productive investments. Instead, new debt issuance has increasingly been funding share buybacks and dividends on the corporate side (Mason, 2015) and mortgages for (mostly already existing) real estate on the household side (Turner, 2015a, p. 61ff.). Such lending does not necessarily create much economic value in aggregate but does drive up asset prices, inequality, and debt vulnerabilities. Sustaining aggregate demand in this way seems neither sustainable nor equitable over the long run (cf. Giraud and Grasselli, 2021; Mian, Straub and Sufi, 2021; Minsky, 1986).

3. MORE EFFECTIVE AND MORE EQUITABLE: OUTRIGHT TRANSFER (OT)

In contrast to QE and ultra-low/negative interest rates, OT would not only be more equitable by avoiding the negative side-effects on wealth inequality, direct transfers to households would also be more effective and positively affect rebalancing processes within currency unions and the global economy. Rather than relying on an increase of private and non-central bank public sector debt, OT would simultaneously expand base *and* broad money without creating new liabilities for firms, households, and governments.[11] OT would raise the real net private wealth of the private sector, thereby setting in motion a virtuous cycle of increased consumption and investment, higher capacity utilization, and greater confidence. This section will discuss macroeconomic and distributional aspects pertaining to OT, how it could be calibrated to achieve monetary policy objectives, and different methods of implementing

OT in practice. Accounting aspects and economic consequences of the corresponding newly created central bank liability will be analyzed in Sections 3.6 and 4, while Section 5 dives deeper into the differences between a debt- or money-financed fiscal stimulus.

3.1   Evidence from the MPC Literature, Survey Data, and Ricardian Considerations

The increase in disposable funds and purchasing power can be used by households to spend, save, or deleverage, depending on their financial position and marginal propensity to consume (MPC). It is reasonable to expect a household response that is similar to cash transfers from the government, as, for instance, implemented in the US in response to COVID-19 or the global financial crisis (GFC). Studies have shown that such lump-sum payments have had sizable impacts in economies hit by negative demand shocks.[12] In a seminal paper on the effect of the 2008 economic stimulus payments on household spending in the US, Parker et al. (2013) estimate an MPC of between 0.5 and 0.9 within the first two quarters of receipt, increasing further in the following months. In a natural experiment study based on an exogenous and unanticipated cash transfer in Singapore in 2011, Agarwal and Qian (2014) come to similar conclusions, detecting an MPC of 0.8 over the first ten months, which was mainly driven by the strong response of liquidity-constrained households.

The above-mentioned studies have focused on transfers from the fiscal authority, which typically involved an element of means testing. It is therefore instructive to also look at survey data on how transfers from the central bank would be perceived. According to Djuric and Neugart (2017), individuals would spend about 38 percent of a direct transfer from the central bank in the same period, use 19 percent to pay down debt, and save the rest, based on a representative panel of 5000 German households. Van Rooij and de Haan (2016) not only find comparable results for a representative panel of 2000 Dutch individuals, but also that direct transfers would be much more favorably perceived by the public than other monetary policy measures such as asset purchases or negative interest rates on saving accounts. Specifically, helicopter money would decrease trust in the ECB among 18 percent of the respondents while purchases of public and corporate debt or negative interest rates on saving accounts would decrease trust among 23 percent, 30 percent, and 50 percent, respectively. Similarly, a study by ING (2016) across 12 euro area countries and 12 000 participants suggests that 54 percent of survey respondents would perceive direct transfers favorably while only 14 percent would be skeptical.

Survey data does not suggest the presence of significant Ricardian effects but rather spending behavior that is comparable to empirical evidence from tax rebates or direct cash transfers from the government. Theoretically, this should not be surprising as the empirical evidence for Ricardian behavior by households in response to fiscal policy changes is not strong to begin with (Romer, 2009). Moreover, the associated public sector liability that arises from OT on the central bank balance sheet is not only more opaque and harder to understand for most households, but also a permanent one that in principle never has to be rolled over or repaid, akin to a perpetual bond that is remunerated at the prevailing short-term interest rate on excess reserves. The effectiveness of OT in $t = 0$ is irrespective of whether the central bank intends to keep the liability resulting from OT on its balance sheet forever, in which case it would either incur associated reserve remuneration costs or impose an implicit tax on the banking sector (cf. Section 4.5), or pay it down using future seigniorage. As discussed in detail in Section 5, unlike classical government debt, future servicing costs for the central bank would be *state dependent* and only arise if the policy measure actually achieves its intended purpose of boosting nominal GDP at the ELB, thereby alleviating potential Ricardian effects. The same holds true for a potential inflation tax on the private sector or an implicit tax on the banking sector.[13] Ricardian effects are further attenuated as the net present value (NPV) of future seigniorage itself is endogenous to whether and when OT is implemented (cf. Section 4.4).

Using a New Keynesian dynamic stochastic general equilibrium (DSGE) framework, Galí (2020) shows that even with fully Ricardian households, helicopter money (in the form of a money-financed tax cut) would have a positive effect on aggregate demand and welfare due to the presence of nominal price rigidities. As prices take time to adjust, private net wealth would increase in both nominal and real terms, leading to an increase in aggregate demand.[14]

Relatedly, Benigno and Fornaro (2018) show that an economy characterized by weak aggregate demand, involuntary unemployment, and pessimistic expectations about the future can be lifted out of such a 'stagnation trap' by aggressive policy interventions that shift growth expectations. Buiter (2014) formalizes how such an outcome can always be achieved through helicopter money in a theoretical model. Jorda, Singh and Taylor (2020) provide empirical evidence for the non-neutrality of monetary policy even over the long run due to hysteresis effects.

3.2   Positive Spillovers and Rebalancing

Beyond OT's immediate domestic effects, it also entails sizable positive spillovers to other economies within and outside a currency area, as part of the increase in domestic demand will go into imports of goods and services. It would thereby promote intra-currency area rebalancing processes as it would be most impactful in those parts of the country or currency union where macroeconomic policy support is needed most. While the effect on countries' current account balances is not clear-cut, OT would promote rebalancing in a broader economic sense by counteracting the divergence in real economic growth and competitiveness, which has been observed between many core and peripheral member countries since the adoption of the euro.

As households in regions that are hardest hit by a crisis are likely to have higher MPCs – for example, due to an increase in unemployment or other cash constraints – one can expect a larger share of the transfer to be spent in such regions, boosting regional demand.[15] In regions that are relatively less affected by an economic downturn, more of the transfer will be saved. Moreover, the part that is being spent would have a greater impact on nominal price and wage growth relative to regions with a larger negative output gap. These regions would in turn become more competitive, further supporting intra-currency area rebalancing. While this effect would be particularly pertinent in the euro area with its lack of a central fiscal capacity and corresponding automatic risk-sharing mechanisms, it also extends to other currency areas with heterogeneous regions hit by asymmetric shocks.[16]

In contrast, QE is a fairly blunt tool that depresses yields across a currency area, with the corresponding economic impulse from increased credit growth possibly being larger in those regions that are doing relatively well already due to a better growth outlook. Additionally, QE partly works through the exchange rate channel – that is, a depreciation-induced improvement of a currency area's current account. However, reliance on external demand and other countries' (more expansionary) policies is not a sustainable approach, especially for large currency areas, and can contribute to the widening of global imbalances.

The exchange rate effects of OT, on the other hand, are ambiguous. A strengthening economy, greater confidence, and higher interest rates would tend to attract capital inflows and lead to exchange rate appreciation while the monetary expansion could work in the opposite direction. In the euro area, OT would likely lead to a reduction of its current account surplus – in particular, in countries such as Germany where it has been significantly above a level that can be justified by fundamentals. By analogy, the current account deficit would widen in currency areas such as the US, where it has been negative to begin with.

3.3   Magnitude, Calibration, and Accounting

Like any other monetary policy instrument, OT would have to be employed judiciously, monitoring its effect on prices, output, and unemployment closely. As direct transfers could always be stepped up if need be, and given little practical experience, a cautious and gradual approach appears warranted.

While this chapter does not intend to provide a quantitative general equilibrium assessment of OT, a back-of-the-envelope calculation can indicate an approximate figure that is required to achieve a certain desired impulse to nominal GDP.[17]

As Table 9.2 illustrates, OT would be particularly effective in a depressed economy with cash-constrained households, characterized by a high multiplier and MPC. If policymakers in the euro area wanted to achieve a boost to nominal GDP of ca. 1 percent (€100 billion), this would require a transfer of ca. €460 to every adult citizen (ca. 270 million) under the baseline assumption of an MPC of 0.8 (over four quarters) and a multiplier of 1, which is at the lower end of the spectrum of fiscal multiplier estimates at the ELB.[18] If one wanted to include citizens under the age of 18 as well, the number of recipients would be around 340 million, reducing the individual transfer correspondingly to ca. €370. These numbers are very close to estimates by Renault and Savatier (2021) and an associated proposal by Martin et al. (2021), who reckon that a transfer of around 1 percent of GDP (or €385 per person, including children below the age of 15 with a weight of 50 percent) would be needed to generate a 1 percent boost to nominal GDP, half of which attributable to inflation. The estimate is also comparable to an early suggestions by Muellbauer (2014) to provide a transfer of €500 to each adult citizen in the euro area.

Table 9.2   *Required amount of OT to achieve €100 billion (ca. 1%) boost to euro area nominal GDP over four quarters*

| | | Total (in billion) | | | | | Per capita* | | |
		Multiplier					Multiplier		
		0.5	1	2			0.5	1	2
MPC	1	200	100	50	MPC	1	741	370	185
	0.8	250	125	63		0.8	926	463	231
	0.4	500	250	125		0.4	1852	926	463

Note: * Assumes 270 million eligible recipients, based on adult population.

In this example, the transfers would require a *permanent* increase in central bank money of around €125 billion, which amounts to less than 1.5 percent of the Eurosystem's October 15, 2021 balance sheet size of €8.337 trillion. It would also amount to about five times the Eurosystem's average yearly seigniorage of ca. €25 billion, meaning that all else equal, the reduction in central bank equity resulting from the newly created liability could be replenished within five years with the current annual level of seigniorage alone. Traditionally, seigniorage is largely transferred to the governments of member states according to their capital key but nothing prevents the ECB and the

Eurosystem's central banks from withholding seigniorage to strengthen their equity position, which has indeed been common practice in recent years in the form of increased risk provisioning.[19]

3.4 Distributional Considerations and Transfer Options

All monetary policy measures entail redistributive consequences of one sort or the other. Monetary policy should, however, strive to achieve its mandate as effectively as possible while minimizing the redistributive impact of its policies since active choices about redistribution should be undertaken by the government (cf. Section 6.2). Against this backdrop, OT appears more appropriate than alternative monetary policy measures at the ELB from both an economic and an institutional legitimacy perspective.[20]

Accordingly, direct transfers from the central bank should be distributed as equitably as possible. There are several dimensions to be considered by monetary policymakers when deciding on the potential recipients' eligibility criteria and relative magnitude of transfers.

3.4.1 Transfers of equal size

The most straightforward approach would be an equal absolute amount for every citizen, who are, after all, the ultimate 'owners' of the central bank. This is consistent with the notion of central bank money being a form of social equity as characterized by Allen et al. (2020). While equal in magnitude, direct transfers would nonetheless have an element of progressivity as they would reduce relative inequality. Moreover, the welfare effect on lower-income households would be higher due to the decreasing marginal utility of income. It would also be easy to introduce a further and more direct element of progressivity to equal transfers by taxing them at individuals' marginal tax rates according to the existing progressive national income tax schedule (as opposed to exempting them or taxing them at a flat capital income rate).[21]

3.4.2 Transfers according to capital key

A second approach that could be applied in the euro area would be to distinguish transfers across different member states according to their capital key, which is based on a country's population size and GDP in equal measure. Economically stronger countries would be allocated a relatively higher per capita OT share, which may be justified on the grounds of fairness due to the likewise generally higher cost of living in these countries and the ownership structure of the central bank.[22] Alternatively, transfers could be adjusted by national consumer price levels directly to reflect differences in the cost of living. While these approaches could make OT more equitable from a purchasing power perspective, it would attenuate the rebalancing effect of OT to a certain extent (see Section 3.2). It would also be more complex to communicate and may therefore result in lower public acceptance and risk political division. By analogy, it seems hard to imagine higher government-provided cash transfers going to richer states within one country such as the US.

3.4.3   Means-tested transfers

A third approach would be to distinguish transfers according to income level and phase them out beyond certain thresholds, similar to government-provided cash transfers. Such transfers could raise their efficacy (and thereby require a smaller overall amount of OT) as lower-income households have a higher MPC.[23] However, means-tested transfers would require a degree of cooperation from fiscal authorities and tax agencies to provide corresponding records, raising organizational and data privacy challenges. Moreover, while the reduction of excessive inequality is a desirable and important policy goal by itself to promote strong, sustainable, and inclusive growth,[24] fiscal policymakers are better placed and legitimized to undertake appropriate steps in the form of structural fiscal measures such as higher progressivity in the tax system and the provision of social security and public services. Against this backdrop, direct lump-sum transfers to households actually appear to be a more suitable policy tool for central banks than for governments, since the latter have a much wider array of tools to provide targeted support to the economy at their disposal.[25] Generally speaking, OT is not necessarily preferable to more targeted fiscal support at the ELB. OT should rather be considered in lieu of asset purchases if fiscal support is not forthcoming in sufficient ways, including to help achieve price stability objectives at the ELB, due to economic or political constraints, which loom particularly large in the euro area (see Section 5.5).

3.5   Practical Implementation

There are different ways in which OT can be implemented in practice within the existing institutional frameworks and financial market infrastructure. This subsection will outline the following potential options and some key operational aspects: checks, CBDCs, and perpetual targeted long-term refinancing operations (PTLTROs).

3.5.1   Checks and central bank-issued digital currencies (CBDCs)

The first option, and the one operationally most similar to government-provided cash transfers, would be to send out checks to every eligible recipient. Names and addresses could be obtained from publicly accessible electoral registers, circumventing fiscal authorities. Including minors would be more complex, but not unfeasible. Citizens can then deposit or cash these checks at any commercial bank, which in turn is credited the same amount in central bank money in the form of reserves upon delivering the check to the central bank.[26] The setup of a centralized digital register could allow the central bank to keep track of payments and prevent errors or fraud.[27] National or regional central banks' local branches, which have public cashiers' offices, could also be used to cash checks directly.

The introduction of a central bank digital currency, through which households could obtain direct access to central bank money, would greatly facilitate the delivery of direct transfers as it would obviate the need for commercial banks as intermediaries and allow the central bank to provide (and possibly withdraw) central bank money practically in real time (cf. Bateman and Allen, 2021; Bossone and Natarajan, 2020; Coronado and Potter, 2020a). However, it would give rise to other challenges related to a CBDC payments infrastructure and associated financial stability considerations that go beyond the scope of this chapter.[28]

3.5.2 Perpetual targeted long-term refinancing operations (PTLTRO)

A third option, perpetual targeted long-term refinancing operations (PTLTRO), has been proposed by Lonergan (2016). Its primary appeal would be that it could be easily implemented within current monetary policy frameworks by building on the existing established relationships and payments infrastructure between the central bank, commercial banks, and private households. Under PTLTRO, the central bank would provide perpetual zero-coupon loans to banks under the condition that loans of identical condition are passed on to households, akin to the current TLTRO setup in the euro area (see also Coronado and Potter, 2020b for a similar proposal for the US). Being administered through the banking system, this approach would not require much in terms of additional infrastructure, except for a centralized electronic loan register for monitoring purposes and to prevent abuse. Under this option, there may be the need for additional financial incentives for banks to act as intermediaries and to take on newly created reserves on their asset side, which would initially not be or negatively remunerated due to the economy being at the ELB. Banks could, for instance, be incentivized by a commission or administration fee, capped by the central bank at a few basis points (bps), which would be deducted from the loan up-front before it is extended to households. After liftoff from the ELB, different scenarios for reserve remuneration, including higher non-remunerated minimum reserves, are imaginable to preserve central bank policy solvency and will be discussed in Section 4.5.

3.6   Accounting for OT on the Central Bank Balance Sheet

OT creates a new liability in the form of reserves. This liability is perpetual by nature as no corresponding interest-bearing asset is acquired that could be sold to reduce the reserves again.[29]

To balance its books, the central bank can either book an instantaneous loss to equity, potentially leading to a negative equity position, or create a new matching but not interest-bearing asset – for example, related to PTLTRO and covered by future seigniorage gains. While booking such a deferred asset has been common practice at the Federal Reserve Bank of New York (Carpenter et al., 2013), a perpetual zero-coupon bond would have to be valued at its mark-to-market value of zero according to standard accounting rules and best practices regarding central bank transparency. As Stella (2002), Dziobek and Dalton (2005), and the IMF (2020) stress, adherence to prudent accounting standards is key for central banks' credibility. In effect, the central bank can therefore not circumvent recognizing a loss to its equity following OT. That being said, it could still find booking a corresponding asset preferable to a negative equity position as it creates a standalone position on the balance sheet that can be easily traced over time and may facilitate communication with the public (Figure 9.4).

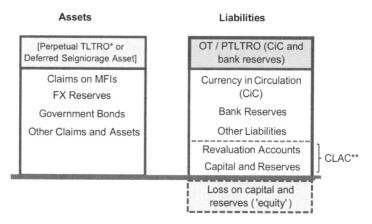

Note: * TLTRO: targeted longer-term refinancing operation; ** CLAC: conventional loss-absorption capacity; MFI: monetary financial institutions; FX: foreign exchange.

Figure 9.4   *Stylized central bank balance sheet after OT*

For commercial banks, OT would cause a balance sheet extension as both deposits and reserves would increase by the same amount (Figure 9.5). While the effect on banks' income position would be broadly neutral initially, this could change over time subject to interest rate dynamics and central banks' policy choices regarding reserve remuneration (see Section 4.5).

For households, OT – implemented through either checks or PTLTRO – would lead to an increase in net wealth for each individual citizen in equal magnitude, corresponding to the decrease in the central bank's net wealth.

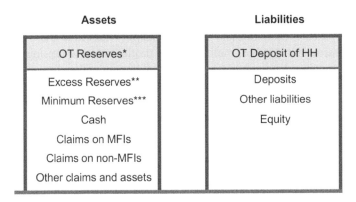

Note: * Remunerated at the policy rate on deposits or the rate on minimum reserves (policy choice by central bank to adjust reserve requirements upwards); ** remunerated at the policy rate on deposits (unless exempted due to tiering); *** remunerated at the rate on minimum reserves; HH: households.

Figure 9.5   Stylized commercial bank balance sheet after OT

This stands in stark difference to QE, which does not alter the net wealth of either sector mechanically but only through second-round price effects, that impact individual households very differently.

Going forward, the central bank could choose to keep the negative equity position or the matching asset on its balance sheet indefinitely as it would not impinge on the central bank's ability to control inflation for moderate amounts of OT (see Section 4). Alternatively, it could choose to reduce its overall liabilities and thereby its outstanding stock of base money through the sale of other existing assets. Future policymakers could also opt to eliminate the OT liability entirely over time using future seigniorage, which would involve choices over the intertemporal distribution of seigniorage.[30]

Taking the ECB as an example, Article 33 of its Statute lays out provisions for the allocation of net profits and losses, which is determined by the

Governing Council: 'In the event of a loss incurred by the ECB, the shortfall may be offset against the general reserve fund of the ECB and, if necessary, following a decision by the Governing Council, against the monetary income of the relevant financial year.' While the Statute is not explicit regarding losses that cannot be covered in a given year, the ECB has clarified that such losses would be offset with future income from seigniorage.[31] This is similar to the legal provisions at the Federal Reserve where realized losses would be booked as a deferred asset and lead to a suspension of remittances to the Treasury until the loss has been recouped with future earnings.[32]

As Buiter (2020b) has pointed out, the particular setup of the profit/loss sharing arrangement of the ECB and the Eurosystem's national central banks inherently creates economic and political instability risks from QE. This is due to the agreement that only a small part of the profits and losses arising from QE operations, which have led to concentrated holdings of national sovereign debt by individual national central banks, would be shared across different national central banks.[33] This problem would be obviated by OT, which would pool risks across the currency union (Section 5.4).

4.   CENTRAL BANK POLICY SOLVENCY CONSIDERATIONS

This section will discuss aspects related to the impact of OT on the strength of the central bank balance sheet and potential risks to central bank policy solvency. These risks are not germane to OT per se but similarly apply to QE.

4.1   Negative Central Bank Equity and Policy Solvency from a Theoretical Perspective

While a central bank that issues its own currency can never become financially insolvent as its liabilities can always be serviced, a sufficiently strong central bank balance sheet is nevertheless important to preserve policy solvency – that is, the central bank's ability to independently control inflation.[34] In the case of the Eurosystem's corridor system, where the interbank rate is closely tied to the deposit rate in the presence of large excess reserves, the ECB would have to raise the deposit rate on excess reserves in line with the main refinancing rate and incur the associated remuneration costs.

To preserve policy solvency over the medium term, a central bank needs to be able to cover its operational costs and the costs from its monetary policy operations – that is, the payment of interest on reserves, through its seigniorage profits (cf. Del Negro and Sims, 2015; Hall and Reis, 2015). Otherwise, it would be forced to meet its obligations by printing new central bank money, which may prevent it from running a sufficiently contractionary monetary policy. While there is no precise tipping point beyond which a central bank loses its policy solvency, its balance sheet strength can provide some orientation. The strength of the central bank's balance sheet can generally be assessed by estimating its capacity to absorb losses, which depends both on its current structure and assumptions about its future evolution.

Accordingly, negative central bank equity does not present a danger to policy solvency per se but only at unsustainable levels that would give rise to an explosive negative central bank equity path (cf. Stella, 1997). Reis (2016, pp. 36–7) derives a theoretical intertemporal solvency constraint, which illustrates the conditions under which a central bank can retain its policy solvency even in the face of large negative equity (or an equivalent deferred asset). It should be noted though that policy solvency also depends on much harder-to-gauge factors such as the public's confidence in the currency and expectations regarding the future path of monetary policy. To preserve the public's trust and safeguard its credibility, central banks should therefore always strive to maintain strong balance sheets that provide a large margin of safety to their loss-absorption capacities. In the extreme, the loss of confidence in a currency could lead to a currency crisis characterized by large-scale capital flight, rapid depreciation, and subsequent higher inflation due to increased import prices and domestic wage push inflation. However, this is not a realistic scenario under any reasonable calibration of OT in reserve currency-issuing economies with strong institutions such as the euro area.

4.2 Assessing a Central Bank's Loss-Absorption Capacity

This subsection illustrates the assessment of a central bank's capacity to absorb losses by zooming in on the Eurosystem's balance sheet.

Following the approach of Buiter and Rahbari (2012), the Eurosystem's consolidated *conventional loss-absorption capacity* (CLAC) stood at around €622 billion as of end-2020. The CLAC consists of capital and reserves (€109 billion) as well as revaluation accounts (€512 billion), which constitute unrealized gains on gold, foreign-exchange reserves, and securities. The Eurosystem's consolidated *non-inflationary loss-absorption capacity* (NILAC), which additionally includes the outstanding stock of currency in circulation and discounted future seigniorage gains, is a multiple of the CLAC. Using conservative and non-explosive assumptions for annual seigniorage growth (1 percent) and the discount rate (2 percent in line with target inflation), the NPV of future seigniorage, which in 2020 stood at around €25 billion, amounts to around €4.5 trillion (Figure 9.6). This NILAC/CLAC ratio of around seven is very close to estimates by Buiter and Rahbari (2012).

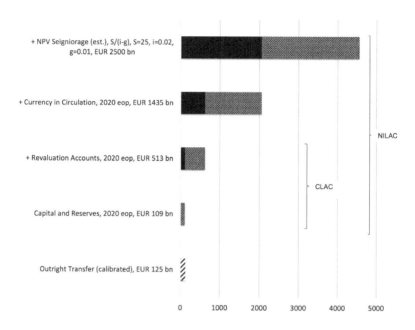

Note: eop: end of period; dotted shading indicates share of capital and reserves in the CLAC; hatched shading indicates OT.
Source: Haver, ECB, own calculations.

Figure 9.6   *Eurosystem non-inflationary loss-absorption capacity (NILAC)*

4.3   Negative Central Bank Equity and Policy Solvency from an Empirical Perspective

While unproblematic at moderate levels, negative central bank equity can pose risks to the central bank's policy solvency if it approaches or even exceeds the central bank's NILAC. In such a situation, absent a recapitalization through the fiscal authorities, this could lead to a loss of confidence in the central bank to control inflation, excessive money growth, and eventually a currency crisis (cf. Stella, 2008).

While there are well-known examples of central banks losing policy solvency due to excessive monetary financing and the subsequent deterioration of central bank balance sheets such as the Weimar Republic or Zimbabwe and Venezuela more recently, there are also plenty of examples of prudent central banks operating with negative central bank equity for prolonged periods of time without negative repercussions on their ability to control inflation, preserve a stable currency, or maintain credibility among the general public. Prominent examples include Chile, Israel, or the Czech Republic (cf. Benecka et al., 2012). Ryan-Collins (2015) provides a case study of Canada that pursued close monetary–fiscal cooperation between 1935 and 1975 without concomitant high inflation.

A less well-known case is post-World War II Germany, where its central bank[35] effectively operated with negative central bank equity throughout many years in the first decades of its existence (Bibow, 2018). This was due to the costs associated with the currency reform of 1948, including costs for the recapitalization of commercial banks after the war. In later years, the appreciation of the Deutsche Mark following the end of the Bretton Woods system in 1971 gave rise to large FX valuation losses. Accounting-wise, to avoid an outright negative equity position, a claim on the government was booked on the asset side of the balance sheet, the so-called '*Sonderposten Ausgleichsforderungen*' (broadly translating to 'special item: equalizing claim'), that has been remunerated with 1 percent p.a. and remained on the Bundesbank's balance sheet up to this day, with amortization slated to begin in 2024.[36] This approach was repeated by the Bundesbank in 1990 following the reunification of West and East Germany. Although the informal market exchange rate had been around 8 Eastern German Mark per Western German Deutsche Mark, Eastern German households were allowed to exchange their currency at much more favorable official rates of 1 up to a fixed amount and at a rate of 2 beyond that for political reasons (Zinsmeister, 2009), contributing to an increase in the money supply and inflation as a result of the skewed conversion rates. The associated costs to the Bundesbank's balance sheet were assumed by the German government through another special item on its asset side, the so-called '*Ausgleichsfonds Währungsumstellung*' (broadly translating to 'equalization fund currency conversion'), which amounted to ca. €30 billion in 1994.

Above examples, including that of Deutsche Bundesbank as a paragon of monetary stability, illustrate that negative central bank equity is no issue per se for central bank policy solvency at moderate levels. Rather, it is the strength of institutions and monetary policy frameworks that matters, which allows central banks to independently pursue an appropriately tight (or loose) monetary policy stance. These findings are corroborated by Bindseil, Manzanares and Weller (2004), who show that negative central bank equity at varying levels does not impinge on central banks' abilities to control interest rates. However, they also caution that maintaining a strong balance sheet position remains generally advisable for political economy reasons. A weak equity position could weaken a central bank's perceived independence or entice the central bank to pursue looser policies than warranted in an attempt to shore up profitability. Empirical analysis by Adler, Castro and Tovar (2016) suggests a negative link between a central bank's financial strength and its performance in controlling inflation, although a meta-analysis of the literature by Hampl and Havranek (2018) indicates that this nexus is not particularly strong. Benecka et al. (2012) detect the presence of strong non-linearities, with results driven by financially very weak outliers.

4.4   OT vs QE Effects on Balance Sheet Strength, Seigniorage, and Ease of Exit

While OT would be highly effective in lifting an economy out of a low growth and inflation equilibrium, a cautious approach in employing OT is warranted as it creates an unmatched liability for the central bank and a corresponding instantaneous reduction in central bank equity. However, as OT in the magnitude suggested in Section 3.3 would only constitute a small fraction of the NILAC, the expected losses on equity resulting from the newly created and unmatched reserves would not present material risks to policy solvency.

At the same time, this also underscores why OT should be strictly limited to exceptional circumstances in the current fractional reserve banking system.[37] These circumstances arise when other more traditional monetary policy levers have been exhausted (see Section 2) and fiscal policy is either economically or politically incapable of providing the needed support to an economy that is operating with spare capacity at below-target inflation.

It should be noted that the long-term general equilibrium effects of OT on the strength of the central bank's balance sheet could well be positive as it would contribute to a faster economic recovery, higher growth in real money demand, and ultimately greater seigniorage. Future seigniorage is endogenous to monetary policy operations and difficult to forecast as it depends on a host of different factors. In 'normal' pre-crisis times with full allotment and little excess reserves, seigniorage tends to increase with nominal GDP growth as money demand grows and the interest rate differential between a central bank's assets and its monetary base, remunerated at zero (currency in circulation) and the short-term policy rate (reserves), is strictly positive for an upward-sloping yield curve. While OT would lead to a more direct reduction of central bank equity up-front, it is therefore not clear a priori whether it would outweigh the costs and risks of large-scale asset purchases in terms of the expected NPV of future seigniorage for a given desired amount of monetary stimulus.[38]

QE not only exposes the central bank to a potential increase in excess reserve remuneration costs but also to mark-to-market losses on the central bank's assets. While the cost to the central bank of OT is more direct and transparent as no corresponding asset is acquired, the cost of QE is more akin to a contingent liability, which may or may not be greater than that of OT in NPV terms for a similar monetary policy impulse on inflation. As inflation and bond yields pick up, the central bank would either have to sell assets acquired under QE at a loss – which it may be pressured to do to absorb excess liquidity – or incur mark-to-market losses if it chooses to hold on to its assets temporarily or until maturity. These mark-to-market losses – which would be reflected in the central bank's annual financial statement according to standard accounting practices – would be amplified by actual losses from a more adverse interest rate differential between its assets and liabilities, if liabilities are remunerated at the policy rate. The central bank therefore faces a much larger interest rate risk under QE than under OT, making exiting from it more difficult.

Figure 9.7 illustrates the potential losses to the Eurosystem's balance sheet that may arise from OT and QE, both calibrated to have the same expected impulse on nominal GDP in year 1 following an increase in the deposit rate from its current level of –0.5 percent. Based on the calculations in Section 3.3, the example assumes that €125 billion of direct transfers would be needed to provide a 1 percent boost to nominal GDP. It is not straightforward to derive the equivalent amount of QE needed to achieve a similar effect on nominal GDP as estimates in the literature vary a lot across time, countries, and researchers (Fabo et al., 2020), with interest rate policy and QE becoming increasingly ineffective as interest rates fall and the yield curve flattens (Bernanke, 2020; Brunnermeier and Koby, 2018; Gopinath, 2021). Agur et al. (2022) provide empirical estimates regarding the effectiveness of an expansion of the monetary base on inflation, finding that the nexus is very weak and potentially insignificant when inflation is low, central bank independence is high, and fiscal deficits are small. This precisely describes the circumstances laid out in this chapter under which OT should be considered. Against this backdrop, and informed by the literature on the actual and expected effectiveness of QE (cf. Dell'Ariccia, Rabanal and Sandri, 2018; Hutchinson and Smets, 2017), the example conservatively assumes required asset purchases of €1500 billion, around 15 percent of GDP, to achieve a 1 percent impulse to nominal GDP.[39] The associated central bank balance sheet expansion is more than an order of magnitude higher than under OT, underscoring that due to its much more direct transmission, OT can achieve the central bank's monetary policy goal(s) much more effectively.

In order to gauge the potential valuation losses from a rise in interest rates, it assumes that the acquired assets have a weighted average maturity of 8 years and an average return of 0 percent, similar to the ECB's actual portfolio. The example further assumes that these are zero-coupon bonds, such that their duration is equal to the weighted average maturity, and a parallel shift of the yield curve following an increase in the deposit rate by the same amount. Moreover, no reserve tiering or new net asset purchases are assumed. While this is a highly stylized example, it nevertheless allows us to visualize some key differences in the costs of OT and QE. Under OT, an upfront non-recurring loss of €125 billion would be incurred, with recurring reserve remuneration costs being fairly small for all deposit rate increase scenarios, ranging from €–0.6 billion p.a. for a negative deposit rate of –0.5 percent and €3.1 billion p.a. for a deposit rate of 2.5 percent. Under QE, these effects are reversed. Although there is no upfront cost to QE, it exposes the central bank to large interest rate risks through both reserve remuneration expenditures, with costs ranging from €–7.5 billion p.a. to €37.5 billion p.a., and (one-off) valuation losses ranging from €0 billion to €316 billion. While valuation losses may not have to be realized if assets are held until maturity, they would nonetheless have to be booked against the central bank's revaluation accounts or even its equity.

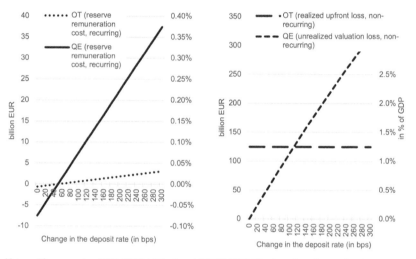

Note: The amounts of OT (€125 billion) and QE (€1500 billion) are based on estimates to achieve a stimulus to nominal GDP of €100 billion (around 1% of GDP). The starting deposit rate is assumed to be –0.5%. See text for details and assumptions.

Figure 9.7   *Stylized costs of OT and QE following an increase in interest rates: recurring (left panel) and non-recurring (right panel)*

From a risk–return perspective, OT may therefore be preferable to QE as it is more costly up-front, but less costly and risky down the road. This tradeoff, inter alia, depends on the shape of the yield curve and the associated amount of asset purchases needed to achieve a certain level of stimulus. With OT being easier to calibrate to the desired level of stimulus, it has the additional advantage of being more transparent and predictable in its consequences for the balance sheet. Future research could undertake a more comprehensive comparison that assesses the efficacy of OT vs QE in a dynamic setting that takes into account the position in the business cycle, the level and shape of the yield curve, as well as other potentially relevant circumstances.

It should be noted that the maximization of profits – or minimization of losses – is not a policy objective of the central bank by itself. However, the above profit–loss considerations are relevant in so far as they may impact the conduct of monetary policy. The following section will discuss central banks' options to preserve policy solvency, including potential reserve requirement and remuneration policies.

4.5   Preserving Central Bank Policy Solvency: the Role of Reserve Requirements and Remuneration

In principle, if an overheating economy warrants monetary tightening, central banks can start by adjusting their forward guidance and reducing the size of their balance sheet through open-market operations – that is, by mopping up excess liquidity through selling the assets they have acquired over the past years, which would induce a steepening of the yield curve.[40] Central banks can also raise deposit and lending rates to further shift up rates at the short end of the yield curve. While this would curb inflation, it would also create large costs for central banks given the expansion of central bank balance sheets, which is unlikely to be unwound significantly anytime soon (see Section 5.3).

To preserve both policy solvency and the health of its balance sheet, central banks could in principle tier reserve remuneration rates in an upswing to achieve a sufficiently high effective policy rate without incurring high reserve remuneration costs. This would be analogous to the tiering of deposit rates at the ELB currently pursued by the ECB, which is partially offsetting the costs of negative interest rates for banks and supporting their profitability.[41]

Such tiering would allow for newly created reserves to be remunerated at zero or any level below the desired policy rate (see also Figures 9.4 and 9.5). However, this would require adjusting minimum reserve requirements (MRRs) upwards to cover these reserves to anchor interbank rates close to the main deposit rate on excess reserves.[42] As excess reserves are reduced over time, the interbank rate would start trending closer to the main lending rate again. It would be the central bank's prerogative to remunerate either all minimum reserves or just the fraction that is attributable to OT at below its policy rate. Figure 9.8 shows the corridor of past policy rates in the euro area and illustrates a hypothetical path forward under a scenario, in which policy rates are gradually raised, excess reserves reduced, and minimum reserves remunerated at the main refinancing rate or zero, whichever is lower.

The practice of actively using reserve requirements – and their (non-) remuneration – as a policy tool has gone out of fashion at advanced economies' central banks in favor of open-market operations since the early 1980s, while they still play a prominent role in emerging market economies such as China.[43] Given large legacy central bank balance sheets and excess reserves in advanced economies, the approach of forgoing this monetary policy tool may need to be reconsidered to find the best policy mix to remove tail-risks to central bank policy solvency and to deal with potential above-target inflationary pressures in the macroeonomically least disruptive manner.[44]

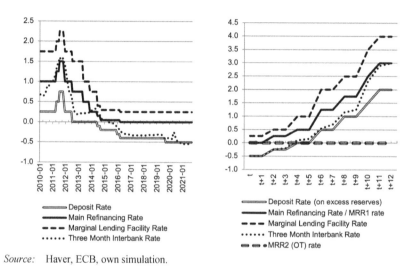

Source: Haver, ECB, own simulation.

Figure 9.8   *Interest rate corridor in the euro area: past (left panel) and hypothetical future path under OT (right panel) (%)*

Naturally, the benefits of actively using reserve requirement and remuneration policies must be weighed against their costs, foremost the tax that it imposes on the banking sector. Such a tax, akin to financial repression, cannot be avoided but could theoretically be passed on to banks' customers (similar to current negative deposit rates). However, this would be a feature, not a bug, as it would amplify the desired contractionary effect.[45]

Moreover, given that the ECB's current tiering and TLTRO III system provide substantial implicit transfers to banks of what would otherwise have been seigniorage gains accruing to the general public, it is hard to argue that the tiering of reserves in the opposite direction during the recovery phase should not be permissible. This may also be justifiable due to the favorable treatment of banks with regard to other private sector firms, be it through the right to originate money through credit, implicit subsidies from government guarantees, or by being exempted from sales/value-added taxes in the provision of financial services.[46]

A solvent fiscal authority could, of course, always choose to recapitalize the central bank on its own volition, obviating the need for tiering. However, this may not be realistic or feasible for several reasons (see Section 5). OT and tiering would thereby expand options to smooth the intertemporal consolidated budget constraint of the state including both the central bank and fiscal entities.[47] Over time, excess reserves would decline organically as nominal GDP and demand for money and required reserves increase. Additionally, using seigniorage to reduce any negative central bank equity position resulting from OT or QE would reduce reserves by an equivalent amount.

Naturally, the introduction of active reserve requirement and remuneration policies cannot be looked at in isolation. After all, the banking sector would be in a much better position to absorb associated costs in a cyclical upswing, which had been enabled and supported by the central bank's policies (QE and/ or OT) in the first place. Such an upswing would bring about higher credit volumes, lower non-performing loan ratios, increased net interest margins due to a steepening of the yield curve and a corresponding increase in profits from maturity transformation. The net effect on bank profitability – and financial stability – may therefore well be positive from a general equilibrium perspective depending on the extent and calibration of the reserve tiering. While a comprehensive general equilibrium cost–benefit analysis is beyond the scope of the chapter, future research into the tradeoffs involved with actively employing reserve requirement policies with regard to other policy choices could provide valuable insights.

As OT would create much fewer new reserves than QE to achieve the same impact on inflation, the costs to the banking sector associated with the tiering of reserves would be far smaller (see Figure 9.7), underscoring the advantages of OT over QE also over the medium run with a view to the unwinding of expansionary monetary policy stances. For instance, the creation of €125 billion in OT would – if fully tiered – create an annual cost to the banking sector of only €2.5 billion for an interest rate differential between required and excess reserves of 200 bps. This would be significantly lower than forgone seigniorage revenue from the current tiering system for excess reserves remuneration, which had lowered Eurosystem banks' interest rate expenditures on excess reserves by close to €5 billion between October 2019 and December 2020 (Deutsche Bundesbank, 2021). It would also be far below the forgone seigniorage revenue from lending below the policy rate under TLTRO III, where direct transfers from the Eurosystem's central banks to its commercial banks could amount to an annual subsidy of around €11 billion for an outstanding volume of €2.2 trillion and an interest rate differential of 50 bps if all banks satisfy the lending target (Da Silva et al., 2021).

In conclusion, while it is highly unlikely that central bank policy solvency would be at risk for moderate levels of negative central bank equity that are well below a central bank's NILAC, this risk can be addressed by the judicious tiering of reserves if need be. Tiering might be desirable to increase central bank equity faster to rebuild central bank policy space. It would also allow the central bank to avoid any potential explosive dynamics if negative central bank equity increases to unsustainably high levels. However, the central bank should remain mindful of the costs that tiering would impose on the banking sector and/or bank customers. Policy solvency is therefore a policy choice of the central bank for moderate levels of negative central bank equity.

4.6   A More Active Role for Fiscal and Structural Policies to Support Price Stability Objectives

Generally speaking, there can be other policies outside the control of the central bank that would be more effective in curbing inflationary pressures than raising interest rates, selling assets, or raising reserve requirements, which tend to be rather blunt tools that all come with individual drawbacks. For instance, in the current environment it could be argued that interest rate hikes might not be the best tool to curb inflation if price pressures are primarily driven by non-monetary factors such as supply chain disruptions, real private and public underinvestment, corporate market power, pandemic-related sectoral reallocations from services to goods, one-off fiscal support measures, or trade barriers, and regulations. To safeguard stable prices in the least disruptive manner to the economy, the employment of fiscal and structural policies to reduce inflationary pressures and increase potential output might be more growth-friendly and equitable.

For instance, the semiconductor shortage, which had large knock-on effects on the price of cars and consumer goods in 2021, was, inter alia, attributable to high and rising demand from cryptocurrency mining, drawing scarce global real resources away from productive and welfare-enhancing activities and eventually leading authorities in several countries to ban cryptocurrency mining outright. Another example is imputed rents from owner-occupied housing, which have risen markedly in line with higher housing prices. Expanding housing supply and/or tightening macroprudential policy tools while exempting first-time home buyers could dampen price pressures and improve affordability for large parts of the population. Over the medium term, targeted public policies that promote an efficient allocation of resources, competition, innovation, and strategic investments to address supply-side bottlenecks or market failures can both boost growth and dampen price pressures (cf. Hasanov and Cherif, 2019).

In the case of an economy where 'too much money is chasing too few goods,' fiscal policy can play an important role in curbing excessive inflationary pressures by reducing purchasing power – and removing money from circulation – through levying higher taxes and paying down debt. While progressive taxation reduces the disinflationary impact due to high-income earners' lower MPC, it could nonetheless be desirable to ensure fair burden sharing. On the spending side, containing current expenditures on items with a low multiplier could likewise attenuate inflationary pressures without strong adverse effects on growth.

In line with the fiscal theory of the price level (FTPL), similar to how expansionary fiscal policy (or OT) would help to achieve price stability objectives at the ELB, a contractionary fiscal policy should do so in an over-heating economy. The optimal mix of fiscal, structural, and monetary policies should take the tradeoffs involved with either into account, informed by country-specific circumstances.

5. DISTINCT DIFFERENCES BETWEEN DEBT-FINANCED FISCAL STIMULUS AND MONETARY FINANCING

While it has been argued that OT would be equivalent to the issuance of short-term government debt from a consolidated public sector balance sheet perspective,[48] this argument does not stand up to closer scrutiny. This section provides an overview of a number of important but often overlooked differences between central bank-issued liabilities and government-issued debt, summarized in Table 9.3.

5.1 A State-contingent and Perpetual Liability

As described in the preceding sections, OT would create a long-term liability for the central bank – and thereby the public sector – that would traditionally be remunerated at the short-term deposit rate on excess reserves. As central banks set the policy rate based on price developments, the rate at which the OT liability would be remunerated is *state-contingent* in contrast to short-term debt issued by the government. While the short-term rate a government faces is usually closely tied to economic developments and the central bank's policy rate, there may be large deviations – in particular, in a currency union in times of crisis – when the interest rate paid on short-term debt can vary considerably across different countries and be substantially higher than the deposit rate on reserves. The central bank will therefore only find itself in the situation of (potentially) having to remunerate the newly created reserves if they actually had their intended effect – that is, a rise in nominal GDP driven by a mix of

Table 9.3   *Differences between OT, QE, and a debt- or money-financed fiscal stimulus*

	OT	QE	Permanent QE	Money-financed Fiscal Stimulus	Debt-financed Fiscal Stimulus
State-contingent liability	x	x	x	x	Not usually
Perpetual liability / no rollover risk	x		x	x	Not usually
Direct and significant effect on real economic activity and consumer prices	x	x	x	x	x
Can be employed rapidly	x	x	x	May require lengthy coordination	x
Not subject to fiscal rules	x	x	x		
Does not require fiscal cooperation or ability/willingness to support economy	x	x	x		
Can be employed irrespective of fiscal space/market access	x	x	x	x	
Does not violate monetary financing prohibition/taboo	x	Under certain limits			x
Does not give rise to fiscal dominance risks	Not for moderate amounts	Not for moderate amounts	x	x	Not for moderate amounts
Does not create an unmatched liability for the central bank		x			x
Does not give rise to central bank solvency concerns	Depends (i.a. on amount)	Depends (i.a. on amount)	Depends (i.a. on amount)	Depends (i.a. on amount)	x
Currency union specific (no or very limited central fiscal capacity)					
Improves risk-sharing in a currency union	x	To a limited extent	To a limited extent	Depends	
Contributes to intra-currency area rebalancing	x	To a limited extent	To a limited extent	Depends	
Contributes to external rebalancing	x	Depends (demand vs. exchange rate)	Depends (demand vs. exchange rate)	x	Depends
Can be implemented at the country level					x

Note: i.a.: inter alia.

higher real economic activity and inflation. This makes OT liabilities much more akin to a perpetual GDP-linked bonds or floating rate consol than to short-term government debt with fixed coupons and maturity. Although increased issuance of perpetual and potentially GDP-linked government debt would indeed be economically desirable (cf. Soros, 2020), historically, much higher long-term interest rates may have prevented the emergence of such markets. Moreover, the issuance of longer-dated or even perpetual debt is often being complicated by myopic public debt management strategies that display a bias towards issuing short-term debt, which – while cheaper in the short run – exposes a country to interest rate and rollover risks in the future (*The Economist*, 2020). Although improvements to the type and maturity structure of public liabilities could be made irrespective of the presence of OT, OT would help to diversify the composition of the consolidated public sector's liabilities.

As Turner (2015b) shows, the state-dependent character of OT liabilities renders OT fully effective even in the presence of fully Ricardian households.[49] Beyond the state dependency of the newly created liability, central banks' control over the way reserves are remunerated is another important distinction to short-term government debt (see Section 4.5).

Besides a principal that never has to be repaid, interest payments on the OT liability are made in central bank money, another distinguishing feature of government debt. Accordingly, OT liabilities do not face any *rollover risk* and are not exposed to speculative attacks or sudden stops, something experienced by several European countries at the height of the euro crisis (cf. Krogulski, Korczak and Bakker, 2019).[50]

It should be noted, however, that just like other expansionary policies, OT faces an inflation or real resource constraint, based on the economy's real production capacities.[51] At the same time, future contributions to base money growth from interest payments on OT reserves would be small and could be sterilized at the discretion of the central bank.

5.2   Differences Between OT and Money-financed Fiscal Stimulus

Cecchetti and Schoenholtz (2016), among others, have argued that direct transfers from the central bank would be equivalent to a money-financed fiscal stimulus of equal magnitude. Despite some obvious similarities, this is an oversimplistic and incorrect assertion.

First, it neglects the legal and institutional context under which central banks in advanced economies operate, which – in the case of the euro area – explicitly prohibit monetary financing while OT could potentially be implemented within existing institutional frameworks (see Section 6.3 for a discussion of associated legal complexities). Indeed, a different treatment appears justified as the political economy implications and fiscal dominance risks are quite different (see Section 5.3).

Second, although acquired government bonds could theoretically be held on the central bank's balance sheet indefinitely (similar to the quasi-permanent nature of OT), there may be political or legal pressures to reduce the stock of government debt held by the central bank after a crisis. Anticipating such unwinding and future contractionary effects, the effect of a money-financed fiscal stimulus on the spending patterns of households and firms may be smaller than an OT operation of equal magnitude.[52]

Third, while OT could be implemented instantaneously by the central bank with the appropriate technical infrastructure in place (see Section 3.5), a money-financed fiscal stimulus – even if legal – would raise complex coordination issues – in particular, in a currency union with many member states – and be subject to considerable time lags.

Fourth, the risk of fiscal inaction, implementation lags, and pro-cyclicality, which has been a commonly observed feature of fiscal policy across many countries (Fatás, 2019), is a major part of the *raison d'être* for OT in the first place. So, while OT may be a useful addition to the monetary policy toolkit even in the presence of appropriate fiscal policy due to its unique characteristics as described in this chapter, the biggest argument for its introduction would be overcoming fiscal policy inadequacies in the pursuit of macroeconomic stability through a rapid and data-driven mechanism. In the case of the euro area, the pursuit of optimal fiscal policy is further constrained by outdated and suboptimal fiscal rules (see Section 5.5).

5.3   OT Reduces Risks of Fiscal Dominance and Enables Faster Liftoff from the ELB

With central banks holding large amounts of government bonds on their balance sheets as a result of different asset purchase programs,[53] central banks will face difficult choices regarding whether, when, and how fast these holdings should be unwound in the future. While central bank officials have been stressing that this will be guided by macroeconomic conditions, debt sustainability and broader economic stability considerations will inevitably factor into these decisions – in particular, with a view to countries where elevated debt-to-GDP ratios will not be sustainable under a less favorable $r - g$ differential. These debt sustainability considerations extend beyond their macroeconomic and fiscal dimension to central banks' balance sheets, which would be directly exposed to large losses in the case of a currency union member's default. It remains to be seen how the ECB will deal with this challenge, including the requirement imposed by the European Court of Justice (ECJ) that government bond purchases by the ECB are only permissible under the Treaty on the Functioning of the European Union (TFEU) as long as these are strictly temporary in nature (Mersch, 2020). It is clear, however, that the de facto scope to raise interest rates to counter inflationary pressures is constrained by the extent to which high and rising government debt is held by the central bank as also expressed by the House of Lords (2021). If central banks had chosen to employ OT rather than QE in the past, these fiscal dominance risks and exit challenges would pose much less of a challenge now and going forward. In the future, a switch from QE towards OT could help to prevent the build-up of associated risks further.

By the same token, OT would actually present the 'drawback' that the more rapid liftoff from the ELB would obviate the need for purchases of government debt, thereby potentially driving up government yields and leading to faster mark-to-market losses for existing assets on central banks' balance sheets than would otherwise have occurred. If policymakers wanted to remedy this drawback, OT could in theory be combined with a type of yield curve control (YCC) to support (nominal) debt sustainability without the need for continued large asset purchases.[54] And naturally, the central bank should continue to fulfill its lender-of-last-resort function in response to liquidity risks or speculative attacks.

It is beyond the scope of this chapter to discuss strategies to address debt overhang and solvency risks in detail. Beyond what is achievable through higher real GDP growth, it is largely a distributional issue to be determined by public choice between higher taxes, lower expenditures, inflation, financial repression, and – if need be – outright debt restructuring or reprofiling. As certain combinations are better suited to ensuring a strong, equitable, and green recovery from the crisis, these choices should be informed by the large body of literature on the growth and distributional effects of different measures. In any case, the distributional choices that are required to ensure debt sustainability should be taken through the political process and not indirectly by central banks through their balance sheet operations.

5.4   OT Improves Risk-Sharing in a Currency Union Without a Central Fiscal Capacity

OT constitutes a liability that is shared across a currency area. This may not matter much in a currency area that just comprises one country such as the US or Japan, where a central fiscal capacity allows for a sizable degree of risk-sharing in a crisis situation where different areas may be very differently affected. However, the absence of such a central fiscal capacity – or other forms of meaningful fiscal risk-sharing elements such as the large-scale joint issuance of debt instruments – have long been identified as the key shortcoming in the euro area's institutional design, also in view of other missing features of an optimal currency area such as labor mobility and synchronized business cycles across regions.[55] During the height of the euro crisis between 2010 and 2012, the premature withdrawal of fiscal support and lack of adequate risk-sharing mechanisms hampered effective crisis responses and contributed to the double-dip recession that the euro area was experiencing in 2012 in contrast to other advanced economies (cf. Bützer, 2017).

Accordingly, countries in the euro area have been much more susceptible to rollover risks and diverging interest rates, as witnessed during the euro crisis, creating large negative spillovers for other euro area countries and the global economy. Consequently, and in view of the difficulties in establishing a central fiscal capacity, greater risk-sharing through the central bank balance sheet would lower risks and refinancing costs in aggregate, improve economic conditions for all member countries, and raise welfare across the currency area. While such increased risk-sharing is already happening to a certain extent in the context of the ECB's asset purchases and expansion of its balance sheet, profits and losses from QE are explicitly not being pooled across national central banks. OT would be more transparent and less prone to risks of fiscal dominance and moral hazard concerns pertaining to the mutualization of public debt. It could thereby usefully augment the outright monetary trans-actions (OMT) program, which has been effective in removing tail-risks and preventing economic collapse in the euro area in the summer of 2012 (cf. Altavilla, Giannone and Lenza, 2014).

Although the creation of the Next Generation EU recovery fund in the mag-nitude of €750 billion and the concomitant issuance of joint debt in response to the COVID-19 shock will at last introduce a small element of much-needed risk-sharing across the euro area, it is explicitly temporary in nature and therefore does not constitute a true 'Hamiltonian moment.' Moreover, due to the lengthy political approval process and legal challenges, the disbursement of funds will come with a long time lag that is far removed from the initial contractionary shock in early 2020. As the disbursement will be stretched over several years between 2021 and 2026, yearly amounts relative to GDP will generally be fairly small – in particular when just looking at the grant element of €390 billion.[56] While providing some fiscal space to countries in the future, the recovery fund does not obviate the need to create an euro area-wide mecha-nism for a jointly financed macroeconomic response to deteriorating economic conditions that can be rapidly employed such as OT.

5.5   OT Addresses Political Economy Constraints to Pursuing Optimal Fiscal Policy

Beyond the technical differences between OT and a debt- or money-financed fiscal stimulus, OT could remedy some of the most problematic and outdated constraints to pursuing optimal fiscal policy. These are particularly pertinent in the euro area, on which this section will therefore focus.

While the fiscal policy response to the COVID-19 shock in 2020 has been forceful in the euro area, calls for a swift return to fiscal consolidation and adherence to fiscal rules have already been growing louder, raising concerns that the policy mistakes of 2010–12 will be repeated once again.

Unless the fiscal rules are adjusted substantially, they will continue to enshrine a contractionary bias due to the systemic underestimation of potential output, which in turn determines the permissible structural balance.[57] This would be especially relevant for Southern European countries, which – despite having been hardest hit by both the euro crisis and the COVID-19 crisis – would face the biggest consolidation pressures from the current fiscal rule framework given their highly elevated debt ratios.[58] The current fiscal rules also hinder the use of fiscal space to undertake Pareto-improving investments, for which the scope might be much larger than previously thought, as pointed out by Blanchard (2021) and Mian et al. (2021).

In principle, fiscal rule reform could take the form of drastic simplification towards a nominal expenditure rule (Darvas, Martin and Ragot, 2018; Gaspar, 2020) or even the abandonment of quantitative targets in favor of qualitative standards, which take changing macroeconomic and country-specific circumstances into account (Blanchard, Leandro and Zettelmeyer, 2021), foremost the secular improvement in the $r - g$ differential over the past decades.

However, as changes to the fiscal rule framework require unanimity among EU members, it is unlikely that the needed comprehensive reforms to fiscal rules will occur, even if a majority of member states and European citizens wanted to see these amended. This economic detrimental and rather undemocratic status quo could be remedied to a certain extent by OT. It could counteract the effects of pro-cyclical fiscal consolidation, which could derail a nascent recovery in 2022 and beyond, and help to prevent lasting economic scarring and macroeconomic instability.

Further distinguishing it from a fiscal operation, OT would be grounded in the central bank's monetary policy framework and guided by the central bank's mandate, insulating key macroeconomic stabilization objectives – in particular, regarding inflation and deflation risks – from political myopia and electoral cycle considerations.

Central banks, with their highly trained technical staff and expert senior management, are well placed to help their economies overcome such inadequacies and, of course, have been doing so in years past (Draghi, 2020).[59]

6.   CENTRAL BANK INDEPENDENCE, INSTITUTIONAL LEGITIMACY, AND LEGAL CONSIDERATIONS

While the previous sections have outlined economic and practical implementation aspects of OT, this section discusses broader institutional aspects and associated concerns with regard to central banks' independence, legitimacy, and legal considerations.

6.1   Central Bank Independence

The idea of direct transfers from the central bank has been criticized in the past on the grounds that while it could constitute an effective monetary policy tool, it could raise unwarranted expectations among politicians and the general public that such transfers can be made at will in the future, irrespective of economic conditions. This, in turn, could endanger the independence of the central bank and its ability to fulfill its mandate.

Examining this argument closer, however, reveals that the exact same argument could be made for any type of central bank policy, be it the lowering of policy rates or asset purchases, both of which affect a government's refinancing costs much more directly. In fact, OT would help to attenuate fiscal dominance risks with regard to other policy instruments at the ELB as described in Section 5.3.

Moreover, it is precisely for such risks that strong institutional safeguards for the separation between the central bank and fiscal authorities exist, including independent decision-making mechanisms that guard against political abuse, independent of the type of chosen monetary policy instrument. While it is correct that a strong central bank balance sheet, whose equity position does not require fiscal support to avoid breaching its NILAC, supports central bank independence, the central bank would not come close to that limit for any reasonable calibration of OT (see Section 4.2). In addition, and as discussed in Section 4.4, it is not evident that the central bank's balance sheet would be weaker under OT than under a large asset purchase-driven expansion of its balance sheet in NPV terms.

In any case, it would be key to clearly communicate to the public that OT is an extraordinary policy measure that is geared towards the extraordinary circumstances at the ELB. The volume – and potential future rounds – of OT should be strictly conditional on inflation dynamics – for example, in the form of pre-determined quantitative thresholds beyond which OT would be inadmissible. For instance, the 'Sahm' rule (Sahm, 2019), which proposes automatic cash transfers to households to stabilize economies in view of impending recessions as indicated by an increase of the three-month moving average of the unemployment rate by 0.5 percentage points or more over its trough during the preceding 12 months, could provide rules-based guidance for the timing of OT. As the economy lifts off from the ELB, no more OT would be needed as the central bank could revert to its more traditional interest rate tools. Furthermore, adherence to prudent and transparent accounting stand-ards, as outlined in Section 3.6, would be essential to preserve and strengthen people's trust in the central bank's actions.

Accordingly, and similar to considerations on monetary finance (cf. Agur et al., 2022), OT would only be suitable for central banks with strong institutional frameworks that provide safeguards against undue political interference and risks of abuse. The ECB, for instance, would be well-placed to implement OT, given its independence, strong operational framework, and analytical capacities.

At the same time, economies without these central bank characteristics do not typically face the problem of idle domestic capacities at the ELB and associated deflationary pressures, which OT is geared towards addressing. Moreover, unconventional policy measures such as direct transfers or govern-ment bond purchases may have adverse effects on confidence, capital flows, and the exchange rate in less developed economies due to generally weaker institutional safeguards, a lower level of reserves, and an associated higher susceptibility to sudden stops.

In contrast, in reserve currency-issuing economies, OT would strengthen confidence – and possibly the exchange rate – as it would support a strong and swift economic recovery without jeopardizing price stability or central bank policy solvency. While being a reserve currency-issuing economy is itself endogenous to the pursuit of prudent macroeconomic policies and robust institutional frameworks, in the described circumstances OT may actually be the more prudent – and central bank independence-enhancing – policy choice than the available monetary policy alternatives.

6.2   Institutional Legitimacy

Modern central banks generally try to achieve their policy goal(s) by working through the financial sector while not directly interacting with households and non-financial firms. A major critique of direct transfers to households pertains to such transfers being outside the realm of eligible monetary policy instruments within the division of powers and responsibilities between differ-ent public entities (van 't Klooster, 2023). According to this argument, direct transfers are a type of fiscal policy that should only be undertaken by the government through its fiscal authority. Members of the government, legisla-ture, and the general public could see OT as a quasi-fiscal activity beyond the central bank's mandate, involving direct losses on the central bank's capital. As OT would likely be politically controversial, it would not be appropriate for the central bank to rely on an arguable interpretation of the flexibility provided in central bank laws (see Section 6.3) and introduce OT under its own discretion, which could risk exposing the central bank to legal and political challenges (cf. Bateman and Allen, 2021).

While these are legitimate concerns, they are attenuated by a number of factors:

1. It is widely agreed that questions of redistribution should be the prerogative of fiscal policy, undertaken by government officials through targeted measures in the tax and spending system. From this perspective, OT would be preferable to QE given that its redistributive consequences would be largely neutral and much less opaque. OT would also avoid the distortion of asset prices and risk of both financial and real resource misallocation, thereby making it a lot more justifiable from an institutional legitimacy perspective as a market and distribution neutral monetary policy choice at the ELB.
2. Every monetary policy measure has fiscal consequences, with interest rate policy and asset purchases being no exception. Whether a policy is more monetary or fiscal in nature should not exclusively be judged by whether it relies on credit creation and the financial sector as an intermediary, but to what extent it redistributes wealth and income within an economy. Moreover, while it is true that OT would result in a direct loss to a central bank's equity, asset purchases similarly expose the central bank to losses over the medium term, which are, however, much more opaque and uncertain by nature.
3. Beyond interest rate cuts and asset purchases, some central banks have resorted to even more extreme measures, such as equity purchases by the Bank of Japan or the tiered reserve remuneration system of the ECB, which effectively constitutes a transfer of central bank profits to the banking system that would otherwise have accrued to the general public. While there may be economic arguments in favor of such measures, these policy tools appear less straightforward from an institutional legitimacy point of view as they directly benefit one group – such as asset owners and bank shareholders in the above examples – more strongly than the rest of society, even if they have a net positive effect on the economy as a whole through second-round effects.
4. Last, central banks and their officials do not operate without accountability to the public or outside democratic processes in major advanced economies. They act with the objective to achieve their politically given mandates as stipulated – and constrained – by the relevant legal provi-

sions. Reserve currency-issuing central banks adhere to strict reporting requirements and are subject to the rule of law before the relevant courts.

6.3   Legal Considerations

This subsection touches on legal aspects of OT, with a focus on the euro area, where legal disputes over monetary policy and the problem of insufficient fiscal support have been front and center of the policy debate over the past years. It is not meant to provide a legal judgment but a discussion of key considerations.

Although advanced economy central banks have traditionally tried to fulfill their mandate by relying on the financial sector to provide (and absorb) credit, this does not imply that other means of conducting monetary policy such as OT should not be explored, particularly if they can achieve policy goals more effectively without exacerbating inequalities or financial stability risks. That being said, OT would constitute a significant departure from more established forms of monetary policy operations due to its much more direct interaction with the non-financial sector, questioning the fundamental tenets of modern central banking law, which could pose a major constraint for its introduction and subject it to legal and political challenges.

Therefore, if OT were to be introduced by a central bank, it should ideally have a sound and clear legal foundation in the central bank law. As public entities governed by public law, central banks can only do what is authorized by law (the 'legality'/'attributed powers' principle of administrative law). In relation to monetary policy tools, central bank laws establish objectives, functions, and specific powers. To legally conduct OT, the law should provide explicit or at least implicit powers to conduct that operation. Although it is up to each authority to interpret its central bank law, central bank laws currently do not typically provide a clear and unambiguous legal foundation for OT.

To illustrate this point, while the Statute of the European System of Central Banks (ESCB) and of the ECB explicitly allows for open-market and credit operations (Article 18), it also allows for the use of 'other instruments of monetary control' (Article 20) that can be decided under an exceptional decision-making procedure by the Governing Council if deemed necessary to fulfill the central bank's mandate.[60] However, given the vagueness of this article, it is not unambiguously clear whether it would cover OT – a direct and permanent increase of both base and broad money – as also reflected in former ECB president Mario Draghi's remark who called it an 'interesting concept' that 'clearly involves complexities, both accounting-wise and legal-wise' (Draghi, 2016, n.p.). Former ECB chief economist and Governing Council member Peter Praet considered OT to be legally feasible, stating that in principle the ECB 'can issue currency and...distribute it to people,' while calling it 'an extreme sort of instrument' (Praet, 2016). It is important to note that OT would not violate the monetary financing prohibition in the Statute (Article 21), contrary to the proposals floated by Galí (2020), Boivin et al. (2019), Sims (2016), or Turner (2015a).

It is also worth recalling that Article 2 of the Statute not only tasks the ESCB with maintaining price stability but – without prejudice to the objective of price stability – to support the general economic objectives of the European Union, which, inter alia, include full employment, social progress, economic, social and territorial cohesion, solidarity among member states, and a sustainable balance of payments.[61] Beyond being more effective at achieving price stability, the general economic objectives would likewise appear better served by OT than QE. Moreover, while Article 2 would not be sufficient as a legal basis for the ESCB to conduct OT, it does require the ESCB to pursue its goals 'favouring an efficient allocation of resources.' From an economic perspective, this would similarly favor OT over QE as OT would not have a distortionary impact on relative prices.

While a court case against OT would be all but guaranteed, concerns that loomed large in prior court cases – in particular, regarding the monetary financing prohibition and corresponding quantity and time limits to asset purchases – would not apply to OT. While not binding in the current COVID-19 crisis context, legal pressures to enforce issue share limits by constraining the share of outstanding government debt that the ECB may hold are likely to ramp up in the coming years due to the monetary financing prohibition. OT could also allay the concerns expressed by the German Constitutional Court regarding the proportionality of the ECB's action and its distributional impact as redistributive effects and financial stability risks would be kept to a minimum. More generally, it would be hard to fathom a court ruling, either on the German or European level, that would deny the ECB the opportunity of direct transfers as an operational method of monetary control after having criticized and/or limited alternative policies in previous rulings based on concerns that OT would not be subject to. It would also be difficult to imagine from a broader political and institutional perspective, as OT would likely garner overwhelming public support – in particular, with regard to continued asset purchases and negative interest rates. Moreover, and as described in Section 4.5, direct transfers from the central bank to private agents are already a de facto element of the monetary policy toolkit in the euro area as the current tiering of reserves and TLTRO III lower the Eurosystem's remittances to the fiscal authorities and its ability to increase provisions for general risks (cf. Da Silva et al., 2021; Deutsche Bundesbank, 2021). In contrast to OT, these implicit targeted transfers are more opaque and less equitable as they only accrue to commercial banks.

As regards the option of using reserve requirement policies more actively, the Statute is very clear, stating that '[s]ubject to Article 2, the ECB may require credit institutions established in Member States to hold minimum reserve on accounts with the ECB and national central banks in pursuance of monetary policy objectives. Regulations concerning the calculation and determination of the required minimum reserves may be established by the Governing Council' (Article 19).

To conclude, OT would constitute a monetary policy innovation, which would address many of the concerns raised in previous lawsuits against the ECB. There would, however, be legal uncertainty regarding the interpretation of Article 20, which would ultimately require a ruling by the ECJ. Against this backdrop, it would generally be desirable to have an endorsement for OT by the legislature, including a corresponding central bank law amendment, to remove legal uncertainties. Such an amendment should spell out the conditions under which OT can be employed to provide safeguards against abuse (cf. Section 6), akin to existing central bank laws in many countries that allow central banks to provide credit to the government under certain qualitative and quantitative conditions.

7.   CONCLUSION

In an economy at the ELB, well-calibrated OT from the central bank to households would constitute an equitable and effective monetary policy tool to achieve price stability objectives and stimulate aggregate demand. In both regards, OT would be superior to asset purchases and negative interest rates. Moreover, OT would automatically provide stronger policy support in those regions of a currency area that are particularly hard hit by an economic shock due to different marginal propensities to consume, which, in turn, would contribute to internal and external rebalancing. In practice, OT could be operationalized through physical checks, CBDC, or perpetual zero-coupon-targeted long-term lending operations, building on the existing financial market infrastructure and payment systems.

The benefits of direct transfers must be weighed against their costs as they create a liability for the central bank that is not matched by interest-bearing assets. This can create a risk for a central bank's policy solvency when taken to unsustainable levels. At the same time, prolonged large-scale asset purchases not only carry similar risks to central bank equity, they also exacerbate already large pre-existing wealth inequalities, rely on new and potentially excessive credit creation, distort relative prices, and give rise to concerns of fiscal dominance. For moderate and carefully calibrated amounts of OT that are strictly conditional on inflation dynamics, the risk of policy solvency appears small in reserve currency-issuing economies with strong monetary and fiscal institutions, robust central bank balance sheets, and well-established safeguards in place to prevent unwarranted or excessive use. For a central bank's negative equity to remain well below its non-inflationary loss-absorbing capacity, OT should be reserved as a monetary policy tool for stagnation traps, characterized by sizable slack and depressed interest rates. Even under those extraordinary circumstances, more targeted fiscal policy measures that are means-tested and raise the economy's productive capacities in a sustainable, green, and inclusive way, would in principle be more desirable if politically and economically feasible.

That being said, OT is distinctly different from a debt-financed fiscal stimulus as the arising central bank liability would be state-contingent, not subject to rollover risk, and entail an implicit risk-sharing element across different fiscal entities of a currency area. It could therefore provide a particularly important and welfare-improving addition to a currency union that lacks a central fiscal capacity such as the euro area. Although similar in its immediate economic impact, OT is also different from a money-financed fiscal stimulus as it reduces rather than increases the risks of fiscal dominance relative to asset purchases on the secondary market. Moreover, a money-financed fiscal stimulus is legally prohibited in the euro area and would, even if permitted, require the cooperation of fiscal policymakers.

While the fiscal response to the COVID-19 crisis has been rightfully large in most advanced economies, it remains to be seen whether the post-GFC mistakes of premature fiscal consolidation will be avoided this time around. If not, direct central bank transfers to households would constitute a powerful addition to the monetary policy toolkit that would help to achieve policy objectives in an effective and equitable manner.

NOTES

1. The views expressed herein are those of the author and should not be attributed to the IMF, its Executive Board, or its management. The author would like to thank Shekhar Aiyar, Bas Bakker, Ulrich Bindseil, Marijn Bolhuis, Damien Capelle, Marco Casiraghi, Piet Philip Christiansen, Simon Gray, Marco Gross, Maurizio Habib, Vikram Haksar, Gerhard Illing, Stan Jourdan, Sylvio Kappes, Jens van 't Klooster, Tobias Krahnke, Marc Lavoie, Jesper Lindé, Eric Lonergan, William Oman, Brett Rayner, Neil Shenai, Manmohan Singh, Arthur Sode, Livio Stracca, Steffen Strodthoff, Robert Unger, Miklos Vari, Akihiro Yoshinaga, and Jeromin Zettelmeyer for very useful comments and invaluable discussions that helped to shape this chapter. He would also like to thank seminar participants at the IMF MCM Policy Forum and EUR Webinar, the Fourth Conference on Law and Macroeconomics, and the Future of Central Banking Conference in Talloires for their comments and suggestions.
2. QE and asset purchases by the central bank are used interchangeably in this chapter.

3. The original idea goes back to Friedman (1969), although it has only gained renewed attention in recent years as central banks have been running out of traditional monetary policy space at the ELB.
4. ECB and Eurosystem are used interchangeably in this chapter.
5. Note that QE can induce increased bank lending through the lowering of interest rates and not the expansion of base money itself. Contrary to common textbook presentations of the money multiplier, the expansion of base money has no direct or causal link to broad money growth, as newly created reserves can never leave the financial system or be 'multiplied' out by banks; cf. Borio and Disyatat (2009); McLeay, Radia and Thomas (2014); Sheard (2013).
6. At the current juncture, the inflationary pressures in the euro area still appear mostly attributable to temporary factors, including pandemic-induced global value chain disruptions, commodity price increases, base effects, and the reversal of the VAT rate cut in Germany.
7. For a detailed overview of the wealth distribution in Europe, see Eurofound (2021).
8. Globally, the frequent divergence of relative and absolute indicators of inequality is a well-documented phenomenon; cf. Niño-Zarazúa, Roope and Tarp (2017).
9. The underrepresentation and underreporting of ultra-high net-worth individuals in survey and tax data-based measures of inequality further skew results downwards; cf. Saez and Zucman (2020).
10. This includes currency in circulation, whose quantity is driven by the demand from households, firms, and banks, rather than being exogenously 'injected' into the economy by the central bank.
11. The increase in broad money would be smaller than the amount of OT as the private and public sector's money demand would not increase exactly in line with OT, leading to an offsetting effect through early or accelerated repayments of outstanding debt.
12. See Sahm (2019) for an overview of the literature.
13. For a more detailed discussion of related Ricardian considerations, see Agur et al. (2022); Turner (2016a, 2016b).
14. Galí (2020, p. 10): '[T]o the extent that the money-financed tax cut raises the discounted sum of real seigniorage, current tax cuts will be perceived as net worth by each individual household (since they will not be fully offset by future tax increases), inducing an increase of individual consumption in partial equilibrium, i.e. given the initial level of output, prices and interest rates… The resulting increase in aggregate consumption, combined with the assumed stickiness of prices, will then trigger several general equilibrium effects, including an increase in output and inflation… In a rational expectations equilibrium, the household's perceived increase in net worth that triggered such a response will prove to be correct ex-post, thus justifying the initial increase in consumption.'
15. This is confirmed by Drescher, Fessler and Lindner (2020), who find considerable heterogeneity in the MPC across different European countries and a negative correlation with income, using microdata from the Eurosystem Household Finance and Consumption Survey.
16. Throughout this chapter, currency area may refer to both a single country such as the US or a currency union such as the euro area.
17. Galí (2020) provides quantitative estimates for the effects of a money-financed fiscal stimulus, which would be broadly similar to those of OT.

18.   For the sake of simplicity, this calculation assumes no leakage of the stimulus to imports, which would rise and provide a boost to economies outside the currency area. This, in turn, would stimulate exports to these countries, albeit to a smaller degree. An MPC of 0.8 over four quarters is consistent with the litera- ture (see Section 3.1) and a typical advanced economy savings rate of far below 20 percent. The COVID-19-induced increase in private saving rates in many advanced economies is likely to be a transitory phenomenon that is related to the restrictions in spending disposable income – in particular, on services.
19.   See Section 4 for a detailed discussion.
20.   To the extent that OT is successful in bringing inflation back to target and achieving broader economic goals, second-round effects on wealth and income distribution are related to the central bank's mandate and not the policy measure itself.
21.   Unless exempted, OT would provide an additional source of tax revenue to governments. The same second-round effect on tax revenues is, of course, similarly present with asset purchases. However, just like increased tax revenues that result from asset purchase programs, this would not be considered monetary financing or bear its political economy risks.
22.   I am grateful to Olivier Blanchard for bringing this point to my attention.
23.   See Coenen et al. (2012) for a comparison of fiscal multipliers of general and targeted transfers.
24.   Cf. Berg and Ostry (2017); Ostry, Loungani and Berg (2019).
25.   For instance, as Summers (2021) observed, instead of massive COVID-19-related cash transfers to most households (which far exceed the OT calculations in this chapter), the US government could have provided smaller but means-tested fiscal support to households in need and spent more on productive capacity-enhancing investments in infrastructure or green technologies, thereby promoting long-term growth and containing risks of overheating.
26.   Commercial banks would have to accept these central bank checks just like cash, reserves, or government-provided stimulus checks.
27.   If electoral registers were not accessible to the central bank in certain countries, a centralized digital register could also allow citizens to claim OT payments in person or electronically upon provision of their national identity card or passport.
28.   For a more in-depth discussion see, for instance, Bindseil (2020) and Kumhof and Noone (2018).
29.   For an in-depth discussion on the nature of central bank liabilities and whether they should be considered as such at all from a more holistic and legal point of view, see Allen et al. (2020).
30.   See Bunea et al. (2016) for a cross-country overview of seigniorage distribution policies and best practices.
31.   European Central Bank (2017, n.p.): 'Almost every year since it was founded, the ECB has reported a net profit, but of course it is also possible for the central bank to make a loss. If the ECB recorded a loss, it would first use the money set aside in previous years. If this were not enough, the ECB might ask the national central banks of the euro area countries to cover the remaining loss with the income from their monetary policy operations. Any further amount may be recorded on the ECB's balance sheet, to be offset against any net income received in the future.'
32.   Bonis, Fiesthumel and Noonan (2018, n.p.): 'Moreover, in the unlikely scenario in which realized losses were sufficiently large enough to result in an overall net income loss for the Reserve Banks, the Federal Reserve would still meet

its financial obligations to cover operating expenses. In that case, remittances to the Treasury would be suspended and a deferred asset would be recorded on the Federal Reserve's balance sheet, representing a claim on future net earnings that the Reserve Banks would need to realize before remittances to the Treasury would resume.'

33. See Kyriakopoulou and Ortlieb (2021) for a more detailed discussion of the Eurosystem's current risk-sharing arrangements.

34. While policy solvency typically describes the ability of the central bank to contain inflationary pressures, it could be argued that policy solvency is a symmetric concept that should similarly apply to containing the risk of deflation, with OT being the ultimate tool to preserve policy solvency in that direction.

35. Bank deutscher Länder between 1948 and 1957, Deutsche Bundesbank afterwards.

36. Deutsche Bundesbank (2020, p. 60).

37. Theoretically, direct transfers could become modus operandi of monetary policy implementation in a potentially welfare-improving full-reserve banking system (cf. Baeriswyl, 2017; Kumhof and Benes, 2012).

38. Naturally, as long as QE fails to bring up inflation and interest rates, it generates sizable profits for the central bank. In this case, however, QE not only fails to achieve its *raison d'être*, it would also come at the cost of rising financial stability risks, wealth inequality, and risks to the central bank balance sheet over the medium term.

39. This is for illustrative purposes only. The amount could vary a lot in both directions depending on macroeconomic circumstances and the shape of the yield curve.

40. This may be harder in the euro area than in other currency areas due to concerns over the effect on spreads between euro area countries.

41. 'ECB introduces two-tier system for remunerating excess liquidity holdings,' European Central Bank press release, September 12, 2019, accessed March 1, 2022 at https://www.ecb.europa.eu/press/pr/date/2019/html/ecb.pr190912_2 ~a0b47cd62a.en.html.

42. The Federal Reserve only started remunerating reserves in 2008, following the expansion of its balance sheet.

43. See, for instance, Feinman (1993) for the US; Deutsche Bundesbank (1995, pp. 119–30) for Germany; and Schobert and Yu (2014) or Geiger (2010, pp. 78–83) for China. At the low levels prevailing in advanced economies, reserve requirements do not constrain money creation from commercial banks as these are always provided with the needed reserves ex post against the provision of adequate collateral (cf. Borio and Disyatat, 2009). Accordingly, some countries such as the US, Canada, or Australia have abolished reserve requirements altogether or set them to zero. In countries with much higher and varying reserve requirements, such as China, minimum reserve requirement rates are actively employed as a monetary policy tool to manage liquidity.

44. Bindseil (1997, p. 44) notes that 'even if the reserve requirements are reduced for other reasons to zero for some while, the instrument should be preserved such that it could be reactivated any time. This would contribute to the confidence of economic agents into the capacity of the central bank to determine in all eventualities the scarcity of central bank money and thus to control indirectly its purchasing power.' Carlson and Wheelock (2014) show that changes in minimum reserve requirement were in fact the Fed's primary monetary policy

tool in the U.S. between the mid-1930s and 1951, a time period of similarly unusual fiscal-monetary conditions.

45. Widespread financial repression in advanced economies after World War II helped to reduce high public debt levels without discernible adverse effects on economic growth or the functioning of the financial sector; cf. Reinhart and Sbrancia (2015).

46. Bindseil (1997, p. 1) points out that the non-remunerated reserve requirements tax 'may be efficient from the point of view of the theory of optimal taxation or it may be perceived as a "fair" price for some central bank services for the private banking sector.' Relatedly, Deutsche Bundesbank (1995, p. 126) mentions a number of justifications for the non-remuneration of minimum reserves: '[B]anks opportunity cost deriving from the minimum reserves is accompanied by a number of concessions and competitive advantages, such as the low-interest funding available through the discount window and the fact that minimum reserve balances may also be used as working balances, with the Bundesbank, moreover, providing relatively generous short-term finance.' Bossone (2016) argues that since reserves do not carry liquidity or default risk, their non-remuneration would remove a form of subsidy.

47. Reis (2016, p. 17) makes a similar point for seigniorage more broadly.

48. See, for instance, Rogoff (2019) or Borio, Disyatat and Zabai (2016).

49. Any Ricardian effects, whose presence is unlikely to begin with, particularly at the ELB (see, for example, Choi and Devereux, 2006), are further attenuated by OT's perpetual character.

50. In principle, a central bank could, of course, choose to unconditionally backstop national government's debt to eliminate local currency rollover risks (cf. Agur et al., 2022). However, this would be at odds with the ECB's legal framework and monetary financing prohibition. Accordingly, while the ECB's outright monetary transactions (OMT) program was effective in bringing down spreads following its announcement in 2012, it did not eliminate them and can only be employed in the presence of strict country-specific conditionality.

51. For an analytical presentation of the real resource constraint that fiscal and monetary policymakers jointly face, see Buiter (2020a).

52. This argument also applies to the simultaneous increase of fiscal deficits and government bond purchases by central banks on the secondary market that have been commonplace in many countries during the COVID-19 crisis.

53. In the euro area, for instance, 26 percent of all outstanding government debt was held by the Eurosystem as of end-2020 (Martin et al., 2021).

54. See Higgins and Klitgaard (2020) for a discussion of Japan's recent experience with YCC, and Garbade (2020) for an analysis of YCC in the US in the 1940s.

55. See, for instance, Godley (1993) for a prescient assessment. Berger, Dell'Ariccia and Obstfeld (2019) and Barkbu et al. (2018) offer proposals to reform the European Monetary Union (EMU) fiscal architecture to allow for greater risk-sharing.

56. See Darvas (2020) for estimates by year and country.

57. Cf. Heimberger and Kapeller (2017). See also Jarocinski and Lenza (2016) for an empirical assessment of the extent of the underestimation of potential output, and Aiyar and Voigts (2019) for a theoretical model that elucidates the structural underestimation bias in traditional output gap calculation techniques.

58. While the European Stability Mechanism (ESM) could provide liquidity to a cash-strapped EU country, stringent fiscal rules-determined conditions may not

only be difficult to implement politically but could also undermine growth and thereby long-term debt sustainability. Moreover, the ESM's size would not be sufficient in the case of a systemic crisis or a large country case.

59. See Section 6.2 for a discussion of institutional legitimacy considerations.
60. European Union (2016): Article 20: 'The Governing Council may, by a majority of two thirds of the votes cast, decide upon the use of such *other operational methods of monetary control as it sees fit*, respecting Article 2. The Council shall, in accordance with the procedure laid down in Article 41, define the scope of such methods if they impose obligations on third parties' (emphasis added).
61. Article 2: 'In accordance with Article 127(1) and Article 282(2) of the Treaty on the Functioning of the European Union, the primary objective of the ESCB shall be to maintain price stability. Without prejudice to the objective of price stability, it shall support the general economic policies in the Union with a view to contributing to the achievement of the objectives of the Union as laid down in Article 3 of the Treaty on European Union. The ESCB shall act in accordance with the principle of an open market economy with free competition, favouring an efficient allocation of resources, and in compliance with the principles set out in Article 119 of the Treaty on the Functioning of the European Union.'

REFERENCES

Adler, G., P. Castro and C.E. Tovar (2016), 'Does central bank capital matter for monetary policy?' *Open Economies Review*, **27**, 183–205.

Agarwal, S. and W. Qian (2014), 'Consumption and debt response to unanticipated income shocks: evidence from a natural experiment in Singapore,' *American Economic Review*, **104**, 4205–30.

Agur, I., D. Capelle, G. Dell'Ariccia and D. Sandri (2022), 'Monetary finance: do not touch, or handle with care?' *IMF Departmental Papers No. DP/2022/001*, International Monetary Fund.

Aiyar, S. and S. Voigts (2019), 'The negative mean output gap,' *IMF Working Papers No. 19/183*, International Monetary Fund.

Allen, J., W. Bateman and S. Gleeson et al. (2020), 'Central bank money: liability, asset, or equity of the nation?' *CEPR Discussion Papers No. 15521*, Centre for Economic Policy Research.

Altavilla, C., D. Giannone and M. Lenza (2014), 'The financial and macroeconomic effects of OMT announcements,' *Working Paper Series No. 1707*, European Central Bank.

Ampudia, M., D. Georgarakos and J. Slacalek et al. (2018), 'Monetary policy and household inequality,' *Working Paper Series No. 2170*, European Central Bank.

Andersen, A.L., N. Johannesen, M. Jørgensen and J.L. Peydró (2020), 'Monetary policy and inequality,' *CEPR Discussion Papers No. 15599*, Centre for Economic Policy Research.

Baeriswyl, R. (2017), 'The case for the separation of money and credit,' in F. Heinemann, U. Klüh and S. Watzka (eds), *Monetary Policy, Financial Crises, and the Macroeconomy*, Cham: Springer, pp. 105–21.

Barkbu, B., H. Wang and H.E. Ture et al. (2018), 'A central fiscal stabilization capacity for the euro area,' *IMF Staff Discussion Notes No. 2018/003*, International Monetary Fund.

Barrdear, J. and M. Kumhof (2016), 'The macroeconomics of central bank issued digital currencies,' *Bank of England Working Papers No. 605*.

Bateman, W. and J. Allen (2021), 'The law of central bank reserve creation,' *The Modern Law Review*, 85 (2), 401–34.

Benecka, S., T. Holub, N. Kadlcakova and I. Kubicova (2012), 'Does central bank financial strength matter for inflation? An empirical analysis,' *Working Papers No. 2012/03*, Czech National Bank.

Benigno, G. and L. Fornaro (2018), 'Stagnation traps,' *Review of Economic Studies*, **85**, 1425–70.

Berg, A.G. and J.D. Ostry (2017), 'Inequality and unsustainable growth: two sides of the same coin?' *IMF Economic Review*, **65**, 792–815.

Berger, H., G. Dell'Ariccia and M. Obstfeld (2019), 'Revisiting the economic case for fiscal union in the euro area,' *IMF Economic Review*, **67**, 657–83.

Bernanke, B. (2016, April 11), 'What tools does the Fed have left? Part 3: helicopter money,' *Brookings.edu* [Blog], accessed September 1, 2019 at https://www.brookings.edu/blog/ben-bernanke/2016/04/11/what-tools-does-the-fed-have-left-part-3-helicopter-money/.

Bernanke, B. (2020), 'The new tools of monetary policy,' *American Economic Review*, **110**, 943–83.

Bibow, J. (2018), 'Unconventional monetary policies and central bank profits,' *IMK Studies No. 62*.

Bindseil, U. (1997), 'Reserve requirements and economic stabilization,' *Discussion Paper No. 1/97*, Deutsche Bundesbank.

Bindseil, U. (2020), 'Tiered CBDC and the financial system,' *Working Paper Series No. 2351*, European Central Bank.

Bindseil, U., A. Manzanares and B. Weller (2004), 'The role of central bank capital revisited,' *Working Paper Series No. 0392*, European Central Bank.

Blanchard, O. (2021, December 21), 'Why low interest rates force us to revisit the scope and role of fiscal policy: 45 takeaways,' *Piie.com*, Peterson Institute for International Economics.

Blanchard, O.J., A. Leandro and J. Zettelmeyer (2021), 'Redesigning EU fiscal rules: from rules to standards,' *Working Paper Series No. WP21-1*, Peterson Institute for International Economics.

Boivin, J., E. Bartsch, S. Fischer and P. Hildebrand (2019, August 15), 'Dealing with the next downturn,' *Blackrock.com*.

Bonifacio, V., L. Brandao-Marques and N. Budina et al. (2021), 'Distributional effects of monetary policy,' *IMF Working Papers No. 2021/201*, International Monetary Fund.

Bonis, B., L. Fiesthumel and J. Noonan (2018), 'SOMA's unrealized loss: what does it mean?' *FEDS Notes No. 2018-08-13-2*, Board of Governors of the Federal Reserve System.

Borio, C. and P. Disyatat (2009), 'Unconventional monetary policies: an appraisal,' *BIS Working Papers No. 292*, Bank for International Settlements.

Borio, C., P. Disyatat and A. Zabai (2016, May 24), 'Helicopter money: the illusion of a free lunch,' *VoxEU.org*, accessed June 1, 2016 at http://voxeu.org/article/helicopter-money-illusion-free-lunch.

Bossone, B. (2016, September 5), 'The true costs of helicopter money,' *VoxEU. org*, accessed July 1, 2022 at https://cepr.org/voxeu/columns/true-costs-helicopter-money.

Bossone, B. and H. Natarajan (2020, July 15), 'Getting funds to those in need and enabling access to money during COVID-19, part 3: central bank digital currencies and other instruments,' *VoxEU.org*, accessed July 1, 2022 at https://cepr.org/voxeu/

columns/getting-funds-those-need-and-enabling-access-money-during-covid-19
-part-3-central.

Brunnermeier, M. and Y. Koby (2018), 'The reversal interest rate,' *NBER Working Papers No. 25406*, National Bureau of Economic Research.

Buiter, W. (2014), 'The simple analytics of helicopter money: why it works – always,' *Economics – The Open-Access, Open-Assessment EJournal* (Kiel Institute for the World Economy– IfW), **8**, 1–51.

Buiter, W. (2020a), *Central Banks as Fiscal Players: The Drivers of Fiscal and Monetary Policy Space*, Cambridge, UK: Cambridge University Press.

Buiter, W. (2020b, October 1), 'The Eurosystem: an accident waiting to happen,' *VoxEU.org*, accessed May 1, 2021 at https://voxeu.org/article/eurosystem-accident-waiting-happen.

Buiter, W. and E. Rahbari (2012, February 27), 'Looking into the deep pockets of the ECB,' *Citi: Global Economics View*.

Bunea, D., P. Karakitsos, N. Merriman and W. Studener (2016), 'Profit distribution and loss coverage rules for central banks,' *Occasional Paper Series No. 169*, European Central Bank.

Bunn, P., A. Pugh and C. Yeates (2018), 'The distributional impact of monetary policy easing in the UK between 2008 and 2014', *Bank of England Working Paper No. 720*, March.

Bützer, S. (2017), '(Monetary) policy options for the euro area: a compendium to the crisis,' in F. Heinemann, U. Klüh and S. Watzka (eds), *Monetary Policy, Financial Crises, and the Macroeconomy*, Cham: Springer, pp. 125–62.

Caballero, R., E. Farhi and P.-O. Gourinchas (2015), 'Global imbalances and currency wars at the ZLB,' *NBER Working Papers No. 21670*, National Bureau of Economic Research.

Carlson, M.A. and D.C. Wheelock (2014), 'Navigating constraints: the evolution of Federal Reserve monetary policy, 1935–59,' *Working Papers No. 2014-13*, Federal Reserve Bank of St. Louis.

Carpenter, S., J. Ihrig and E. Klee et al. (2013), 'The Federal Reserve's balance sheet and earnings: a primer and projections,' *Finance and Economics Discussion Series No. 2013-01*, Board of Governors of the Federal Reserve System.

Cecchetti, S. and K. Schoenholtz (2016, August 19), 'A primer on helicopter money,' *VoxEU.org*, accessed June 1, 2021 at https://voxeu.org/article/primer-helicopter-money.

Choi, W.G. and M.B. Devereux (2006), 'Asymmetric effects of government spending: does the level of real interest rates matter?' *IMF Staff Papers*, **53**, 1–8.

Coenen, G., C.J. Erceg and C. Freedman et al. (2012), 'Effects of fiscal stimulus in structural models,' *American Economic Journal: Macroeconomics*, **4**, 22–68.

Coronado, J. and S. Potter (2020a), 'Reviving the potency of monetary policy with recession insurance bonds,' *PIIE Policy Briefs No. 20-5*, Peterson Institute for International Economics, accessed July 1, 2022 at https://www.piie.com/publications/policy-briefs/reviving-potency-monetary-policy-recession-insurance-bonds.

Coronado, J. and S. Potter (2020b), 'Securing macroeconomic and monetary stability with a Federal Reserve-backed digital currency,' *PIIE Policy Briefs No. 20-4*, Peterson Institute for International Economics, accessed July 1, 2022 at https://www.piie.com/publications/policy-briefs/securing-macroeconomic-and-monetary-stability-federal-reserve-backed/.

Da Silva, E., V. Grossmann-Wirth, B. Nguyen and M. Vari (2021), 'Paying banks to lend? Evidence from the Eurosystem's TLTRO and the euro area credit registry,' *Banque de France Working Paper Series No. 848.*

Darvas, Z. (2020, November 12), 'Next Generation EU payments across countries and years,' *Bruegel.org* [Blog].

Darvas, Z., P. Martin and X. Ragot (2018), 'European fiscal rules require a major overhaul,' *Bruegel Policy Contribution No. 18.*

Del Negro, M. and C. Sims (2015), 'When does a central bank's balance sheet require fiscal support?' *Journal of Monetary Economics*, **73**, 1–19.

Dell'Ariccia, G., P. Rabanal and D. Sandri (2018), 'Unconventional monetary policies in the euro area, Japan, and the United Kingdom,' *Journal of Economic Perspectives*, **32**, 147–72.

Deutsche Bundesbank (1995), *The Monetary Policy of the Bundesbank*, Frankfurt am Main: Deutsche Bundesbank.

Deutsche Bundesbank (2020), *Geschäftsbericht 2020*, Frankfurt am Main: Deutsche Bundesbank.

Deutsche Bundesbank (2021), *The Two-tier System for Reserve Remuneration and its Impact on Banks and Financial Markets*,' monthly report, January, pp. 59–79.

Djuric, U. and M. Neugart (2017), 'Helicopter money: survey evidence on expectation formation and consumption behavior,' paper presented at the Annual Conference 2017 (Vienna), Verein für Socialpolitik/German Economic Association.

Draghi, M. (2016), 'Speech at the Annual Meeting of the Asian Development Bank,' Frankfurt am Main, May 2.

Draghi, M. (2020), 'Farewell remarks,' remarks by Mario Draghi, President of the ECB, at the farewell event in his honour, Frankfurt am Main, October 28.

Drescher, K., P. Fessler and P. Lindner (2020), 'Helicopter money in Europe: new evidence on the marginal propensity to consume across European households,' *Economics Letters*, **195** (C), Article 109416.

Dziobek, C. and J. Dalton (2005), 'Central bank losses and experiences in selected countries,' *IMF Working Papers No. 2005/072*, International Monetary Fund.

Eurofound (2021), *Wealth Distribution and Social Mobility*, Luxembourg: Publications Office of the European Union.

European Central Bank (2017, February 16), 'Does the ECB make a profit?' accessed March 24, 2021 at https://www.ecb.europa.eu/explainers/tell-me-more/html/ecb _profits.en.html.

European Union (2016), 'Consolidated version of the Treaty on European Union: Protocol (No. 4) on the Statute of the European System of Central Banks and the European Central Bank,' *Official Journal of the European Union*, C 202/230.

Fabo, B., M. Jancokova, E. Kempf and L. Pástor (2020), 'Fifty shades of QE: conflicts of interest in economic research,' *CEPR Discussion Papers No. 15449*, Centre for Economic Policy Research.

Fatás, A. (2019), 'Fiscal policy, potential output, and the shifting goalposts,' *IMF Economic Review*, **67**, 684–702.

Feinman, J. (1993), 'Reserve requirements: history, current practice, and potential reform,' *Federal Reserve Bulletin*, June, 569–89.

Friedman, M. (1969), *The Optimum Quantity of Money: And Other Essays*, Chicago, IL: Aldine Pub. Co.

Galí, J. (2020), 'The effects of a money-financed fiscal stimulus,' *Journal of Monetary Economics*, **115** (C), 1–19.

Garbade, K.D. (2020), *Managing the Treasury Yield Curve in the 1940s: Staff Reports 913*, Federal Reserve Bank of New York.

Gaspar, V. (2020), 'Future of fiscal rules in the euro area,' Keynote Address, Workshop on 'Fiscal Rules in Europe: Design and Enforcement,' DG ECFIN, Brussels, January 28.

Geiger, M. (2010), 'Monetary policy in China: institutions, targets, instruments and strategies,' doctoral dissertation, Julius-Maximilians-Universität Würzburg.

Giraud, G. and M. Grasselli (2021), 'Household debt: the missing link between inequality and secular stagnation,' *Journal of Economic Behavior & Organization*, **183**, 901–27.

Godley, W. (1993), 'Maastricht and all that,' *London Review of Books*, **14** (19), 3–4.

Gopinath, G. (2021), 'The interaction of fiscal and monetary policy,' paper presentation at the 2021 Jackson Hole Symposium, August 27.

Hall, R. and R. Reis (2015), 'Maintaining central-bank financial stability under new-style central banking,' *NBER Working Papers No. 21173*, National Bureau of Economic Research.

Hampl, M. and T. Havranek (2018), 'Central bank capital as an instrument of monetary policy,' *Working Papers No. IES 2018/25*, Charles University Prague, Faculty of Social Sciences, Institute of Economic Studies.

Hasanov, F. and R. Cherif (2019), 'The return of the policy that shall not be named: principles of industrial policy,' *IMF Working Papers No. 2019/074*, International Monetary Fund.

Heimberger, P. and J. Kapeller (2017), 'The performativity of potential output: pro-cyclicality and path dependency in coordinating European fiscal policies,' *Review of International Political Economy*, **24**, 904–28.

Higgins, M. and T. Klitgaard (2020, June 22), 'Japan's experience with yield curve control,' Federal Reserve Bank of New York, Liberty Street Economics [Blog].

House of Lords (2021), *Quantitative Easing: A Dangerous Addiction? Economic Affairs Committee, 1st Report of Session 2021–22*.

Hutchinson, J. and F. Smets (2017), 'Monetary policy in uncertain times: ECB monetary policy since June 2014,' *Manchester School*, **85**, 1–15.

IMF (2020), 'The central bank transparency code,' *IMF Policy Paper*, July.

ING (2016), *Helicopter Money: Loved, Not Spent*, ING International Survey special report, Amsterdam: ING.

Jarocinski, M. and M. Lenza (2016, July 1), 'How large is the output gap in the euro area,' *ECB Research Bulletin*, European Central Bank.

Jorda, O., S. Singh and A. Taylor (2020), 'The long-run effects of monetary policy,' *Federal Reserve Bank of San Francisco, Working Paper Series No. 2020-10*.

Juselius, M., C. Borio, P. Disyatat and M. Drehmann (2017), 'Monetary policy, the financial cycle, and ultra-low interest rates,' *International Journal of Central Banking*, **13**, 55–89.

Kappes, S. (2021), 'Monetary policy and personal income distribution: a survey of the empirical literature,' *Review of Political Economy*, ahead-of-print, https://doi.org/10.1080/09538259.2021.1943159.

Koo, R. (2011), 'The world in balance sheet recession: causes, cure, and politics,' *Real-world Economics Review*, (58), 19–37.

Krogulski, K., M. Korczak and B. Bakker (2019), 'Unemployment surges in the EU: the role of risk premium shocks,' *IMF Working Papers No. 2019/056*, International Monetary Fund.

Kumhof, M. and J. Benes (2012), 'The Chicago plan revisited,' *IMF Working Papers No. 2012/202*, International Monetary Fund.

Kumhof, M. and C. Noone (2018), 'Central bank digital currencies – design principles and balance sheet implications,' *Bank of England Working Papers No. 725*.

Kyriakopoulou, D. and P. Ortlieb (2021, January 27), 'Does central bank capital matter?' *OMFIF.org*, accessed May 1, 2021 at https://www.omfif.org/2021/01/does - central-bank-capital-matter/.

Lonergan, E. (2016, February 24), 'Legal helicopter drops in the Eurozone,' *Philosophyofmoney.net* [Blog], accessed September 1, 2019 at https://www.philosophyofmoney.net/legal- helicopter-drops-in-the-eurozone/.

Martin, P., E. Monnet and X. Ragot (2021), 'What else can the European Central Bank do?' *Les notes du conseil d'analyse économique*, No. 65, June.

Mason, J.W. (2015, February 25), 'Disgorge the cash: the disconnect between corporate borrowing and investment,' *Roosevelt Institute Working Paper*.

McLeay, M., A. Radia and R. Thomas (2014), 'Money creation in the modern economy,' *Bank of England Quarterly Bulletin*, **54**, 14–27.

Mersch, Y. (2020), 'Legal aspects of the European Central Bank's response to the coronavirus (COVID-19) pandemic – an exclusive but narrow competence,' Keynote Speech at the ESCB Legal Conference, Frankfurt am Main, November 2.

Mian, A., L. Straub and A. Sufi (2020), 'The saving glut of the rich and the rise in household debt,' *CESifo Working Paper Series 8201*, Center for Economic Studies.

Mian, A., L. Straub and A. Sufi (2021), 'Indebted demand,' *The Quarterly Journal of Economics*, **136** (4), 2243–307.

Minsky, H.P. (1986), *Stabilizing an Unstable Economy*, New Haven, CT: Yale University Press.

Muellbauer, J. (2014, December 23), 'Combatting Eurozone deflation: QE for the people,' *VoxEU.org*, accessed May 1, 2016 at http://voxeu.org/article/ combatting-eurozone-deflation-qe-people.

Niño-Zarazúa, M., L. Roope and F. Tarp (2017), 'Global inequality: relatively lower, absolutely higher,' *Review of Income and Wealth*, **63**, 661–84.

Ostry, J.D., P. Loungani and A. Berg (2019), *Confronting Inequality: How Societies Can Choose Inclusive Growth*, New York: Columbia University Press.

Parker, J., N. Souleles, D. Johnson and R. McClelland (2013), 'Consumer spending and the economic stimulus payments of 2008,' *American Economic Review*, **103**, 2530–53.

Praet, P. (2016), 'Interview with *La Repubblica*: interview with Peter Praet, Member of the Executive Board of the ECB, conducted by Ferdinando Giugliano and Tonia Mastrobuoni on 15 March 2016 and published on 18 March 2016,' European Central Bank.

Reinhart, C. and B. Sbrancia (2015), 'The liquidation of government debt,' *Economic Policy*, **30**, 291–333.

Reis, R. (2016), 'Can the central bank alleviate fiscal burdens?' *NBER Working Papers No. 23014*, National Bureau of Economic Research.

Renault, T. and B. Savatier (2021), 'What impact does helicopter money have on inflation?' *Focus du conseil d'analyse économique*, No. 63-2021, June.

Rogoff, K. (2019), 'Is this the beginning of the end of central bank independence?' *Occasional Paper No. 95*, Group of Thirty.

Romer, D. (2009), *Advanced Macroeconomics* (3rd edition), New York: McGraw-Hill.

Ryan-Collins, J. (2015), 'Is monetary financing inflationary? A case study of the Canadian economy, 1935–75,' *Working Paper Series No. 848*, Levy Economics Institute.

Saez, E. and G. Zucman (2020), 'Trends in US income and wealth inequality: revising after the revisionists,' *NBER Working Papers No. 27921*, National Bureau of Economic Research.

Sahm, C. (2019), 'Direct stimulus payments to individuals,' in H. Boushey, R. Nunn and H. Shambaugh (eds), *Recession Ready: Fiscal Policies to Stabilize the American Economy*, Washington, DC: The Hamilton Project, pp. 62–92.

Schmelzing, P. (2020), 'Eight centuries of global real interest rates, RG, and the "suprasecular" decline, 1311–2018,' *Bank of England Working Papers No. 845*.

Schobert, F. and L. Yu (2014), 'The role of reserve requirements: the case of contemporary China compared to postwar Germany,' in F. Rövekamp and H.G. Hilpert (eds), *Currency Cooperation in East Asia*, Cham: Springer, pp. 143–61.

Sheard, P. (2013, August 13), 'Repeat after me: banks cannot and do not "lend out" reserves,' *Standard & Poor's RatingsDirect*.

Sims, C. (2016), 'Fiscal policy, monetary policy, and central bank independence,' paper presented at the Economic Policy Symposium, Jackson Hole, August 25–27, Kansas City Fed.

Soros, G. (2020, April 20), 'The EU should issue perpetual bonds,' *Project-syndicate. org*.

Stella, P. (1997), 'Do central banks need capital?' *IMF Working Papers No. 1997/083*, International Monetary Fund.

Stella, P. (2002), 'Central bank financial strength, transparency, and policy credibility,' *IMF Working Papers No. 2002/137*, International Monetary Fund.

Stella, P. (2008), 'Central bank financial strength, policy constraints and inflation,' *IMF Working Papers No. 2008/049*, International Monetary Fund.

Summers, L. (2021, February 4), 'The Biden stimulus is admirably ambitious. But it brings some risks, too,' *Washington Post*, accessed March 1, 2021 at https://www .washingtonpost.com/opinions/2021/02/04/larry-summers-biden-covid-stimulus/.

The Economist (2020, December 10), 'After the pandemic, will inflation return?'

Turner, A. (2015a), *Between Debt and the Devil: Money, Credit, and Fixing Global Finance*, Princeton, NJ: Princeton University Press.

Turner, A. (2015b), 'The case for monetary finance – an essentially political issue,' paper presented at the 16th Jacques Polak Annual Research Conference, hosted by the International Monetary Fund, Washington, DC, November 5–6.

Turner, A. (2016a), 'Why a future tax on bank credit intermediation does not offset the stimulative effect of money finance deficits,' Institute for New Economic Thinking, August.

Turner, A. (2016b), 'Why a money financed stimulus is not offset by an inflation tax,' Institute for New Economic Thinking, May.

van Rooij, M. and J. de Haan (2016), 'Will helicopter money be spent? New evidence,' *DNB Working Papers No. 538*, Netherlands Central Bank.

van 't Klooster, J. (2023), 'Central banks,' in R. Bellamy and J. King (eds), *The Cambridge Handbook of Constitutional Theory*, Cambridge, UK: Cambridge University Press (forthcoming).

Woodford, M. (2012), 'Methods of policy accommodation at the interest-rate lower bound,' paper presented at the Federal Reserve Bank of Kansas City Symposium on 'The Changing Policy Landscape,' Jackson Hole, Wyoming, August 31.

Zinsmeister, F. (2009), 'Die Finanzierung der deutschen Einheit – zum Umgang mit den Schuldenlast der Wiedervereinigung,' *Vierteljahrshefte zur Wirtschaftsforschung*, **78** (2), 146–60.

10. On interest and interest-rate policy

Massimo Pivetti

1. INTRODUCTION

In this chapter, the real effects of interest-rate policy are discussed, together with its impact on inflation, once the traditional concept of a 'natural' real rate of interest is discarded and interest is viewed as a monetary phenomenon, a true policy variable subject to a wide range of policy objectives and constraints, which contributes to determining normal production costs. Attention will then be focused on the merits of cheap money, whilst it will be maintained that a persistent *zero* real interest-rate policy would ultimately be incompatible with capitalist production. The chapter concludes by pointing out the implications of the main arguments put forward in the previous sections for the status of the central bank and the question of capital control.

2. THE TRADITION, KEYNES AND THE CONNECTION BETWEEN INTEREST AND PROFIT

An important corollary of any economic theory that postulates the existence of a 'natural' real rate of interest, or of a normal rate of return on capital employed in production determined by real factors, is scepticism that interest-rate policy can *persistently* affect the real economy – the denial, in other words, of any substantial power on the part of monetary authorities.

Thus, within the various formulations of the neoclassical approach, and quite independently of whether money is regarded as exogenous or endogenous, the existence of a natural equilibrium of time preference by consumers–savers and the marginal productivity of capital ultimately makes long-term real interest rates beyond the reach of policy, and monetary neutrality is hardly disputable. Given the state of productivity and thrift, the impact on the price level, or on real output and accumulation, of any lasting discrepancy between the course of the market rate of interest and that of the natural real rate would force the authorities to act so as to make the former move in sympathy with the latter. If the central bank knew the level of the natural rate of interest, then the best monetary policy would be one that kept the actual real rate at its natural level through time in order to keep output at potential while at the same time ensuring price stability.

The main challenge for those in charge of monetary policy would simply be that of not yielding to the political temptation of keeping the real rate below its natural level, with a view to bringing output and employment above their natural levels. So, to the extent that monetary policy was performed at its best, money would be neutral in the short and the long run alike. But even if monetary policy could not be performed at its best, possibly owing to an 'imperfect estimate' of the 'unobservable' equilibrium real rate by the central banks, it is nevertheless believed to be capable of tracking the natural equilibrium of the economy and the corresponding equilibrium real rate of interest by *inferring* its course from the changes in the price level.[1] If inflation rises, a raising of nominal interest rates by the bank, provided it is sufficiently large to also raise real rates, will succeed in lowering inflation, while keeping output near potential. In sum, according to the whole neoclassical tradition, monetary policy can affect only nominal variables in the long run.[2]

The neoclassical notion of a natural rate of interest also seriously pollutes Keynes's interpretation of interest as a monetary phenomenon, together with his conviction that under capitalism, monetary phenomena are central to the explanation of real phenomena. Notwithstanding his claim in the *General Theory* (1936, p. 243) that he 'no longer' regards the concept of a 'natural real rate' as 'a most promising idea', the natural rate is still there, as the rate that would ensure equality between full employment savings and investment decisions. Keynes's underemployment equilibrium is ultimately the result of a limited flexibility of the money rate of interest in the face of discrepancies between full employment savings and investment decisions. Since he shares the neoclassical tenet of an inverse relation between the rate of interest and investment decisions – derived from the principle of substitution between capital and labour – this limited flexibility is actually all he has to offer as a basis for his non-orthodox concept of interest as a monetary phenomenon. The neoclassical synthesis could thus quite easily maintain that the determination of the current rate of interest by the intersection of the supply and the demand schedule of money, while adequate for showing that the flexibility of the interest rate is not of an automatic nature, is, however, insufficient to sustain the thesis of its *limited* flexibility. And if current money interest can normally be brought to and kept at its natural level – provided that monetary authorities act with a sufficient 'measure of persistence and consistency of purpose' (Keynes, 1936, p. 204) – then the neoclassical real forces of productivity and thrift may still be regarded as the ultimate determinants of the equilibrium rate of interest.[3]

Keynes's interpretation of interest as a monetary phenomenon is also incompatible with the so-called Keynesian theory of distribution, unless one is prepared to deny any long-run connection between the rate of interest and the rate of profit. This connection was certainly not denied by Keynes, who, consistent with his monetary explanation of interest, regarded the latter as 'setting the pace' in the necessary equalization of 'the advantages of the choice between owing loans and assets': 'instead of the marginal efficiency of capital determining the rate of interest' – he wrote – 'it is true…to say that it is the rate of interest which determines the marginal efficiency of capital' ([1937] 1973, pp. 122–3).[4] The development of Joan Robinson's position on interest as her life's work progressed, neatly reflects the incompatibility that has just been pointed out: she eventually stressed that no matter how large a measure of persistence and consistency of purpose the monetary authorities applied to their action, neither a situation of high interest rates nor one of cheap money could be maintained irrespective of the 'underlying reality' represented by the course of the rate of accumulation. In 1951, in the last section of her widely circulated article 'The rate of interest',[5] she had written with respect to the possibility of a cheap-money policy: 'If the authorities take it gently and do not try to push the rate down too fast, and if they stick consistently to the policy, once begun, so that the market never has the experience of today's rate being higher than yesterday, it is hard to discern *any limit* to the possible fall in interest rates' (Robinson, 1952, p. 30; emphasis added). But in the first reprint of the article (1960) that followed *The Accumulation of Capital* (1956), its last section was omitted, obviously because in her main work she had argued that 'there is, at any moment, a low level of interest such that, if obtained, inflation would set in…and a high level such that if obtained would be regarded as intolerable and some kind of reaction would set in to get it brought down. The two levels…are governed, roughly speaking, by the prospect of profit on investment… Actual interest rates must be somewhere between these two levels' (1956, pp. 399–400). In 1979, 'The rate of interest' was again reprinted, this time in full, at the end of her volume *The Generalisation of the General Theory and Other Essays*, but in the introduction to the volume she referred to the essay on interest as 'quite old fashioned', and explicitly criticized as 'unnatural' the concept of the rate of interest as an independently determined monetary phenomenon that governs the rate of profit: 'Over the long run' – she wrote, reversing Keynes's point of view – 'the interest that rentiers can exact is determined by the profits that entrepreneurs can earn, not the other way round' (1979, p. xxii).[6] As to Luigi Pasinetti, he has stressed that the theory of rate-of-profit determination through the money rate of interest and Kaldor's rate-of-profit determination through the rate of growth 'are *alternative*' (Pasinetti, 1990, p. 462; original emphasis), so that they cannot both hold true.

Finally, the interpretation of interest as a conventional monetary phenomenon, determined from outside the system of production, is incompatible with the classical and Marxian concept of a normal rate of profit determined by the real wage, given production techniques. But while the long-run dependence of money interest on normal profit is most clearly stated by Ricardo,[7] it cannot be so easily disposed of as far as Marx's views on interest are concerned. Indeed, Marx did not share Ricardo's view that lasting changes in the rate of interest must reflect changes in the normal rate of profit. He regarded instead 'the average rate of interest prevailing in a certain country' as a magnitude determined by socio-economic and institutional circumstances unrelated to the real forces that govern the normal rate of profit (see Marx, [1894] 1977, pp. 425, 427, 431–2). The problem is that Marx's 'autonomous determination' of the rate of interest is accompanied by a marked weakening of the connection between this variable and the normal rate of profit, since the latter still depends in his analysis, as in that of Ricardo, on the real wage. For Marx, both rates are thus capable of being determined independently of each other, with the corollary that 'assuming the average profit to be given, the rate of the profit of enterprise is…determined by the rate of interest. It is high or low in inverse proportion to it' (ibid., p. 379). This is, however, a hardly acceptable view, in the light of the conviction, shared by Marx, that since 'to represent functioning capital is not a sinecure like representing interest-bearing capital' (ibid., p. 446), a positive profit of enterprise *must* constitute a component part of normal profit, so that it cannot be high or low irrespective of the elements of risk that justify its existence.

In the actual conditions of modern capitalism, it is difficult in any case to share the classical and Marxian view of the real wage rate as the independent or given variable in the relationship between wages and profits. The difficulty ultimately stems from the fact that the direct outcome of wage bargaining is a certain level of the money wage, while the price level cannot be determined before and independently from money wages: given the methods of production and normal distribution, the level of prices *depends* on the level of money wages (see Pivetti, 1991, pp. 36–7).

3.   THE RATE OF INTEREST AS AN AUTONOMOUS
       COMPONENT OF NORMAL PRODUCTION
       COSTS AND THE OTHER DETERMINANTS OF
       NORMAL GROSS PROFIT MARGINS

But if, in normal conditions, one can hardly accept the idea of an 'average profit', determined by the real wage rate, which can be taken as the *primum movens* in the long-run relationship between profit and interest, and if, on the other hand, the neoclassical tenet of an investment demand schedule is ill-founded, so that also such a thing as a 'natural' rate of interest cannot be postulated, then the door is wide open to an interpretation of interest as a true policy-determined variable – a monetary phenomenon, that is to say, determined from outside the system of production. Moreover, since interest-rate policy decisions are taken under a wide range of policy objectives and constraints, which have different weights both among the various countries and for a particular country at different times, it can be said that interest-rate determination is not subject to any general law and is actually largely intertwined with the parties' relative strengths (more on this below).

With such an interpretation of interest, its necessary long-run causal relationship with normal profit, as traditionally envisaged by the bulk of economic theory, must, of course, be reversed: rather than the normal rate of profit determining the long-term rate of interest, it is the latter that will 'set the pace' by contributing to determining normal gross profit margins and the ratio of prices to money wages. The policy-determined long-term interest rate – that is, the rate of interest to be earned on long-term riskless financial assets – is thus viewed as constituting an autonomous determinant of normal money production costs, quite independently of the kind of capital employed in production (borrowed, shares or a firm's own capital). Everything else remaining the same, a persistent change in the long-term rate of interest causes a change in the same direction in the level of prices in relation to the level of money wages, thereby generating a corresponding change in the rate of profits and an inverse change in the real wage. Wage bargaining and monetary policy come out of this view as the main channels through which class relations act in determining distribution and they are seen as acting primarily upon the profit rate, via the policy-determined rate of interest, rather than upon the real wage as maintained by both the classical economists and Marx. The level of the real wage prevailing in any given situation is regarded as the final result of the whole process by which distribution of income between workers and capitalists actually occurs.

This long-run causal relationship from interest to profit is blurred by the fact that the long-term rate of interest is but one of the determinants of normal gross profit margins, the others being, in addition to normal profits of enterprise, depreciation expenses per unit of capital and top-management remuneration. For any given course of the long-term interest rate, each one of these other components of normal gross profits may experience over time some change, such as to bring about a *non-parallel* movement of interest and profit from which one might be led to infer an absence of any connection between the two variables. But it would be erroneous, in my view, to derive such a want of connection from a non-parallel movement of interest and profit, even if it persisted over significant time spans.

Focusing, for example, on the US case, a shortening of the average life of equipment is widely acknowledged to have brought about over the last four decades an increase in depreciation allowances per unit of capital,[8] while social changes connected with the acceptability of very high compensations resulted in huge increases in top-management remunerations.[9] Finally, and most importantly, a general weakening of the incentives to invest throughout the economy and the increased relative weight of the financial sector are very likely to have resulted in significantly higher profits of enterprise (or business profits). The epoch-making policy shift away from full employment that took place at the end of the 1970s did actually reduce the incentive to invest throughout advanced capitalism, lowering the rate of growth of fixed capital formation to less than half of what it had been in the 30-year period following World War II. The point here is that a reduction of the incentive to invest is one and the same thing as an increase of the risk of productively employing capital, which must perforce result in a rise in the normal component of profit necessary to remunerate it.[10] As to the increased weight of the financial sector, it is widely acknowledged to have increased the share of business profit in total value-added, as well as the ratio of total value-added to money wages.

Because of these changes, profit margins soared notwithstanding a markedly decreasing trend of long-term interest rates, and real wages stagnated in the face of rising outputs per hour. But without decreasing interest rates, gross profit margins and the ratio of prices to money wages would have been even higher. Indeed, especially since the mid-1990s, decreasing interest rates appear to have somewhat checked the negative impact on real wages of the rise in the other three components of normal profits.[11]

4.   ON THE REAL EFFECTS OF INTEREST-RATE POLICY AND INFLATION

Interest-rate policy thus primarily affects income distribution, and it is chiefly through this channel that it will also impact on activity levels, with the implication that its influence on employment is much more complex than that postulated by a Keynesian investment demand schedule.[12] A priori, one can only affirm that, *ceteris paribus*, a low interest-rate policy contributes to sustain the economy's propensity to consume through its impact on distribution between profits and wages in the latter's favour. Moreover, that low interest rates are likely to sustain consumption also through their effects on the burden of household debt, the prices of fixed-interest securities and most ordinary shares, as well as the value of houses. Actual experience over these last 30 years has clearly shown that both a lesser burden of debt and higher stock exchange and house prices positively affect the willingness of large sectors of the public to purchase goods and services in general. Finally, since in the interpretation of interest as an autonomous determinant of normal money production costs, as is put forward here, interest rates and the price level tend to be positively rather than inversely correlated, cheap money may positively affect the real income and consumption of social classes and groups other than the capitalists and wage earners. In sum, it is principally through consumption that a cheap-money policy is capable of exerting a positive influence on output and employment. The picture is much more problematic as to the influence of interest-rate policy on the incentive to invest. Certainly, the possibility cannot be ruled out of situations in which a positive impact on the incentive to invest is exerted by higher rates of utilization of existing productive capacity resulting from the rise in consumption caused by cheaper money. The fact is, however, that there is no functional relationship that allows one to establish which will be, in general, the direction of the influence of persistent changes in interest rates on the incentive to invest. In other words, the impact of changes in income distribution on the incentive to invest is bound to be different in each different concrete situation, and may go either way (see on this, Pivetti, 1991, pp. 43–6).

As to inflation, a raising of interest rates by the central bank, *ceteris paribus*, raises the price level because it raises the firms' mark-ups. A dearer-money policy is thus by itself inflationary.[13] But its overall net impact on the price level essentially depends on the effects that the policy-determined interest rates will eventually exert on aggregate demand and employment, through their impact on income distribution and the other channels by which changes in interest rates are bound to affect activity levels, including the leverage they exert on net exports through the exchange rate (in a flexible exchange-rate regime). Should the overall net impact of a dearer-money policy on aggregate demand and employment be negative, then the higher price/wage ratio brought about by it might eventually be accompanied by lower inflation if the repercussions of a weakening wage earners' bargaining power on the dynamic of money wages were sufficiently robust. It can therefore be said that higher interest rates may succeed in checking inflation if the higher ratio of prices to money wages they bring about, through their direct impact on mark-ups, is more than counter-balanced by the lowering of prices of imported inputs (expressed in domestic currency) through the exchange-rate channel, and by a reduction or slower rise of money wages as a result of the likely negative impact on employment of the contractionary effects on consumption spending and net exports caused by higher interest rates. Finally, to the extent that a dear-money policy is made effective by means of lasting programmes of credit restrictions, a check on the rise in prices might come about via the negative impact of the restrictions (in the availability of funds, relative to the demand for them) on activity levels and hence, again, on the level of employment and of money wages.[14]

But since both the impact of changes in distribution on aggregate demand and the responsiveness of money wages to changes in employment are bound to be different in each concrete situation, the direction of the long-run effects of a country's interest-rate policy on the rate at which its price level changes remains highly uncertain. This said, one can, however, quite confidently maintain, on the basis of the view of money interest and its role put forward here, that it is rather a *cheap*-money policy that should be regarded as the most promising, in the context of a fixed exchange-rate regime, to ensure low and stable inflation without at the same time negatively impinging upon activity levels. Capital control would, of course, have to become a component part of the overall policy stance to make cheap money consistent with the fixed exchange-rate regime. As to the dynamic of money wages, it would have to be dealt with, and kept under control, by means other than increases in unemployment: essentially by income policies – that is, through the expansion of the welfare state, which would in turn be rendered financially more viable by cheap money and the consequent lesser weight of interest payments in the public budget.

Different from mainstream interpretations of inflation, with their emphasis on the degree of central bank independence and the credibility of its commitment to price stability, there is hardly anything mechanical in the complex interpretation of the behaviour of the general level of prices that can be reached on the basis of the framework expounded here. As a matter of fact, one of its most significant bearings concerns precisely the status of the central bank, an issue that will be dealt with in the last section of the chapter.

5. OBJECTIVES AND CONSTRAINTS OF INTEREST-RATE POLICY

The concept of the rate of interest as a policy variable that, given production techniques, contributes to governing the ratio of prices to money wages, does not imply postulating that at all times and places interest-rate policy is dominated by the distributive struggle between wage earners and profit earners, nor by the decisive impact of this struggle on activity levels and inflation rates. An outstanding part has clearly been played in several concrete situations by objectives and constraints of a non-distributional character, such as public debt management objectives or balance-of-payments and exchange-rate constraints. Moreover, owing to the relevance gained by financial markets within several national systems of retired security, also social as well as political constraints are most likely to have acted upon interest-rate policies. With respect, for example, to the US case, the massive return in the period since 1980 to individual-based retirement security, by dramatically exposing the living conditions of elderly households (a significant section of the population) to the behaviour of stock market prices, is likely to have contributed to a call for a policy of progressive lowering of interest rates.[15] Still more importantly, such a policy was eventually imposed on the authorities of a few major capitalist countries by a growth strategy crucially based on the expansion of household debt.[16] Finally, interest rates are often dictated to this or that country by the need to check outflows of funds incompatible with the exchange-rate policy and regime chosen by its authorities. In sum, as has already been emphasized in Section 3 above, interest-rate determination can be properly described in terms of sets of objectives and constraints, on the action of the monetary authorities, which have different weights both among the various countries and for a specific country at different times.

Having settled this, it must nevertheless be emphasized that interest-rate policy is in *any case* also constrained by the level of the real wage, irrespective of any awareness by this or that monetary authority of the presence of such a constraint and of any given interest-rate policy having actually been acted upon by it. To acknowledge that the real wage constitutes the residual variable in the relation between profits and wages is not to concede that the real wage may move to any level whatsoever. In the presence of independent factors, such as increasing normal profits of enterprise and top-management remu-nerations, which keep on pushing up the price level/money wage ratio in the economy, beyond certain limits, which will vary from one situation to another, a compensatory effect will have to be sought in the level of interest rates.[17] This point is fully consistent with the classical and Marxian tradition, which correctly tends to regard as a self-evident fact that in any given set of social and historical conditions, the real wage cannot be lower than the cost that must be incurred to endow the process of production a minimum of workers' sanction to continue in an orderly manner. Within the framework of interest-rate deter-mination defended here, this translates precisely into the fact that the level of the real wage, owing to its 'cost' or 'necessary' component (see Pivetti, 1999), constitutes in any case an important constraint on the freedom of monetary policy to establish the level of interest rates.

As hinted in Section 3 above, 'the respective powers of the combatants' (Marx, [1898] 1950, p. 402) are strictly intertwined with the policy objectives and constraints to which interest-rate policy decisions are subjected. Consider, for example, a country that adheres to a fixed exchange-rate regime *cum* financial liberalization, and is compelled by it to stick to a comparatively dear-money policy. Concern would then mount over time over the impact of dear money on domestic costs and the competitiveness of domestic products. This, in turn, would put pressure on wage earners to restrain wage demands so that cheap labour might compensate for dear money. At the same time, the high cost of servicing the government debt would put pressure on budgetary policy, with the formation of primary surpluses tending to be pursued to service the debt and check its rise. Now, it is difficult to conceive that such a series of events – from the abolition of restrictions on capital movements to the high interest policy and the budgetary stringencies – could come about and be allowed to persist, unless wage earners of the countries concerned happened to find themselves in an increasingly weak position. Wage earners, by contrast, would be in a relatively strong position if, in the face of rising money wages and increases in the price level, objectives and constraints of a non-directly distributional character compelled the monetary authorities not to raise nominal interest rates. In such a situation, distribution would tend to change in favour of wages. This because competition among firms within each industry causes the rate of profit to adapt to the *real* rate of interest; it is, in fact, the latter, not the nominal rate, that constitutes the actual opportunity cost of any capital, be it borrowed or not, invested in production.[18]

There can be no doubt that from the end of World War II up to the end of the 1970s, both in the US and the other major capitalist countries, cheap money did constitute a decisive ingredient of an overall expansionary policy stance that brought about what came to be termed the Golden Age of capitalism. Let us here recall that, still reflecting the spirit of the Employment Act of 1946, in the United States the Humphrey–Hawkins Act re-established as late as 1978 the principle that monetary policy had to be conducted to promote the goals of full employment, stable prices, and moderate long-term interest rates. With real long-term interest rates maintained on average throughout advanced capitalism well below growth rates, the rise in public debt to GDP ratios was checked even in the presence of large primary deficits, which in turn could keep on sustaining growth. 'Moderate long-term interest rates' and comparatively low public debts to GDP ratios also contributed to containing over those three decades the share of interest payments in national incomes, thus helping to ensure overall distributive conditions especially favourable to long-run growth.

6.   A ZERO INTEREST-RATE POLICY?

But if cheap money is good, couldn't capitalism work even better with a zero long-term real interest rate? Is a situation of persistent zero real interest conceivable?

One may dismiss as quite irrelevant the question of the impact of a zero real interest-rate policy on savings. Outside a neoclassical way of reasoning, persistent zero real interest would not have to exert any significant negative effect on the propensity to save; by itself, it would certainly not induce spending the entire national income on consumption at any given level of employment. Through a possible higher value of the multiplier, *ceteris paribus*, zero interest might actually leave the supply of savings unaltered, or even increase it owing to higher equilibrium levels of employment. The relevant question then is that of its impact on the inducement to invest and on the accumulation of capital.

With a persistent zero long-term real interest rate, the pure remuneration of capital would be nil, together with the price for the use of capital and the opportunity cost of any capital employed in production. Through the competition among firms within each industry, the normal rate of return on capital employed in production would therefore necessarily be lower and the real wage correspondingly higher. Provided it is this normal rate of return that constitutes the fundamental regulator of capitalist accumulation – since when some new capacity is being installed, the investor naturally expects that it will be operated at normal levels[19] – then the impact of a zero interest-rate policy on accumulation should ultimately be negative, unless the 'void' left by the long-term rate of interest was filled by some other element, or component part, of normal profit.

In light of the recent experience of advanced capitalism, one might be led to believe that the 'void' left in normal profit margins by the long-term rate of interest could perhaps be filled by some rate of return on *speculative* financial investment – that is, by persistently higher stock prices/earnings ratios that would thus become the new opportunity cost of capital employed in production. But different from investment in long-term fixed-interest securities substantially devoid of risk (governments usually pay back their debts), speculative financial investment *is* normally risky. So some substitution of the rate to be obtained on speculative financial investment for the long-term rate of interest might take place, but arguably only as a temporary phenomenon, as a result of exceptional conditions that couldn't, however, persist indefinitely: as long-term interest rates approached zero, stock prices would eventually fall – the 'bubble' would burst – because of rising expectations of a general rise in interest rates. Over the last three decades, the true alternative to the productive employment of capital may actually have ceased to be investment in long-term riskless fixed-interest securities, and may have become speculative financial investment – an alternative certainly more risky but *significantly* less risky than it used to be, precisely owing to generalized policies of continuous lowering of interest rates.[20]

But the relevant point here is, in my view, that under capitalism, private ownership of wealth, as distinct from ownership of productive capital, cannot permanently cease to yield an income, independently of the forms of its employment. Nor can the bulk of that income be permanently ensured by speculation and capital gains. In the context of a permanent zero interest-rate policy, mere private ownership of wealth would cease to be a sinecure, the credit system would collapse, and capital income could continue to exist only as profits of enterprise. The net output or surplus of the economy would thus accrue to labour, but for the remuneration of the risks incurred in the various productive employment of wealth. A state of 'euthanasia of the rentier' – that is, practically our having escaped capitalism – would thus have been achieved simply through monetary policy, without any social revolution. In Marxian terms, permanent zero real interest would imply that in the first phase of the circuit $M - C - M'$, M could never be anticipated by someone who was not themselves the operating capitalist. For all those who did not intend to transform their money into productive capital themselves, hoarding would obviously be the best choice: '[t]he miser's plan would be far simpler and surer; he sticks to his 100 pound sterling instead of exposing it to the dangers of circulation' (Marx, [1887] 1954, p. 147). After having stressed that a large part of social capital is not employed by its actual owners, Marx points out that with the development of loan capital '[t]he last illusion of the capitalist system, that capital is the fruit of one's own labour and savings, is destroyed. Not only does profit consist in the appropriation of other people's labour, but the capital with which the labour of others is set in motion and exploited consists of other people's property, which the money capitalist places at the disposal of the industrial capitalists, and for which he in turn exploits the latter' (Marx, [1894] 1977, p. 496). He finally emphasizes that 'as long as the capitalist mode of production continues to exist, interest-bearing capital, as one of its forms, also continues to exist and constitutes in fact the basis of its credit system' (p. 594).[21]

Modern Keynesian economists do not seem to grasp this point. Some of them actually view a zero real interest-rate policy as the best possible monetary policy in that it would be 'neutral' with respect to income distribution: by ceasing to favour the wealthy, it is argued, 'zero real interest would hurt rentiers and help borrowers with low incomes and a higher propensity to consume' (Altesoglu and Smithin, 2006, p. 678; see also Smithin, 2004, 2007). Others, while substantially sharing this view, point out, however, that in the case of deflation, zero real interest would require a policy of *negative* nominal interest rates, which beyond certain very low levels would cause financial disintermediation and create financial instability (cf. Pressman, 2019; see also Palley, 2019).[22] In sum, within the Keynesian tradition, a persistent zero real interest context tends to be viewed as perfectly compatible with capitalism, but for its financial shortcomings in situations of significant price deflation.

Overall, the idea of a possible persistent zero real interest rate can be regarded as a component part of an awkward (pre-COVID-19) imaginative effort to cope with stagnation, brought about by the deep changes in overall distributive conditions that advanced capitalism as a whole has experienced over the last few decades, without resorting to 'big government' – that is, without giving up public budget austerity and the privatization drive. It belongs, in other words, with the same family as massive bank bailouts, monstrous 'quantitative easing' interventions and eventual pathetic monetizations of private consumption spending through various forms of alms, such as 'basic income' injections or miserable 'helicopter money' policies.

7.   THE STATUS OF THE CENTRAL BANK AND CAPITAL CONTROL

Let us conclude this chapter by pointing out the implications of our arguments in Sections 3–5 above for the status of the central bank. The absurdity of the dominant tenet nowadays that central banks must be politically independent stems precisely from the relevance of the rate of interest and its changes for income distribution and aggregate demand, for the balance of payments and the exchange rate, for the public budget and government fiscal operations. Being such a crucial component of any government *general* economic policy, interest-rate determination cannot be disposed of by a single self-contained body that pursues its own independent objectives. As a matter of fact, this was long the dominant view and the convenience of a subordinate position of the central bank with regard to the central government was extensively dealt with in widely circulated official documents, such as the Radcliffe Report on the working of the monetary system at the end of the 1950s (Radcliffe Committee, 1959, paras. 660–675). Especially explicit and lucid was the dissociation by the authors of that influential report from the view 'that the public interest requires that the central bank should be assured complete independence from political influence' (ibid., p. 273):

> We do not share this view…because it seems to us that it either contemplates two separate and independent agencies of government of which each is capable of initiating and pursuing its own conception of what economic policy requires or else assumes that the true objective of central bank is one single and unvarying purpose, the stability of the currency and the exchanges. The first alternative would, we think, be out of harmony with the general conceptions of responsible government that prevail in this country, even if it were not to prove stultifying in itself; the second, while it rightly stresses that this stability is the special and continuing concern of any central bank, ties such a bank down to a single objective which is both too limited in scope and at the same time incapable of achievement without concurrent action on the part of the central Government.
>
> It follows that [the central Government's] economic policy, whatever form it may take from time to time, must include the general planning of monetary policy and monetary operations and that the policies to be pursued by the central bank must be from first to last in harmony with those avowed and defended by Ministers of the Crown responsible to Parliament. (Radcliffe Committee, 1959, pp. 273–4)

Concepts such as these remained dominant up until the end of the 1970s and major monetary policy decisions continued to fall within the orbit of general economic policy – whatever form this took from time to time – with the government of the day bearing full responsibility for them. But acknowledging that interest-rate decisions are a crucial component of general economic policy, while, on the one hand, led to the view that conferring political independence on the central bank was an unreasonable step, on the other rendered unacceptable any giving up of a government's capability to retain a fair amount of control on the level of domestic interest rates. It is here that the question of capital control entered forcibly into the picture: if interest-rate decisions were a crucial aspect of general economic policy, then any deliberate step towards losing national control over the level of the domestic rate of interest was to be seen as an ill course of policy action, no less than endowing the central bank with a politically independent power of decision on it.

In fact, already in 1942, at the very eve of the Bretton Woods settlement, Keynes wrote in a letter to Harrod on the forthcoming conversations with the Americans on post-war planning:

> In my view the whole management of the domestic economy depends upon being free to have the appropriate rate of interest without reference to the rates prevailing elsewhere in the world. Capital control is a corollary to this…my own belief is that the Americans will be wise in their own interest to accept this conception. (Keynes, [1942] 1980, p. 147)

And he kept stressing the same conception in 1943 and 1944:

> It is not merely a question of curbing exchange speculation and movements of hot money, or even of avoiding flights of capital due to political motives; though all this is necessary to control. The need, in my judgement, is more fundamental. Unless the aggregate of the new investments which individuals are free to make overseas is kept within the amount which our favourable trade balance is capable of looking after, we lose control over the domestic rate of interest. (Keynes, [1943] 1980, p. 275)

> We intend to retain control of our domestic rate of interest, so that we can keep it as low as suits our own purposes, without interference from the ebb and flow of international capital movements or flights of hot money…whilst we intend to prevent inflation at home, we will not accept deflation at the dictate of influences from outside. In other words, we abjure the instrument of Bank rate and credit restrictions operating through the increase of unemployment as a means of forcing our domestic economy into line with external factors. (Keynes, [1944] 1980, p. 16)

The view of the rate of interest that emerges from these passages is clearly that of a policy-determined variable, which, as a crucial component of general economic policy, the government of each country should endeavour to keep as much as possible under its control – hence the primacy eventually given in the Bretton Woods settlement to national macroeconomic autonomy, with the explicit right accorded to every member government to control all capital movements.[23] It is well known how far we have moved from all this over the last 40 years. Indeed, most economists, especially in Europe, have ended up regarding any loss of policy autonomy on the part of national governments with undiluted favour. Full capital mobility, in particular, has come to be viewed as an irreplaceable source of discipline, or non-discretion, in the conduct of economic policy, as it impedes deficit financing at low interest rates and stands in the way of capital taxation.

It is obviously to be wished that throughout Europe economic policy will soon return to draw its chief inspiration from the experience of the 30-year period that followed World War II, when the commitment to high employment by the major nations was accompanied by their reiterated efforts to retain sovereignty in monetary policy.

NOTES

1. Think of Wicksell's monetary theory and of the entire inflation-targeting frame-work inspired by it (cf. on this, Pivetti, 2010).
2. This, of course, raises the question that if inflation was actually neutral with respect to the level and composition of output, then such an overriding importance attached by the neoclassical tradition to price stability or low and stable inflation would be somewhat difficult to swallow. As has been observed: 'After all, if all the central bank can control is the price level in the long run, and if the rate at which the price level increases has no implications for the level of real economic activity, then one inflation rate is just as good in welfare terms as another. There is no reason to prefer a steady-state inflation rate of 2 percent over one, say, of 20 percent' (Wynne, 2008, p. 222).
3. Pierangelo Garegnani was the first to point out, in the light of the neoclassical synthesis, that 'the idea of an investment demand schedule constitutes an obstacle which a monetary theory of interest cannot easily overcome' ([1964–65] 1979, p. 78).
4. On the interest–profit connection in economic theory, see Pivetti (1991), Part II.
5. According to F. Hahn (1985, p. 909), Joan Robinson's best work, together with her other contributions to monetary economics contained in *The Rate of Interest and Other Essays* (1952).
6. On Joan Robinson's change of view on the rate of interest, cf. Pivetti (1996).
7. 'The rate of interest, though *ultimately* and *permanently* determined by the rate of profit, is however subject to *temporary* variations from other causes' (Ricardo, [1821] 1951, p. 297; emphasis added).
8. According to data from the US Bureau of Economic Analysis, the consumption of fixed capital in percentage of the price per unit of output was 15 per cent on average in 1951–80, against more than 20 per cent over the last 40 years. Arguably, the phenomenon of a shortening life of capital equipment was linked to the diffusion of ICT technologies and the connected increase in the relative weight of the services-producing sector. On the connection between ICT investment and the enlargement of the service sector, see Barba and Pivetti (2012, pp. 130 and 133).

9. According to Piketty and Saez, social, fiscal and union pressure to contain a fast growth of top compensations would have been significantly reduced over the past few decades, which would have greatly enhanced the top managers' capability to increase their own compensations (see Piketty and Saez, 2003, pp. 34–5; see also Piketty, 2013, pp. 524–9).

10. According to some authors, however, the non-parallel movement of policy interest rates and normal profits would have been brought about, not by an increase in the risk of productively employing capital, hence in normal profits of enterprise, but by an increase in the risk of bank lending to non-financial firms, which, especially after the global financial crisis, would have increased the mark-up between the lending rate and the policy rate; see on this, Gambacorta, Illes and Lombardi (2014). I am grateful to Fabio Petri for directing my attention to this contribution.

11. Over the second half of the 1990s, a slight upward trend in real wages did actually take place in the USA, parallel to the decline in interest rates (see Joint Economic Committee, 2003, p. 16; Juhn, Murphy and Topel, 2002; Mishel, Bernstein and Shierholz, 2003).

12. It can actually be said that the chief limits of the Keynesian analysis of employment derive precisely from the role that he assigns to the rate of interest in the determination of activity levels. In fact, on the basis of his 'marginal efficiency of capital' schedule, all the shortcomings of the system would ultimately be due to the presence in it of obstacles, of an essentially monetary nature, that make it difficult to bring and keep the rate of interest on long-term loans at its full-employment level. All the disasters of unemployment, in other words, would boil down to an insufficient downward flexibility of the rate of interest (see on this, Robinson, 1942, p. 56).

13. Empirical work on firms' pricing behaviour has provided robust evidence of the fact that interest rates are regarded as a cost, with the corollary that they look to establish a price rise in response to increased interest rates. In the words of an early chairman of the US Joint Economic Committee, 'raising interest rates to fight inflation is like throwing gasoline on fire' (W. Patman, quoted in Seelig, 1974, p. 1049; see also Patman, 1957, p. 134).

14. This overall picture appears to be supported by empirical evidence, which seems to show that when so-called inflation-targeting policies succeeded in lowering inflation, they did so by also causing slower growth and higher unemployment (see Akerlof et al., 2002; Ball, 2005; Bodkin and Neder, 2003; Debelle, 1997; Fortin, 1996; Laidler and Robson, 1993).

15. See on this, Pivetti (2004, pp. 234–7).

16. Declining interest rates succeeded in containing over several years the share of disposable personal income of indebted households required to service the increasing outstanding stock of their debts, thus significantly protracting the macroeconomic sustainability of a massive process of substitution of loans for wages (see Barba and Pivetti, 2009, pp. 127–9).

17. Thus the post-1995 US policy of progressive lowering of interest rates might have *also* been dictated by a real wage constraint, although its primary objective was most likely that of delaying for as long as possible the *redde rationem* of recourse to household debt as the chief demand management tool (cf. the previous note).

18. On real vs nominal interest within the framework of the monetary theory of distribution, see Pivetti (1990) (with the attached comments and replies); Pivetti (1991, ch. 6); Stirati (2001, pp. 430–39).

19.   See on this, Pivetti (2015), Section 7.
20.   Alternatively, the reduced risk of speculative financial investment might have simply contributed to increasing in each production sphere the component part of normal profit necessary to remunerate the risk of productively employing capital (see Section 3 above on the rise over the last few decades of this component part of normal profits).
21.   Marx continues by observing that '[o]nly that sensational writer, Proudhon…was capable of dreaming of a *crédit gratuit*, this monster that was supposed to realize the pious wish of small capitalist production' (ibid.).
22.   Pressman, for example, argues that with a negative nominal rate beyond –0.7 per cent, financial institutions would experience large withdrawals: 'we have a lower bound of interest rates which is *not* zero; but some small negative number due to the carrying costs associated with holding cash and a desire to ensure one's assets' (2019, p. 149; original emphasis).
23.   In addition to according to every member government the explicit right to control all capital movements, Article VI of the IMF Articles of Agreement (IMF, 1944) even contemplated the possibility of *requiring* member countries using the resources of the Fund to exercise the control of the outflow of capital: 'If, after receiving such a request, a member fails to exercise appropriate controls, the Fund may declare the member ineligible to use the general resources of the Fund' (from Article VI, Section I of the Agreement). Keynes could thus declare in the House of Lords that what in the pre-war system 'used to be a heresy', in the field of international capital movements, 'is now endorsed as orthodox' (Keynes, [1944] 1980, p. 17).

REFERENCES

Akerlof, G.A., Dickens, W.T., Fortin, P. and Perry, G.L. (2002), 'Inflation and unemployment in the US and Canada: a common framework', *Cahier de recherche du Département des sciences économiques, UQAM, No. 20-16*.
Altesoglu, S. and Smithin, J. (2006), 'Inflation targeting in a simple macroeconomic model', *Journal of Post Keynesian Economics*, **28**, 673–88.
Ball, L. (2005), 'Commentary on M. Goodfriend, "The monetary policy debate since October 1979: lessons for theory and practice"', *Federal Reserve Bank of St. Louis Review*, **87** (2, Part 2), 243–62.
Barba, A. and Pivetti, M. (2009), 'Rising household debt: its causes and macroeconomic implications – a long period analysis', *Cambridge Journal of Economics*, **33**, 113–37.
Barba, A. and Pivetti, M. (2012), 'Distribution and accumulation in post-1980 advanced capitalism', *Review of Keynesian Economics*, Inaugural Issue, 126–42.
Bodkin, R.G. and Neder, A.E. (2003), 'Monetary policy targeting in Argentina and Canada in the 1990s: a comparison, some contrasts, and a tentative evaluation', *Easter Economic Journal*, **29** (3), 339–58.
Debelle, G. (1997), 'Inflation targeting in practice', *IMF Working Paper No. 97/35*, International Monetary Fund.
Fortin, P. (1996), 'Presidential address: the great Canadian slump', *Canadian Journal of Economics*, **29** (4), 761–87.

Gambacorta, L., Illes, A. and Lombardi, M.J. (2014), 'Has the transmission of policy rates to lending rates been impaired by the Global Financial Crisis?', *BIS Working Paper No. 477*, Bank for International Settlements.

Garegnani, P. ([1964–65] 1979), 'Notes on consumption, investment and effective demand: II', *Cambridge Journal of Economics*, **3**, 63–82.

Hahn, F. (1985), 'Robinson–Hahn love–hate relationship: an interview', in G.R. Feiwell (ed.), *Joan Robinson and Modern Economic Theory*, New York: New York University Press, pp. 895–910.

Humphrey–Hawkins Act (1978), *The Full Employment and Balanced Growth Act of 1978: Public Law 95-523—Oct. 27, 1978, 92 Stat. 1887*, enacted by the 95th United States Congress, May 10, 1979.

International Monetary Fund (IMF) (1944), *Articles of Agreement of the International Monetary Fund, adopted by United Nations Monetary and Financial Conference, Bretton Woods, New Hampshire, July 22, 1944*. Washington, DC: International Monetary Fund.

Joint Economic Committee (2003), *Economic Indicators* (March), prepared for the Joint Economic Committee by the Council of Economic Advisers, Washington, DC: US Government Printing Office.

Juhn, C., Murphy, K.M. and Topel, R.H. (2002), 'Current unemployment, historically contemplated', *Brookings Papers on Economic Activity*, **1**, 79–116.

Keynes, J.M. (1936), *The General Theory of Employment, Interest and Money*, London: Macmillan.

Keynes, J.M. ([1937] 1973), 'The general theory of employment', *Quarterly Journal of Economics*, **51** (2), 209–23, reprinted in *The Collected Writings of John Maynard Keynes. Vol. XIV: The General Theory and After: Part II*, edited by D.E. Moggridge, London: Macmillan for the Royal Economic Society, pp. 109–23.

Keynes, J.M. ([1942] 1980), 'Letter to R.F. Harrod, 19 April 1942', in *The Collected Writings of John Maynard Keynes, Vol. XXV*, edited by D.E. Moggridge, London: Macmillan, pp. 146–51.

Keynes, J.M. ([1943] 1980), 'Speech before the House of Lords, 18 May 1943', in *The Collected Writings of John Maynard Keynes, Vol. XXV*, edited by D.E. Moggridge, London: Macmillan, pp. 269–80.

Keynes, J.M. ([1944] 1980), 'Speech before the House of Lords, 23 May 1944', in *The Collected Writings of John Maynard Keynes, Vol. XXVI*, edited by D.E. Moggridge, London: Macmillan, p. 17.

Laidler, D.E.W. and Robson, W.P.B. (1993), *The Great Canadian Disinflation: The Economics and Politics of Monetary Policy in Canada, 1988–93*, Toronto: C.D. Howe Institute.

Marx, K. ([1887] 1954), *Capital, Vol. I*, London: Lawrence & Wishart.

Marx, K. ([1894] 1977), *Capital, Vol. III*, London: Lawrence & Wishart.

Marx, K. ([1898] 1950), *Wages, Price, and Profit*, in K. Marx and F. Engels, *Selected Works in Two Volumes (Vol. 1)*, London: Lawrence & Wishart, p. 402.

Mishel, L., Bernstein, J. and Shierholz, H. (2003), *The State of Working America, 2008–2009*, Ithaca, NY: Cornell University Press.

Palley, T. (2019), 'The fallacy of the natural rate of interest and zero lower bound economics: why negative interest rates may not remedy Keynesian unemployment', *Review of Keynesian Economics*, **7** (2), 155–73.

Pasinetti, L.L. (1990), 'Comment' [on M. Pivetti, 1990], in K. Bharadwaj and B. Schefold (eds), *Essays on Piero Sraffa: Critical Perspectives on the Revival of Classical Theory*, London: Unwin Hyman, pp. 460–61.

Patman, W. (1957), *Hearings before the Subcommittee on Economic Stabilization of the Joint Economic Committee, Congress of the United States, Eighty-Fourth Congress* (2nd Session, December 10–11, 1956), Washington, DC: US Government Printing Office.

Piketty, T. (2013), *Le Capital au XXI Siècle*, Paris: Editions du Seuil.

Piketty, T. and Saez, E. (2003), 'Income inequality in the United States, 1913–1998', *Quarterly Journal of Economics*, **CVIII** (1), 1–39.

Pivetti, M. (1990), 'On the monetary explanation of distribution' (with the comments by R. Ciccone, J. Steindl and L.L. Pasinetti), in K. Bharadway and B. Schefold (eds), *Essays on Piero Sraffa: Critical Perspectives on the Revival of Classical Theory*, London: Unwin Hyman, pp. 432–53.

Pivetti, M. (1991), *An Essay on Money and Distribution*, London: Macmillan.

Pivetti, M. (1996), 'Joan Robinson and the rate of interest: an important change of view on a topical issue', in M.C. Marcuzzo, L.L. Pasinetti and A. Roncaglia (eds), *The Economics of Joan Robinson*, London and New York: Routledge, pp. 75–80.

Pivetti, M. (1999), 'On Sraffa's "cost & surplus" concept of wages and its policy implications', *Rivista Italiana degli Economisti*, **IV** (2), 279–300.

Pivetti, M. (2004), 'La teoria monetaria della distribuzione e il caso americano', *Rivista Italiana degli Economisti*, **IX** (2), 225–44.

Pivetti, M. (2010), 'Interest and the general price level: some critical notes on "The new consensus monetary policy model"', in A. Birolo, D.K. Foley and H.D. Kurz et al. (eds), *Production, Distribution and Trade*, London and New York: Routledge, pp. 216–32.

Pivetti, M. (2015), 'Marx and the development of critical political economy', *Review of Political Economy*, **27** (2), 134–53.

Pressman, S. (2019), 'How long can we go? The limits of monetary policy', *Review of Keynesian Economics*, **7** (2), 137–50.

Radcliffe Committee (1959), *Report of the Committee on the Working of the Monetary System*, Cmnd. 827, London: HMSO.

Ricardo, D. ([1821] 1951), *On the Principles of Political Economy and Taxation*, in *The Works and Correspondence of David Ricardo Vol. I*, edited by P. Sraffa with M.H. Dobb, Cambridge, UK: Cambridge University Press, p. 227.

Robinson, J. (1942), *An Essay on Marxian Economics*, London: Macmillan.

Robinson, J. (1951), 'The rate of interest', *Econometrica*, **19**, 92–11.

Robinson, J. (1952), *The Rate of Interest and Other Essays*, London: Macmillan.

Robinson, J. (1956), *The Accumulation of Capital*, London: Macmillan.

Robinson, J. (1960), *Collected Economic Papers, Vol. II*, Oxford: Blackwell.

Robinson, J. (1979), *The Generalisation of the General Theory and Other Essays*, London: Macmillan.

Seelig, S. (1974), 'Rising interest rates and cost push inflation', *Journal of Finance*, **29** (4), 1049–61.

Smithin, J. (2004), 'Interest rates operating procedures and income distribution', in M. Lavoie and M. Seccareccia (eds), *Central Banking in the Modern World*, Cheltenham, UK and Northampton, MA, USA: Edward Elgar Publishing, pp. 57–69.

Smithin, J. (2007), 'A real interest rate rule for monetary policy?', *Journal of Post Keynesian Economics*, **30**, 101–18.

Stirati, A. (2001), 'Inflation, unemployment and hysteresis: an alternative view', *Review of Political Economy*, **13**, 427–51.

Wynne, M.A. (2008), 'Core inflation: a review of some conceptual issues', *Federal Reserve Bank of St. Louis*, **90** (3, Part 2), 205–28.

11. The distributional impacts of inflation-targeting strategies[1]

Sergio Rossi

1.   INTRODUCTION

Inflation-targeting strategies have been in fashion since the early 1990s, after the Reserve Bank of New Zealand adopted this monetary policy regime in 1989, soon followed by other advanced countries, and then also by emerging and developing countries (see Rochon and Rossi, 2006a, 2006b; Rossi, 2009).

Generally speaking, there is a consensus that inflation is an increase in some relevant price level, which induces various microeconomic and macroeconomic costs that should be avoided by central banks' policy interventions. An analogous consensus exists, at least within the mainstream of the economics profession, that such an increase is the result of demand-led factors on the product market, where consumers and the general government sector exert a demand for goods and services that could put an upward pressure on the price level if their supply cannot be increased because of full-capacity constraints. Hence, the government should have a balanced budget over the medium run (if not yearly), while the central bank should provide price stability on the product market. With respect to the latter objective, monetary authorities should be independent of governments (to avoid the 'monetization' of public deficits) and target an inflation rate that is compatible with the definition of price stability. Owing to some technical and methodological biases, however, price stability does not correspond to a zero rate of measured inflation, but is considered to occur when the rate of inflation is between 1 and 2 per cent (see Rossi, 2001, Ch. 2 for analytical elaboration).

Nevertheless, inflation-targeting strategies did not impede the global financial crisis (GFC) in 2008, which occurred as a result of various credit bubbles that banks had been inflating (both in Europe and the United States) in the previous decade. This means that price stability (as measured on the product market) and financial stability are false friends, to wit, that the former does not automatically imply the latter. The belief that monetary authorities should focus on price stability only – thus ignoring financial stability – has been encapsulated in the so-called 'Jackson Hole consensus' among central bankers: the latter were indeed led to believe they should not intervene to avoid asset-price inflation, as they are not in a position to know whether the increase in asset prices is the result of an inflating credit bubble or is supported by real economic growth. As a matter of fact, when banks inflate such a bubble, the debt–income discrepancy that this generates at the macroeconomic level cannot be revealed by the evolution of any price level on the market for produced goods and services. Hence, this does not pose a threat, apparently, for the financial stability of the whole economic system – as maintained, for instance, by Greenspan (2004) when the real-estate bubble was inflating in the United States from 1996 to 2006 (see also Greenspan, 1999).

Let us first expand on the characteristics of inflation targeting, before addressing its major shortcomings for the economic system as a whole with regard to income and wealth distribution. We will then propose an alternative framework for taking monetary policy decisions considering their distributional impacts. The last section concludes and summarizes the main arguments of this chapter.

2.   THE CHARACTERISTICS OF INFLATION-TARGETING STRATEGIES

Inflation-targeting strategies have a number of characteristics that Bernanke et al. (1999, p. 4) encapsulated in five points, as follows (see also Rossi, 2015, p. 254):

- a public announcement of the targeted rate of inflation over a given time horizon;
- an institutional commitment to price stability as the monetary policy's primary long-run goal, and a commitment to achieve the inflation target in any case;
- an information-inclusive strategy in which many economic variables are considered in taking monetary policy decisions;
- a communication strategy to inform the public about the plans as well as the objectives of the central bank; and
- an increased accountability of the central bank for attaining its inflation target.

These characteristics show that inflation targeting is a revised version of monetarism as advocated by Friedman (1960, 1968, 1969). In its original version, monetarism claimed that '*inflation is always and everywhere a monetary phenomenon* in the sense that it is and can be produced only by a more rapid increase in the quantity of money than in output' (Friedman, 1987, p. 17; original emphasis). In its revised version – which is still fashionable within central banks as well as universities – monetarism considers that a central bank should aim at price stability on the market for produced goods and services (measured with some price index capturing the evolution of consumer prices), since it can affect the relevant price level through some monetary policy transmission channels; the most important of which stems from steering the policy rates of interest (we address this point later).

Let us now expand on each of the characteristics of inflation targeting indicated above. First, inflation-targeting central banks announce the targeted rate of inflation. Generally speaking, this target is expressed with regard to a consumer price index, excluding some goods or services whose prices are extremely volatile owing to (geo)political factors or other reasons. There are two possible frameworks in this regard. Some central banks, like the Bank of England, announce a point target for the inflation rate their policy aims to achieve. This rate may be decided by the central bank itself or, as is the case for the United Kingdom, established by the country's government, which is intended as being representative of the people's desires in a democratic system. Be that as it may, such a point target gives a precise indication for economic agents to include it in their own expectations about the rate of inflation that will be observed if the central bank is in a position to hit its own target over the relevant time horizon. Other central banks, such as the Bank of Canada, announce a target range (with or without a mid-point target) within which they aim at keeping the inflation rate. In the Canadian case, for instance, there is an inflation-control target range of 1 to 3 per cent, and the central bank aims to keep the rate of inflation at the 2 per cent mid-point. This is intended to take into account that inflation is a variable that central banks cannot control precisely, so that a target range for the rate of inflation is in a better position to reduce the loss of credibility (and hence reputation) the central bank could suffer if the inflation target is not met over the relevant horizon. The target range, nevertheless, should not be too wide (say, not wider than 200 basis points), in order to still affect agents' expectations about the rate of observed inflation. There is actually no reason to have a large target range, since in such a case the central bank would not be in a position to affect (or to steer) agents' expectations in this regard.

Second, inflation-targeting central banks consider the achievement of price stability as the first (if not unique) objective of their policy decisions over the long run. This can in some cases harm other policy goals, defined with regard to exchange rates or employment levels, for instance. This hierarchy of monetary policy objectives results from what has been called 'New Consensus Macroeconomics' (see Arestis, 2013), which considers a 'dichotomized' eco-nomic system, where nominal variables (such as the policy rates of interest) can only influence other nominal variables (like the price level, hence the rate of inflation), while real variables (say, the rate of unemployment) remain unaffected by monetary policy decisions. This supports the (monetarist) view that price stability must be the first (if not unique) objective that monetary authorities pursue, as being instrumental in achieving other general economic policy objectives, such as maximum employment levels and real economic growth. In this perspective, trying to influence a real variable like the employment level through monetary policy interventions could make it more difficult, if not impossible, to hit the inflation target, particularly within the framework of rational expectations, where agents anticipate that an expansionary monetary policy aiming at reducing unemployment will increase the (expected) price level, thereby increasing the nominal wage level in such a way that leaves the rate of unemployment eventually unaffected.

Third, inflation-targeting strategies consider several economic variables beyond the so-called monetary aggregates and the prices of goods and services (imported or produced domestically) that these aggregates are considered to ultimately affect – in line with the quantity theory of money (see Fisher, [1911] 1931; Friedman, 1956, 1969; Hume, [1826] 1955). Contrary to monetarism and its practical outcome – namely, monetary targeting (to wit, a monetary policy strategy that focussed exclusively on the causal relation between a given monetary aggregate and some relevant price level) – inflation targeting enlarges the number of economic variables that could have some impact on the price level during the relevant period (usually two or three years after a monetary policy intervention like a change in the policy rates of interest). In spite of this larger spectrum of variables, the money supply (usually captured by a broad monetary aggregate like M3) still takes a prominent position when the central bank has to decide its policy stance regarding the inflation forecast that it generally publishes to inform the public about its expectations with respect to the targeted rate of inflation.

Indeed, the fourth characteristic of inflation targeting is to communicate with the public much more than central banks were used to doing under monetary targeting – the first and most famous version of monetarism, in which central banks target the rate of growth of the monetary aggregate that is best correlated with the evolution of some price level on the goods market. The communication strategy of inflation-targeting central banks aims at informing economic agents, particularly across financial markets, about their policy decisions, in order to ultimately influence these agents' expectations and behaviour. In this perspective, central banks regularly publish their own inflation forecasts, a variety of reports and monetary statistics, and in a number of cases even the minutes of their meetings, to inform the public at large about the whole decision-making process during the relevant period. In fact, the general public understands what an inflation target is much better than it does the strategy of communicating monetary targeting: announcing some target for a monetary aggregate implies that economic agents know what the latter represents, which is questionable. This is even more so when it comes to announcing the targeted rate of growth of the relevant monetary aggregate. Inflation targeting is thereby also a way of making the central bank more transparent and efficient in communicating with the public at large.

Fifth, inflation targeting increases central banks' accountability, at least *ex post*, which many consider as essential, particularly to ensure that central bankers do not pursue some private interests that could conflict with those objectives that monetary authorities must achieve by statute or mandate (see de Haan, Amtenbrink and Eijffinger, 1999). Indeed, an inflation-targeting central bank must explain, and convincingly so, why its inflation target was not met in the past (*ex-post* accountability). It may even have to provide the reasons for a change in its policy stance if the inflation forecast shows that the targeted rate of inflation would not be otherwise met (*ex-ante* accountability). It is true, however, that the rate of measured inflation depends on a number of variables other than those a central bank can control or at least influence over time. Also, the central bank can always explain that the targeted rate of inflation has not been met for a number of reasons that lie beyond its own field of influence. In fact, the economic system is so complex and its variables are so interconnected that it is impossible to maintain that the central bank can affect a variable (say, the price level) to a precise extent with one or more instruments it may put into practice. Indeed, both before and after the GFC in 2008, there have been several cases where a given variable moved in the opposite direction from what the so-called monetary policy 'transmission channels' would have implied in (mainstream) economic theory.

Let us expand on these channels in the next section with regard to their impacts on both income and wealth distribution.

3. THE DISTRIBUTIONAL IMPACTS OF MONETARY POLICY CHANNELS

Monetary policy decisions affect income and wealth distribution through a variety of 'transmission channels', the most important of which is the so-called 'interest-rate channel'. This channel affects other channels like the 'balance-sheet channel', the 'asset-price channel', the 'bank-credit channel' and the 'exchange-rate channel'.

The largest channel stems from the central bank's decisions regarding the policy rates of interest, which are those rates that monetary authorities control in order to affect the whole structure of market rates of interest and, thereby, eventually, the (targeted) rate of inflation. There are different ways to make this channel operational. A central bank may announce the interest rate that banks will have to pay when they borrow what used to be called 'reserves' (or settlement balances in technical jargon). The interbank market, where banks must settle their own debts by the end of the day (if not in real time, as it occurs in real-time gross-settlement systems), needs central bank money for the paying bank to finally pay its counterparty across this market. A final payment occurs when the 'seller of a good, or service, or another asset, receives something of equal value from the purchaser, which leaves the seller with no further claim on the buyer' (Goodhart, 1989, p. 26). This cannot happen when a bank issues its own means of payment to pay for its own debt, as in this case there is a promise of payment that represents a claim by the receiving bank on the paying bank – which therefore does not pay finally unless it disposes of a sum of central bank money (see Rossi, 2007, pp. 67–78 for an analytical elaboration).

By determining the rate of interest that banks must pay when borrowing from the central bank, the latter can affect interbank market rates of interest (such as the London Interbank Offered Rate, the so-called LIBOR). Indeed, usually, a bank may choose to borrow from other banks (on the interbank market) or from the central bank (often considered as a lender of last resort), depending on the interest-rate levels. If the policy rate of interest goes up, this induces banks to borrow more across the interbank market, thereby also pushing up the market rates of interest – in line with the central bank's expectations regarding the impact of this on aggregate demand and hence, eventually, on the rate of measured inflation.

Another way for a central bank to steer the whole interest-rate structure is to announce a so-called 'corridor'. In this case, the central bank sets two policy rates of interest: one for the borrowing banks and the other for the deposits that banks may have with them. The latter banks, indeed, may decide to keep their deposits with the central bank or to lend them across the interbank market, according to the interest-rate differential (namely, the difference between the deposit rate of interest paid by the central bank and the lending rate of interest on the interbank market). By moving up or down such a 'corridor', the central bank can affect the level of interbank market rates of interest, because banks are induced to switch to or from the interbank market for both their borrowing and lending activities in light of the interest-rate differential with regard to the policy rates.

Be that as it may, in respect of the central bank's operational framework for the setting of policy rates of interest, these rates originate the 'interest-rate channel' that affects the whole series of interest rates and thereby also income and wealth distribution. This can occur along different lines (or 'sub-channels'), the most direct of which consist of a direct impact on the volume of credit lines that banks open for any kind of customer.

This 'narrow view' of the interest-rate channel considers that the central bank's policy rates of interest affect the volume of banks' credit directly, thereby impacting on demand for goods and hence on the rate of inflation. With regard to income distribution, therefore, the central bank's decision to reduce the policy rates of interest leads to a higher total demand on the market for produced goods and services, which is likely to increase the firms' profit according to their sales figures. If so, then the profit share in national income increases, thereby reducing the wage share. Further, the wage share consists of managers' and their employees' wages: hence, the reduction of the wage share that results from lowering the policy rates of interest can impact the employees' wages more than the managers', particularly because of involuntary unemployment that provides a 'reserve army' of unemployed people willing to work for the current wage level. In short, unskilled and low-skilled workers are much more impacted than high-skilled workers and their managers, when the 'interest-rate channel' impacts on income distribution by increasing the profit share to the detriment of the wage share.

A similar reasoning applies when the central bank increases its policy rates of interest. On the one hand, such an increase reduces firms' investment and the employment level, particularly for unskilled and low-skilled workers. On the other hand, it makes sure that creditors receive a higher interest income, notably the wealthy people who have huge funds, transnational corporations as well as banks and non-bank financial institutions with their major shareholders. These agents will thus be largely prone to 'park' a large part of their income and wealth on financial markets, where they expect to earn higher interests, thereby inducing an upward pressure on the prices of financial assets. In this case, the downward pressure on these prices that results from an increase in the policy rates of interest is (more than) compensated by the upward pressure stemming from the possibility to earn higher interest income across the financial markets. This means that wealthy people and financial institutions benefit in any event of a change in the interest rates that central banks control: this occurs either through a wealth effect or an income effect that impact on income and wealth distribution in favour of the wealthy and to the detriment of the rest of the population.

These impacts on income distribution are further affected by other 'sub-channels' that can operate in the monetary policy transmission mechanism, such as the 'balance-sheet channel'. Indeed, firms' balance sheets are affected when the central bank changes its policy rates of interest: a reduction of the latter, generally speaking, enables firms to have a higher cash flow, owing to a reduction of the interest they must pay to the banking sector when they borrow from it. This usually results in an increase in the profit share, hence in higher dividends to firms' shareholders, which could be problematic if these dividends are not spent on the market for produced goods and services (but spent across financial markets, thereby inflating asset prices on these markets). Further, such an increase in dividends induces a higher demand for firms' financial assets, whose price increases, thereby also increasing the wealth of those individuals holding them in their portfolio.

There is also an 'asset-price channel' through which monetary policy decisions, particularly in an inflation-targeting regime, affect income and wealth distribution. This 'sub-channel' operates for both firms and households. Firms are impacted through it when the prices of those (real or financial) assets they possess increase or decrease as a result of a change in the policy rates of interest. If the latter diminish (increase), there will be a higher (lower) demand for real or financial assets, hence a likely increase (reduction) in their prices that increases (reduces) the valuation of the firms' portfolio where these assets are recorded. This makes these firms more prone to borrowing, at lower rates of interest, since they can offer better guarantees of solvency (in the form of collateral) to their lenders, particularly banks in the case of small and medium-sized firms that are not in a position to borrow across the capital market. Now, if firms borrow to invest productively, this generates a higher level of economic activity and probably also of employment, thereby supporting the wage share and, eventually, consumption. However, owing to a lack of effective demand, as a result of income distribution that has been reducing the purchasing power of the middle class, a number of firms do not borrow to produce more but only to extract higher rents from financial markets, thereby exerting an upward pressure on asset prices in these markets.

The 'asset-price channel' also operates as regards to households, particularly those in the upper class, whose wealth is relevant in terms of both real and financial assets, and whom monetary policy decisions affect considerably. As a matter of fact, a reduction in the policy rates of interest induces an increase in the prices of both real and financial assets. Their owners in the household sector benefit directly from such an increase if they decide to sell (part of) these assets. Also, there may be a so-called 'wealth effect' when households decide to spend more on the market for produced goods and services as a result of the fact that their wealth has increased owing to a reduction in the policy rates of interest that pushes up the prices of real and/or financial assets. This eventually increases the profit share in the distribution of income, as firms are in a position to sell more goods and services to the wealthier consumers.

There are two other 'sub-channels' in the monetary policy transmission mechanism. On the one hand, owing to money endogeneity, the 'bank-credit channel' operates when a bank decides to open a credit line to any kind of borrower, considering the policy rate of interest that is relevant in this regard. Again, in this case, bank credit lines may induce what Werner (2012, p. 29) has called 'non-GDP-based transactions' – that is, those transactions that are not linked in any way to production activities, hence that generate an inflationary gap in the money-to-output relation even though this gap does not appear in the measured rate of inflation on the market for produced goods and services, because these credit lines are used to purchase financial assets – thereby inflating their prices but without any reaction from the central bank with regard to financial stability.

On the other hand, there is an 'exchange-rate channel', which concerns the impact that a change in the policy rates of interest has on the domestic currency's exchange rates. If the central bank reduces (increases) its policy rates of interest, this makes the national currency less (more) interesting to purchase across the foreign-exchange market. As a result, the exchange rates of this currency are expected to depreciate (appreciate) – on the *ceteris paribus* hypothesis – thereby affecting this country's balance of payments because of higher (lower) exports and lower (higher) imports. This is likely to have an eventual impact on the price level, hence also on the measured rate of inflation. As a result, again, income and wealth distribution could vary in line with the evolution of the profit share, respectively of the wage share that goes to the top managers and upper class of high-skilled workers. If the central bank reduces its policy rates of interest to affect the exchange rates of the national currency, this can impact wealth and income distribution in favour of the upper class, since their income and wealth can increase to the detriment of the middle and lower classes. Hence, consumption could diminish, thereby inducing firms not to invest their net profits productively, 'parking' them across the financial market – which will further increase the wealth of the upper-class individuals in a self-reinforcing spiral that could eventually lead to the bursting of a financial bubble (particularly when the central bank decides to increase the policy rates of interest), as observed in the United States during the subprime crisis.

4. AN ALTERNATIVE FRAMEWORK FOR MONETARY POLICY DECISIONS

In light of the distributional impacts of central banks' decisions, monetary authorities do play a prominent role in the dynamics of the economic system as a whole – that is, with respect to both real and nominal variables. It is therefore important that monetary policy decisions are also taken with regard to income and wealth distribution, at least since this affects price stability as well as financial stability – to wit, the two (major) objectives of central banks to pursue according to their mandate.

With regard to price stability, central banks should take into account the distributional impact of their policy decisions, particularly at the time of writing, since their rates of interest affect households' consumption and firms' investment through a number of the so-called 'transmission channels' we explored in the previous section. The so-called 'negative interest-rate policy' (NIRP) that various central banks have been putting into practice since the GFC in 2008 has a relevant impact on income and wealth distribution, but does not really affect the level of economic activity as imagined by monetary authorities. Rather, financial actors and institutions have been profiting much more than the so-called 'real economy' as a result of the NIRP – which has widened the gap between income classes and inflated asset prices much beyond the so-called 'fundamentals' of the relevant firms or the economy as a whole.

As a matter of fact, first the 'zero interest-rate policy' (ZIRP) and then the NIRP have been inducing a number of banks to significantly increase their lending for non-GDP-based transactions, in order for them to earn an interest income that compensates the reduction of their earnings stemming from the credit lines they granted to firms aiming to invest productively. Indeed, the latter investment has greatly lowered as a result of the negative impacts of the GFC on consumption, through a reduction in the employment level and also in the wage level of a number of workers. Banks have also greatly expanded their lending for real-estate transactions – a dynamics that has been induced by ZIRP and NIRP, since both borrowers and lenders on the real-estate market want to benefit from this monetary policy stance for different reasons. Borrowers want to become homeowners, or to earn an income by renting their real estate, while lenders (particularly banks) want to earn interest income from a variety of mortgage loans. This inflates real-estate prices, thereby contributing to the widening gap between the top and the bottom of the social pyramid with regard to the distribution of wealth (see Rossi, 2019).

In this regard, central banks must consider that reducing their policy rates of interest could inflate the prices of real or financial assets through a credit bubble growing as far as banks are induced to expand their lending volumes to earn a higher profit across real-estate and financial markets. Rather than split-ting their monetary policy toolbox into two parts, one for price stability and the other for financial stability – as occurs at the time of writing with, on the one hand, policy rates of interest and, on the other, liquidity or capital ratios that banks must respect – central banks should go beyond a Taylor-rule approach (see Taylor, 1993) to integrate the distributional impacts of their policy rates of interest in their so-called 'reaction function'. In so doing, central banks should consider that reducing the policy rates of interest cannot be enough to support economic activity if both banks and firms are unwilling to expand the volume of credit lines concerning GDP-based transactions. In such a case, the reduc-tion of policy rates of interest should concern only those credit lines that banks open for GDP-based transactions, which are the only transactions that can have a positive impact on the employment level, as well as on the wage level of the middle class. Further, central banks should also consider in the setting of their policy rates of interest that a number of GDP-based transactions are actually damaging the environment. In this case, only those GDP-based transactions that are environmentally friendly should benefit from a reduction in the policy rates of interest – hence banks should also be induced to steer their portfolio decisions with regard to such a crucial issue, thereby contributing to 'greening' the economic and financial system.

These behavioural considerations are not enough, however, for monetary policy decisions to have a long-lasting, positive impact on financial stability for the economic system as a whole. A structural-monetary reform must be put into practice in this regard, as proposed by Cencini and Rossi (2015, Ch. 10). Monetary authorities should therefore require that commercial banks split their ledgers into two departments, where they should record their monetary emissions (first department) and the opening of credit lines (second department). This is instrumental in ensuring that the emission of money does not create a credit bubble – to wit, to prevent banks creating money *ex nihilo* to pay for non-GDP-based transactions that affect income and wealth distribution to the advantage of the upper class and against the general interest. Those banks that want to open credit lines for such transactions will therefore have to finance them by previously existing deposits, rather than with a newly issued number of money units that cannot have purchasing power unless they are associated with a new production process and the relevant payment of wages. Such a structural reform of banks' book-keeping ensures that financial stability prevails, since all new monetary emissions will be linked to an equivalent production of income in the form of bank deposits that will be originally earned by workers. If so, those banks complying with this two-department book-keeping structure may benefit from a lower policy rate of interest when they borrow from the central bank in connection with their lending for GDP-based transactions.

Such an operational framework for central banks' decisions is likely to reduce income and wealth inequalities, as far as banks are more prone to lend for production purposes rather than for speculation across financial markets. This will also positively affect the wage share, notably with regard to both lower- and middle-class workers, and thereby support consumption, employment levels, as well as economic growth. By contrast, those banks that do not split their ledgers into two book-keeping departments will not benefit from a reduction in the policy rates of interest, and might even be punished with a penalty rate of interest when they need to borrow from the central bank. This could be enough to damage their own reputation, inducing them to switch to the two-department book-entry structure rapidly, in their own interest and that of their shareholders, as otherwise they might also be asked to pay a higher rate of interest on the interbank market, owing to their lower reputation and higher risk of illiquidity (if not insolvency).

Overall, a monetary policy framework that takes into account distributional issues within a central bank's decision-making process is more likely to induce a higher level of financial stability for the whole economic system than is actually the case under an inflation-targeting regime. It also contributes to ensuring there is a higher level of employment and therefore more prosperity and social cohesion across the economic system as a whole.

5.   CONCLUSION

This chapter has presented the distributional impacts of inflation-targeting strategies – to wit, those monetary policy strategies that consider price stability on the product market as being the most important (if not unique) task a central bank must fulfil. It explained that central banks' decisions affect income and wealth distribution to the advantage of the wealthy, generally speaking, through a variety of transmission channels that originate from changing the policy rates of interest in light of inflation forecasts against a given inflation target defined with regard to the market for produced goods and services. It then provided an alternative framework for the decision-making process of central banks, which takes into account the distributional impacts of their decisions at both the behavioural and structural levels. From the latter perspective, this chapter suggested that a structural-monetary reform is put into practice, aiming at splitting the banks' ledgers into two book-entry departments, one for the recording of all new money emissions and the other for keeping track of all those credit lines that banks decide to open to any kind of borrowers. Such a 'departmentalization' of banks' books will be enough to guarantee that financial stability prevails within an economic system where income and wealth distribution can be less problematic on both economic and social grounds.

NOTE

1.   The author is grateful to the co-editors of this volume for their invitation to contribute this chapter, and to Carryl Oberson and Maurizio Solari for their comments on an earlier version of it. The usual disclaimer applies.

REFERENCES

Arestis, P. (2013), 'Economic policies of the New Consensus Macroeconomics: a critical appraisal', in J. Pixley and G.C. Harcourt (eds), *Financial Crises and the Nature of Capitalist Money*, London: Palgrave Macmillan, pp. 196–215.
Bernanke, B.S., T. Laubach, F.S. Mishkin and A.S. Posen (1999), *Inflation Targeting: Lessons from the International Experience*, Princeton, NJ: Princeton University Press.
Cencini, A. and S. Rossi (2015), *Economic and Financial Crises: A New Macroeconomic Analysis*, London: Palgrave Macmillan.
de Haan, J., F. Amtenbrink and S.C.W. Eijffinger (1999), 'Accountability of central banks: aspects and quantification', *Banca Nazionale del Lavoro Quarterly Review*, **52** (209), 169–93.

Fisher, I. ([1911] 1931), *The Purchasing Power of Money: Its Determination and Relation to Credit, Interest and Crises*, New York: Macmillan.

Friedman, M. (ed.) (1956), *Studies in the Quantity Theory of Money*, Chicago, IL: University of Chicago Press.

Friedman, M. (1960), *A Program for Monetary Stability*, New York: Fordham University Press.

Friedman, M. (1968), 'The role of monetary policy', *American Economic Review*, **58** (1), 1–17.

Friedman, M. (1969), *The Optimum Quantity of Money and Other Essays*, Chicago, IL: Aldine Publishing.

Friedman, M. (1987), 'Quantity theory of money', in J. Eatwell, M. Milgate and P. Newman (eds), *The New Palgrave: A Dictionary of Economics, Vol. IV*, London: Macmillan, pp. 3–20.

Goodhart, C.A.E. (1989), *Money, Information and Uncertainty* (2nd edition), London: Macmillan.

Greenspan, A. (1999), 'Testimony by Alan Greenspan, Chairman Board of Governors of the Federal Reserve System before the Joint Economic Committee, June 17', accessed 23 November 2022 at https://fraser.stlouisfed.org/docs/historical/greenspan/Greenspan_19990617.pdf.

Greenspan, A. (2004), 'The mortgage market and consumer debt, remarks by Chairman Alan Greenspan at America's Community Bankers Annual Convention, Washington, DC, October 19', accessed 23 November 2022 at http://www.federalreserve.gov/BoardDocs/Speeches/2004/20041019/default.htm.

Hume, D. ([1826] 1955), *The Philosophical Works, Volume III*, reprinted in *Writings on Economics*, edited by E. Rotwein, Edinburgh: Nelson.

Rochon, L.-P. and S. Rossi (2006a), 'Inflation targeting, economic performance, and income distribution: a monetary macroeconomics analysis', *Journal of Post Keynesian Economics*, **28** (4), 615–38.

Rochon, L.-P. and S. Rossi (2006b), 'The monetary policy strategy of the European Central Bank: does inflation targeting lead to a successful stabilisation policy?', in E. Hein, A. Heise and A. Truger (eds), *European Economic Policies: Alternatives to Orthodox Analysis and Policy Concepts*, Marburg: Metropolis Verlag, pp. 87–110.

Rossi, S. (2001), *Money and Inflation: A New Macroeconomic Analysis*, Cheltenham, UK and Northampton, MA, USA: Edward Elgar Publishing.

Rossi, S. (2007), *Money and Payments in Theory and Practice*, London: Routledge.

Rossi, S. (2009), 'Inflation targeting and monetary policy governance: the case of the European Central Bank', in C. Gnos and L.-P. Rochon (eds), *Monetary Policy and Financial Stability: A Post-Keynesian Agenda*, Cheltenham, UK and Northampton, MA, USA: Edward Elgar Publishing, pp. 91–113.

Rossi, S. (2015), 'Inflation targeting', in L.-P. Rochon and S. Rossi (eds), *The Encyclopedia of Central Banking*, Cheltenham, UK and Northampton, MA, USA: Edward Elgar Publishing, pp. 254–5.

Rossi, S. (2019), 'The dangerous ineffectiveness of negative interest rates: the case of Switzerland', *Review of Keynesian Economics*, **7** (2), 220–32.

Taylor, J.B. (1993), 'Discretion versus policy rules in practice', *Carnegie-Rochester Conference Series on Public Policy*, **39** (1), 195–214.

Werner, R. (2012), 'Economics as if banks mattered: a contribution based on the inductive methodology', *The Manchester School*, **79** (2), 25–35.

Index